UN Co
Development Thinking
and Practice

United Nations Intellectual History Project

Ahead of the Curve? UN Ideas and Global Challenges
  Louis Emmerij, Richard Jolly, and Thomas G. Weiss

Unity and Diversity in Development Ideas: Perspectives from the
UN Regional Commissions
  Edited by Yves Berthelot

Quantifying the World: UN Ideas and Statistics
  Michael Ward

The UN and Global Political Economy: Trade, Finance, and Development
  John Toye and Richard Toye

UN Contributions to Development Thinking and Practice

Richard Jolly, Louis Emmerij,
Dharam Ghai, and Frédéric Lapeyre

Indiana University Press

Bloomington and Indianapolis

This book is a publication of

Indiana University Press
601 North Morton Street
Bloomington, Indiana 47404-3797 USA

http://iupress.indiana.edu

Telephone orders   800-842-6796
Fax orders   812-855-7931
Orders by e-mail   iuporder@indiana.edu

The paper used in this publication meets the minimum requirements
of American National Standard for Information Sciences—Permanence
of Paper for Printed Library Materials, ANSI Z39.48-1984.

Manufactured in the United States of America

Library of Congress Cataloging-in-Publication Data

UN contributions to development thinking and practice /
Richard Jolly . . . [et al.].
    p.   cm. — (United Nations intellectual history project)
Includes bibliographical references and index.
    ISBN 0-253-34407-7 (cloth : alk. paper) — ISBN 0-253-21684-2 (pbk. : alk. paper)
    1. Economic development—International cooperation—History. 2. United Nations—
History. 3. Human rights—Economic aspects. 4. Poverty—Prevention. I. Title: United
Nations contributions to development thinking and practice. II. Jolly, Richard.
III. Series.
    HD82.U18 2004
    338.9—dc22   2003026468

1 2 3 4 5 09 08 07 06 05 04

Contents

Part III. Outcomes and the Future

Boxes, Tables, and Figures

Boxes

Tables

Figures

Foreword

It is surprising that there is no comprehensive history of the United Nations family of organizations, either institutional or intellectual. True, a few of the funds or specialized agencies have written or are in the process of writing their institutional histories. This is, indeed, what all UN organizations should do, along with making enhanced efforts to organize their archives so that independent researchers can also document and analyze dispassionately the problems and contributions of multilateral institutions in the last half-century.

Faced with this major omission, which has substantial implications for the academic and policy literatures, we decided to undertake the task of beginning to write an intellectual history—that is, a history of the ideas launched or nurtured by the United Nations. Readers should not be put off by what may strike them as a puffed-up billing. Our working assumption behind this effort is straightforward: ideas and concepts are a main driving force in human progress, and they arguably have been one of the most important contributions of the world organization.

The United Nations Intellectual History Project (UNIHP) was launched in 1999 as an independent research effort based in the Ralph Bunche Institute for International Studies at The Graduate Center of The City University of New York. The project also maintains a liaison office in Geneva. We are grateful for the enthusiastic backing of the Secretary-General and other staff and governments within the UN system. Generous financial support from five foundations and eight governments ensures total intellectual and financial independence. Details of this and other aspects of the project can be found at our Web site: www.unhistory.org.

The work of the United Nations can be divided into two broad categories: economic and social development, on the one hand, and peace and security, on the other. The UNIHP is committed to producing fourteen volumes in the first arena and a further three volumes if sufficient resources are mobilized to include the latter. Indiana University Press will publish all these volumes as a series. In addition, the project has completed an oral history collection of some seventy-five lengthy interviews of persons who have played major roles in launching and nurturing UN ideas—and sometimes in hindering them! Extracts from these interviews will be published in 2004 in *UN Ideas: Voices from the Trenches and Turrets*. Authors of the project's various volumes, including this one, have drawn on these interviews to highlight substantive points made in their texts. Full transcripts of the oral histories will be disseminated in electronic form at the end of the project to facilitate work by other researchers and interested persons worldwide.

There is no single way to organize research, and certainly not for such an ambitious project as this one. The way we have structured this history is to select topics—ranging from trade and finance to human rights, from transnational corporations to development assistance, from gender to sustainability—and tease out the history of ideas under each of these topical headings. We have selected world-class experts for each topic, but they have been given freedom and responsibility to organize their own digging, analysis, and presentation of material. Guidance from ourselves as the project directors, as well as from peer-review groups, is provided to ensure accuracy and fairness in depicting where the ideas came from, what happened to them within the UN system, and what happened afterward.

As lifelong participants in and observers of multilateral development work and diplomacy, we are convinced that the UN story deserves to be better documented if it is to be better understood and appreciated. The Bretton Woods institutions, in this respect, are far ahead. The World Bank published two massive histories—one on the occasion of its twenty-fifth anniversary and the other (two volumes and more than 2,000 pages) on its fiftieth.[1] The International Monetary Fund (IMF) has an in-house historian who ensures that its place in history is captured with regular publications.

We are pleased to be part of what we hope will be a long and varied journey for the UN. As Kofi Annan, the UN Secretary-General, kindly wrote in the Foreword to *Ahead of the Curve? UN Ideas and Global Challenges:* "With the publication of this first volume in the United Nations Intellectual History Project, a significant lacuna in twentieth-century scholarship and international relations begins to be filled."[2]

UN Contributions to Development Thinking and Practice is another significant step in this intellectual adventure. We welcome as co-authors Dharam Ghai, a distinguished and long-standing contributor to development thinking and practice and former director of the UN Research Institute for Social Development (UNRISD), and Frédéric Lapeyre, a rising star in development studies, who assisted us with *Ahead of the Curve.*

We hope that readers will enjoy this journey through time. As they proceed, they should keep in mind a challenging observation from an early feminist, Midge Decter:

> Ideas are powerful things, requiring not a studious contemplation but an action, even if it is only an inner action. Their acquisition obligates each man in some way to change his life, even if it is only his inner life. They demand to be stood for. They dictate where a man must concentrate his vision. They determine his moral and intellectual priorities. They provide him with allies and make him enemies. In short, ideas impose an interest in their ultimate fate which goes far beyond the realm of the merely reasonable.[3]

Louis Emmerij
Richard Jolly
Thomas G. Weiss

Preface and Acknowledgments

All four of us are grateful for research support from a number of creative and energetic assistants. These include Severine Deneulin, who spent many hours digging up basic sources and material and helping to summarize what were the intellectual contributions in such a mass of material and contributed directly to Chapter 1. We are grateful to a number of others: in Geneva, Maria Alvarez, Ibrahima Dia, and Carla Bellota; in Sussex, Christopher Buttler and Philip Middleton of the Institute of Development Studies; and in New York, Jason Schulman of The CUNY Graduate Center. Thanks go to Julia Brown, who helped with typing and checking the manuscript. We would also like to recognize the invaluable contribution of Effie MacLachlan, who performed all the final tasks necessary for transforming this volume into a publishable work.

We have also benefited from the comments on earlier drafts from a variety of friends and colleagues—too many to be all mentioned by name, including a number who participated in a UNIHP review meeting in Uppsala hosted by the Dag Hammarskjöld Foundation. For their detailed comments, we must single out Margaret Joan Anstee, Gerry Helleiner, and Ann Tickner.

A word is in order about the structure and logic of the volume. We have presented it in three parts, since it did not seem appropriate simply to follow a chronological outline. Part I—Values and History—provides some essential background: the values and criteria underlying our work and our perspectives on development thinking before the UN. Part II—Ideas and Action—presents the evolution of development thinking within the UN from 1945 to 2000, decade by decade, with some attention to how ideas shifted with the changing situation in developing and transition countries. This section focuses on UN contributions to thinking on the human foundations of development and on sectoral change, two cross-sectoral areas where a decade-by-decade treatment does not easily fit. The emphasis on action is also stronger here, since in Chapter 10 we attempt to relate UN thinking to the actual record of development. Part III—Outcomes and the Future—draws conclusions from this record for the

UN's work in the years ahead, fulfilling our commitment to try to make this a future-oriented history.

Since development theory did not start with the beginning of the world organization in 1945, this volume devotes its second chapter to some of the early distinguished thinkers in this field, from Adam Smith to John Maynard Keynes. This volume shows how much vision and creative thinking emerged from the first generation of UN leaders and how great was the input of their colleagues and academic consultants, many of whom later were awarded Nobel Prizes. We think, for instance, of people such as Jan Tinbergen, W. Arthur Lewis, Gunnar Myrdal, James Meade, Theodore Schultz, Richard Stone, Wassily Leontief, and Lawrence Klein.

In later decades, and particularly since the 1980s, the vision became less clear, the ideas more blurred, and the UN, at least in the development arena, often sidelined. There were exceptions, which the authors have been happy to underline. And in the 1990s, with a new emphasis on human rights and human development, there was a revival of UN vision and intellectual creativity and a new visibility often linked to the global conferences and summits.

The Millennium Summit in September 2000 outlined a new development agenda for the UN and opened possibilities for a new and more balanced partnership with the Bretton Woods institutions and the World Trade Organization (WTO). Our reading of the record of the previous fifty years has convinced us that this is desperately needed. At the time of writing, in early 2003, it is exceptionally difficult to assess whether or not these new possibilities are likely to be carried forward into action, since preoccupations with terrorism and war have moved to center stage. But this study has left us in no doubt that development remains a central priority for the new millennium and that the UN with its universal membership and truly worldwide concerns is in a unique position to contribute to new thinking about it. Indeed, without such new thinking, action toward the eradication of poverty, economic and ecological sustainability, and a world of greater justice will not be achieved.

Richard Jolly
Louis Emmerij
Dharam Ghai
Frédéric Lapeyre

Abbreviations

ACAST	Advisory Committee on the Application of Science and Technology to Development
CDF	UN Capital Development Fund
CDP	Committee for Development Planning
CEDAW	Convention on the Elimination of All Forms of Discrimination against Women
CID	Centre for Industrial Development
CIEC	Conference on International Economic Cooperation
CIS	Commonwealth of Independent States
CRC	Convention on the Rights of the Child
DAC	Development Assistance Committee
DMFAS	Debt Management and Financial Analysis System
DPI	Department of Public Information
ECA	Economic Commission for Africa
ECE	Economic Commission for Europe
ECAFE	Economic Commission for Asia and the Far East (ESCAP after 1974)
ECLA	Economic Commission for Latin America
ECLAC	Economic Commission for Latin America and the Caribbean (changed from ECLA in 1984)
ECOSOC	Economic and Social Council
EPTA	Expanded Program of Technical Assistance
ESAF	Enhanced Structural Adjustment Facility

ESCAP	Economic and Social Commission for Asia and the Pacific (changed from ECAFE in 1974)
EWLP	Experimental World Literacy Programme
FAO	Food and Agriculture Organization
FFHC	Freedom from Hunger Campaign
FIVIMS	Food Insecurity and Vulnerability and Mapping Systems
G-7	Group of 7
G-77	Group of 77
GATT	General Agreement on Tariffs and Trade
GDI	Gender-Related Human Development Index
GDP	Gross Domestic Product
GEF	Global Environment Facility
GEM	Gender Empowerment Measure
GNP	Gross National Product
HDI	Human Development Index
HDR	Human Development Report
HIPC	Highly Indebted Poor Countries
HIV/AIDS	Human Immunodeficiency Virus/Acquired Immunodeficiency Syndrome
HPI	Human Poverty Index
IAP	Immediate Action Program
IBRD	International Bank for Reconstruction and Development (World Bank)
IDA	International Development Association
IDEP	Institut Africain de Développement Economique et de Planification (African Institute of Economic Development and Planning)
IDS	Institute of Development Studies
IFAD	International Fund for Agricultural Development
IFC	International Finance Corporation
IIA	International Institute of Agriculture
IIEP	International Institute of Education Planning

ILO	International Labour Organization
IMF	International Monetary Fund
INSTRAW	UN International Research and Training Institute for the Advancement of Women
IOM	International Organization of Migration
ISI	import-substituting industrialization
IUCN	International Union for the Conservation of Nature (The World Conservation Union)
LDCs	Least-Developed Countries
NGO	Non-Governmental Organization
NIEO	New International Economic Order
ODA	overseas development assistance
OECD	Organisation for Economic Co-operation and Development
OIHP	L'Office International d'Hygiene Publique (International Office of Public Health)
OPEC	Organization of Petroleum Exporting Countries
PAHO	Pan American Health Organization
PAMSCAD	Programme of Action to Mitigate the Social Costs of Adjustment
R and D	research and development
SAF	Structural Adjustment Facility
SNPA	Substantial New Program of Action
SUNFED	Special United Nations Fund for Economic Development
TAB	Technical Assistance Board
TAC	Technical Assistance Committee
TDDS	Third Development Decade Strategy
UN	United Nations
UNCTAD	United Nations Conference on Trade and Development
UNDP	United Nations Development Programme
UNEDA	United Nations Economic Development Administration
UNEP	United Nations Environmental Program

UNESCO	United Nations Educational, Scientific and Cultural Organization
UNFPA	UN Fund for Population Activities
UNICEF	United Nations Children's Fund
UNIDIR	UN Institute for Disarmament Research
UNIDO	United Nations Industrial Development Organization
UNIFEM	United Nations Development Fund for Women
UNIHP	UN Intellectual History Program
UNITAR	United Nations Institute for Training and Research
UNRISD	United Nations Research Institute for Social Development
UNRRA	United Nations Relief and Rehabilitation Administration
UNU	United Nations University
USSR	Union of Soviet Socialist Republics
WEC	World Employment Conference
WFC	World Food Conference
WFP	World Food Programme
WHO	World Health Organization
WISTAT	Women's Indicators and Statistical Database
WID	women in development
WIDER	World Institute for Development Economics Research
WTO	World Trade Organization
WWF	World Wildlife Fund

Part I. Values and History

1

Has There Been Progress?
Values and Criteria for UN History

- **Beauty in the Eye of the Beholder**
- **The UN Charter and the Universal Declaration of Human Rights**
- **The Right to Development**
- **The Growing Consciousness of Gender**
- **The Millennium Summit: Agenda and Goals**
- **A Definition of Development**

Beauty in the Eye of the Beholder

Beauty is in the eye of the beholder. Whether looking back at the early days of the UN in the mid-twentieth century or looking forward half a century later, the progress one sees, or the setbacks and failures, is enormously influenced by the values and beliefs one holds. Every UN action has its political side. And development is necessarily a value-laden activity. In order to assess the record of the UN's work, the standards we apply—our values and criteria—need to be made clear to the reader.

What values and criteria should be used? Is the process of development to be assessed primarily as economic advance in terms of countries becoming economically richer, their populations enjoying rising living standards, the countries becoming economically stronger or less vulnerable to natural disasters or to financial shocks? Is the process to be judged in terms of social achievements, fulfillment of human rights,[1] or expansion of freedoms? What weight is to be given to issues of distribution—the extent to which economic and social advance, even democratic benefits, are concentrated on some rich or better-off segment of the population or are distributed more evenly among the population as a whole?

All of these questions have international dimensions, dimensions which are both important and often controversial for the United Nations. Is development to be weighed as a national process of advance or also as a regional or an international process? If it is to be evaluated in part as a regional or international process, what standards are to be applied to these international aspects? Is it enough for individual countries to advance, or must their progress also be assessed relative to the progress of other countries within the region or globally? Should account be taken of the external repercussions of their advance and to the differences such advance creates in economic wealth or political power within the world at large?

The answers given to these questions will reflect the values and criteria used in forming the judgments underlying them as well as views and ideas about the nature of power and interaction between countries. A work of international history needs to make these explicit. But this raises complications. Are the values and criteria, the views and ideas, to be those which command widespread support today or those which received support at the time under review, when the events were taking place? In the case of the UN, there are further crucial questions: Whose values and whose criteria, whose views and whose ideas? Those of the governments (which our history refers to as the "first UN")[2] or those of the UN Secretariat, led by its Secretary-General (which we call the "second UN")? Or indeed, those of concerned citizens and organizations outside—which perhaps should be called the "third UN"? And if the values are to be those of governments, which governments—bearing in mind that the UN has some 190 member governments from all regions of the world?

There are, and always have been, sharp differences between the views and the concerns of UN member states—related in part to the values embodied in their own political systems and their own different economic and social situations and histories. Important today are the large economic differences between rich, poor, and transition countries. In the era of the Cold War, differences between the Western bloc and the Soviet bloc were a major polarizing factor within the UN, just as at the beginning were the differences between those major powers with colonies and the eighty or so countries which were or had recently been colonies. In the 1970s, differences sharpened between the industrial countries and the developing countries, the Group of 77, and later also between the industrial and transition countries. All of these differences come to the surface and add to the complications of specifying the values and criteria by which to assess the UN's contributions to development theory and practice.

The ambition of this first chapter is to clarify the position taken by the authors on these difficult questions. We begin by examining the core norms and values underpinning the UN system as defined in its two founding documents, the Charter of the United Nations and the Universal Declaration of Human Rights. Even though these have often failed to be translated into practice by countries or by the UN itself, the values laid down in these two documents constitute the core of accepted UN values. We will en passant give some explanations for the frequent gap between rhetoric, on one hand, and practice, on the other. But the purpose of the chapter is to explain how and why these values are the appropriate ones for assessing the UN's contributions to development.

We end the chapter by referring to the Declaration on the Right to Development (1986)[3] and the United Nations Millennium Declaration (2000),[4] in which the heads of state and government of 147 countries and representatives of some forty others reaffirmed the continuing commitment of their governments to the Charter and the Universal Declaration and adopted a set of fundamental values and principles, goals, and strategic actions which they considered "essential to international relations in the twenty-first century." These reaffirm the continuing relevance of the Charter and the Universal Declaration as criteria by which to assess the UN contributions to development, both in the early years of the UN and in the final years of the twentieth century, the era of globalization.

The UN Charter and the Universal Declaration of Human Rights

The UN Charter is a political and organizational document. Its nineteen chapters and 111 articles deal mostly with the structure and procedures of the UN system. The political and peacekeeping roles of the UN form an important part of the document. But contrary to popular impressions, the document is infused with human values and human concerns from its opening words:

We the peoples of the United Nations determined

to save succeeding generations from the scourge of war, which twice in our lifetime has brought untold sorrow to mankind, and

to reaffirm faith in fundamental human rights, in the dignity and worth of the human person, in the equal rights of men and women and of nations large and small, and

to establish conditions under which justice and respect for the obligations arising from treaties and other sources of international law can be maintained, and

to promote social progress and better standards of life in larger freedom

This opening paragraph immediately moves on to the underlying values which must guide the response of member states toward these objectives: tolerance, good neighborliness, unity in strength to maintain international peace and security, the rejection of armed force for national ends, and the employment of "international machinery for the promotion of the economic and social advancement of all peoples."[5]

These objectives are elaborated under the purposes and principles of the UN in Chapter I of the Charter. The third of these purposes deals directly with what would today be called development:

> To achieve international co-operation in solving international problems of an economic, social, cultural, or humanitarian character, and in promoting and encouraging respect for human rights and for fundamental freedoms for all without distinction as to race, sex, language, or religion.[6]

The UN's roles and obligations with respect to international economic and social cooperation are later spelled out more fully in Chapter IX, Article 55:

> With a view to the creation of conditions of stability and well-being which are necessary for peaceful and friendly relations among nations based on respect for the principle of equal rights and self-determination of peoples, the United Nations shall promote:
> a. higher standards of living, full employment, and conditions of economic and social progress and development;
> b. solutions of international economic, social, health and related problems; and international cultural and educational co-operation; and
> c. universal respect for, and observance of, human rights and fundamental freedoms for all without distinction as to race, sex, language or religion.[7]

At the time, these words were extraordinary and unprecedented. The Charter recognized the need for development action on a global scale—to improve the standards of living of people universally and to promote full employment and conditions of economic and social progress in all parts of the world. The economic and social advances were also to be pursued with full respect for human rights and fundamental freedoms. As mentioned in *Ahead of the Curve,* the first volume of this series, these visionary goals and objectives were at the time breathtaking in their boldness, far ahead of their time in the world of 1945—a world in which half the global population lived in colonies and a significant proportion of the rest in conditions of dictatorship.[8]

The Universal Declaration of Human Rights followed three years later. Its thirty articles give life and detail to the broad commitments to human rights embodied in the UN Charter. Together the articles cover the full range of rights—political, civil, economic, social, and cultural. As with the Charter, the most remarkable feature was the recognition that rights were universal. As Article 1 declared, "All human beings are born free and equal in dignity and rights. They are endowed with reason and conscience and should act towards one another in a spirit of brotherhood." Those words were courageous and challenging.[9]

The words of Article 2 were equally extraordinary for the direct manner in which they made clear beyond any doubt their universal application:

> Everyone is entitled to all the rights and freedoms set forth in this Declaration, without distinction of any kind, such as race, color, sex, language, religion, political or other opinion, national or social origin, property, birth or other status.
>
> Furthermore, no distinction shall be made on the basis of the political, jurisdictional or international status of the country or territory to which a person belongs, whether it be independent, trust, non-self-governing or under any other limitation of sovereignty.[10]

Other articles spelled out the specifics of these rights in twelve broad categories, from life, liberty, and security of person to the rights to education and to an adequate standard of living. This is not the place to summarize them in detail, let alone deal with the further elaborations that have followed over the half-century since 1948. Suffice it to say that major elaborations have taken place in all of the main components of human rights:

- Nondiscrimination
- Freedom of thought and assembly
- Rights of participation and democracy
- Cultural pluralism and diversity
- Freedom from want
- Social justice
- Rights to self-determination, a nationality, and asylum
- Equality on a global basis

Toward the end of the Universal Declaration came two articles important for the universal realization of the preceding rights:

> Everyone is entitled to a social and international order in which the rights and freedoms set forth in this Declaration can be fully realized.
>
> Everyone has duties to the community in which alone the free and full development of his personality is possible.[11]

Despite adoption of the Universal Declaration of Human Rights in 1948, concern with and promotion of human rights as such often played little part in the UN's early work on economic and social development. The fulfillment of many economic and social rights was certainly implicit in UN concerns and actions for economic and social advance, but references to rights in this work were few and far between. Moreover, political and civil and even cultural rights mostly got forgotten or ignored in economic writing on development[12] and were treated more as a matter of political and ideological debate in the UN. Indeed, in development discussion, the belief became popular that authoritarian regimes had some advantage and even some justification because of their ability to take the tough decisions required—for example, to raise the rate of savings in poor countries. It was argued that more democratic leaders would find it difficult to take these hard decisions.[13]

Is the UN's early failure to refer to rights a clinching argument against using human rights today as criteria for assessing the UN's development work? To adopt this attitude would be illogical for at least three reasons.

In the first place, the fact that it took some years for the UN to give serious attention to the full range of human rights in development is no reason for suggesting that rights—all human rights—are not important as criteria against which to assess UN performance. After all, at no time did the UN ever suggest that human rights were not important, let alone renounce them. And for at least some parts of the UN, such as the United Nations Educational, Scientific and Cultural Organization (UNESCO), the World Health Organization (WHO), the Commission on Human Rights, and the UN Secretariat itself, human rights were quoted and used as guidelines from their earliest days.

Second, during the last two decades, human rights have become increasingly important within the UN as a whole and for the day-to-day operations of many of its specialized development funds and agencies. A rights-based approach to development is now accepted policy in a number of the UN's development funds and agencies. It would be difficult today to argue that human rights have no relevance for assessing the focus and effectiveness of the UN's work, even over the entire period of its existence, even applied retrospectively.

Third, it is not clear what other standards could be used which would command the same level of international allegiance and legitimacy. The literature of economic analysis is large and rich. It gives close attention to many elements of the development process: economic growth, structural change, living standards, poverty reduction, women's advance, income distribution, environmental sustainability, institutional development, freedom, and economic justice. In principle, it would be possible to evaluate the UN's contribution to development ideas and thinking by reference to any one or several of these ideas—or more. But to do so would be to focus on certain features of the development process which are often idiosyncratic and frequently reflect the cultural biases of their proponents, mix means with ends, and, in most cases, choose criteria which lack formal international endorsement. Basing our standards on human rights as endorsed by the UN system avoids these problems.

To judge the UN's development performance by reference to human rights does not imply being locked in to an unchanging set of standards. Over the UN's life, human rights have not only been given more detail—for instance, the rights of workers in various conventions of the International Labour Organization (ILO) in the early years of the UN and rights for women and for children in the two major conventions of 1979 and 1989[14]—but have been taken into new areas of concern, such as rights for refugees,[15] migrant workers,[16] and national minorities. In 1966, the International Covenant on Civil and Political Rights[17] and the International Covenant on Economic, Social and Cultural Rights[18] made more specific the elements of the Universal Declaration, and two years later, the International Conference on Human Rights, organized by the UN in Teheran on the occasion of the twentieth anniversary of the Universal Declaration of Human Rights, made the link between human rights and development more explicit and stronger.[19]

The Right to Development

The inclusion of human rights in the UN's development thinking culminated in December 1986, when the General Assembly adopted the Declaration on the Right to Development. This established the right to development as "an inalienable human right by virtue of which every human person and all peoples are entitled to participate in, contribute to, and enjoy economic, social, cultural and political development, in which all human rights and fundamental freedoms can be fully realized."[20] It added that "equality of opportunity for development is a prerogative both of nations and of individuals."[21]

If human rights provide the values and criteria by which to assess the UN's work in development, why is there so little reference to human rights in the orthodox literature on development? One can speculate on at least four reasons. First, the literature on development has been dominated by economists who have focused overwhelmingly on the process of economic development rather than the broader processes of economic, social, cultural, and political advance. If the lead in development had been taken by sociologists or anthropologists or political scientists, the focus and emphasis would almost certainly have been different, though whether human rights would have been at the center is debatable. Second, much of the analysis of development has focused on the process of economic development, often treating increases in incomes as unambiguous evidence of human improvement and playing down evidence of other outcomes.

Third, neglect of human rights values and criteria in the literature of development is in some respects more apparent than real. Mainstream economic thought rests on certain key assumptions about the virtues of free markets in ensuring at least a core of political and civil rights for consumers and the public at large. A main argument, powerfully analyzed by Nobel Prize winner Friedrich von Hayek, was that free markets and democracy go hand in hand. Indeed this argument led him and many of his followers to the belief that economic planning and all government controls necessarily involve a violation of human rights.

In addition to these links between market economies and political and civil rights, economic development was expected to bring advances in the fulfillment of economic and social rights, and it often did so. But the assumption that this would happen provided something of a complacent expectation that what was expected to happen always would occur. Often it did not. Moreover, the links between development and rights became embroiled in Cold War debate. The West put the emphasis on political and civil rights—pointing to the lack of freedoms in the Eastern bloc and the USSR. The USSR and the Eastern bloc put the emphasis on economic and social rights, pointing to the persistence of poverty in the West and thus to the failure to ensure economic and social rights for all.

Fourth, and finally, neoclassical economics has prided itself on not making value judgments. The early classical economists, as set out in the next chapter, had no such reservations—or illusions that objectivity was possible. Indeed, Adam Smith's university appointment in Glasgow was to the chair of moral philosophy. But by the mid-twentieth century, the discipline of economics thought it had largely separated itself from normative issues. Mainstream economists, newly fortified by mathematical skills, sought to recreate economics as a value-free science, if not on a par with physics and the other hard sciences at least the queen of the social sciences. Though careful analysis of the strict conditions for making value-free statements later showed this to be unrealizable in all but the most trivial of situations, the vision of a value-free positive economic analysis was still held up as the Holy Grail.

The result is that when development economics began to emerge slowly and somewhat shyly as a separate discipline in the early 1950s, it defended its arrival by wearing the colors of mainstream economics: a preoccupation with economic relationships, the search for generalizations, and the avoidance of value judgments, except for what was seen as the most basic and least controversial, namely that increasing living standards by increasing economic growth and per capita income in the poorer countries was a desirable goal. An interesting example of that ambition to build a value-free development concept could be seen, for example, in Arthur Lewis's book *The Theory of Economic Growth*.[22] Lewis's discussion about the desirability of economic growth was pushed back to the end of the book in a little appendix.

For most of the past half-century, economic development thinking, which was strongly rooted in the utilitarian philosophical tradition, became dominated by a view of human well-being defined in terms of an individual's preferences, disregarding the values behind those preferences.

The Growing Consciousness of Gender

It was only in the mid-1970s with the arrival of thinking about basic needs that systematic concern for human living conditions and human well-being became an active topic for discussion among the circles of development economists and the utilitarian foundations of economic theory began to be questioned.[23] Over this same period, pioneering work began to appear on the role of women in development that contributed to and reflected growing consciousness of the neglect of the contributions of women in development studies and growing demands by women in both developing and developed countries that analysis of their roles and concerns become a core focus of development.[24] Later this work evolved into a broader analysis of gender and development, sometimes into a range of "subversive deconstructing tendencies of feminist analysis" of development.[25]

All of these changes meant that development theory and practice began to be more formally linked with the nature of the lives that human beings were living. By the 1980s, development thinking that was explicitly linked to human living conditions began to be referred to as "human development." Those approaching development from a human rights perspective began to find a more welcoming reception and more theoretical support from economists who were developing new tools to tackle human rights along with development. This "new" conception of development was popularized by the United Nations Development Programme (UNDP) through the inauguration in 1990 of an annual series of Human Development Reports.[26]

Over the last decade of the twentieth century, analysis within the frame of human development began to elaborate the concepts, frameworks, and policy agendas needed to link the legal world of human rights with the dynamic world of economic and social development.[27] Human development constructed a people-centered analysis of the goals and processes of development in which concepts and tools were linked systematically to the policies and actions, norms and institutions which over time will lead to the fulfillment of rights. It directs attention to the socioeconomic context in which human rights can be realized— or threatened. The human development approach thus serves as a bridge from the legal concepts of rights to the dynamic economic and social processes of development with which countries gradually build up the resources and institutions that enable them to achieve human rights on a national scale.

The Millennium Summit: Agenda and Goals

By the year 2000, a new consensus had been established about the central importance of people in the process of development. In September 2000, the Millennium Summit was held at the United Nations in New York and the Millennium Declaration was adopted.[28] In this declaration, heads of state and government reaffirmed their "commitment to the purposes and principles of the Charter of the United Nations [adding that] indeed, their relevance and capacity to inspire have increased, as nations and peoples have become increasingly interconnected and interdependent."[29]

In the declaration, the heads of state and government declared that six fundamental values were "essential to international relations in the twenty-first century." These included:

Freedom: Men and women have the right to live their lives and raise their children in dignity, free from hunger and from the fear of violence, oppression or injustice. Democratic and participatory governance based on the will of the people best assures these rights.

Equality: No individual and no nation must be denied the opportunity to benefit from development. The equal rights and opportunities of women and men must be assured.

Solidarity: Global challenges must be managed in a way that distributes the costs and burdens fairly in accordance with basic principles of equity and social justice. Those who suffer or who benefit least deserve help from those who benefit most.

Tolerance: Human beings must respect one another, in all their diversity of belief, culture, and language. Differences within and between societies should be neither feared nor repressed, but cherished as a precious asset of humanity. A culture of peace and dialogue among all civilizations should be actively promoted.

Respect for nature: Prudence must be shown in the management of all living species and natural resources, in accordance with the precepts of sustainable development. Only in this way can the immeasurable riches provided to us by nature be preserved and passed on to our descendants. The current unsustainable patterns of production and consumption must be changed in the interest of our future welfare and that of our descendants.

Shared responsibility: Responsibility for managing worldwide economic and social development, as well as threats to international peace and security, must be shared among the nations of the world and should be exercised multilaterally. As the most universal and most representative organization in the world, the United Nations must play the central role.[30]

This led to more specific commitments in seven areas of action: peace, security, and disarmament; development and eradicating poverty; protecting our common environment; human rights, democracy, and good governance; protecting the vulnerable; meeting the special needs of Africa; and strengthening the United Nations.

A Definition of Development

In summary, we provide a definition of development that will be used in this study.

The goal of development is the improvement of human well-being and the quality of life. This involves the eradication of poverty, the fulfillment of basic needs of all people, and the protection of all human rights and fundamental freedoms, including the right to development. It requires that governments apply active social and environmental policies and that they promote and protect all human rights and fundamental freedoms on the basis of democratic and widely participatory institutions.

This definition is in fact that given in the UN Agenda for Development, issued by the Secretary-General in 1997.[31] It represents a considerable advance from the early UN years, when the essence of successful development was seen "merely" as a sustained increase in a country's per capita income, a sustained increase in a country's total production, a long-term evolution of a country's economic structure and institutions, and a country's movement toward becoming a more industrialized economy of greater self-reliance.

Human well-being has been made central to the definition of development. The focus has shifted to how a country's population has been affected by the process of development and how people have been strengthened as subjects of the process, not just as objects and recipients.

None of this is to ignore development as a process of economic growth and structural change. But the definition focuses on the significance of growth and structural change for people. Unless we know how people have been affected by growth and structural change and how these changes have affected people's capabilities to make choices, we do not have the information needed to judge whether or not the whole process should be counted as progress. An expansion of human freedoms—and the capabilities to fulfill them—becomes the goal of development.

Moreover, the process of development in broadening choices and strengthening human capabilities is also important and must be assessed. Has it been a process of freedom? Has it provided opportunities for *all* the population? Has it strengthened the capabilities of all, or have some groups been left marginalized? How has the position of women and children been changed with the process of development, especially in relation to gender equality and the advance of women (and girls) in society at large? Gender advance and equity becomes part and parcel of development, as stated in the Universal Declaration and elaborated in the Convention on the Elimination of All Forms of Discrimination against Women (CEDAW).[32]

Questions about the sustainability of the process also become crucial. Is the whole process sustainable? How well have choices been kept open for the future? Questions about sustainability must now focus on whether opportunities and choices are being preserved for future generations.

Some might ask whether incorporating human rights in the criteria of development is to set the hurdle too high. Can we really apply the standards of human rights to periods long before the rights were taken seriously? As mentioned earlier, in the 1950s and 1960s, human rights became sharply polarized, with the West emphasizing political and civil rights and the Soviet bloc emphasizing economic, social, and sometimes cultural rights. Human rights too often became more of a political football to kick at the other side than a serious test by which to judge one's own progress. Is it fair therefore to apply to development the test of whether it enlarged people's rights—political and civil as well as economic and social and cultural rights? This is precisely the point. Today's human-focused approach would and should assess progress not only by how much people's economic and social standards have advanced but by whether the process of development has been one in which human freedoms in political and civil and cultural space have been protected.

In the world of today, no country or community is an island unto itself. Progress in individual countries and communities is closely linked with progress in other countries and communities and with the world as a whole. So global policy and action to expand choices and opportunities for people in all countries, including the poorest, is also important.

From the beginning, the UN has been centrally concerned with this global situation—what could be called "building an enabling framework on a global scale." In terms of human development, this involves concern for international action to ensure the opportunities that allow countries and individuals to develop their capacities and exercise their human capabilities.

1. Economic, social, and cultural frameworks, both national and international, which are dynamic and responsive to human needs and concerns and in which individuals are free to exercise their capabilities;
2. Democratic and legal frameworks, within which elected governments can operate and flourish, that practice inclusive democracy and that include separation of powers; laws, courts, and judges; and national and international structures which ensure justice and accountability;
3. Political and social stability in a peaceful and sustainable environment that avoids extreme and unsustainable levels of inequalities.

This list of elements required for an enabling international and national framework is far from exhaustive, and there are overlapping items in the categories. But it provides a checklist against which the focus and range of UN concerns in the promotion and support of development should be assessed.

Such are the values and criteria, goals and considerations that will underlie our intellectual history of the UN's contributions to development thinking and action over the second half of the twentieth century. To this we now turn—but first we explore the perspectives of development pioneered by the economic giants of the nineteenth and early twentieth centuries.

2

The History of Development Thinking from Adam Smith to John Maynard Keynes

- **The Classical Economists**
- **The Neoclassical and Later Economists**
- **Concluding Observations**

Ideas do not just emerge. Many have a birth date and are born in an identifiable place. But like all children, they draw on the genes of their parents and their character and growth reflect the situation of their birth and upbringing.

In this chapter we set the historical stage of this book by reminding the reader of the extraordinary richness of ideas and thinking on issues of economic and social development from the eighteenth century to the onset of World War II—from Adam Smith to Maynard Keynes. In doing so, we briefly review the pioneering ideas of a core of writers, all of whom have left an imprint on the world as it is today.

We start with the classical economists—Adam Smith, Thomas Malthus, David Ricardo, John Stewart Mill, and Karl Marx. We note some of the dissident voices—Alexander Hamilton and Friedrich List. We move on to Joseph Schumpeter and John Maynard Keynes. UN writers on development made few references to these giants, even though postwar analysis on development often drew on the huge contributions of these early thinkers. The same is true of the UN development debates. Some of the issues most hotly contested in matters of population and development policy, trade, or planning were often reflecting questions raised a century or more earlier by such figures as Malthus and Mill, Hamilton and List, and, more recently, Keynes and Schumpeter. But these debates did not make much reference to earlier times.

If we are to understand the evolution of ideas, we need to refer back to these important antecedents. There are dangers, of course, in taking modern concepts and concerns and imposing them on writers of a different era. But there are dangers also in neglecting the lessons of earlier times. Those who do not learn from history may find themselves repeating it, mistakes and all. Whether considering the case for a laissez-faire economy or socialist planning, open trade or protection of domestic industry, one important lesson from history is that one must take account of the circumstances in which the strategy was first developed and the circumstances in which it is today applied.

The UN as an institution was born with the help of many who were highly aware of the failures of the League of Nations and determined, this time, to fashion a Charter and international institutions sufficient to put an end to war. In matters of economic and social development, one can argue—as we will—that there was too much focus on the economic failures of the Great Depression as they affected the industrial countries of Europe and the United States and too little focus on, or even consciousness of, the weaknesses and failures of development in the developing countries. More attention to the early experience of nineteenth-century development in the industrial countries might have helped to avoid this.

The reader may well ask why we tell here a story that has been told many times before.[1] The answer is that we tell the story not in general but with a specific focus on its relevance for the development problems of the second half of the twentieth century and beyond. As we proceed in this chapter, the reader will see example after example of discussions first held 100 or 200 years ago that still have an eerie modern ring to them. Perhaps the world—politicians and diplomats—could solve things quicker today by being more aware of those earlier debates instead of repeating them, often in clumsier and less clear terms. One example is the modern debate about trade liberalization, another is the relevance of the neoclassical upsurge of the last twenty years, and a third is the need for stronger structures of governance. All need to be interpreted with more attention to the stages of a country's development. We shall, of course, come back to the lessons of these in the concluding observations at the end of this chapter.

The Classical Economists

Adam Smith

In the introduction to *An Inquiry into the Nature and Causes of the Wealth of Nations* (commonly referred to as *The Wealth of Nations*),[2] Adam Smith made it clear that his leading theme was economic development: the long-term forces that govern capital accumulation and economic growth. *The Wealth of Nations* appeared in the same year that James Watt patented the perfected steam engine. The book paid little attention to machines, factories, or industrial production; the production it described was still craft based. The industrial revolution in the United Kingdom really took off toward the end of the eighteenth century, and therefore it is hardly surprising that Smith failed to anticipate it. This helps to account for the fact that he neglected fixed capital and his conviction that agricultural production was the principal source of Britain's wealth.

In *The Wealth of Nations,* Adam Smith did not make a distinction between development and growth, although he covered many social and ethical problems, particularly in his other writings. For him, development was economic growth and growth was rooted in the increasing division of labor that broke down big tasks into many components, which enhanced efficiency:

> This great increase of the quantity of work which, in consequence of the division of labor, the same number of people are capable of performing, is owing to three different circumstances: first to the increase of dexterity in every particular workman; secondly, to the saving of the time which is commonly lost in passing from one species of work to another; and lastly, to the invention of a great number of machines which facilitate and abridge labour, and enable man to do the work of many.[3]

Productive labor, to Smith, fulfilled two important requirements. First, it led to the "production of tangible objects." Second, labor needed to "create a surplus" which could be reinvested in production. The objective of development was to create a social order in which the individual, in pursuing his or her own self-interest, necessarily contributed to the general interest of society. The propensity of human nature "to truck, barter and exchange one thing for another" was conducive to harmonious relations among people and between people and their government, given a policy of laissez-faire.[4]

Adam Smith differentiated several stages of social development, culminating in "commercial civilization," a state of extensive and increasing national wealth. A nation's wealth consisted in the well-being of the mass of ordinary citizens. Hence, Smith saw the wealth of commercial nations as well diffused. As we have seen, the division of labor boosts labor productivity. The increase in productivity in rural occupations, according to Smith, could not occur in Europe until towns and long-distance trade had developed because of the importance of property as an incentive to improving production. The natural progress of wealth was from agriculture to manufacture, as food was the first thing that had to be set aside before anyone could specialize in manufacture and town manufactures used materials from the country. In Smith's words: "According to the natural course of things . . . the greater part of the capital of every growing society is, first, directed to agriculture, afterwards to manufactures, and last of all to foreign commerce."[5]

Adam Smith explained how the commerce of the towns contributed to the improvement of the countries to which they belonged:

First, by affording a great and ready market for the rude produce of the country, they gave encouragement to its cultivation and further improvement. . . . Secondly, the wealth acquired by the inhabitants of cities was frequently employed in purchasing such lands as were to be sold, of which a great part would frequently be uncultivated. . . . Thirdly, and lastly, commerce and manufactures gradually introduced order and good government, and with them, the liberty and security of individuals, among the inhabitants of the country, who had lived before almost in a continual state of war with their neighbors, and of servile dependency upon their superiors.[6]

Smith stated that the division of labor was limited by the extent of the market. The advent of water transportation widened the market: "It is natural that the first improvements of art and industry should be made where this conveniency opens the whole world for a market to the produce of every sort of labour, and that they should always be much later in extending themselves into inland parts of the country."[7] Cities on the seacoast or on navigable rivers were not dependent on the country in their neighborhood and had the world as a market.

The central theme that inspired *The Wealth of Nations* was the working of the "invisible hand": it is not to the benevolence of the baker but to his self-interest that we owe bread.[8] How did Smith see the question of inequalities in such a system? He clearly saw the inequalities of power and wealth emerging under incipient capitalism. The interests of capitalists ("masters") and laborers are by no means the same. The workmen desire to get as much as possible, the masters to give as little as possible:

We rarely hear, it has been said, of the combinations of masters, though frequently of those of workmen. But whoever imagines, upon this account, that masters rarely combine, is as ignorant of the world as of the subject. Masters are always and everywhere in a sort of tacit, but constant and uniform combination, not to raise the wages of labour above their actual rate. . . . Masters, too, sometimes enter into particular combinations to sink the wages of labour even below this rate. These are always conducted with the utmost silence and secrecy, till the moment of execution, and when the workmen yield, as they sometimes do, without resistance, though severely felt by them, they are never heard of by other people.[9]

Smith also discussed inequalities due to the "policy of Europe" which placed restrictions on the market's freedom. It restricted competition on some jobs ("employments"), primarily by giving exclusive privileges to corporations requiring long apprenticeships, therefore limiting the number of apprentices. It overstocked other professions and drove down wages in those professions by educating aspirants at public expense. Hence scholarships to encourage the education of the clergy resulted in low pay for clergymen and also for writers and teachers. Smith claimed that "the usual reward of the eminent teacher bears no proportion to that of the lawyer or physician, because the trade of the one is crowded with indigent people who have been brought up to it at the public expense, whereas those of the other two are encumbered with very few who have not been educated at their own."[10] How little has changed during the past 230 years!

Smith's view on inequality, therefore, was dim. In Book Two, this came out with particular clarity:

> Wherever there is great property, there is great inequality. For one very rich man, there must be at least five hundred poor, and the affluence of the few supposes the indigence of the many. The affluence of the rich excites the indignation of the poor, who are often both driven by want, and prompted by envy, to invade his possessions. It is only under the shelter of the civil magistrate that the owner of that valuable property, which is acquired by the labour of many years, or perhaps of many successive generations, can sleep a single night in security.[11]

As implied in this quote, Adam Smith was not satisfied to argue that a free-market economy secures the best of all possible worlds. He was very much preoccupied with specifying the exact institutional structure that would guarantee the beneficent operation of market forces. He was aware of the fact that self-interest is just as likely to hinder as to promote the public welfare and must therefore be surrounded by an appropriate legal and institutional framework.

Adam Smith covered a large surface: he had quite a few things to say about religion and how "the gradual improvement of arts, manufactures, and commerce" destroys the power of the clergy.[12] There are also many references to education and training. According to Mark Blaug, however, it is not true, as has been frequently maintained, that Smith and other classical economists originated the theory of human capital or that they approved of the now-standard belief in the principle of free but compulsory schooling.[13]

Finally, Smith's laissez-aller and laissez-faire can, of course, lead to antisocial behavior. One could construct a science of manners around the need for people to recognize the effects of their personal actions on others and to take care to mitigate those which are most irritating and negative to others. There is an interaction between manners and laws that affects the freedom that people can enjoy. Laws and manners are to some extent substitutes. A system of ethics and the inculcation of socially defensible habits could replace coercion and bureaucratic control as a regulating principle of society. Adam Smith was aware of some of those interactions when he expounded his doctrine of the invisible hand.

Long before *The Wealth of Nations,* Adam Smith had published *The Theory of Moral Sentiments,*[14] in which he wrote: "Prudence was of all virtues that which is most helpful to the individual. Humanity, justice, generosity and public spirit, are the qualities most useful to others."[15] This suggests that he had tried to develop a theory of *social* interest long before he expounded his theory of *self-*interest. The "Adam Smith problem" consists precisely of this paradox: on the one hand, production and exchanges should better be guided by self-interest, but on the other, prudence and benevolence should guide behavior. Self-interest is always prudent self-interest; that is, "the wise conduct directed towards the care of health, of the fortune, rank and reputation of the individual."[16] It is here that the thinking of Adam Smith relates most clearly to what was said in Chapter 1 about values and criteria in the development process.

Thomas Robert Malthus

Malthus published his famous *Essay on the Principle of Population* in 1798,[17] a good twenty years after Smith's *The Wealth of Nations.* Malthus's theory, in its simplest form, can be stated as follows: the biological capacity of man to reproduce himself exceeds his physical capacity to increase the food supply. He introduced the famous distinction—repeated many times since to illustrate analogous impossibilities—between two kinds of progression, the geometrical increase in numbers (2, 4, 8, 16, 32, etc.) and the arithmetical increase in food (100, 103, 106, 109, etc.). Additional people could reproduce themselves—hence the compound factor—whereas additional food could not. According to Malthus, a rapid increase in foodstuffs is out of the question because the supply of land is limited and technical improvements in agriculture do not come fast and hard enough. This assertion was later baptized as the law of diminishing returns.

> The constant effort towards population, which is found to act even in the most vicious societies, increases the number of people before the means of subsistence are increased. The food therefore which before supported seven millions must now be divided among seven millions and a half or eight millions. The poor consequently must live much worse, and many of them be reduced to severe distress. The number of labourers also being above the proportion of the work in the market, the price of labour must tend towards a decrease, while the price of provisions would at the same time tend to rise. The labourer therefore must work harder to earn the same as he did before.[18]

However, Malthus argued not that land was augmentable only at increased cost but that capital accumulation and technical change could not offset limitations in natural resources. With hindsight, it is clear that for Malthus the

law of diminishing returns was a static proposition ruling out the technological progress the world has known since 1800.

But the important point to make here is that Malthus's theory had analytical consequences that made it an integral part of classical economics that has
lasted long after he was proven wrong in his vision concerning population. By
emphasizing the rigid dependence of population growth on the food supply,
Malthusian theory lent support to the subsistence theory of wages and prepared the way for the Ricardian preoccupation with the land-using bias of
economic progress. By explaining poverty in terms of a race between population and the means of subsistence, Malthus provided the touchstone for all
classical thinking about economic policy and inequalities.

> The true cause of the advance in the price of labour is thus concealed, and the
> rich affect to grant it as an act of compassion and favour to the poor, in consider-
> ation of a year of scarcity, and, when plenty returns, indulge themselves in the
> most unreasonable of all complaints, that the price does not again fall, when a
> little rejection would show them that it must have risen long before but from an
> unjust conspiracy of their own. But though the rich by unfair combinations con-
> tribute frequently to prolong a season of distress among the poor, yet no possible
> form of society could prevent the almost constant action of misery upon a great
> part of mankind, if in a state of inequality, and upon all, if all were equal.[19]
>
> Where there is any inequality of conditions, and among nations of shep-
> herds this soon takes place, the distress arising from a scarcity of provisions
> must fall hardest upon the least fortunate members of the society. This distress
> also must frequently have been felt by the women, exposed to casual plunder in
> the absence of their husbands, and subject to continual disappointments in
> their expected return.[20]

By focusing attention on the limited supply of land, Malthusian theory led
not only to the concept of diminishing returns but also to a theory of the
nature of ground rent. Both Malthus and Ricardo saw the law of diminishing
returns as applicable only to agriculture by showing that the growth of population forces recourse to inferior soil. If this was true, then it would follow
that price would be regulated by the least favorable circumstance under which
production was carried on and that, in consequence, rent would be the excess
of the product over the outlays of the marginal farmer for capital and labor.
This excess went to the landlord as rent. This led straight to Ricardo and John
Stuart Mill. Ricardian theory had it that ground rent was eminently suitable
for taxation, and Mill drew the obvious corollary that all future increments in
rent could be taxed away without serious harm. As one can imagine, the idea
of confiscating the income of a leading social class was deeply shocking, in
those days as well as (again) in ours.

David Ricardo

If the major problem of economics is growth and development, Adam Smith contributed more than David Ricardo. But Ricardo's writings helped to make free trade a popular objective of policy. It could be said that he unwittingly provided the theoretical justification for the long-range solution to the growth problem of Great Britain in the nineteenth century: Britain became "the workshop of the world" and bought most of its food abroad.[21] Thus, even if Ricardo has little to say about economic growth per se, his work[22] on international trade and the so-called Ricardo effect make him extremely relevant to our problem.

What has survived of Ricardo above all is the law of comparative advantage. This was his way of demonstrating how international factors are introduced in the analysis:

> Under a system of perfectly free commerce, each country naturally devoted its capital and labour to such employments as are most beneficial to each. This pursuit of individual advantage is admirably connected with the universal good of the whole. By stimulating industry, by rewarding ingenuity, and by using most efficaciously the peculiar powers bestowed by nature, it distributes labour most effectively and most economically, while, by increasing the general mass of productions, it diffuses general benefit, and binds together, by one common tie of interest and intercourse, the universal society of nations throughout the civilized world. It is this principle which determines that wine shall be made in France and Portugal, that corn shall be grown in America and Poland, and that hardware and other goods shall be manufactured in England.[23]

Specialization based on the theory of comparative advantage (to be precise, we should talk about the law of comparative cost and the method of comparative static analysis) leads to an increase in production which benefits all of the world economy. The point of Ricardo's analysis is to show that the conditions that make international trade possible are different from the conditions under which domestic trade will arise. Within a nation, trade between two places requires an absolute difference in costs, but a comparative difference is a sufficient condition for the existence of international trade.

Ricardo was struck by the fact that measured in money of constant purchasing power, a rise in wages would raise the price of labor-intensive goods relative to the price of capital-intensive goods. Under such conditions, the price of a labor-intensive good such as wheat would rise, while that of a capital-intensive good such as cloth would fall in price. This is the so-called Ricardo effect.[24]

Ricardo believed that wages naturally tended toward a minimum level corresponding to the subsistence needs of the workers. Movements in wages depend upon the proportion between capital and population. Any time wages rise above the natural (subsistence) level—because the pace of capital accumulation exceeds that of population—the population will increase and thus cause wages to go down again. In describing this "iron law of wages," Ricardo distinguished between "natural" and "market" price:

> However much the market price of labour may deviate from its natural price, it has, like commodities, a tendency to conform to it. It is when the market price of labour exceeds its natural price, that the condition of the laborer is flourishing and happy, that he has it in his power to command a greater proportion of the necessaries and enjoyments of life, and therefore to rear a healthy and numerous family. When, however, by the encouragement which high wages give to the increase of population, the number of laborers is increased, wages again fall to their natural price, and indeed from a reaction sometimes fall below it.
>
> When the market price of labour is below its natural price, the condition of the laborers is most wretched: then poverty deprives them of those comforts which custom renders absolute necessaries. It is only after their privations have reduced their number, or the demand of labor has increased, that the market price will rise to its natural price, and that the laborer will have the moderate comforts which the natural rate of wages will afford.[25]

Ricardo predicted that the landlords would receive an increasing share of the national income while capitalists would get ever less. This shift in income distribution and in the distribution of wealth would lead to economic stagnation. Every rise in a laborer's wage would lead to that laborer having more and more children, which in turn would compete his wages down to bare subsistence. Capitalists would find their wage costs and their rents getting ever higher while their profits got smaller. Thus the landlords would alone get wealthier and wealthier, while the rest of society—both capitalists and laborers—would get poorer and poorer.

The leading Ricardian doctrine, therefore, states that the productivity of labor in agriculture governs the rate of return on capital as well as the secular changes in the distribution shares. This has been a hotly debated issue, but the central problem that Ricardo posed—namely, how the changes in the relative shares of land, labor, and capital are connected with the rate of capital accumulation—remains one of the abiding concerns of modern economists.

But when everything is said and done, the one thing that has really survived of Ricardo is the law of comparative cost and the method of comparative static analysis. We owe to Ricardo the entire subsequent development of comparative and competitive advantages as well as the discussion on the terms of trade. It was a giant contribution that had major implications for policy and practice, then as today. Yet Ricardo's analysis and conclusions reflected the situation of Great Britain at the time quite accurately. In Britain, the industrial revolution was well under way. British industries were well established and had the strength to outcompete those of other countries, even to the extent of preventing competitors from getting established. It is not surprising that those analyzing trade from the perspective of weaker countries came to different conclusions. This was the position of List and Hamilton.

Friedrich List

Friedrich List published his most important work in 1841, twenty years after Ricardo but well before Mill and Marx.[26] List pleaded in favor of a *Zollverein* (a customs union) as a way to unite the many German states and principalities. He found his political counterpart in Otto von Bismarck, who led the way to the unification of Germany with List's book in hand.

List, who emigrated from Germany to the United States in 1825 and returned in 1834 as the American consul at Leipzig, set out a theory focused on the expansion and growth of productive power: "The power of producing wealth is . . . infinitely more important than wealth itself; it insures not only the possession and the increase of what has been gained, but also the replacement of what has been lost."[27] "The prosperity of a nation is not, as Say believes, greater in proportion in which it has amassed more wealth (i.e. values of exchange), but in the proportion in which it has more *developed its power of production.*"[28]

List saw no real contradiction between free trade and protection, as neither is an end in itself but is rather merely a means to develop the productive power of a nation. Which of the two is preferable depends on how developed the nation is in relation to the level of development of other nations. A loss under protection is justifiable if it leads to greater gains in the future:

> It is true that protective duties at first increase the price of manufactured goods; but it is just as true, and moreover acknowledged by the prevailing economic school, that in the course of time, by the nation being enabled to build up a completely developed manufacturing power of its own, those goods are produced more cheaply at home than the price at which they can be imported from foreign parts. If, therefore, a sacrifice of *value* is caused by protective duties, it is made good by the gain of a *power of production,* which not only secures to the nation an infinitely greater amount of material goods, but also industrial independence in case of war.[29]

It is interesting that the United States was the birthplace of the protection of infant industries, adopting policies designed by Alexander Hamilton, the first secretary of the treasury in the post-Revolution government of George Washington. Hamilton believed that manufacturing was necessary for economic development and a strong economy. He argued that a protected home market was needed until American industry was strong enough to resist the onslaught of the (already) industrializing European nations. In addition to protective tariffs, Hamilton argued in favor of government investments in infrastructure, unification of the thirteen former colonies into a single market without internal tariffs, and establishment of a unified creditworthy financial system.[30] The U.S. not only followed these policies for a century and a half but also remained the world's most heavily protected economy until World War II.[31]

List had a more subtle analysis of how countries should modify their trading systems according to the stages of their own development. Initially, they should adopt free trade with more developed nations as a way to stimulate their own development and make agricultural advances. They then should enact commercial restrictions to promote the growth of manufactures, fisheries, navigation, and foreign trade. Ultimately, and "after reaching the highest degree of wealth and power," they should progressively revert to free trade principles and de-restrict competition in national and foreign markets to ensure that their agriculturalists, manufacturers, and merchants would not grow slothful and would retain their commercial domination.

Regarding manufactures and agriculture, List argued:

> The productive power of the cultivator and of the laborer in agriculture will always be greater or smaller according to the degree in which the exchange of agricultural produce for manufactures and other products of various kinds can proceed more or less readily. That in this respect the foreign trade of any nation which is but little advanced can prove in the highest degree beneficial, we have shown in another chapter by the example of England. But a nation which has already made considerable advances in civilization, in possession of capital, and in population, will find the development of a manufacturing power of its own infinitely more beneficial to its agriculture than the most flourishing foreign trade can be without such manufactures.[32]
>
> With regard to the interchange of *raw products,* the [free trade] school is perfectly correct in supposing that the most extensive liberty of commerce is, under all circumstances, most advantageous to the individual as well as to the entire State. One can, indeed, augment this production by restrictions; but the advantage obtained thereby is merely apparent. We only thereby divert, as the school says, capital and labour into another and less useful channel.[33]

With respect to the stages listed above, List wrote in 1841: "In the first stage, we see Spain, Portugal, and the Kingdom of Naples; in the second, Germany and the United States of North America; France apparently stands close upon the boundary line of the last stage, but Great Britain alone at the present time has actually reached it."[34]

List said of the English of his time:

Through their position as the manufacturing and commercial monopolists of the world, their manufactories from time to time fall into a state which they call "glut," and which arises from what they call "overtrading." At such periods everybody throws his stock of goods into the steamers. . . . The English manufacturers suffer for the moment, but they are saved, and they compensate themselves later by better prices.[35]

List also wrote insightfully of Venice:

If we carefully consider the commercial policy of Venice, we see at a glance that that of modern commercial and manufacturing nations is but a copy of that of Venice, only on an enlarged (i.e. national) scale. . . . It has been recently asserted in defense of the principle of absolute and unconditional free trade, that her protective policy was the cause of the downfall of Venice. That assertion comprises a little truth with a great deal of error. . . . Unrestricted freedom of trade was beneficial to the Republic in the first years of her existence. . . . But a protective policy was also beneficial to her when she had arrived at a certain stage of power and wealth, for by means of it she attained to manufacturing and commercial supremacy. Protection first became injurious to her when her manufacturing and commercial power had reached that supremacy, because by it all competition with other nations became absolutely excluded, and thus indolence was encouraged. Therefore, not the introduction of a protective policy, but perseverance in maintaining it after the reasons for its introduction had passed away, was really injurious to Venice.[36]

In this, one can hear echoes of debates that would reverberate a hundred or more years later. The above quote could have been of Raúl Prebisch, as we shall see in the next chapter. And some of the economic difficulties of Latin America today are due to the fact that, like Venice, many countries of the continent continued too long with import-substituting policies instead of moving—like East Asia did—to an export-promoting stance.

Though Britain in the mid-nineteenth century might have been described as having reached the highest degree of wealth and power, it was still far from industrialized. Factories and machines were not yet central to the whole economy. They had played only a modest role in the economics of David Ricardo, who lived from 1772 to 1823. Neither factory workers nor bankers can be found in the novels of Jane Austen, England's perceptive social critic at the turn of the nineteenth century. We have to wait for Honoré de Balzac and Charles Dickens—that is, the middle of the nineteenth century—to see bankers, the stock exchange, and the factory system make their appearance. Dickens's *Hard Times: For These Times*[37] is the first industrial novel, the powerful story of a bitter strike in a cotton mill and class war at its starkest.

John Stuart Mill

Mill published the first edition of his *Principles of Political Economy* in 1848.[38] His aim was—as he said in the preface—to write an updated *Wealth of Nations* "adapted to the more extended knowledge and improved ideas of the present age."[39] The five books of Mill's *Principles of Political Economy* remained the main source of economic wisdom during the entire second half of the nineteenth century, and only toward its end did Alfred Marshall's treatise begin to be the major influence.

In his sketch of economic development since ancient times, Mill made a sharp distinction between the laws of production laid down by technical conditions and the laws of distribution governed by "human institutions" and the "laws and customs of society." Nothing could be done about the laws of production, for they are given by "the character of physical truths." But the laws of distribution are subject to human decision and are capable of being altered even under a regime of private property.[40] Mill saw, therefore, a greater potential for mankind to influence the laws of economics than many had seen before him. This led him to be more optimistic than Malthus, by whom he was otherwise very influenced. To defeat Malthus's predictions, more active state intervention was both possible and necessary, Mill argued. Though worried about industrial concentration, he was hopeful that governments could help stabilize economic development:

> [We] yet looked forward to a time when society will no longer be divided into the idle and the industrious; when the rule that they who do not work shall not eat, will be applied not to paupers only, but impartially to all; when the division of the produce of labour, instead of depending, as in so great a degree it now does, on the accident of birth, will be made by concert on an acknowledged principle of justice; and when it will no longer either be, or be thought to be, impossible for human beings to exert themselves strenuously in procuring benefits which are not to be exclusively their own, but to be shared with the society they belong to.[41]

There is a clear echo here of what we said in the previous chapter about values and criteria. Mill predicted an increase in the scale of business firms in the course of economic development, a prediction that is often attributed to Marx as one of his accurate forecasts. The advantages of scale must be set off against the dangers of oligopoly and spontaneous agreements to restrict entry and to keep up prices: "Where competitors are so few, they always end up by agreeing not to compete. They may run a race of cheapness to ruin a new candidate, but as soon as he has established his footing they come to terms with him."[42] Natural monopolies must be nationalized, Mill concluded.

Mill noted the "improvement in the business capacities of the general mass of mankind," even though he was "inclined to believe that economical progress has hitherto had a contrary effect on human sagacity."[43] Mill also argued that we should sacrifice economic growth for the sake of the environment and should limit population as much to give ourselves breathing space as to fend off the risk of starvation for the overburdened poor.

Concerning the essence of the economic and social development process, Mill recognized the importance of technological advance:

> Of the features which characterize this progressive economical movement of civilized nations that which first excites attention . . . is the perpetual, and so far as human foresight can extend, the unlimited, growth of man's power over nature. Our knowledge of the properties and laws of physical objects shows no sign of approaching its ultimate boundaries. . . . This increasing physical knowledge is now, too, more rapidly than at any former period, converted, by practical ingenuity, into physical power. The most marvelous of modern inventions . . . the electro-magnetic telegraph sprang into existence but a few years after the establishment of the scientific theory which it realizes and exemplifies. . . . Another change, which has always characterized, and will assuredly continue to characterize, the progress of civilized society, is a continual increase of the security of the person and property.[44]

On matters of international trade, Mill was a classical liberal; foreign commerce, he said, leads to "a more efficient employment of the productive forces of the world."[45] The tendency of every extension of the market is "to improve the process of production."[46] But he claimed not only that free trade was essential to realize collective security but also that the establishment of an international organization to supervise free trade practices was a crucial part of instituting genuinely free trade and a peaceful international environment. Mill considered the enacting of protectionist measures to be threats to security as well as impediments to free trade and a vigorous political economy.

Mill held that nations may, like individual dealers, be competitors with opposite interests in the markets of some commodities, while in others they are in the more fortunate relation of reciprocal customers. The benefit of commerce did not consist, as it was once thought to do, in the commodities sold; but since the commodities sold were the means of obtaining those which are bought, a nation would be cut off from the real advantage of commerce, the imports, if it could not induce other nations to take any of its commodities in exchange; and in proportion as the competition of other countries compelled it to offer its commodities on cheaper terms, on pain of not selling them at all, the imports which it obtained by its foreign trade were procured at greater cost.[47]

In discussing the laws of distribution, Mill presented the first discussion of socialism in a major treatise of economics. However, it must not be forgotten that he wrote before Marx. When dealing with socialism, therefore, his focus was on the ideas of Saint-Simon and Fourier, which bear little resemblance to those of Marx. Mill's treatment of socialist theory is sympathetic but differs from socialists on one fundamental question. He traced the social ills experienced under capitalism to rampant individualism and inadequate safeguards against the abuses of property rights, not to the private ownership of property. Mill also drew a distinction between communism—a society in which income is equalized regardless of the productivity of individuals—and socialism, which retains the incentives of differential pecuniary rewards.[48] This distinction is identical to the one Marx drew between "each according to his ability" under socialism and "each according to his need" under communism.

As to why women are paid less than men, Mill claimed that the reason is either customary prejudice that makes "almost every woman, socially speaking, an appendage of some man" or that the "degree of overcrowding [of women's particular professions] may depress the wages of women to a much lower minimum than those of men."[49] Furthermore, there were "kinds of labour of which the wages are fixed by custom, and not by competition. Such are the fees or charges of professional persons: of physicians, surgeons, barristers, and even attorneys."[50]

Mill declared some strong views on distribution which could make him a patron saint of the Green movement today. "It is only in the backward countries of the world that increased production is still an important object; in those most advanced, what is economically needed is better distribution."[51]

Mill, in general, was in favor of laissez-faire unless state intervention was required "for some greater good." An important example of the latter was his recommendation of compulsory education and a state system of examinations because the consumer of education is not a "competent judge of the commodity." Mill also approved the regulation of hours of work on the ground that public action is sometimes necessary to give effect to the self-interest of individuals.[52] In this respect, Mill differs from the classical economists. He left no doubt that he regarded both the quantity and quality of private education in England as seriously inadequate.[53] He asserted: "I hold it therefore the duty of the government to supply the defect, by giving pecuniary support to elementary schools."[54]

Almost a century before the creation of the UN, Mill thus worked over many of the ideas which would be raised time and again in relation to postwar development. He developed and analyzed many proposals for economic reform and social improvement. He was not a socialist, despite his sympathetic treatment of the theory, but a "classical liberal." He attributed the social ills he saw around him not to private ownership of the means of production but to the untrammeled exercise of private property rights, as we have seen above. His attitude to capitalism as an economic system was free from dogmatism; he thought it premature to dispense with the profit motive while there were still ample prospects of improvements under the present economic order.

Karl Marx

Marx was undoubtedly a great classical economist. His leitmotif was the theory of surplus value, and he stood at the cradle—later further developed by Lenin—of the Marxian theory of imperialism. It is a theory of the nature of foreign policy of capitalist governments and a theory of economic development that traces the causes of the gap between rich and poor countries to the dynamics of foreign investment in capitalist countries. It was Lenin rather than Marx who developed all the implications of the argument, but Marx stands at its origin. And though Marx wrote about capitalism rather than socialism, the thinking of Marx was at the origin of the worldwide efforts to create socialist systems in many parts of the world in the twentieth century. Marx and Marxist analysis also inspired many later critiques of the global capitalist system, including dependency theory.

The first volume of Marx's *Das Kapital* was published in 1867, the second volume in 1885 (after his death in 1883), and the third volume in 1894.[55] Friedrich Engels edited volumes two and three, but we have his word that the drafts of these two volumes were completed by Marx before his death.[56]

In his devastating critique of capitalism, Marx analyzed the mechanism at its core: "Accumulate, accumulate! That is Moses and the prophets."[57] Capitalist firms exist to make profits. Capitalists sell commodities for more money than they pay for the inputs that produce them. Thus, over the whole system, capitalists appropriate a surplus value. The worker, using contemporary machinery and technology, performs the "socially necessary quantity of labor" in the production process.[58] He is normally able to reproduce in value the cost of his own work in a matter of a few hours per day. But the worker is paid not just to work the few hours during which he reproduces the cost of his own labor power, but for many more hours per day. Thus, the capitalist recovers not only the cost of the wages but also the surplus value produced during the remaining hours of labor. Moreover, absolute surplus value is extracted through lengthening the working day; relative surplus value is extracted through intensified exploitation.

Marx described the "laws of motion" of the capitalist development process as consisting of several long-term tendencies:

- The capitalist's compulsion to accumulate
- The tendency toward technological revolutions
- The capitalist's unappeasable thirst for the extraction of surplus value
- The tendency toward growing concentration and centralization of capital
- The tendency of the rate of profit to decline
- The tendency toward growing objective socialization of labor

For Marx, technological innovation was a central part of the process, directly enhancing the productivity of labor: "Like every other increase in the productiveness of labour, machinery is intended to cheapen commodities, and, by shortening that portion of the working day in which the labourer works for himself, to lengthen the other portion that he gives, without an equivalent, to the capitalist. In short, it is a means for producing surplus value."[59] The capitalist, therefore, tries to introduce modern technologies in order to increase the number of hours during which the worker produces surplus value.

Marx explained that the greater the amount of capital investment required to start a factory capable of competing with existing factories, the harder it is to become an independent capitalist. Competition inevitably gobbles up smaller factories[60] that merge in self-defense. Larger enterprises with their superior economies of scale and technologies cheapen commodities at a faster rate than smaller enterprises. Thus, they drive the latter out of business or simply buy them out. Ownership and control are steadily centralized.

Marx saw an inevitable long-term tendency for rates of profit to fall. As capital accumulates from the creation of surplus value, capitalists in competition with each other will normally reinvest more of that surplus value into "constant capital" (i.e., technology embodied in machinery) than into "variable capital" (i.e., wages for labor). Thus, as capital accumulates, the proportion of constant capital to variable capital will increase. This in turn will result in a fall in the relative value of variable capital and hence in the amount of surplus value.

Marx, in a colorful and biting passage, brought together these tendencies, illustrated the workings of the laws of motion, and looked forward to the long-term result of this historical tendency of capitalist accumulation:

> The expropriation of the immediate producers is accomplished with merciless vandalism, and under the stimulus of passions the most infamous, the most sordid, the pettiest, the most meanly odious. Self-earned private property (of

the peasant and handicraftsman), that is based, so to say, on the fusing together of the isolated, independent laboring individual with the conditions of his labor, is supplanted by capitalist private property, which rests on exploitation of the nominally free labor of others. . . . That which is now to be expropriated is no longer the laborer working for himself, but the capitalist exploiting many laborers. This expropriation is accomplished by the action of the immanent laws of capitalist production itself, by the centralization of capital. One capitalist always kills many. Hand in hand with this centralization, or this expropriation of many capitalists by few, will develop, on an ever extending scale, the co-operative form of the labor-process, the conscious technical application of science, the methodical cultivation of the soil, the transformation of the instruments of labor into instruments of labor only usable in common, the economizing of all means of production by their use as the means of production of combined socialized labor, the entanglement of all people in the net of the world market, and with this the international character of the capitalist regime. Along with the constantly diminishing number of the magnates of capital, who usurp and monopolize all advantages of this process of transformation, grows the mass of misery, oppression, slavery, degradation, exploitation; but with this too grows the revolt of the working class, a class always increasing in numbers, and disciplined, united, organized by the mechanism of the process of capitalist production. The monopoly of capital becomes a fetter upon the mode of production, which has sprung up and flourished along with and under it. Centralization of the means of production and socialization of labor at last reach a point where they become incompatible with the capitalist structure. The integument is burst asunder. The knell of capitalist private property sounds. The expropriators are expropriated.[61]

As Marx said in *The Communist Manifesto* in 1848,[62] capitalism seeks everywhere to make the world in its image: bourgeoisie and proletariat. Everywhere capitalism spreads, it brings industrialization and urbanization, creating conditions of penury and misery among wage laborers. The pressures of the forces of production proletarianize all middle strata. Every occupation that retained a remnant of status from previous modes of production (doctors, teachers, artists, and clergy) is made a form of wage labor. The one-world economy is characterized by a continual search for new products, new methods, new markets, new workforces, and so forth; it is a world in which all producers become separated from the means of production and in which employers must constantly innovate to remain in business. This line of reasoning inevitably led to the thesis of economic imperialism.

Marxist theory supposes that a closed capitalist economy must suffer from a chronic shortage of effective demand, from a basic imbalance that can only be corrected by the opening of foreign markets. Imperialism, the direct or indirect exploitation of backward areas, was therefore seen as an inherent feature of advanced capitalist economies. Marx, and for that matter John Stuart Mill, argued that the export of capital counteracts the decline in the rate of profit by draining off excess savings—hence the proposition that the inability to dispose profitably of goods and capital at home leads inevitably to imperialist ventures. This theory of imperialism was elaborated by Lenin, who combined the high-profit pull of backward areas with the low-profit push of late-stage capitalism in his emphasis on foreign investment:

> In these backward countries profits are usually high, for capital is scarce, the price of land is relatively low, wages are low, raw materials are cheap. The possibility of exporting capital is created by the fact that numerous backward countries have been drawn into international capitalist intercourse; main railways have either been built or are being built there; the elementary conditions for industrial developments have been created etc. The necessity of exporting capital arises from the fact that in a few countries capitalism has become "over-ripe" and (owing to the backward state of agriculture and the impoverished state of the masses) capital cannot find "profitable" investment.[63]

Marx's analysis of inequalities under capitalism has already been summarized. Under capitalism, workers are free to sell their labor power to whatever capitalist chooses to employ them. But the asymmetry of power behind this ostensibly "free exchange" is that while the capitalists own the means of production, workers have only their labor power to sell. One can understand the appeal of this analysis to the trade union movement and to many in developing countries.

The Neoclassical and Later Economists

After 1870, preoccupation with increases in the quantity and quality of resources and the dynamic expansion of economic growth, needs, and wants moved to the back of the stage in economic theory. These effects had been regarded by the classical economists as essential to the improvements of economic welfare. The classical preoccupation with economic development was replaced by a focus on the analysis of general equilibrium within an essentially static framework.

Neglect of development issues was a stronger feature of the neoclassical theorists of the Lausanne and Austrian Schools than those of the English School, which was dominated by Alfred Marshall, and above all, his magnum opus, *Principles of Economics*—for many years the bible of British economics. Marshall had learned his economics from John Stuart Mill and never entirely abandoned the deep-rooted classical belief that economic welfare depends as

much on capital accumulation and population growth as on efficiency in resource allocation. Moreover, Marshall's writings on economic growth very
much echo those of John Stuart Mill forty years earlier.[64] Nonetheless, though
the brilliant contributions of Alfred Marshall and those of such luminaries as
William Stanley Jevons, Philip Henry Wicksteed, Gustav Cassel, and Leon
Walras did much to refine the science of economics and to lay its foundations
as a quantitative science, in terms of development, the long-term effect of
their contributions was to establish a deep divide from the classical preoccupations with capital accumulation, growth, and development. Indeed, the divide was so deep and sustained that it lasted for over half a century. Other
problems took center stage, such as equilibrium analysis, business cycles, and
other microeconomic problems. Not until after World War II and the founding of the United Nations would growth and development move back to center stage—and then only for part of the economic profession.

Joseph A. Schumpeter

Along this long *traversée du désert,* one of the few oases to be encountered
is Joseph Schumpeter's theory of innovations-generated growth. The classical economists had mostly seen the sources of growth in the accumulation of
capital and in growth of population and the labor force. Schumpeter shifted
this emphasis to innovation as the engine of growth, putting "creative chaos"
at the center of his theory.[65]

> Continuous changes, which may in time, by continual adaptation through in-
> numerable small steps, make a great department store out of a small business,
> come under the "static" analysis. But "static" analysis is not only unable to pre-
> dict the consequences of discontinuous changes in the traditional way of doing
> things; it can explain neither the occurrence of such productive revolutions
> nor the phenomena that accompany them. . . . What we are about to consider is
> that kind of change arising from within the system *which so displaces its equi-*
> *librium that the new one cannot be reached from the old one by infinitesimal*
> *steps.* . . . Development in our sense is defined by the carrying out of new com-
> binations [of productive means].[66]

Marginal-productivity theory had neglected the problem of technical change
as falling outside the purview of economic analysis. In his *Theory of Economic
Development,* Schumpeter filled this gap, insisting on the importance of "innovations"—broadly defined as the introduction of new methods, new products, new sources of supply, and new forms of industrial organization—for
the understanding of economic progress. The source of dynamic change in
the Schumpeterian system is the "innovating entrepreneur" who stimulates

investment and innovation, thereby causing "creative destruction." Creative destruction occurs when innovation makes old ideas and technologies obsolete; the slowing down of profits from old methods provides the incentive to innovate.

Schumpeter argued that economic development is dependent on shifting capital from old firms that use established methods of production to firms that use innovative new methods. He claimed that this process takes place through credit expansion. Banks create credit through the reserve system and then lend money to firms specializing in new production methods, which then raise the price of production goods and consumer goods in an attempt to pay for their required production goods. He describes innovation as:

- The creation of new goods or quality of goods;
- The creation of new production methods;
- The opening of new markets;
- Capturing new sources of supply; and
- Creating new organizations of industry—for example, creating and destroying monopolies.[67]

Putting this in a somewhat more formal manner, Schumpeter analyzed how successful innovations stimulate the growth of the economy through three channels. The first is the investment channel. The innovating entrepreneur must invest to be able to exploit his discovery or the discovery of others. Most probably there will be imitators who wish to jump on the bandwagon. This multiplies the amount of investment, which in itself is good for economic growth. The second is the additive nature of these investments. Since they concentrate on new ventures, no substitution occurs. In other words, the capital required is not taken from ongoing activities. This is so because once the process is under way, profits will be plowed back into the economy. But where does the money come from in the first place? Here we find the third channel. Schumpeter believed that the investments necessary for developing the innovations and starting to exploit them would be financed by an expansion of bank credits, with the normal stimulating (and possibly inflationary) consequences.

Schumpeter's theory is consistent with observed patterns of economic growth, especially their unevenness. Economies rarely develop along a regular trend. On the contrary, they move along a bumpy road, with booms alternating with slumps. The booms reflect the investment-induced innovative periods. Examples include the railroad boom, the automobile boom, and, most recently, the electronics boom. Schumpeter explained through his theory the phenomenon of business cycles, each being a response to a fresh discontinuous innovation. But his work also foreshadowed the "big bang," the "great spurt," and the "take-off" theories of the postWorld War II period, which will be introduced in the next chapter.

Thirty years later, Schumpeter published his most-quoted book, *Capitalism, Socialism, and Democracy,*[68] where he asserted that the role of the individual innovating entrepreneur had been taken over by the research laboratories of big business. Entrepreneurship had been made routine. Big government and big business—both of which were bureaucracies—had moved closer together to the point where the former would swallow the latter. Schumpeter argued that capitalism as we have known it would blend into a socialism as we have not yet known. It was uncertain, according to Schumpeter, whether democracy as we know it would survive. Schumpeter predicted that capitalism would eventually be undermined by its own success. He believed that the links between government and special-interest groups would be intensified, which in turn would lead to replacing entrepreneurship with a centrally planned socialist state:

> The actual and prospective performance of the capitalist system is such as to negate the idea of its breaking down under the weight of economic failure, but . . . its very success undermines the social institutions which protect it, and "inevitably" creates conditions in which it will not be able to live and which strongly point to Socialism as the heir apparent.[69]

This conclusion—which for the time being has been proven wrong—can be traced, among other things, to the ever-increasing and dominant role of banks and financial institutions. But Schumpeter saw other reasons that pertain to culture rather than to economics.

Capitalism, in the view of Schumpeter, "creates a critical frame of mind."[70] Capitalism develops rationality. Schumpeter argued that rationality first appears with regard to matters of economic necessity and material needs and then extends to other aspects of human existence. Capitalism perpetuates this extension, initially because it depends on rational cost-profit calculations through double-entry bookkeeping.[71] Capitalist success popularized the habit of calculation and encouraged the development of science and rational methods. Schumpeter suggested that all the features and achievements of modern civilization are due to capitalism, "the propelling force of the rationalization of human behavior."[72] In his words: "Although the modern hospital is not as a rule operated for profit . . . capitalist rationality supported the habits of mind that evolved the methods used in these hospitals."[73] He added, "The capitalist process rationalizes behavior and ideas and by so doing chases from our minds, along with metaphysical belief, mystic and romantic ideas of all sorts. Thus it reshapes not only our methods of attaining our ends but also these ultimate ends themselves."[74]

Modern management would delight in this early recognition of what they now so often claim. But unlike modern management, Schumpeter went on to forecast what he saw as the eventual result of these tendencies: an anti-capitalist intelligentsia. The trend toward rationalization and of capitalist firms to become increasingly bureaucratized—particularly in their entrepreneurial tasks—would increase anti-capitalist sentiment among intellectuals and within the labor movement. Because of this, Schumpeter argued, capitalism would eventually give way to socialism—not through revolution but through the steady capture of the private sector by different levels of the state and the increasing regulation of what remained of the private sector.

Schumpeter also predicted the decline of the bourgeois family due to the spread of calculating rationality:

> As soon as men and women . . . acquire the habit of weighing the individual advantages and disadvantages of any prospective course of action—or, as we might also put it, as soon as they introduce into their private life a sort of inarticulate system of cost accounting—they cannot fail to become aware of the heavy personal sacrifices that family ties and especially parenthood entail under modern conditions.[75]
>
> With the decline of the driving power supplied by the family motive, the businessman's time living on shrinks, roughly, to his life expectation. . . . [T]he same economic process that undermines the position of the bourgeoisie by decreasing the importance of the functions of entrepreneurs and capitalists, by breaking up protective strata and institutions [aristocratic survivals], by creating an atmosphere of hostility, also decomposes the motor forces of capitalism from within. . . . The capitalist order not only rests on props made of non extra-capitalist material but also derives its energy from extra-capitalist patterns of behaviour which at the same time it is bound to destroy.[76]

John Maynard Keynes

Finally we must refer to the contribution of Keynes, the person who participated directly in the creation of the Bretton Woods institutions and whose economic ideas directly influenced the economic elements of the UN's founding Charter. Keynes had started out as a neoclassical economist, albeit a highly original and freethinking one. But faced in the 1930s with the misery of mass unemployment during the Great Depression and the failure of orthodox neoclassical economics to come up with an adequate explanation, Keynes developed an alternative theory, set out in his magnum opus, *The General Theory of Employment, Interest and Money.* As he wrote in the preface, only with difficulty did he break loose from neoclassical economic ideas, which "ramify . . .

into every corner of our minds."[77] Keynesian ideas on policies to avoid unemployment and his later work in setting out the structure for an international clearing union[78] had a profound influence on the economic thinking underlying the structures and economic priorities of the United Nations and the Bretton Woods institutions. And for the next twenty-five years, until the 1970s, Keynesian ideas exercised a major influence on economic policymaking in the leading industrial countries.

Keynes asserted that "the outstanding faults of the economic society in which we live are its failure to provide full employment and its arbitrary and inequitable distribution of wealth and incomes."[79] The essence of Keynesian thought is that no mechanism in a competitive economy guarantees full employment. Keynes focused on the determinants of effective demand in a country's economy. If investment slackens or if consumers are not willing to continue to purchase all that the economy is capable of producing, then effective demand declines and the actual level of production will fall below the full-employment level.[80] Because consumers are limited in their spending by the size of their incomes, they are not the source of business-cycle fluctuations. The dynamic actors are business investors and governments.

The origins of unemployment and depression are caused by inadequate effective demand. When demand is low, sales and jobs suffer; when it is high, all is well. With falling demand, expected future revenues are adjusted downward and corporations may further cut back on investment spending. The economy may thus move into a sustained decline. It is then the responsibility of the government to restore aggregate demand to full-employment levels.

International factors do not figure prominently in *The General Theory of Unemployment.* However, during World War II, Keynes increasingly turned his thoughts to the design of international economic and financial institutions aimed at stimulating reconstruction and limiting the risks of depression. In making his suggestions, Keynes obviously had in mind to avoid the slump and inflation which followed World War I.[81] Keynes saw the need to stabilize the prices of primary products, put pressure on surplus as well as deficit countries to move toward a world currency, and monitor and coordinate international economic and financial policies. He was clear about the effects of deflationary pressures on the world economy generated by countries amassing large current-account surpluses in their balance of payments. Deficit countries restrict demand, production, and employment opportunities with no analogous pressure on the surplus countries to expand activity or to lend or invest abroad. The surplus countries export unemployment to the rest of the world; the deficit countries export employment.

In the words of Paul Streeten:

> Keynes foresaw the need to prevent the violent fluctuations in the prices of exported primary commodities that wreak havoc with the incomes and livelihoods of small farmers in developing countries and cause inflation and unemployment in the importing industrial countries. . . . Keynes also saw the need for a world currency—he called it Bancor. It was to be initially fixed in terms of thirty primary commodities (of which gold was one), which would stabilize the average prices of commodities. . . . He proposed an International Clearing Union with powers that represented a step towards a global Central Bank. Excessive accumulation of both deficits and surpluses was to be penalized by an interest charge. . . . The big difference would have been that pressures would have been put on countries with surpluses to reduce them. They would have been taxed at the rate of one percent per month on their surpluses and required to adopt measures to expand their economies.[82]

Though most of these ideas were too far ahead of contemporary thinking to be incorporated into the International Monetary Fund (IMF) and the World Bank, there is no doubt that Keynesian thinking had a great influence on their creation. In his writings and in his role as a negotiator for Britain, Keynes made a mark on the major international economic institutions and on international economic policy that was to last for the last half of the twentieth century.[83]

Concluding Observations

The early economists, mostly the classicists, initiated a whole series of debates—on economic growth, distribution of income, international trade, the international division of labor, and the ethics of development—many of which are still with us today. They set the stage for the debates on development in the United Nations, even if their early contributions were only dimly recalled. But in terms of the intellectual origins of the ideas explored from the 1940s onward, the early economists had already elaborated many of the basic arguments in seven major areas of policy and concern:

- International trade and development, including the question of liberalization and protection
- The role and place of agriculture and industry in development
- The role of the market and government in furthering development
- The importance of population questions and technology
- Wages, profits, and the distribution of income
- The importance of a legal and institutional framework
- The sense of ethics and justice that should prevail

Adam Smith opened the debate on international trade, as he did so many other issues. Adam Smith was in favor of open trade and against the restricted-import practices of the mercantilists. Ricardo's law of comparative advantage—extended later and by other authors to competitive advantage—provided the technical rationalization for the argument. Ricardo showed that a difference in comparative cost is a sufficient condition for international trade to start and continue on a free trade basis to the benefit of the countries (and their inhabitants) in question. But Friedrich List (and earlier Alexander Hamilton) developed a systematic attack on free trade by developing the "infant industry" argument as an indispensable stage in a country's development. By this they showed that the benefits of international trade to some parties in the short run could be outweighed by their long-run gains if protection for a period led to the establishment of industries which would develop a comparative advantage in the future. The validity of this latter contention has come under serious scrutiny in the contemporary debate on the terms of trade question, as we shall see later. The classicists argued in favor of what Marx called a "one world economy," which he questioned because it led to a continuous search for new products and foreign markets and to economic imperialism. This line of reasoning would come back after the war as the import-substitution argument.

Given that the early classicists wrote before the industrial revolution became visible, it is not surprising that when it came to the role of agriculture and industry in development, Adam Smith and David Ricardo gave pride of place to agriculture. In their opinion, the sector sequence had to be agriculture first, industry second, and commerce third. This has remained a controversial issue as reflected in the reasoning of heavy industry of the 1950s and 1960s and the already-mentioned debate over terms of trade and in light of technological progress.

John Stuart Mill explored the role of the market versus the role of government, an argument perhaps underplayed by economists in postwar discussion until the 1970s or even later. Mill also introduced concern for the equitable treatment of individuals—foreshadowing the UN's concern with human rights, though again relating this to development in a way that was neglected within the UN for the first two or three decades of its thinking on development. Mill recognized that in order to protect individual rights, a more active intervention of the state was essential. While the laws of production are imposed by technical and technological conditions, the laws of distribution are created by human institutions and customs of society. Mill was an early believer in the "makeability" of society, a belief that has known its ups and downs since 1848, the year Mill developed (and set the stage for) a debate that continues to flourish to this day.

He believed in the income-generating effects of public spending and that natural monopolies should be nationalized. He also believed in the positive effects of trade unions as a countervailing power to the force of employers. Mill would be called today a social democrat, albeit of the "third way" variety.[84]

The role of population growth and of technology in economic development was an early contribution. Malthus presented the problem as the result of the difference between population growing at a geometric rate and food production growing only at an arithmetic rate. This was bound to produce a crisis—and the argument still has a superficial appeal today. However, John Stuart Mill introduced the more sophisticated proposition that economic progress must be conceived as a race between technical changes and diminishing returns in agriculture. When Mill wrote in the 1840s and 1850s, the first results of the industrial revolution had become visible. Since about 1820, technical change has outstripped population pressures in England. However, population has not gone away as a problem, as will emerge very clearly in the chapters that follow. And technological change, including technological transfers and the role of transnational corporations, has remained a burning issue to this day.

The classicists have a lot to say about the role of wages, profits, and distribution of income in economic growth. Malthus's concern with population growth and his support for the subsistence theory of wages prepared the way for Ricardo's preoccupation with the land-using bias of economic progress and his explanation of poverty in terms of a race between population and the means of subsistence. Malthus provided the touchstone for all classical thinking about economic policies and inequalities when he noted that the limited supply of land would lead to diminishing returns in agriculture because of the way population growth led to the use of inferior types of soil. This trend would lead, according to Ricardo, to two things. First, it would lead to falling levels of profits because of population growth and the forced use of poor lands. These lower rates of profits in turn would in the end put a halt to capital accumulation and hence to production. This is Ricardo's "growth pessimism." Second, wages would tend toward a minimum level corresponding to the subsistence needs of workers. This is the iron law of wages, which distinguishes between the natural price and the market price of labor. Population increase is to a large degree the result of paying the natural price of labor, so wages tend to go down to the market-price level. Karl Marx reinforced this point by bringing the notion of the reserve army of labor into the analysis. In Ricardo's growth- and income-distribution model, the landlords will get an increasing part of national income because the excess in rent on the good as well as the poor lands goes to him, the capitalists in industry will get less because of growth pessimism, and the laborers will get poorer because of the iron law of wages. The sum total of these three assertions is bound to lead to economic stagnation.

But with hindsight, it is clear that the law of diminishing returns was interpreted in a static context that ruled out the enormous technological progress which the world has seen since the time Malthus and Ricardo were writing. Technological advance was central to the model of economic progress of Joseph Schumpeter, who, for the first time, brought innovation and technological change to the very center of the debate. He "dynamized" the classical concentration on increases in population and in the stock of capital and labor. His emphasis on the role of the innovative entrepreneur, creative destruction, and the creative chaos theory was truly novel, and the debate over his ideas has continued ever since. Much more debatable was his thesis that capitalism would fade into socialism, an argument which has lost much of its appeal since the collapse of the socialist economies in the late 1980s. But his reasoning has more to it than his oversimple prediction. His contention that capitalistic firms tend to become bureaucratized and dependent on state intervention has been vindicated many times over. The same applies to his other assertion that capitalist rationality would generate an anti-capitalist attitude in the intelligentsia. Both trends have been observed, and it could be maintained that the political reaction since 1980—as embodied in the economic and financial policies pursued over the last twenty to twenty-five years—was in part because of these trends.

Adam Smith analyzed how income distribution was negatively affected by what he called the "masters" (meaning the capitalists) and their tendency to keep wages down as much as possible. He summed the issue up in one single sentence: "Wherever there is great property, there is great inequality."[85]

John Stuart Mill brought government action into the debate by observing that the laws of distribution are manmade and hence subject to improvement in the sense of increased social justice. He was sympathetic to the early socialist ideas of Saint-Simon and Fourier. This is reflected in a statement that we have heard frequently since to the effect that poor countries should be preoccupied by economic growth and rich countries by better income distribution. As for declining rates of profits according to the law of diminishing returns, both Mill and Marx argued that capital export to poorer countries would counteract this trend, in which both of them believed.

All in all, the classicists had a complete model of growth and distribution, and we had to wait a long time before this scheme of things would be taken up again and altered significantly.

Adam Smith introduced the international aspects of the division of labor into the debate on economic growth. Over the last fifty years, the international dimension has moved to center stage. The problem of a rational international division of labor has been debated in economic theory and practice. Jan Tinbergen tried to revive the debate in the 1970s, mainly from the point of view of enhancing income in the developing countries, without losing sight of the size-of-the-market argument. The former Soviet Union put it into practice in Central and Eastern Europe in a rather negative manner. But the point Smith made has remained valid and has continued to be discussed in a variety of ways, of which the most recent one comes under the guise of globalization and regionalization.

Adam Smith had already stressed the importance of a legal and institutional framework to protect the capitalist and the working of the market. John Stuart Mill developed the argument, bringing the interests of the workers into play and emphasizing the important role of trade unions. This was the beginning of a debate that now flourishes under the heading of "good governance." It is striking how early this issue was perceived by the classicists and how frequently it has been neglected since, most recently in the transition policies of the former communist countries in Europe.[86]

John Maynard Keynes developed a structural macroeconomic model that not only linked important elements in classical thinking but also laid the foundation for the structural analysis of developing countries. It is true that over much of the postwar period, the neoclassical echo was louder than the structuralist. Keynes was the first economist to focus on the employment problem in industrial countries by making the distinction between full-employment output and the actual level of production. Aggregate demand was the key, and it was the responsibility of the government to restore aggregate demand to full-employment levels. Keynes provided policymakers with a consistent macroeconomic model and a coherent theory of the determination of national income and employment.

During World War II and at Bretton Woods, Keynes focused on international factors, and his proposal for an even-handed treatment of both surplus and deficit countries remains as important today as it was fifty-five years ago.

Finally, it is important to note that the classical authors had much to say about the role of ethics and justice in economic development and society. They were much concerned with the interaction between social and individual interests, the end objectives of growth and development, and how moral virtues and sentiments are crucial to the well-being of the individual and the well-functioning of society. In his *Theory of Moral Sentiments,* Adam Smith was much more explicit about ethics and justice than in *The Wealth of Na-*

tions. In these two works seen as a whole, self-interest cannot be seen separately from other moral sentiments such as prudence, sympathy, and benevolence. Self-interest is always prudent self-interest that is "the wise conduct directed towards the care of the health, of the fortune, rank and reputation of the individual."[87] Prudent self-interest, according to Smith, is the only means to achieve collective material well-being. Prudence and benevolence in the sphere of private relations are translated into sympathy in the sphere of public relations and economic exchanges. Since economic exchanges are on the whole impersonal, they should be based on rules of justice rather than on benevolence.

Adam Smith's concept of the invisible hand must be interpreted in this context. A society guided by self-interest is more prosperous because, in order to satisfy their desires, individuals would be propelled to create new activities and new opportunities that could be profitable to others. Instead, a society of non-self-interested individuals implies that everyone is happy with the status quo and consequently the society in question would quickly stagnate. A lot more can, and maybe should, be said about the approach of Adam Smith to the problems of the economy and of society. However, the important point to make is that this approach was based on a profound conviction of the importance of ethics and justice and was much more subtle and comprehensive than is so frequently claimed by those who have not read him.

These great thinkers had a major impact on the ideas and policies adopted for development over the last half of the twentieth century, 100 years or more after most of them had first written. What is surprising is not that they had such influence but that their influence, apart from that of Marx, was so little recognized. Moreover, their influence was often selective and distorted. Adam Smith was remembered for his invisible hand, not for what he said about the need for societies to protect the weak and vulnerable and the importance of institutions and strong moral values in society to achieve this goal. The early thinkers, to the extent that they are remembered, are recalled for what the dominant members of present society want to hear, not for what they truly said. Most important, the early thinkers wrote in relation to the issues and challenges of development as they saw them at the time. Many were analyzing development in the context of Great Britain, the dominant economic power of the early to mid-nineteenth century. Just as their writing reflects this context, so in drawing on their work one must take full account of this context. Interests and priorities change with the evolving stages of development. Perhaps this is the most important lesson to draw from past writings on development.

Part II. Ideas and Action

3

The 1940s and 1950s: The Foundations of UN Development Thinking and Practice

- **The Process of Economic Development and the UN's Early Work**
- **Trade and Economic Development**
- **ECLA's Doctrine and Development Strategy**
- **Measures for the Economic Development of Underdeveloped Countries**
- **Industrialization, Agriculture, and Balanced vs. Unbalanced Growth**
- **Domestic Savings and Foreign Capital**
- **The Development of Technical Assistance**
- **The Story of SUNFED**
- **Concluding Observations**

In the postwar period, economic development became an important, if always somewhat sidelined, theme of economic thinking and analysis. The growing concern with development among economists resulted from three different challenges: the reconstruction of Europe after 1945, the development of the socialist countries and the Cold War, and the priorities of national development in the South. Newly independent countries considered economic development to be their main challenge and pushed, especially within the UN, for that issue to be put high on the international agenda. In Africa, colonialism lasted until 1960 for the most part. Eighteen countries became independent in 1960, ten others from 1961 to 1965, and five others from 1966 to 1969. The decolonization process oriented the early stages of development thinking in the 1950s toward Latin America and South and Southeast Asia.

There was something of a Eurocentric bias in development theory. Development thinking in the 1950s and the early 1960s was heavily influenced by the concrete experience of Western economic history. It was the great period of the modernization paradigm and dual models. The path to development was provided by the Western model of development, which underdeveloped countries were supposed to reproduce.

The expression "underdeveloped" rapidly gained currency and was almost universally accepted after President Truman's inaugural address in January 1949.[1] Truman was the first to use the word "underdeveloped," in the same speech in which he launched the idea of an expanded technical assistance program. He also established the hegemony of the modernization paradigm by dividing the world into developed and underdeveloped countries, between the countries which had reached modernity and those which had not. As Gustavo Esteva has argued:

> Underdevelopment began, then, on January 20, 1949. On that day, two billion people became underdeveloped. In a real sense, from that time on, they ceased being what they were, in all their diversity, and were transmogrified into an inverted mirror of other's reality: a mirror that belittles them and sends them off to the end of the queue, a mirror that defines their identity, which is really that of a heterogeneous and diverse majority, simply in the terms of a homogenizing and narrow minority.[2]

During the 1950s, the modernization paradigm became mainstream. It emphasized the dualistic nature of underdeveloped countries. This analytical framework opposed the modern sector to the traditional sector and found the obstacles to economic, political, and social development in the latter, which was seen as backward, characterized by low productivity, rigid social structures, and inadequate mentality for economic and technological progress.[3] The framework linked the process of development to the expansion of the modern sector and the shrinking of the traditional sector, which meant first and foremost the channeling of resources from the traditional to the modern sector. The main strategy for doing that was industrialization. This reasoning was caught in W. Arthur Lewis's dual model for a strategy of economic development in underdeveloped countries that were characterized by "unlimited supplies of labour."[4]

The Process of Economic Development and the UN's Early Work

When the United Nations started to get involved in the debate on economic and social development in underdeveloped countries, there were but few contemporary studies. Eugene Staley's work for the ILO and Kurt Mandelbaum's book *The Industrialisation of Backward Areas*, which was published as early as 1945,[5] were the exceptions, as was Paul N. Rosenstein-Rodan's

1943 article, "Industrialization of Eastern and South-Eastern Europe."[6] The contemporary pioneers of development, such as W. Arthur Lewis, Gunnar Myrdal, Ragnar Nurkse, Albert Hirschman, and Walter W. Rostow, would not publish their classics until the mid- to late 1950s. Nevertheless, toward the end of the 1940s and in the early 1950s two outstanding documents were published by the UN which had far-reaching repercussions for development thinking and practice during the decade and even after. These two major intellectual contributions were: 1) Prebisch's document *The Economic Development of Latin America and Its Principal Problems,* published by the UN in 1950,[7] and the development of his structuralist approach in *The Economic Survey of Latin America,* published in 1951[8]; and 2) the report of the UN group of experts, which included Theodore W. Schultz and W. Arthur Lewis, *Measures for the Economic Development of Underdeveloped Countries,* which was published in 1951.[9]

One of the more interesting discoveries that digging into the UN archives of the 1950s brings out is the central role of the UN in development thinking regarding two major issues which have been at the genesis of the emergence of development economics as an autonomous branch of knowledge and which even today are at the heart of the debate on development. These are the role of the state versus the role of the market and the role of external versus internal factors.

The work of the UN regarding economic development in the 1940s and 1950s focused mainly on the ways to get development going. The UN view was clearly on the side of interventionist strategy, in which public intervention and strengthened government capacity played a key role.[10] The dominant paradigm of economic development had its roots in a very specific historical context, namely the Great Depression and the wartime experience in industrialized countries. In addition, several Latin American countries must be given credit for effective government action to maximize output and mobilize output for economic progress and full employment. The Latin American experience also showed that the paradigm was replicable in underdeveloped countries. The postwar pioneers of development were profoundly marked by the Keynesian revolution. Albert Hirschman argues about this period:

> Keynes had firmly established the view there were two kinds of economics: one the orthodox or classical tradition—which applied to the "special case" in which the economy is fully employed; and a very different system of analytical propositions and of policy prescriptions (newly worked out by Keynes) that took over when there was substantial unemployment of human and material resources.[11]

Although Keynes had been writing mainly about management of short-term demand in industrial countries, the principle of proactive economic policy was carried over to thinking about developing countries. The result of the impact of Keynesian thinking was a strong consensus in the UN arena that economic development in the underdeveloped countries would not be secured unless national governments played a significant role, especially in the mobilization and allocation of available resources.[12] The idea of the "special case" led to the strong belief among most of the pioneers of development thinking that economic development was not spontaneous, as in the classical capitalist pattern, but was consciously achieved through planning.[13]

How to mobilize domestic capital and channel it to economic growth was considered to be a central problem and a major feature of the UN's analysis of development. Public intervention had a key role to play in increasing savings and investment as ways to initiate or accelerate the pace of economic development. Tibor Scitovsky, like many others at that time, was pessimistic about the capacity of market forces to promote economic development. He emphasized the point that if the industrialization of underdeveloped areas were to be left to private enterprise, the process would be slower, there would be less investment and lower national income, and the economic structure of the region would be different.[14]

The UN and its specialized agencies turned their attention from the beginning to such development problems as how to finance economic development, land reform, distribution of national income, and technical assistance to hasten the development process. In the 1940s and 1950s, the General Assembly and the Economic and Social Council (ECOSOC) repeatedly recommended to the underdeveloped countries that they should adopt integrated programs of development that were based on the harmonious development of their natural and human resources and the mobilization of available domestic capital in order to raise the living standards of the population as a whole. Resolution 198 (III) adopted by the General Assembly in 1948 requested the Council to give "further and urgent consideration to the whole problem of the economic development of underdeveloped countries in all its aspects."[15]

A second feature related to the responsibility of countries for their own economic development. The UN expressed its conviction on many occasions that governments of underdeveloped countries should remain in command. Any foreign assistance that might flow to the underdeveloped countries should retain the character of a supplement to the efforts and resources of the countries in question. A third feature was general recognition that accelerating economic development required support from outside on concessionary terms.

Many resolutions and recommendations concerning economic development were adopted during the late 1940s by the General Assembly, ECOSOC, and the Economic and Employment Commission. Of particular importance was the creation of a Sub-Commission on Economic Development in ECOSOC in 1946.[16] The aim of this sub-commission was to study and advise on the principles and problems of long-term economic development with particular attention to what it called "the inadequately developed parts of the world."

This sub-commission was composed of representatives of the U.S., the USSR, major underdeveloped countries (China, India, Brazil, and Mexico), and Czechoslovakia. According to the sub-commission, the objective was the promotion of higher standards of living, full employment, conditions of economic and social progress, and development in the countries concerned. The manner for achieving this was a sound, efficient, and fuller utilization of manpower, natural resources, energy, and capital.[17]

The sub-commission's approach to economic development was largely through industrialization.[18] The key problem was how to accelerate the accumulation of physical capital and the adoption of modern technological methods. The sub-commission suggested that countries on the threshold of economic development should examine the experience of countries that had already undergone a substantial measure of industrialization and take deliberate steps to create conditions for accelerated industrial development. This included drawing on the experience gathered by the more-developed economies, particularly with respect to the machinery such countries used to promote their own economic development. To achieve this objective, the sub-commission outlined the necessity of:

- Diversification of the economy through the development of as many sectors as possible, including the diversification of the export trade;
- Establishment of key industries in the country, even though such industries might not satisfy strictly economic criteria in terms of comparative costs;
- Diversification of technology;
- International economic cooperation;
- Development of agriculture, particularly the production of food, in national development programs

In contrast to the optimistic view of self-sustained growth which had emerged from the growth models of the Harrod-Domar type or the classical and neoclassical international trade theories,[19] the general picture which developed in the postwar decade within the UN system was more pessimistic. UN economists emphasized the obstacles that could prevent a process of self-sustaining economic growth from becoming established. This led to an emphasis on the need for some kind of exceptional "big push" to ensure the internal conditions for self-sustaining growth.

Hence, most early attention was focused on how to start and nurture economic development. Igniting a process of industrialization became a central concern for the pioneers of development economics. Their work has been labeled by a series of catchphrases and metaphors aimed at explaining the process of economic development: the "take-off" metaphor of Rostow, Lewis's "snowball," or Rosenstein-Rodan's "big push" are cases in point. Lewis, for example, used the snowball metaphor to describe the critical minimum effort to get out of the poverty trap: "Once the snowball starts to move downhill, it will move of its own momentum, and will get bigger and bigger as it goes along. . . . You have, as it were, to begin by rolling your snowball up the mountain. Once you get it there, the rest is easy, but you cannot get it there without first making an initial effort."[20] In the same line, Rosenstein-Rodan used Rostow's "take-off" metaphor to argue that "there is a minimum level of resources that must be devoted to a . . . development programme if it is to have any chance of success. Launching a country into self-sustaining growth is a little like getting an airplane off the ground. There is a critical ground speed which must be passed before the craft can become airborne."[21] He had already conceived of this "big push" argument in his well-known 1943 article, "Industrialization of Eastern and South-Eastern Europe."

Among the ideas developed or promoted by the UN in the 1940s and 1950s, one can identify four major contributions to development thinking and practice:

1. Identification of the obstacles to economic development and policy recommendations to speed up economic progress;
2. Analysis of the difficulties of international trade for economic development, leading to a rationale for industrialization and diversification, and moving away from primary commodities production;
3. Elaborating a rationale and proposals for a large-scale capital fund for economic development;
4. Understanding the need for a large-scale capital fund for economic development.

The need for soft financing for development was developed at the same time as the work on terms of trade, with a clear intellectual link between the two. Hans Singer recalled how revolutionary and subversive both approaches were at the time when the official discourse promoted by the United States was "trade not aid."[22] The United Nations became the place where these new ideas were discussed and promoted.

Trade and Economic Development

One of the major issues during the 1950s within the UN system was the problem of primary commodities. Two important UN studies focused on long-term changes in the terms of trade in the immediate postwar period. These were *Relative Prices of Exports and Imports of Under-Developed Countries* and *Relative Prices of Primary Products and Manufactures in International Trade.*[23] Using U.S. and UK trade statistics as their primary source of information, both studies showed that on the eve of World War II, a given quantity of primary exports would on average pay for only 60 percent of the quantity of manufactured goods it could have bought in the 1870s, eighty years earlier.

This long-term trend had been reinforced by the immediate postwar period experience, which provided further evidence that the terms of trade moved against sellers of food and raw materials and in favor of the sellers of manufactured goods. Singer, in the UN Department of Economic Affairs, and Prebisch, in the Economic Commission for Latin America (ECLA), were the key individuals in the late 1940s to highlight this unfavorable price relation that affected negatively the economic development of underdeveloped countries. The 1949 UN report on *Relative Prices of Exports and Imports on Under-Developed Countries*[24]—which was mostly written by Hans Singer—greatly contributed to this new concern. Contrary to the neoclassical theory about trade, the report observed a long-term downward trend of prices of primary products compared with the prices of manufactured goods. It also pointed out that the production of manufactured goods had increased faster than the production of primary products. Hans Singer summarized his position at the time as follows:

> The specialization of underdeveloped countries on export of food and raw materials to industrialized countries, largely as a result of investment by the latter, has been unfortunate for the underdeveloped countries for two reasons: (1) it removed most of the secondary and cumulative effects of investment from the country in which the investment took place to the investing country; and (2) it diverted the underdeveloped countries into types of activity offering less scope for technical progress, internal and external economies taken by themselves, and withheld from the course of their economic history a central factor of dynamic radiation which has revolutionized society in the industrialized countries. But there is a third factor of perhaps even greater importance which has reduced the benefits to underdeveloped countries of foreign trade-*cum*-investment based on export specialization in food and raw materials. This third factor relates to terms of trade.[25]

However, Singer and Prebisch were not just concerned about the problem of the secular deterioration of the terms of trade of primary commodities; they were also concerned about the problem of short-term volatility of commodity prices. This was a crucial problem for economic development, especially for economic planning. Planning for underdeveloped countries, especially the smaller ones, was impossible if they depended too much on the export of primary commodities that were subject to extreme volatility in prices.

Insofar as investment and economic progress required goods—especially capital goods—from abroad, they were entirely dependent on current export earnings unless there was a net inflow of foreign capital. However, since a net inflow of capital was not large enough for the underdeveloped countries as a group, most of these countries had to rely on the use of part of their export proceeds to finance their economic development. Thus, the special vulnerability of underdeveloped countries to fluctuations in primary-commodity markets and the long-term declines in the price relationship between these products and manufactured products were obvious obstacles to the capacity of underdeveloped countries to press ahead with their economic development.

This is the reason why a UN Commission on Commodity Trade and Economic Development, which was composed of five experts, was set up in 1953. The terms of reference were given by a resolution of the General Assembly, adopted 21 December 1952, which recommended that member states

> ensure that the prices of primary commodities are kept in an adequate, just and equitable relation to the prices of capital goods and other manufactured articles so as to permit the more satisfactory formation of domestic savings in the countries in the process of development and to facilitate the establishment of fair wage levels for the working populations of these countries with a view to reducing existing disparity between their standards of living and those in the highly industrialized world.[26]

Freedom from violent short-term fluctuations was a crucial objective because a greater measure of stability in the prices received for primary products would facilitate the steady economic development of underdeveloped countries and, among other things, improve their ability to estimate their real importing capacity per unit of export.

The report on commodity trade and economic development made two recommendations: first, to develop single-commodity agreements to prevent excessive short-term fluctuations in the price of the commodity—such as the International Wheat Agreement reached in 1949 or the International Sugar Agreement reached in 1953; second, to establish international buffer stocks, which could buy important individual commodities when prices fell below a certain floor and when prices exceeded a specified higher ceiling.[27]

The question of international trade is developed in much more detail in one of our companion volumes.[28]

ECLA's Doctrine and Development Strategy

In the 1950s, ECLA became the promoter of a whole set of new ideas on economic development. ECLA's most important intellectual contributions to development thinking were included in Prebisch's 1950 seminal document *The Economic Development of Latin America and Its Principal Problems* and in *The Economic Survey of Latin America,* published in 1951.[29] Those documents laid the foundation for what came to be called the "Prebisch-Singer doctrine" that was so influential in Latin America and elsewhere during the 1950s. They were a major contribution to the debate on economic development in the post-war period not only because of their unorthodox recommendations but also because they represented a contribution from the South. The center-periphery paradigm developed by Prebisch has also constituted a major building block of structuralist development thinking. His approach was both holistic— analyzing the links between development and underdevelopment—and historical—analyzing the origins of the integration of Latin American economies into the capitalist system as producers of primary commodities.[30]

The ECLA doctrine was built on the idea of a fundamental imbalance in center-periphery relationships and the implications of this for the capacity for capital accumulation in the periphery. The starting point for Prebisch was that the growth rate of productivity was higher in manufacturing industry than in production of primary commodities and, in particular, agriculture. In principle, one would expect this difference to lead, over time, to greater reductions in the prices of industrial products than in prices of primary products and, in turn, to an evolution in the terms of trade to the advantage of countries in the periphery and a more equal international distribution of resources. But because workers and entrepreneurs in the industrialized countries had—and still have—the power to limit the diffusion of technical progress at the international level, they could protect their rate of profit and level of wages by resisting these price declines. Because workers and entrepreneurs in the South generally do not have such power, their prices do decline, and with this follows deterioration in the terms of trade. According to the ECLA view, international trade was not only perpetuating the disparities between the center and the periphery, it was increasing them.

The Prebisch-Singer thesis, then, held that technical progress in manufacturing industries led to an increase in incomes, while technical progress in the production of food and raw materials in underdeveloped countries led to a decrease in prices. The conclusion, as Hans Singer put it, was that "the industrialised countries have had the best of both worlds, as consumers of primary commodities and as producers of manufactured articles; the under-developed countries have had the worst of both worlds, as consumers of manu-factures and as producers of raw materials."[31]

This was a revolutionary thesis at that time because it stressed that one of the main assumptions of international trade theory—that the benefits of tech-nical progress tended to be distributed alike over the whole community—was false. In his now-famous report, Prebisch argued that "the enormous benefits that derive from increased productivity have not reached the periphery in a measure comparable to that obtained by the peoples of the great industrial countries.... In other words, while the Centre kept the whole benefit of tech-nical development of their industries, the peripheral countries transferred to them a share of the fruit of their own technical progress."[32]

Prebisch's main argument was that this left little place within the world economic system for the industrialization of the underdeveloped countries. Latin America was trapped in the production of food and raw materials ac-cording to the existing international division of labor. From this he drew an important conclusion—that industrialization was fundamentally important in the underdeveloped countries if they were to escape from this trap. He argued, "Industrialisation is not an end in itself, but the principal means at the disposal of those countries of obtaining a share of the benefits of techni-cal progress and of progressively raising the standard of living of masses."[33]

Under the circumstances, Prebisch's essay was pessimistic about the theory that exports would be the engine of growth:

> Formerly, before the Great Depression, development in the Latin American countries was stimulated from abroad by the constant increase of exports. There is no reason to suppose, at least at present, that this will again occur to the same extent, except under very exceptional circumstances. These countries no longer have an alternative between vigorous growth along those lines and internal expansion through industrialisation. Industrialisation has become the most important means of expansion.[34]

In order to achieve this objective, Prebisch recommended an import-substitution strategy in developing countries that aimed at domestic manu-facture of substitutes for imports. This vital priority for industrialization underlined the undeniable right of these countries to protect their industries against competition from more highly industrialized countries, in line with the List-Hamilton thesis presented in Chapter 2 and the policy and practice of most industrialized countries in the early stages of their own development.

A more detailed presentation and analysis of the Prebisch-Singer thesis, import-substitution policies, and the center-periphery theorem will be presented in our companion volume *The UN and Global Political Economy: Trade, Finance, and Development.*[35] Suffice it to say here that the success of these ECLA ideas was based not only on the originality of the analysis but also on their clear and direct implications for policy. The immense influence exerted by ECLA on decision makers in Latin America over the 1950s and 1960s led in practice to the adoption and implementation of import-substitution strategies for development on a very wide scale. In the words of Albert Fishlow: "By the end of the decade (i.e. the 1950s) the Commission's policy emphasis on domestic industrialisation had found favour in most Latin American countries. An unusual consensus on both method of analysis and the development strategy it implied pervaded the region."[36]

In many ways, the structuralist approach developed in Latin America by Prebisch and ECLA can be seen as the most advanced analytical contribution to national modernization theory originating in the South. It did not break with the Western model of modernity. The objective was industrialization through the adoption of Western technological paths and the Western model of consumption. The same could be said about India's first Five Year Plan. Jawaharlal Nehru explained in a speech on December 1952 the objectives of the plan:

> We are trying to catch up today with the industrial revolution which came to the Western countries long years ago and made great changes in the course of the century or more. . . . We would be wise not to repeat the errors committed in its earlier stages, we would be wise to profit by them. We talk in terms of industrialisation. It is obvious to me that we have to industrialise India, and as rapidly as possible.[37]

Measures for the Economic Development of Underdeveloped Countries

On 15 August 1950, ECOSOC passed a resolution on full employment[38] that asked the Secretary-General of the United Nations "to appoint a small group of experts to prepare, in the light of the current world situation and of the requirements of economic development, a report on employment and underemployment." This group of experts consisted of T. W. Schultz (United States), Arthur W. Lewis (United Kingdom), Alberto Baltra Cortez (Chile), D. R. Gadgil (India), and George Hakim (Lebanon). Their report, *Measures for the Economic Development of Underdeveloped Countries,* was submitted in April 1951.[39] This report and its recommendations led to in-depth discussion in

ECOSOC during its thirteenth session (August 1951) and had a major impact on development thinking at that time.

According to the report, the main remedy for technological unemployment and for underemployment was to create new employment opportunities rapidly, both in agriculture and in new industries. This was the task of economic development, and it is for this reason that the experts concentrated on measures for economic development rather than on measures to reduce unemployment. Thus, the scope of the report was much broader than indicated in the ECOSOC resolution.

The expert team's analysis of the preconditions for economic development and their recommendations were probably the most radical parts of the report. The experts recommended that the governments of underdeveloped countries make clear to their people their willingness

> to take vigorous action to remove the obstacles to free and equal opportunity which blunt the incentives and discourage the effort of their people. Under this head, we include land reform, abolition of privileges based on race, colour, caste or creed, the establishment of taxation upon a progressive basis, and a programme of mass education.[40]

This 1951 UN expert group, which included two subsequent Nobel Prize winners, Arthur Lewis and Ted Schultz, took strong positions for major social changes toward social justice as a precondition for economic development. Far from many drab international reports that would follow it, *Measures for the Economic Development* included a strong critique of the ruling classes, in particular in its section on land tenure, where the report stated:

> In many under-developed countries, the cultivators of the soil are exploited mercilessly by a landlord class, which perform no useful social function. This class contrives to secure itself the major part of any increase in agriculture yields, and is thus a millstone around the necks of the tenants, discouraging them from making improvements in agriculture and, in any case, leaving them too little income from which they might save to invest in the land. In such countries, land reform abolishing this landlord class is an urgent pre-requisite of agriculture progress.[41]

This argument had been put forward before in a UN 1949 report, which stressed that "if economic development is to achieve its purpose of increasing the security and welfare of the great mass of mankind and enabling them to enjoy a fuller, more fruitful life, its benefits must be widely distributed; it must not serve merely to augment the wealth and power of a small section of the population."[42] However, this radical recommendation led to some strong objections. For instance, Peter Bauer, one of the postwar pioneers in development who promoted first-market approaches from his earliest work, criticized the focus of the report on the preconditions for economic development, which were defined by the experts as psychological, social, legal, and administrative. He rejected the analysis of the expert group on the way "inequality and privilege act as a major obstacle to development," arguing that "at an early stage of economic development preoccupations with egalitarian ideas may serve to retard the growth of real income, including the real income of the poorer classes."[43]

The experts pointed out in their report that a large inflow of capital into the underdeveloped countries was required to accelerate their economic development. The problem was that the flow of private investment was limited and the governments of underdeveloped countries were able to borrow very little in private capital markets, whereas large-scale investment had to take place to improve the human factor—education (basic and technical), training, health, agriculture services—and infrastructure. The paradox was that if they could get this money, these expenditures would themselves stimulate both private investment and government borrowing.

The experts recommended that the World Bank (the International Bank for Reconstruction and Development—IBRD) should set itself the objective, to be reached within the next five years, of lending $1 billion annually to underdeveloped countries. They urged strongly that "some mechanism be created for transferring from the developed to the underdeveloped countries by way of grants-in-aid, a sum of money which should increase rapidly, reaching eventually a level of about $3 billion a year."[44] Criticism from developing countries and scholars of the IBRD and the IMF for not shifting enough capital to underdeveloped nations was repeated during the 1950s, and many demands to reform the statutes of both organizations were made in UN bodies to respond to the changes in the world economic situation and the improbability of any further substantial expansion in the external sources of financing. It was also stated that an increasing proportion of resources of the IBRD should go to the economic development of underdeveloped countries and that the IMF should help underdeveloped countries promote their economic development, particularly with regard to the effect of violent fluctuations in the prices of primary commodities on which they depended for their export proceeds and for helping them maintain the volume of their investment.[45]

The expert team on measures for economic development recognized that movements in the terms of trade had been unfavorable to the underdeveloped countries in the two respects mentioned earlier: the long-term decline and the violent short-term cyclical swings in the price of their export products. In both cases, the experts recommended that national action by developed countries be taken, particularly regarding the effects of sharp fluctuations. The experts emphasized the conclusions of the 1949 report entitled *National and International Measures for Full Employment.*[46] That report had put responsibility for eliminating cyclical fluctuation clearly upon the industrialized countries. One of the earlier recommendations was the stabilization of incomes of primary-product producers, in particular in agriculture, which provided a livelihood to the greater part of the population in underdeveloped countries. The method recommended was the establishment of international stabilization schemes that aimed to stabilize the price of staple commodities in the world market.

In a later expert report—*Measures for International Economic Stability*—published in 1951,[47] measures were proposed to reduce fluctuations in the volume of trade and in prices of primary commodities and thus to moderate the changes in the terms of trade of underdeveloped countries which accompany such movements. In addition, other measures were recommended to enable these countries to maintain their programs of economic development at a reasonably steady rate in the face of such fluctuations. The UN report on *Commodity Trade and Economic Development* argued that a price could be called reasonable as long as it did not show extreme upward and downward movements caused by abnormal and transient conditions. The focus on the terms "fair, just and equitable prices" used in the resolution led the experts to review in detail the various methods of price stabilization.[48]

Box 3.1. The Indian Development Experience

The Indian development experience is of special interest. By the year 2000, India accounted for around 17 percent of the population of developing countries and 40 percent of the world's poor. India was also among the first to embark on systematic planning to enhance its growth rate and improving the living standards of its people. India has enjoyed exceptional political stability and has maintained a democratic system with respect for fundamental human rights and an independent judiciary. It has also pursued a development strategy without radical changes for nearly five decades—albeit with important shifts toward free-market policies in the 1980s and 1990s.

India's first development plan (1950–1955) focused on public investment in infrastructure and agriculture with growth spearheaded by the private sector and resources largely allocated through the market mechanism. The second plan shifted the emphasis to state-led industrialization. This shift reflected the conviction of the political leadership and the planners that rapid growth was possible only through massive industrialization with the state playing a central role not only in guiding resource allocation but also directly participating in establishing enterprises, especially in the heavy-industry and capital-goods sectors. Political leaders and planners both assumed that there was unlikely to be adequate investment in these areas from the private sector because of their technological complexity and scale of operations. This strategy remained essentially intact for nearly three decades, achieving modest but steady progress in economic development.

The state deployed a variety of means to ensure that resources were allocated in line with plan priorities. Imports were controlled through licenses, quantitative restrictions, and high tariffs. Agriculture was supported through price maintenance and subsidized prices for fertilizers, irrigation, and power. The aim was to achieve self-sufficiency in the production of most industrial products, from heavy machinery to light consumer goods. The potential of exports and imports was largely neglected, and little effort was made to attract foreign investment. The development strategy pursued was thus not only largely autarkic but also self-reliant in the generation of resources.

Significant changes in policy began to be made in the 1980s, with some liberalization of imports, relaxation of licensing and foreign exchange restrictions, and external borrowing on commercial terms. More important changes came in 1991, following a serious balance-of-payments crisis. Licensing was largely abolished, quantitative restrictions on imports were greatly eased, tariff rates were lowered, foreign exchange was liberalized, and the rupee was devalued. All this led to an upward trend in economic growth—with per capita growth rising from around 1.5 percent from 1950 to 1980 to over 3.5 percent in the 1980s and just over 4 percent in the 1990s. Major structural changes have taken place over the years—with the share of agriculture declining from 50 percent in 1950 to 37 percent in 1980 and 28 percent in 2000, while the share of industry rose from 16 percent to 26 percent over the same period and to 25 percent in 2000. In parallel, savings, investment, and exports have also risen. External resources have never contributed more than 1 to 2 percent of gross national product (GNP).

Social progress has also been steady, impressive by some human indicators but modest in terms of the reduction of the number of Indians living in poverty. Life expectancy has doubled from 32 years in 1950 to 64 in 2000, and adult literacy over the same period has increased from 25 percent to 67 percent for males and from 8 percent to 43 percent for females. Primary school enrollment ratios have increased from 21 percent in 1950 to almost universal enrollment in 2000. Meanwhile fertility rates have nearly halved—from around 6 percent in 1950 to 3.2 in 2000—and population growth declined from 2.0 percent in 1950 to 1.8 percent in the 1990s, after rising to 2.5 percent in the 1960s.[49]

The proportion of Indians below the Indian income poverty line has been traced from the early years of planning, often with controversy and lively debate. The proportion in poverty was estimated to be about 53 percent in the period 1951–1955 and about the same in 1973/1974; it then declined to 38 percent in 1986/1987 and to 34 percent in 1993. By 2000, there did not seem to have been much progress in reducing poverty, despite high rates of economic growth. Inequality remains moderate by the standards of many developing countries, though after being stable for several decades, it increased slightly over the 1990s.

Sources: Lloyd Reynolds, *Economic Growth in the Third World: 1850–1980* (Yale University Press: New Haven, 1985); World Bank, *World Development Indicators 2000* (Washington, D.C.: World Bank, 2000); UNDP, *Human Development Report 2001* (New York: Oxford University Press, 2001); Jagdish Bhagwati, "The Design of Indian Development," in *Economic Reforms and Development: Essays for Manmohan Singh,* ed. Isher Judge Ahluwalia and I. M. D. Little (Delhi: Oxford University Press, 1998); and Suhkamoy Chakravarty, *Development Planning: The Indian Experience* (Oxford: Clarendon Press, 1981).

Industrialization, Agriculture, and Balanced vs. Unbalanced Growth

As we have seen, industrialization was considered in the 1950s to be the most important factor in the economic development of underdeveloped countries. While the post–World War II pioneers of development thinking acknowledged that economic development was not identical with industrialization due to the importance of agriculture, industrialization was considered to be the decisive element. This view was shared by most of the various bodies and agencies of the United Nations. They all emphasized the connection between the two and underlined the importance of ensuring that industrialization occupies a prominent place in any program of economic development.[50] In the preamble of its resolution 416 (XIV), ECOSOC recognized that "coordinated and integrated policies of economic development must make provision for industrial diversification, in harmony with the development of agriculture production, with a view to ensuring the economic independence of the countries concerned, taking full advantages of the benefits of international trade, and promoting the social welfare of their inhabitants."[51]

We already mentioned Kurt Mandelbaum's pioneering 1945 work, *The Industrialisation of Backward Areas.*[52] He proposed a program for a planned transformation of an agrarian economy into an industrial one. Mandelbaum argued that on the road to economic development an essential complement to agricultural improvement was the expansion and diversification of nonagricultural industries. Industrialization would facilitate capital formation and the provision of capital facilities, with a consequent rise in general productivity and living standards. By increasing the diversity of the economy, industrial development would permit a more efficient use of resources and reduce the vulnerability of underdeveloped countries to economic fluctuations, especially those caused by wide variations in the world demand for primary products. Mandelbaum[53] recalled a conversation around 1950 with a minister of a newly independent Asian country: "When I kept on stressing the need for doing more for agriculture he said that it was the imperialists who always told them to concentrate on agriculture; they had thought that I was an industrialisation man."[54]

During the debate on integrated economic development at the fifteenth session of ECOSOC in 1953, a resolution was adopted requesting the Secretary-General to prepare "a study on the processes and problems of industrialization, which may assist the underdeveloped countries in preparing practical programmes of rapid industrialization."[55] This resolution led to a comprehensive report published in 1955, with contributions from experts such as Arthur Lewis, Jan Tinbergen, Simon Kuznets, and Barbara Ward.[56] The report aimed at identifying the forces which tended to hamper or retard industrial development. The problem of economic development was analyzed in that report in terms of forces of acceleration and deceleration. The objective was to formulate various industrializing policies and measures to overcome the obstacles to industrial progress and increase the speed of development.

This report argued that it was not a matter of choosing between agriculture and industrial development; instead, it was necessary to promote a balanced expansion of all sectors of the economy. Indeed, the UN system contributed to the development of the balanced-growth models, which stressed that agriculture merited attention as well as industry. In general, the development of agriculture had to go simultaneously with, if not in advance of, manufacturing to achieve steady economic progress and avoid structural disequilibria, which might otherwise be a later source of hardship. The approach of balanced growth argued that there was not one path to industrialization; rather, the emphasis was put on the context of the particular underdeveloped country in question, focusing especially on its factor endowment (land, labor, and resources) at the time. In countries where labor was abundant in relation to natural resources, manufacturing industries could be developed by hiring underemployed workers from rural areas, and the efforts to raise agricultural output could be pressed forward simultaneously with the extension of industrial activities. Where labor was in short supply, action to raise productivity in the agricultural and mining sectors would have to precede any withdrawal of workers for employment in industries, unless external capital was available in sufficient amounts to finance the importation of food.[57]

In the report, agrarian reform was an essential aspect of development that primarily required action on the part of the underdeveloped countries themselves. But improvement of agricultural methods in the underdeveloped countries could not be considered in isolation from general economic development.

In particular, development would make it possible to solve the problem of overpopulation and, by raising technical standards and promoting training, pave the way for a satisfactory agrarian reform. Other UN literature clearly brought out in the 1950s that agrarian structure, particularly the system of land tenure and of agricultural credit, hindered the process of economic development and the raising of living standards of agricultural workers in many countries.

Thus, within the UN as a whole, the emphasis moved to balanced economic growth. The process of economic development was defined as the raising of the standard of living through a steady increase in the efficiency of factors of production. Achieving this objective involved the continual transfer of resources from less-productive to more-productive occupations. Thus, a key element of the development process consisted of a movement from agriculture to manufacturing, a process which was defined as industrialization—or in other words, the growth of manufacturing industry. One of the key issues of all those dualistic models was the problem of the transfer of labor from agriculture to manufacturing. Indeed, domestic capital accumulation was to be promoted by utilization of surplus labor, especially in agriculture, and full utilization of the potential of this surplus, called at the time disguised unemployment. The UN thus followed the solution proposed by Ragnar Nurkse in the development literature; namely, a synchronized and simultaneous application of capital throughout the economy in order to bring about a generalized expansion of the market.[58]

Domestic Savings and Foreign Capital

The General Assembly had agreed in the late 1940s that the economic development of the underdeveloped areas of the world would rest primarily on the development of national resources—on the increased productivity of the economies—and should come largely from the effort of the people concerned. From this perspective, the priority was to increase the rate of domestic capital formation, to provide incentives to promote domestic savings, and to direct such saving activities toward capital investment and productivity. Arthur Lewis had stressed the need to stimulate and mobilize domestic savings. He argued that

> the central problem in the theory of economic development is to understand the process by which a community which was previously saving and investing 4 or 5 per cent of its national income or less, converts itself into an economy where voluntary saving is running at about 12 to 15 per cent of national income or more.[59]

The authors of several of the UN reports quoted had also stressed the need not only to increase the rate of investments in those countries but also to see that the rates did not drop sharply in the event of a recession.[60]

Severe capital shortages were a common characteristic of underdeveloped countries, and their causes and consequences were widely analyzed in a number of early UN documents.[61] The UN documents emphasized the fact that in most underdeveloped countries the mass of the population had little or no margin between receipts from wages or the sale of produce and the necessary expenditure on food and other basic needs. The report entitled *National and International Measures for Full Employment* recognized that more rapid development, in particular of production, was essential for raising employment and living standards, for the growth of the world economy as a whole, and for the maintenance of international peace and security.[62] But speeding up development made it necessary to raise levels of productivity in the underdeveloped countries. That was seen as a major challenge for the UN in the 1950s.

In practically all underdeveloped countries there was a gap between domestic savings and investment needs. The contributions from domestic capital needed, therefore, to be complemented by inflows of foreign investment, which could take three forms: private capital, government or international loans, and international grants. The General Assembly and ECOSOC had on many occasions stressed both the necessity of stimulating the formation of domestic capital and the investment of foreign capital in the underdeveloped countries. There was a general agreement that domestic savings constituted the principal source of capital for economic development but was not enough by itself to speed up economic development.

At the end of its 1947 report, the ECOSOC Sub-Commission on Economic Development already was recommending that international provision be made for those underdeveloped countries by way of finance, food, and equipment. Foreign finance was more and more considered to be an important factor in promoting economic development, and underdeveloped countries pleaded in favor of establishing loans for development purposes that should be, for the greater part, long-term loans with low interest rates.[63]

A rapid expansion of production in underdeveloped countries was clearly essential. However, the domestic financial resources of these countries, even when supplemented by foreign capital, was not sufficient at that time to permit such an increase. Indeed, the need for investment in many sectors was so great that it could not be satisfied by private capital and other existing capital flows. The group of experts who wrote the report on *Measures for the Economic Development of Underdeveloped Countries* calculated that those countries required about $19,000 million a year to expand their agricultural production and achieve industrialization, but their total savings were barely $5,250 million. Prebisch in 1950 and the expert team headed by Schultz and Lewis in 1951 emphasized the important role of foreign capital in economic development. For Prebisch, there was a vicious circle, which ran as follows. Productivity is very low owing to lack of capital. The lack of capital is due to the narrow margin of savings resulting from this low productivity. Thus, foreign aid is necessary in the first phase to break this vicious circle without restricting further the already very low consumption level of the people. Once capital invested and productivity increased, domestic savings will increase and can be substituted for foreign capital in the new investment.[64]

A major challenge was thus to fill the gap between the investment needs of the underdeveloped countries and the resources available, including those by means of various forms of international transfer. Underdeveloped countries tended to encounter greater and greater difficulties in the matter of financing, especially in finding the foreign currency essential to private undertakings if they were to carry out programs for extending, modernizing, and renewing equipment and machinery. Because of the recognition of its limitations regarding financing private enterprises, in 1950 the World Bank welcomed the suggestion made by the U.S. International Advisory Board, headed by Nelson Rockefeller, that an international finance corporation be created as an affiliate of the Bank, designed to enable the Bank, through the International Finance Corporation (IFC), to make loans to private enterprises without a governmental guarantee and to make equity investments in partnership with private investors. But the role of the Bank was limited by the creditworthiness of the countries to which money was advanced and the rate of interest, which was too high for many underdeveloped countries. The establishment of the Special United Nations Fund for Economic Development (SUNFED) was the means proposed by the underdeveloped countries to resolve that situation.

The Development of Technical Assistance

Before presenting the debate on SUNFED, a few words on technical assistance are in order. In the early UN days, there was a growing consciousness that the shortage of physical capital was not the only obstacle to development. It was also crucial to develop human resources to respond to the shortage of skills. President Truman raised the idea of technical assistance to the top of the international agenda when he presented his famous "Point 4" proposal to aid the efforts of the peoples of economically underdeveloped areas. In his inaugural address in January 1949, Truman launched the idea of the expanded technical assistance program: "We invite other countries to pool their technological resources in this undertaking. . . . This should be a co-operative enterprise in which all nations work together through the United Nations and its specialized agencies wherever practical. It must be a world-wide effort for the achievement of peace, plenty and freedom." He added, "We must embark on a bold new program for making the benefits of our scientific advances and industrial progress available for the improvement and growth of underdeveloped areas."[65]

Technical assistance was not a completely new idea at that time.[66] The provision of fundamental education—in the first instance, measures to reduce or eliminate illiteracy—was a basic requisite for developing a program of technical training. Important work was done by the ILO in vocational training and by the United Nations Educational, Scientific and Cultural Organization (UNESCO) in elementary education, technical training, and the dissemination of technical literature. It is interesting to note the emphasis put on the diversity of international teams of experts in technical assistance. Such teams would be drawn from different countries and sent out by several specialized agencies. Such balanced multidisciplinary teams were seen as useful not only in advising on specific technical projects or fields of economic development but also in support of overall plans for a country's development.

In December 1948, the General Assembly adopted resolution 200, which enabled the Secretary-General to organize international teams of experts through the United Nations or its specialized agencies to advise governments and offer support in other areas of economic development. This resolution laid the groundwork for further expansion of international action in the field of technical assistance.[67]

In that context, Truman's proposals rapidly generated a strong consensus in favor of providing developing countries with the human skills and human resources to make capital inputs effective. This was to be the principal purpose of technical assistance. On whichever front the problem of economic development was attacked—whether the economic process itself or the necessary social pre-conditions—effective economic development could proceed only where there was both technological knowledge and available finance. By the end of the 1940s, the United Nations had published two reports, each dealing with one aspect of that problem: one on the methods of financing economic development and the other on technical assistance.[68]

Large and increasing investment in the health and hygiene of the people was seen as an essential prerequisite for the successful and continuing economic development of underdeveloped countries. Malaria, smallpox, and other infectious diseases were not only a human disaster but also major obstacles to higher productivity. In addition, educational programs—basic education to abolish illiteracy and technical education and vocational training—were fundamental to the promotion of new knowledge and skills. A further task identified was the development and strengthening of the national administrative services responsible for implementation of the economic development program. One objective was to assist governments to introduce sound methods of personnel selection and training of public officials. We have here some of the roots of the good governance programs that were rediscovered in the 1990s.

The proposals of the technical assistance report were widely debated in 1949 in ECOSOC. The session in conclusion adopted resolution 222, which established: 1) the "expanded programme of technical assistance for economic development of underdeveloped countries," which became known as EPTA; 2) the Technical Assistance Board (TAB), an interagency supervising body composed of the executive heads of the UN and its agencies that was responsible for coordinating the technical assistance activities; and 3) the Technical Assistance Committee (TAC) as a standing body of ECOSOC to examine and approve EPTA activities.[69]

David Owen, the first economist to be appointed to the UN, was nominated as the head of EPTA. For some fifteen years, Owen was EPTA's only director, until 1965, when EPTA was merged with the Special Fund to become the United Nations Development Programme (UNDP). The initial contributions—made on a voluntary basis—to start EPTA's operational activities amounted to some $20 million from fifty-four countries, the United States being the largest donor. The Soviet bloc refused to participate in EPTA or contribute to it until the mid-1950s.

One important innovation of EPTA was the establishment of a field-office network in the developing countries to provide continuous dialogue and exchange of information on development needs. The network progressively expanded to cover 115 developing countries and territories. The idea of EPTA was to create development service centers with professional staff members to meet the specific needs of the country and provide the appropriate technical assistance.

During the early phase of EPTA, the field offices served as experimental stations where the new principles of technical assistance were tested in order to identify good practices. One of the pioneer UN field officers, Margaret Joan Anstee, who later became an assistant and under-secretary-general, recalls, "Everything, it seemed, was improvised that day in July 1952 when I first began to work for the UN Technical Assistance Board in Manila. The office was housed in a disused surgery in the grounds of the Philippine General Hospital, a dilapidated building with a leaking roof. In the rainy season every room was festooned with tin cans and any other receptacles that could be found to catch the drips . . . yet there was a tremendous feeling of enthusiasm and pioneering at that time."[70] This sounds very much like the remark made by Janez Stanovnik: "I must tell you that the United Nations in my time, before 1952 when I was in New York, was a true family of sincere believers, which it is not anymore."[71]

By the end of 1951, EPTA had funded projects in 71 countries for almost $6.5 million, awarded 800 fellowships for specialized studies abroad, fielded 797 project experts recruited from 65 countries, and provided additional training and demonstration equipment. In the following years, EPTA activities grew quickly. By 1956, EPTA was covering 103 countries and territories, providing the services of over 2,300 experts and more than 2,100 fellowships, with 77 governments pledging $28.8 million in support.

In 1955, EPTA adopted a system of country programming drawn up by the governments themselves in consultation with the UN organizations. The objective was to set the priorities and target figures at the country level and then to elaborate the overall program of activities. This new procedure was based on the principle that each requesting country should determine its own priorities for international technical assistance in the light of its own plans for economic and social development. The country-level programming approach encouraged requesting governments to review their needs and in many cases to set up administrative machinery to make such a review, thus strengthening their own planning and coordinating capabilities. This was the principle of country ownership and control in 1955—some forty years ahead of its rediscovery as the necessary ingredient for a successful program of economic adjustment and poverty reduction.

In 1956, the Technical Assistance Board completed a comprehensive review of EPTA. This was transmitted to ECOSOC under the title *The EPTA: A Forward Look.*[72] This report emphasized that despite the modest scale of the program, EPTA had played a constructive role in some 130 countries and territories that had asked for technical support. EPTA had shown that a valuable contribution to economic development could be made by an expansion of the international interchange of technical knowledge through international cooperation. In particular, the program had in fact combined and made use of the experience of many nations with different social patterns and cultural traditions and at different stages of development in order to facilitate progress in the less-advanced countries and to help to solve their technical and economic problems.

With the rapid growth of newly independent countries after the surge of decolonization in the 1960s, the demand for development assistance increased sharply. EPTA and the newly established United Nations Special Fund came under pressure. This led to the recommendation by ECOSOC in August 1964 to merge certain key aspects of EPTA and the Special Fund into a new United Nations Development Programme.[73] The objective was to simplify organizational arrangements and procedures and to facilitate overall planning and coordination of the several types of technical cooperation programs carried on within the UN. A year later, in November 1965, the General Assembly adopted resolution 2029 (XX) requesting the consolidation of the Special Fund and EPTA in a United Nations Development Programme.[74] UNDP started on 1 January 1966 with Paul Hoffman as administrator of the new program and David Owen as co-administrator.[75] Arthur Lewis joined the new UNDP for eighteen months as "deputy administrator." The policy papers he produced over this period must count as some of the most eloquent and penetrating to have been produced within the UN.

Soon after the beginning of the UNDP's activities, its governing body designated Sir Robert Jackson to produce a comprehensive capacity study on relations between the different UN organizations with regard to their aid programs. This was seen as an important step that would tighten up programming and strengthen UN coordination. The study emphasized the complexity of the whole UN assistance machinery, including the UNDP, UNICEF, the United Nations Industrial Development Organization (UNIDO), the United Nations Conference on Trade and Development (UNCTAD), the specialized agencies, and about ten other UN organizations.

The Jackson Report was issued a year later as *A Study of the Capacity of the United Nations Development System,*[76] and it clearly pointed out the shortcomings in technical assistance of each of the partners and the problems of coordination. The study's more than 600 pages proposed sweeping reforms that stirred considerable controversy both inside and outside the United Nations. Jackson's own assessment of UN development assistance was hard-hitting. He pointed out that:

> The constraints here are serious and must give cause for concern. . . . A final point bearing on capacity is based on my personal experience. For many years, I have looked for the "brain," which guides the policies and operations of the UN development system. The search has been in vain. Here and there throughout the system there are offices and units collecting the information available, but there is no group (or "Brain Trust") which is constantly monitoring the present operation, learning from experience, grasping at all that science and technology has to offer, launching new ideas and methods, challenging established practices, and provoking thought inside and outside the system. Deprived of such a vital stimulus, it is obvious that the best use cannot be made of the sources available to the operation. . . . The UN development system has

tried to wage a war on want for many years with very little organized "brain" to guide it. Its absence may well be the greatest constraint of all on capacity. Without it, the future evolution of the UN development system could easily repeat the history of the dinosaur.[77]

The Jackson study generated substantial changes in the UNDP that played a far-reaching role in the programming of technical cooperation. Based largely on its extensive analysis of the difficulties and limitations of existing arrangements and its recommendations for corrective action, a "consensus" resolution was adopted by the UNDP governing council and the General Assembly in 1970. The most significant reforms were the establishment of country-level indicative planning figures, new procedures for country-level programming of UNDP assistance, and internal administrative restructuring to give greater importance to UNDP local offices. Authority for effective programming and implementation at all stages was substantially decentralized from headquarters to the UNDP resident representatives at the country level. The new country-level programming procedures decentralized to the recipient countries the responsibility for the formulation of country programs in order to relate UNDP assistance more closely to national development plans and priorities. Overall coordination of technical assistance programs required in particular that the recipient countries have a good idea of their needs in terms of technical assistance related to their development programs. The UNDP would play a key coordinating role in that process by providing any technical services required to do that work.[78]

In spite of this, technical assistance has been increasingly criticized since the later 1960s. Donors raised the issues of problems with coordination and cost-effectiveness. Developing countries stressed the need to give more attention to building institutional and individual capacities within their own countries instead of sending costly expatriate technicians, teachers, and other technical experts. Another criticism pointed out the frequently hasty and poor design of technical assistance projects, largely due to the inadequate diagnosis of technical assistance needs.[79]

The Story of SUNFED

As we have seen, from the earliest days of the United Nations, it was recognized that the shortage of capital was one of the most serious obstacles to rapid economic development in the less-developed countries. In most underdeveloped countries, the first need was development in such fields as transport, power, communication, and, though they were somewhat less recognized at the time, education and public health. To provide this so-called overhead capital, large investment was often needed in projects which, at least in their early stages, were not self-liquidating, which means they were not producing a "sufficient" return on capital. Obviously, investments that are not self-liquidating cannot be financed by EPTA, which was concerned with technical assistance and had no funds for investment in physical capital, or by private capital, which expects a profit, or even by the IBRD, which charged interest and expected repayment within a reasonable period. Clearly, public financing would be needed. In order to accelerate economic development, it was essential to mobilize all sources of finance, both public and private.[80]

In its third session held in 1949, the Sub-Commission on Economic Development noted that despite the expansion of its activities in financing economic development projects in underdeveloped countries, the IBRD would not be able, in the foreseeable future, to make a significant contribution to the massive investments required for development over a long period. Thus, if economic development was to progress more rapidly, a larger and better-regulated flow of foreign funds than was currently available would have to be promoted by and through the international agencies working within the framework of the UN.

The chairman of the sub-commission, V. K. R. V. Rao, one of the most distinguished Indian economists of the time, made an important suggestion that led to much debate during the following years. Having considered that there was no appropriate international agency for financing basic economic development, he suggested that a new organization be set up, to be called the United Nations Economic Development Administration (UNEDA). This body would have "five fields of activity: technical assistance to underdeveloped countries, coordination of technical assistance as extended by the UN and the Specialised Agencies, assistance to underdeveloped countries in obtaining materials, equipment, personnel, etc. for economic development, financing or helping to finance schemes of economic development which cannot be financed from the country's own resources and for which loans cannot be asked on strict business principles, and the promotion, and, if necessary, the direction and financing of regional development projects."[81]

Rao emphasized that UNEDA should function within the framework of the UN while recognizing that the bulk of the finance required would have to come from the United States. Therefore, the whole project was very dependent on the support and goodwill of the United States. Rao explained that it was worthwhile to put forward this idea in the hope that attention would be drawn to the imperative need for urgent and concrete action by the UN for the rapid promotion of economic development in the underdeveloped countries. "It is my belief," he argued, "that this cannot be done without the setting-up of a new United Nations agency which will, on the one hand, act as a complement to orthodox foreign financing and, on the other, help to coordinate and integrate the supply of technical assistance to underdeveloped countries."[82] This suggestion would fill an existing gap in the international field for financing economic development and would overcome the shortcomings of the World Bank.

However, the Economic and Employment Commission felt there was no need to create a new international agency even if certain of its members felt the proposal deserved further and detailed consideration. Most of the debates of the General Assembly that year (1949) were dedicated to the establishment of the Expanded Program of Technical Assistance. The debate in ECOSOC on financing economic development continued in 1950, but no reference was made to the creation of a new organization. The report *National and International Measures for Full Employment*[83] did not recommend any new agency such as UNEDA for the distribution of grant aid, though it did propose a considerable expansion of the scope of activities of the World Bank and the IMF. However, at its fifth session in 1950, the General Assembly unanimously adopted resolution 400 (V), emphasizing that it was "convinced that the volume of private capital which is currently flowing into underdeveloped countries cannot meet the financial needs of the economic development of the underdeveloped countries and that those needs cannot be met without an increased flow of international public funds."[84]

It was the report *Measures for the Economic Development of Underdeveloped Countries* which gave a new impetus to the matter of financing economic development.[85] The report came back to the suggestion made by Rao and developed the idea of an international development authority. The expert group proposed in its recommendation 14 that "the United Nations should establish an international development authority to assist the underdeveloped countries in preparing, coordinating and implementing their programs of economic development; to distribute to under-developed countries grants-in-aid for specific purposes; to verify the proper utilization of such grants; and to study and report on the progress of development programmes."[86] This report led to very lively discussion at the thirteenth session of ECOSOC in 1951. Two opposing camps emerged—on one side, a number of developing countries such as Chile, Pakistan, the Philippines, and India, and, on the other, most of the developed countries. The proposal to establish an international development authority was rejected by the majority of the council, which confined itself to adopting the recommendation contained in paragraph 14 of resolution 368 (XIII) requesting the Secretary-General, in consultation with the competent specialized agencies, to keep the question under active study.

The U.S. government had always considered the World Bank to be the major international instrument for assisting in the financing of the economic development of underdeveloped countries. Shortly after its creation, it had authorized the Bank to use the total paid-in U.S. contribution for lending purposes. During the 147th meeting of ECOSOC (20 November 1951), Mr. Mansfield (representative of the U.S.) recalled the great caution of the United States toward the recommendation of *Measures for the Economic Development of the Underdeveloped Countries* that a new international organization be developed to provide grants-in-aid to finance basic projects.[87] He recalled that the problems of financing the basic requirements of economic development raised a twofold question concerning the extent to which grants were necessary and the mechanisms through which such grants should be made available. His government recognized that some countries, particularly the least developed, might sometimes require a measure of external grant assistance to provide an initial impetus to basic development (shades of Rosenstein-Rodan's "big push"). He expressed the opinion, which was largely shared by other developed countries, that it would be quite unrealistic and impracticable to assume that there would be wide and substantial participation—without which any institution could not be truly international in character—in any agency organized for the purpose of giving grants-in-aid.

Lord Wakehurst, representative of the United Kingdom, intervening in the debate on the economic development of underdeveloped countries and its financing, said it was a mistake to regard the world as being divided into two camps composed of the developed and the underdeveloped countries. He noted that distinct progress could be made in economic development without having to call on more capital than was available at the moment; the EPTA was doing valuable work in that direction. But the United Kingdom could not accept any further commitments to narrow the gap between the standard of living in industrial and underdeveloped countries.[88] Indeed, the period was marked by acute economic difficulties in both developed and underdeveloped countries caused or aggravated by the war in Korea and the intense rearmament effort to which it had given rise. These difficulties consisted in a shortage of raw materials, a growing disequilibrium in the balance of payments, and increased inflationary pressures in the developed countries and a shortage of industrial products and increased inflationary pressures in the underdeveloped countries.

During the fourteenth session of ECOSOC, a resolution submitted by a group of developing countries was adopted calling for the establishment of a committee of nine members to draft a "detailed plan" for a fund. This committee published its report in 1953. It proposed the establishment of a Special

United Nations Fund for Economic Development, whose acronym SUNFED became widely used in the debate from this date.[89] The sixteenth session of ECOSOC, in 1953, discussed extensively that report—not only the idea of a large-scale UN capital aid fund but also the chosen word SUNFED was subject to intense discussion. Some countries remarked that the initials were suggesting that the UN should feed developing countries. It is interesting to note that originally the body was called United Nations Fund for Economic Development. Hans Singer relates that it was only shortly before translation and printing was due that it was realized that the initials of this new body would read UNFED. That acronym would certainly have been used by the opponents of such a fund, who were pointing out the lack of resources available for it. Thus "special" was rapidly prefixed and UNFED became SUNFED.

A more substantive criticism stressed that the amount recommended by the committee of nine as a starting point—$250 million—was insufficient in the context of the objectives of the fund. Those in favor of the fund at that time mentioned some $400 or $500 million as a minimum requirement. However, even the $250 million went beyond the willingness to pay of the potential contributor countries. Yet it is interesting and significant to note that during the fiscal year 1954, the World Bank made 26 loans totaling approximately $325 million, the U.S. Congress authorized the expenditure of $300 million for economic assistance to underdeveloped countries, and the United Kingdom made available $350 million for such economic assistance.[90]

At the eighth session of the General Assembly in 1953, resolution 724B (VIII) asked the member governments of the UN and the specialized agencies for comments and for "moral and material" support for the proposal of the establishment of SUNFED. Mr. Raymond Scheyven, Belgium, who was president of ECOSOC, was asked to examine the comments of governments, to consult with them, and to report to ECOSOC and the General Assembly in order to "facilitate the establishment of such a fund as soon as circumstances permit."[91] All countries appeared to be convinced of the need of such a fund for financing non-self-liquidating or low-yield investments, but there were still divergences of opinion about the most favorable moment to launch it. The leading industrialized countries made their participation contingent upon general disarmament.

The results of the consultation confirmed the past divergence of views on that issue.[92] In his report, Mr. Scheyven divided the replies from governments into three groups: the first consisted mainly of replies from the underdeveloped countries, which believed that the special fund should be established forthwith; the second group was made up of the principal industrial powers, including the United States, which made their participation conditional on worldwide internationally supervised disarmament; the third group was comprised of all the other industrialized powers, which for the most part believed that the establishment of SUNFED should not necessarily be contingent on the disarmament process and were prepared to participate in that fund only if the major potential contributors also contributed. Indeed, some important changes started to occur in the developed countries' camp with a shift in attitude from Denmark, Norway, and the Netherlands. These three countries adopted a position in 1953 in favor of the establishment of SUNFED without waiting for savings from internationally supervised disarmament. Thus, developing countries pushed for the rapid establishment of the fund and most of the developed countries expressed caution and warned against undue haste.

At the ninth session of the General Assembly in 1954, a new resolution was adopted asking for a new report from Mr. Scheyven to be prepared with the assistance of an ad hoc group of experts.[93] The aim of the report was to give a full and precise picture of the form or forms, functions, and responsibilities which such a SUNFED might have. This report was discussed in 1955 at the twentieth session of ECOSOC and the tenth session of the General Assembly. One important recommendation of the experts was that the money provided by the fund should be directed toward strengthening economic and social infrastructures, which was defined as the basic facilities needed for production—roads, power stations, schools, hospitals, housing, and government buildings. The report notes that experience shows that only under these conditions will production develop smoothly and private initiative participate fully.[94]

The discussion at the General Assembly in 1955 was marked by an atmosphere of optimism regarding the prospects of international disarmament, which strengthened the side of the proponents of SUNFED. However, the resistance of some developed countries to a large-scale UN capital-aid fund led to a compromise resolution under which an ad hoc committee of government representatives was established with the task of analyzing the replies which governments were to give to a questionnaire.[95] This governmental committee was considered by the developing countries to be a big step forward toward the establishment of SUNFED in comparison to a previous resolution calling for expert committees.

The ad hoc committee collected the written views of the governments and presented its report at the twenty-second session of ECOSOC in 1956.[96] The debate at ECOSOC and later at the General Assembly was marked by powerful pressures to draft the statutes of the fund. A majority of the membership of the UN presented a resolution asking the ad hoc committee to work on these statutes. Once again, most developed countries vigorously opposed that move.

In that difficult context, an important suggestion was made by Argentina at that session of the General Assembly; it suggested that a small UN organization be established with a smaller fund than the large-scale fund that had been discussed hitherto. This fund should finance regional training centers and natural resources surveys. But this idea was not presented as a formal proposal, in view of the pressure from the majority of developing countries for SUNFED. During that eleventh session, Paul Hoffman, at the time U.S. representative on the General Assembly's Second Committee, published an article which provoked much informal discussion among the delegates. He suggested "a United Nations experimental fund of $100 million to be used for surveys of mineral, water and soil resources, and for a limited number of pilot projects."[97] The key idea of this article was that large-scale investments, which were essential to raise production and productivity in the underdeveloped countries, would not venture into the unknown. The role of the special fund was to reduce uncertainty and to help prepare for that investment through pre-investment groundwork, which aimed to transform the latent opportunities into actual opportunities. This idea was just a trial balloon sent by the U.S. delegation that was not formally presented to the General Assembly.

During the twenty-fourth session of the ECOSOC, the final and supplementary report of the ad hoc committee was presented. The proponents of SUNFED were in favor of rapid action to establish the new agency, but the major potential contributors were once again strongly opposed to SUNFED's creation. For example, the U.S. representative declared:

> The prospect is that assets of the Fund would consist of a few million dollars in the form of heterogeneous assortment of currencies, and, possibly, some contributions in goods and services. Is it reasonable that a new international financing agency, charged with gigantic tasks, should be established with such pitifully meager resources? Can we pass lightly over all that is being done by private investors, by international lending agencies, and by the United States and other countries through bilateral programmes to direct billions of dollars into economic development? In view of the vast scale of present international development financing, how can it be maintained that the establishment of a Lilliputian SUNFED is the nostrum which will obliterate poverty among millions of people in large parts of the world? So to believe is surely to turn from reality to magic.[98]

The United States, the key actor, made a move before the twelfth session of the General Assembly in 1957 by favoring the establishment of a small UN fund to undertake certain projects and studies which could not be financed from the existing EPTA. This proposed fund was called the Special Project

Fund and would be part of the EPTA machinery. This was followed by difficult negotiations with the proponents of SUNFED who were ready to support the U.S. proposal only if the special fund was a step on the road to
SUNFED. But for the U.S. delegation, the special fund stood entirely by itself
without any other commitments.

On 17 December 1957, the General Assembly adopted resolution 1219 (XII)
to establish "as an expansion of the existing technical assistance and development activities of the United Nations and the specialized agencies, a separate
special fund to provide a systematic and sustained assistance in fields essential to the integrated technical, economic and social development of the less
developed countries." In particular, "it would facilitate new capital investments
of all types—private and public, national and international—by creating conditions which would make such investments either feasible or more effective."
Hans Singer was in charge of the preparatory work for the special fund until
the arrival of Paul Hoffman as managing director. Hoffman was a well-known
U.S. industrialist and former administrator of the Marshall Plan.

Part of the compromise consisted in dropping the term "SUNFED" in favor of the name "Special Fund." However, since the resources "prospectively
available at this time were not likely to exceed $100 million," the resolution
pointed out that the fund would be used to enlarge the scope of EPTA by
financing special projects such as intensive surveys of resources; establishing
training institutes in public administration, statistics, and technology; and
establishing agricultural and industrial research and productivity centers. As
the contributions to the Special Fund were approximately double those of
EPTA, the fund was able to finance large-scale projects such as extensive surveys and feasibility studies that averaged almost $1 million (whereas the aver-
age cost of EPTA projects was around $50,000).[99]

This resolution brought to a close the nine years of highly contentious and
often-tortuous debate on the question of UN funding for the economic development of developing countries. This debate was marked by the conflicts
between developed and developing countries on the extent and provision of
international economic aid toward developing countries. The General Assembly pushed hard for a special fund for economic development, which would
raise money from countries on the basis of their ability to contribute and
distribute it on a grant basis, presumably according to need. The United States,
which would have been the largest contributor, consistently voted against the
project in the Economic and Social Council and finally succeeded in reducing
the proposal to that for a United Nations Special Fund with only $100 mil-
lion, to be used to finance special projects of technical assistance such as resource and pre-investment surveys.

The Special Fund was not to be a lending institution. It provided no investment capital. Its function was to help bring into being some of the preconditions for successful private and public investment. For the most part, it would support relatively large projects, which might be expected to lead to early results and have the widest possible impact in accelerating development in the countries concerned.[100] The essential purposes of the Special Fund were to: 1) help developing countries acquire in-depth knowledge of their resources through surveys of natural resources—geological, soil, hydrological, timber, or fishery surveys—intended to disclose wealth that had not previously been used for the benefit of the country; 2) establish research institutes for applying modern technology to development; and 3) train local personnel—particularly in vocational, scientific, and administrative skills—to increase the productive capacity of increasing numbers of people. According to Hoffman, the success of the Special Fund was not to be judged by the number of reports added to the shelves but by the amount of new investment made possible by the information produced and the skills learned. The aim of the Special Fund was to make an effective use of national resources and thus attract investment and be able to use it productively in order to ultimately become self-sufficient. In a report to ECOSOC in 1964, Mr. Hoffman recalled that experience had shown that with well-placed pre-investment surveys, the Special Fund could foster capital investment in large volume and with only small delay. Indeed, it had been found that twelve surveys costing the Special Fund only $5.8 million had already resulted in investments totaling over $750 million. In other words, the ratio of return on outlay was 130:1.[101]

During its five years of existence, the Special Fund sent to the field more than 1,500 experts, worked with more than 17,000 national project staffs, trained 56,000 people under 124 projects at advanced educational and technical levels, carried out 31 national and physical resource surveys, and established 2 applied-research institutes. The members of the governing council of the Special Fund stressed the importance of field offices, the number of which had increased from 35 at the end of 1959 to 72 by the end of 1964.

After ten years of debate, the General Assembly adopted resolution 1240 (XIII), which established the Special Fund beginning on 1 January 1959. This achievement led the president of ECOSOC, Mr. Davidson, to describe the year 1958 as "the year of the breakthrough."[102] Nevertheless, discussion continued about the possible evolution of the Special Fund into a large-scale capital development fund. This decade of debate brought the developing countries and a few developed countries into opposition against most of the developed countries, including the largest potential contributors. After many endless and fruitless negotiations to establish such a fund, the developing countries proposed in 1966 a resolution which was adopted with 59 in favor and 31 against (most Western countries) and 19 abstentions (including Greece and the Netherlands as the only Western states). This resolution 2186 (XXI) set the statutes of the UN Capital Development Fund (CDF) as an autonomous organ of the General Assembly, as was the case for UNCTAD and UNIDO, aiming to "assist developing countries in the development of their economies by supplementing existing sources of capital assistance by means of grants and loans."[103] But until 1974, there was no progress, as contributions remained minimal. The Netherlands was the first of the developed countries to announce a sizeable contribution to the CDF in the autumn of 1974 following the discussion at the General Assembly about the new international economic order and the problem of the least-developed countries. The idea was to focus the activities of the CDF on the least-developed countries and the most vulnerable groups of the population. Following the Dutch example, Norway first and then other developed countries (the United States in 1978) started to contribute to the CDF.

The establishment of the Special Fund can be interpreted in very different ways. But it remains a good case study of how ideas are promoted and combated and how decisions are made in the UN system.[104] From 1949 to 1955, the developing countries as a group tried to influence the large potential contributors to support the establishment of SUNFED. During this long bargaining period, the developing countries always had a UN majority in favor of the establishment of a large-scale capital aid fund. However, trying to force the decision would have been counterproductive, as they needed the agreement of the potential contributors. Thus, the developing countries always had to search for compromises with the developed countries, and the idea of a large-scale fund for economic development was kept alive for many years despite the opposition of most of the developed countries. In that process, they received the help of some European countries, especially the Scandinavian countries and the Netherlands, who were a positive voice in supporting the move to establish the Special Fund.

The review of the debate on financing economic development shows that there was no opposition from the developed countries to the principle of external assistance to meet certain financial needs which could not otherwise be met. But it is clear that the United States, in particular, preferred mechanisms of bilateral aid and agencies where it had a dominant position and a blocking vote, such as the World Bank. Moreover, from the beginning of the debate on the Special Fund, the United States and some other major potential contributors combined hostility to soft financing with hostility to the idea of a rival to the World Bank. And Eugene Black, then president of the World Bank, was very active within the UN to maintain the leadership of the Bank and discourage the establishment of any soft financing agency that would have competed with the Bank on financing of large-scale economic development projects. The truth is that major potential contributors—such as the United States or Great Britain—were not willing to channel financial aid through the UN, where the developing countries had a majority in decision making; they preferred to work through the World Bank, which they controlled.

In response to a proposal by the United States, the governors of the World Bank at their September 1959 session decided to establish the International Development Association (IDA). The IDA and the International Finance Corporation (IFC), established in 1956, were both created as agents of the World Bank to make different types of loans. The first type of loan was for long-term public infrastructure projects, repayable in local currency, with low interest rates and (frequently) a grace period. The second type of loan was for investment in equities with a view to stimulating private enterprise. The creation of the IDA was partly the result of the pressures in the UN for the creation of a capital development fund. As we have seen above, the creation of a limited special fund for pre-investment activities was a victory for the World Bank and the opponents of SUNFED, who fought against the idea of a new authority that would manage a large-scale fund within the UN. And when Dag Hammarskjöld asked Eugene Black for a "special institutional link" between the newly established IDA and the United Nations, "President Black politely but firmly rejected this suggestion."[105] As Hans Singer said about the attitude of the IMF and World Bank, "Collaboration, yes, co-ordination, no."[106]

To conclude, SUNFED can be seen as an unsuccessful attempt by the underdeveloped countries—with the support of some developed countries such as the Netherlands—to create a major soft-aid mechanism within the United Nations. The long process of negotiations gave birth to a mouse. Indeed, the Special Fund was a mouse both in relation to the initial ambitions for SUNFED and in relation to the enormous task of social and economic development in developing countries. However, the work of EPTA and the Special Fund showed how even relatively modest amounts of multilateral assistance could have an important impact in helping developing countries make their resources available for productive use and put those resources to work for the benefit of their people. The efforts were even intensified with the fusion of the two programs in a single one through the establishment of the UNDP. It is important to point out also that the proposal of a large development fund was revived later by the Brandt Commission, which placed it once again on the international agenda.

Concluding Observations

What, in a nutshell, were the major contributions of the UN to development thinking during the 1940s and 1950s?

First, contrary to classical and neoclassical trade theory, statistical work in the UN during the late 1940s showed that there is a long-term decline in the terms of trade against the developing countries. This finding, which was highly controversial at the time, is now generally accepted as a fact.

This finding led to the conclusion that industrialization is essential. In the wake of Alexander Hamilton and Friedrich List, Raúl Prebisch and his ECLA team elaborated an industrialization strategy that is known as import-substitution policies. These policies served Latin America well for a while, but List's (and Prebisch's) warnings were not heeded and they were continued for too long.

Third, ECLA and Prebisch also contributed the center-periphery thesis, which states that the benefits of international trade go to the rich and not to the poor, leading to unequal exchange—another reason, therefore, to push industrialization and technology development.

Fourth, and in line with John Stuart Mill and other classicists, the role of the state was considered important, especially for breaking through the bottlenecks that occur during the early stages of development.

Fifth, the role of physical and human capital was underlined, leading to technical assistance and the SUNFED proposal. We have shown at some length the tortuous paths to success and failure of these initiatives.

Sixth, the role of foreign capital was underlined to bridge what was supposed to be a temporary gap between national savings and investment needs. This is the one-gap model that, during the 1960s, was transformed into a two-gap model; foreign exchange as well as capital are limiting factors.

4

The 1960s: The UN Development Decade—Mobilizing for Development

- **The Proposals for Action: Growth Plus Change**
- **Planning for Economic Development**
- **The UN's Role in Development Planning**
- **Education and Economic Development**
- **The Challenge of Science and Technology**
- **The World Food Programme**
- **The End of the "Golden Age" of ECLA**
- **UNCTAD and the Emergence of a Unified South**
- **Concluding Observations**

On 25 September 1961 the president of the United States, John F. Kennedy, addressed the UN General Assembly and launched a proposal for a Development Decade.[1] If the United States could commit itself to put a man on the moon before the end of the decade, he said, it would certainly support the idea of improving the living standards of people in the poorest countries over the same period. Some nine months earlier, in his inaugural address, Kennedy had already acknowledged that developed countries, in particular the most advanced of them, the United States, should do something for developing countries. Kennedy developed the theme before the General Assembly:

> Political sovereignty is but a mockery without the means of meeting poverty and illiteracy and disease. Self-determination is but a slogan if the future holds no hope. That is why my Nation which has freely shared its capital and technology to help others help themselves, now proposes officially designating the decade of the 1960s as the United Nations Decade of Development. Under the framework of that Resolution, the United Nations' existing efforts in promoting economic growth can be expanded and co-ordinated.[2]

In spite of the heavy UN involvement in economic development policy and planning in the 1950s, the idea of a development decade came from the

U.S. administration of President Kennedy, not from within the UN. Hans Singer recalls that "when Kennedy uttered his magic words, they came as a complete surprise to me. My recollection is that we had no previous warning in the UN, at least I hadn't."[3]

Soon after Kennedy's declaration, the General Assembly adopted the historic resolution 1710 (XVI), which designated the 1960s as the "United Nations Development Decade. . . . Member States and their peoples [would] intensify their efforts to mobilize and to sustain support for the measures required on the part of both developed and developing countries to accelerate progress towards self-sustaining growth of the economy of the individual nations and their social advancement."[4]

The mood in the UN at the beginning of the 1960s was optimistic. Many people expected that rapid results in terms of development would be achieved during the decade if appropriate measures were taken on the part of both developed and underdeveloped countries. What we refer to now as the First Development Decade was called at the time *the* Development Decade. Not that its supporters thought that all the problems of the developing countries would be solved within a decade. But ten years fit the strong expectation that the job was feasible in a limited period of time.

The resolution on the Development Decade called for action to lessen the gap between developed and underdeveloped countries, to speed up the processes of modernization, and to release the majority of mankind from poverty. More particularly, it called for industrialization; the development of agriculture; effective national planning; the elimination of illiteracy, hunger, and disease; the promotion of education and vocational and technical training; an increase in the flow of public and private capital to developing countries; an increase in the export earnings of the underdeveloped countries; and the utilization of resources resulting from disarmament for the purpose of economic and social development.

As a specific economic target, the General Assembly sought the attainment by the underdeveloped countries of a minimum annual growth rate of 5 percent in aggregate national income by 1970.[5] Though Kennedy had proposed the idea of the Development Decade, the 5 percent target growth rate and the proposals for action came from the UN Secretariat. This target was the result of a back-of-the-envelope calculation based on the Harrod-Domar model, including a rough assumption about the ratio of capital to output. Such a growth rate, it was estimated, would prevent a growing relative gap between developing and developed countries. Within the UN Secretariat, some debate occurred about whether the 5 percent target was too optimistic. Michal Kalecki, for example, was much more skeptical about the ability of developing countries to reach that target by the end of the decade. Concerned with the pre-conditions for growth, he argued that it was politically naive to set up a 5 percent target given the many existing obstacles related to land reform, education, effective planning, and other factors.[6]

The resolution also called upon developed-country member states to pursue policies designed to enable underdeveloped countries to export more at stable and remunerative prices and to increase the inflow of resources—public and private—toward their countries. The General Assembly expressed the hope that the flow of international assistance and capital "should be increased substantially so [that it might] reach as soon as possible approximately 1 per cent of the combined national incomes of the economically advanced countries."[7]

The quantitative objective of 5 percent annual rate of growth in aggregate national income was modest in relation to the general objective of accelerating economic and social progress. Population growth was, at the time, thought to be in the range of 3 to 3.5 percent per annum in many developing countries at the time. The 5 percent specific objective corresponded therefore to an estimated annual increase of only 1.5 to 2 percent in per capita income. In other words, thirty-five to fifty years would have been required to double per capita income.[8]

A link was made during the Development Decade to the economic and social consequences of disarmament. The *Proposals for Action* published by the Secretary-General at the beginning of the decade stressed the importance of worldwide disarmament and the establishment of an international fund within the framework of the United Nations to assist development. It was estimated that the acceleration of growth in aggregate income in underdeveloped countries from 2.5 percent to 5 percent could be financed by a diversion of some 10 percent of the savings resulting from a reduction in armament expenditures by one-half.[9] It was highly significant that at the same time as the Secretariat published *The Development Decade: Proposals for Action*, ECOSOC published "The Economic and Social Consequences of Disarmament."[10] This document broke new ground on thinking about the relationship between development and disarmament.

Just before his tragic death, Secretary-General Dag Hammarskjöld appointed a group of experts to conduct a study on the economic and social consequences of disarmament. Among the ten members of the expert group were some of the most distinguished names in economics, including Oskar Lange, Wassily Leontief, and Alfred Sauvy. The expert group strongly criticized the level of world military spending—estimated at roughly $120 billion annually at that time—which, they argued, represented both a grave political danger and a heavy economic and social burden on most countries. One of the main contributions of the report was its evaluation of the resources devoted to military purposes and its emphasis on the points that "the most fundamental way in which disarmament affects economic life is through the liberation of the resources devoted to military use and their re-employment for peaceful purposes" and that "the promotion of economic and social development in under-developed countries is one of the most important ways in which the resources released by disarmament could be put in use."[11]

The members of the expert group pointed out that a much larger volume of resources could be allocated to investment for productive development in underdeveloped countries even if only a fraction of the resources currently devoted to military purposes were used in this way. Disarmament could thus help accelerate growth in the poorer parts of the world.

The Proposals for Action: Growth Plus Change

The General Assembly resolution on the Development Decade had also requested the Secretary-General to "develop proposals for the intensification of action in the fields of economic and social development by the United Nations system of organisations"[12] in the light of these objectives. The Secretariat, and in particular Hans Singer, was responsible for drafting the proposals in close collaboration with all the UN agencies and many experts, among them Arthur Lewis, Paul Hoffman, Gunnar Myrdal, Julius Nyerere, Barbara Ward, Jan Tinbergen, and Walt W. Rostow.

The United Nations Development Decade: Proposals for Action was submitted to the ECOSOC at its thirty-fourth session, in July 1962.[13] By the time of its publication, a new acting Secretary-General, U Thant, was in place. In his foreword to the report, U Thant explained very clearly the new context (shades of Chapters 1 and 2):

> At the opening of the United Nations Development Decade, we are beginning to understand the real aims of development and the nature of the development process. We are learning that development concerns not only man's material needs, but also the improvement of the social conditions of his life and his broad aspirations. Development is not just economic growth, it is growth plus change. As our understanding of development deepens, it may prove possible, in the developing countries, to compress stages of growth through which the developed countries have passed. It may also be necessary to examine afresh the methods by which the goals of development may be attained.[14]

The report identified six major tasks necessary to achieve the goals of the Development Decade:

1. The development of systematic surveys on physical and human resources in underdeveloped countries for maximum mobilization of domestic resources;
2. The formulation of development plans for social as well as for economic development;
3. An improvement in the machinery of institutional administration and in production incentives for effective national planning;
4. A redirection of science and technology to attack the problems of developing countries;
5. An increase of the export earnings of underdeveloped countries through the increase of manufacture and semi-manufacture exports and the stabilization of export earnings;
6. An increased and a more assured flow of capital on suitable terms to the underdeveloped countries. Social reform and economic strategy were recognized to be two sides of the same coin, "the single strategy of development." Governments should be increasingly concerned with planning for balanced economic and social development.[15]

There were some real successes during the Development Decade: first, in promoting development issues and in mobilizing the international community; second, in facilitating national development planning and stimulating work on international projections; and third, in stimulating creation of an institutional framework for development. In addition to the UNDP, the World Food Programme (WFP) and the United Nations Conference on Trade and Development (UNCTAD) were the true children of the first Development Decade.

Planning for Economic Development

In the early 1950s, several Asian countries had embraced planning for economic development. They established key institutions, such as the Indian Planning Commission in 1950.[16] The Colombo Plan for cooperative economic development in South and Southeast Asia, also established in 1950, gave a strong impetus to development planning in the region. Moreover, the First Five Year Plan established in India in 1952 and in Pakistan in 1955 had quite an influence on the leaders of other developing countries.

Most of the pioneers of development also considered economic planning to be an important tool for breaking the vicious circle of poverty. Paul Rosenstein-Rodan and Ragnar Nurkse[17] proposed investment programs which were both massive and balanced. Others, such as Albert Hirschman[18] or François Perroux,[19] were more concerned with the various bottlenecks in underdeveloped countries and proposed strategies of "unbalanced growth" and "growth poles."

Based on his experience in Colombia, Hirschman was particularly skeptical about comprehensive development plans. Much planning was based on "heroic" estimates by visiting economists and other UN experts.[20] Most of the planners took the position of the Economic Commission for Asia and the Far East (ECAFE) that "in view of generally limited financial resources available for planning and the scarcity of trained personnel, it would be wise to avoid devoting too many resources to the collection of new data as a preliminary to planning."[21]

Though visiting experts attracted criticism, some, such as Jan Tinbergen, were aware of the problems and could make jokes about them. Tinbergen referred to the five-year plan for Afghanistan in which he had participated. Its preface by the king of Afghanistan apparently stated: "Without the necessary data but with the help of Almighty Allah we here present our five-year plan."[22]

In spite of skepticism and lack of data, one of the most striking events of the Development Decade was the widespread adoption of planning as a tool for development.[23] A few years earlier, only a few developing countries—though several in South and Southeast Asia—had rudimentary development plans at the national level. In the 1960s, almost all the developing countries formulated medium-term or long-term plans as a way to assess their requirements for sustained growth and guide their policy decisions. The development of planning activity in the 1960s was also a result of the new independence of many African countries and the launching of the Alliance for Progress in Latin America, for which the United States gave massive support.

In 1963, a UN group of experts issued a report entitled *Planning for Economic Development*. The preface by Secretary-General U Thant stated that "the importance of national planning for economic development is almost universally recognised today.... [N]umerous developing countries as well as more advanced economies have employed planning as a tool for achieving their national economic goals."[24]

This group of experts was chaired by Jacob Mosak from the UN Secretariat and included Celso Furtado. Their report noted the remarkable intensification of interest in national economic planning during the decade; such planning called for long-run transformation of developing countries' economic and social structures. The experts recognized that the forms of planning, and the political significance of those plans, differed considerably among countries with different economic and social systems. They defended a pragmatic vision of planning that fit in with the mixed economies of most developing countries. Planning, for these proponents, was a major instrument that would provide the basis for economic policies and programs which would be comprehensive, consistent, and feasible and would thus help a government reach coherent priorities for achieving rapid economic growth.

Development planning in underdeveloped countries generally assumed a mixed economy in which the state had to take initiatives for development as a result of market failures. As market prices did not signal all the information required for an optimal solution, it was not possible to leave the allocation of investment solely to market forces. The roles of the state and of planning were very similar to what would be called much later "the developmental state" in the context of the "East Asian miracle" countries. It was the responsibility of the state to set the priorities of development and channel resources toward those priorities. In a mixed economy, appropriate incentives were crucial to guide private investment in the right direction. But the public sector also must be active, through public investments, to achieve the plan's targets.

The UN's Role in Development Planning

The work of the UN on development planning became a key contribution to development thinking and practice. During the 1960s, the UN analyzed trends in the world economy and assessed the significance of those trends against the goals set for the Development Decade. Every branch of the UN family became involved in collecting, evaluating, and disseminating the data essential for formulating development policy. Data collection and projections were an indispensable foundation on which to build for a decade of development.

In its *Five Year Perspective, 1960–1964,* the Committee on Programme Appraisal stressed that "great headway has been made in fact-finding and the establishment of internationally comparable statistics and other data."

> More than a start has been made in ascertaining needs and defining problems which call for action, private and public, national and international. Objectives have been formulated and standards set.... As a result of all this, international organisations have become a potent factor in stimulating action by national governments and in assisting them in their efforts to improve economic conditions and raise levels of living.[25]

The United Nations and its specialized agencies undertook special studies and experiments dealing with the process of development itself. For this purpose, the Economic Projections and Programming Center and the Center for Industrial Development were established in 1962 within the United Nations Secretariat. The United Nations Research Institute for Social Development (UNRISD) was created and started operations in 1964. Most ambitious of all, the UNCTAD secretariat was created in Geneva the same year.

In 1966 the Committee for Development Planning (CDP; a subsidiary body of ECOSOC) started its activities with Jan Tinbergen—who three years later would be the first co-winner of the Nobel Prize in economics—as its chairman. Long-term planning and forecasting about key issues for development such as population growth, food and educational needs, industrial production, and international trade became one of the main contributions of the Development Decade. Therefore, the United Nations became a prime source for statistical information about economic, social, and demographic aspects of the world and the member states.[26]

The CDP emphasized that comprehensive plans tended to be too ambitious and to overreach the power and capacity of most governments in mixed economies. Government influence over the private sector was limited. The problems discussed at the CDP were related to the absence of any assured means by which a government could convince the private sector that a given action on its part was necessary for the fulfillment of the plan. The main problem for government was to create conditions conducive to the participation of the private sector.[27] Other causes of failure in development planning were identified. Often, planning activities were disconnected from "present political realities" and were drawn up by a group of technicians working in isolation from the normal governmental process. Another problem was the weakness of the planning machinery at the various political and administrative levels in formulating and, in particular, implementing plans.[28]

Important studies were undertaken on the major trends in world trade in the period 1950 to 1962. They emphasized the international trade of the developing countries[29] and the trends in gross domestic product (GDP) and per capita income between 1950 and 1960 in the developed and the developing market economies.[30] An annual analysis of the more recent trends in the world economy was also made in the 1963 *World Economic Survey*,[31] and the Economic Projections and Programming Center published its first report in 1964, *Studies in Long-Term Economic Projections for the World Economy: Aggregate Models*,[32] and developed a framework for projections of world production and world trade. The regional economic commissions were also engaged in a wide-ranging task that included both methodological and empirical aspects of economic projections and planning. During the mid-1960s, the Economic Commission for Africa made a series of projections running to 1975 about foreign aid, population, and national income for the whole region. ECAFE prepared a report on *Projections of Foreign Trade of the ECAFE Region up to 1980* which was presented in September 1963. ECLA made a systematic compilation of national-accounts data over the previous years in order to provide the basis for specific projections.[33]

At the same time, the United Nations Special Fund, in cooperation with the regional commissions, became active in setting up institutes of economic development and planning in Latin America (1962), Africa (1963), and Asia (1964).

In the field of economic projections, work by the United Nations was organized around three broad themes:

- Elaboration of techniques for long-term projections
- Projections of major economic and social variables
- Appraisal of basic requirements for achieving target growth rates in the developing countries during the Development Decade

Planning for Economic Development dealt in general terms with problems of planning for economic development in economies at different stages of development and with different economic systems. Its main conclusion was that while there were a number of planning methods, most countries accepted the necessity of planning as a major instrument for achieving rapid economic growth. But as Kalecki stressed at that time, "We are all 'planners' today, although very different in character."[34] Both within and outside the UN there was a broad consensus about the need for planning. Jan Tinbergen published his *The Design of Development*,[35] which drew heavily on his experience in the Netherlands, where he had been the creator and first director of the Central Planning Bureau of the Netherlands; in the UN; and in developing countries, where his experience was extensive.

Population projections were essential for planning, as rapid growth of population in many of the developing countries was beginning to be seen as an important handicap to national efforts to achieve economic and social advancement and higher levels of living. Thus, demographic research was particularly relevant to the achievement of the major goals of the Development Decade and, in particular, for the effective development and use of human resources.

When the United Nations was set up, the population explosion was already affecting the development objectives of many countries and territories, but the implications of this situation were not immediately recognized. During the 1950s, there was a slow awakening to the fact that world population was growing at an unprecedented rate, but from the beginning of the United Nations, the population question aroused very emotional debates because of its sensitive nature. However, during the 1960s a growing number of countries came to the conclusion that rapid population growth constituted a serious obstacle to economic and social development and they looked to the UN family for advice and assistance in carrying out family planning programs.[36] This was not without reason. With hindsight, one can now see that the 1960s were the peak of population growth in the less-developed regions, which had increased from around 1 percent per annum in the 1950s to a peak of 2.5 percent per annum in the 1960s.

At the thirty-first session of ECOSOC in April 1961, Eugene Black, president of the World Bank, stressed that "unless population growth [can] be restrained, immediate hopes of economic progress in the crowded lands of Asia and Middle East would have to be abandoned."[37] In that context, the United Nations prepared population projections for the world, the main regions, and individual countries. In addition, several studies of demographic problems in particular developing areas were carried out under technical assistance programs or by direct cooperation of the UN Secretariat.[38] Between 1960 and 1963, under the stimulus of the United Nations World Census Programme (of the UN Population Division), 150 countries and territories carried out population censuses, nine of them for the first time, and in 1963, ninety-two countries undertook industrial censuses.

One can refer to 1965 as the turning point in the history of UN activities regarding the population question. In that year, the UN Technical Assistance Board approved a request from the Indian government for an expert mission to review the Indian family planning program and make recommendations for its intensification. The mission was the first of its kind to be provided by the United Nations. In September of that year, the second world population conference held in Belgrade brought together twice as many participants as there had been at the first conference in Rome in 1954; a large proportion of representatives were from less-developed countries. The Belgrade world population conference provided further evidence of the shift in opinion regarding the seriousness of the demographic situation and the need to control population growth. After that breakthrough, all the different bodies of the UN family, including the World Bank, embarked upon or intensified their activities in the field of population, including operational activities connected with family planning programs. However, the real debate about the relationship between population and development was yet to come at the first UN World Population Conference in Bucharest in 1974. Further details on the UN contributions to thinking on population and development will be found in Chapter 8.

Education and Economic Development

Until the Development Decade, the major constraint in economic growth was generally considered to be the shortage of capital. As of around 1960, however, it became increasingly recognized that the knowledge, skills, and capacities of human beings in a society were at least as important for development. Thus, the development of human resources became much more important in development strategies. In the 1967 report of the Secretary-General on human resources, the problem in the developing countries was stated in the following very simple terms: "There are too few skilled persons and too many unskilled."[39] This situation was further aggravated by the loss of skills resulting from the "brain drain" as highly skilled individuals left the countries of their birth to pursue better-paying jobs abroad.

This was the renaissance of the economics of education—education seen not only as a consumer good but also as an investment in human capital. We say "renaissance" because the classicists were well aware of the importance of education and training in economic growth and development. The academic renaissance took place outside the UN and was spearheaded by academics such as Theodore Schultz, Gary Becker, and Mark Blaug. Within the UN, Singer argued in a paper written in 1961 that "this new insight has been possible by a shift in our whole thinking about development. The fundamental problem is no longer considered to be the creation of wealth, but rather the creation of the *capacity* to create wealth. . . . What is the capacity to create wealth? Essentially, it resides in the people of a country. It consists of brain power."[40]

The acute problem of the shortage of skills in developing countries required a major effort to extend educational and training programs. The challenge was even more difficult given the "demographic explosion"; in many developing countries, the number of people without education and training was increasing from year to year.

The lack of skills was increasingly recognized as a major constraint on economic and social development. The educational system, both formal and informal, rose to the top of the priority list. Special attention was paid in most developing countries to the elimination of illiteracy, universal primary education, and vocational training.

The Challenge of Science and Technology

In 1961, at the beginning of the Development Decade, ECOSOC decided to convene a conference on the Application of Science and Technology for the Benefit of the Less Developed Areas. The conference took place in Geneva in February 1963. This proved to be a decisive event in the Development Decade. The conference was concerned with the observed trend toward greater economic disparity between developed and developing countries—a disparity that progress in science and technology had accentuated, whereas the key objective of the Development Decade was precisely to bridge that gap between the rich and the poor nations.

Conceived initially as a means of exploring the application of recent advances in science and technology, the conference found itself confronted by the much greater problem of ensuring that science and technology make their necessary contributions to development. The conference on science and technology was marked by great optimism on the part of developing countries that thought that the conference would serve to establish guiding principles, enabling the less-developed countries to accelerate their progress by applying many of the latest advances in science and technology to the solution of their economic and social problems.

The conference was also marked by a strong emphasis on the human factor and by the idea that a proper application of knowledge represented by modern technology could largely transform the world and play a major role in realizing the objectives of the Development Decade. However, reality proved rather different. The main finding of the Advisory Committee on the Application of Science and Technology to Development (ACAST)[41] in its third report in 1966 was that "the growing gap between the amount of research and application in developed and developing countries, and between their levels of technology is one of the major factors in the growing gap in living standards."

> One consequence of this is that only a very small fraction of the world's scientific and technical resources is devoted to the problems of the developing countries; the overwhelming proportion of the world's intellectual capital, as well as its physical capital, is applied towards meeting the needs of the highly developed countries.[42]

The World Plan of Action established as a follow-up to the conference aimed at: 1) overcoming the limited capacity of developing countries to do their own scientific and technological work and building up indigenous science and technology resources; 2) changing the structure of research and development (R and D), which was mainly devoted throughout the world to problems that were of interest primarily to the highly developed countries; 3) promoting cooperation in the fields of science and technology; and 4) facilitating transfer of scientific knowledge, research techniques, and technology to developing countries. In a report prepared in 1968 as a contribution to the World Plan of Action, the Sussex Group of Consultants suggested especially:

- That in the aggregate, the developing countries should aim to reach R and D expenditure levels of 0.5 percent of GNP by the end of the Decade,
- That advanced countries should devote some 5 percent of their total R and D expenditure to specific problems of the developing countries.[43]

The issue of science and technology for economic development reached the top of the development agenda in the 1970s in the framework of the debate on the new international economic order and the Green Revolution.[44] However, despite the active and leading role of the UN, which led to many intellectual contributions, the practical contributions in the fields of science and technology have been weak and there has been a lack of concrete results.

The World Food Programme

The World Food Programme was created in December 1961 thanks to the initiative of George McGovern, who was at the time the first director of the newly created Food for Peace program in the executive office of the new president of the United States, John F. Kennedy.[45]

The idea of food aid was much more popular than SUNFED to the U.S. government both for geopolitical reasons and because it was friendly to farmers and not an enemy to the taxpayer. The concept of food for peace, which was developed by McGovern and supported by Kennedy, played an important role in the U.S. farm economy. There were indeed strong elements of domestic U.S. politics in the proposals for a world food program.

The American surplus-disposal policy became a controversial topic in academic literature and in public debate. There was criticism that the misuse of food aid could have harmful effects.[46] However, the U.S. food-aid policy did not change until the 1960s, when it became clear that the problem of surpluses could not be resolved by an expensive protectionist farm policy alone. The U.S. became interested in multilateral aid, since this would make it possible to win the support of other countries and get them to share the responsibilities and the burdens of food aid.[47]

If the WFP owed its origin to the initiative of the U.S. administration, like the Development Decade, the origins of the idea of multilateral food aid can be traced to the pioneering work of the Food and Agriculture Organization (FAO) and to the debate on SUNFED in the 1950s.

In resolution 1496 (XV) adopted in 1960 on the "Provision of Food Surpluses to Food-Deficient Peoples through the United Nations System,"[48] the General Assembly requested the Secretary-General to report to ECOSOC at its thirty-second session on the role the United Nations and the appropriate specialized agencies could play in order to facilitate the best possible use of food surpluses for the economic development of the less-developed countries. The resolution endorsed the challenge of the FAO's "Freedom from Hunger" campaign, which aimed at helping national governments and the peoples of underdeveloped countries break the vicious circle of hunger, poverty, and economic stagnation.

In the end, the World Food Programme was established by the United Nations and the FAO at the end of 1961 as a joint program and was placed within
the orbit of the Freedom from Hunger Campaign.[49] This concerted action
expressed the fundamental interest of both organizations in the major aim of
the program, which was to explore the possibility of stimulating economic
and social development through aid in the form of food. Even though it was
supposed to start its work in 1963, the WFP supplied food aid as early as 1962
to three countries: Iran, which had been hit by an earthquake; Thailand, where
a hurricane left 10,000 victims without food; and Algeria, which had to absorb 5 million refugees who had returned from Morocco and Tunisia.

In the framework of the launching of the World Food Programme, the FAO
was requested to undertake a study of the feasibility and acceptability of additional arrangements, including multilateral arrangements, with the goal of mobilizing available surplus foodstuffs and distributing them in the less-developed
countries. In pursuance of this request, the director-general of the FAO, B. R.
Sen, prepared—with the assistance of a small ad hoc group of "high level, independent experts"—an important report entitled *Development through Food: A
Strategy for Surplus Utilisation.*[50] Among the expert group we find by now well-
known names, such as Hans Singer, Paul Rosenstein-Rodan, and V. K. R. V. Rao.

The report reviewed the basic principles and fundamental considerations
of food aid and economic assistance in general. It stated, in particular, "that
the concept of food aid was not new. It has been debated and accepted in
specialised international groups, and embodied in many bilateral food transfer agreements over recent years. But in the United Nations Resolution the
concept has been expressed as the consensus of world opinion, and as a guiding philosophy for the use of food surplus. This is new."[51]

The director-general of the FAO emphasized the dual role of food in development projects, pointing out that the distribution of food in the areas of
need and the use of food surpluses for economic development could not be
separated from one another. Food aid and economic development were presented as two sides of the same coin. He advocated that these two elements
should be planned and operated as an integrated activity, carefully balanced
with each other. However, in the conclusion of their report to the director-
general, the expert group stressed that

> the chief limiting factor to a surplus food utilisation programme which could
> make major contributions to world economic development lies not so much ...
> in the available supplies but rather in the capacity of the underdeveloped coun-
> tries to absorb these supplies into their economies at an appropriate high stan-
> dard of effectiveness. . . . Without domestic efforts the beneficial effect of this
> opportunity will be lost, or be purely transitory at best.[52]

Although the World Food Programme is one of the main achievements of the Development Decade, it is important to note that since the beginning, food aid has been the subject of much criticism among experts. Most common in the literature on the subject was the argument that food aid created a disincentive for local food producers.[53] Hans Singer, who, as we have seen, was involved from the beginning in food-aid thinking within the United Nations, criticized neoclassical market analysis and the disincentive-effect hypothesis.[54] His first argument was that a disincentive to local production because food aid added to local supply was not so evident as it seemed: food aid was supplied in bulk as balance-of-payment support and was a substitute for commercial imports. These imports would have taken place anyway, so this disincentive effect was the same with or without food aid. Since food aid replaced commercial imports, it did not add to total supply. The effect of food aid and financial aid was the same in this case, since financial aid was also used to import food. Another argument was that the analysis of disincentive effects in a free-market situation is inapplicable because in many countries that receive food aid, prices are set by regulation. Moreover, the market is often dominated by monopolists. Price is just one of many factors in the incentive and disincentive structure. A third argument was that food aid makes possible an expansionist policy on the part of the government. This policy could lead to an increase of demand that would offset the disincentive effect. Therefore, even when the disincentive effect was admitted as a danger, Singer felt that it was the task of government policies to take measures to prevent these effects from happening. The additional government revenue could be used, for example, for dual-price systems, in which producer prices are higher than urban prices (which are subsidized).

The WFP started out with an annual budget of $100 million. By 2000, the WFP had an annual expenditure of almost $1.5 billion, of which 86 percent was spent on relief aid and 14 percent on development aid. It distributed 3.7 million tons of food each year.[55]

In conclusion, food aid is a tool that can be used in an effective or in an ineffective way. Even if misuse occurs in many countries, this does not mean that food aid should be stopped altogether. Food aid is only one part of the solution to world poverty. If used in an effective way, food aid can only help development.

The End of the "Golden Age" of ECLA

In the 1950s, the initial boom atmosphere and rapid successes in terms of industrialization of the early phase of import-substituting industrialization

(ISI) led to great expectations. It seemed possible to break out of the dependent and unequal center-periphery relationship through ISI and a voluntarist development strategy shaped by the state. However, the positive results of ISI started to vanish in the 1960s, and a considerable disenchantment with it grew among Latin America's elite. This shift in the climate of opinion in Latin America resulted from the question of sustainability of ISI strategy, a question that had already been asked and answered by Friedrich List, as we saw in Chapter 2. Since apparently each generation has to learn things all over again, here are some of the problems noted as of the 1960s:

- Once the easy phase of ISI—predominantly based on manufacturing consumer goods that were previously imported—reached its limits, the effect of backward linkages proved to be much more problematic than expected. As Furtado argued in 1966, "The phase of 'easy' development, through increasing exports of primary products or through import substitution has everywhere been exhausted."[56]
- The high protection of domestic industries—if prolonged too long—tends to produce an inward-looking mentality and an expensive and inefficient industrial structure that is unable to compete in the world market. As Prebisch acknowledged when he was still at ECLA: "An industrial structure virtually isolated from the outside world thus grew up in our countries. . . . As is well known, the proliferation of industries of every kind in a closed market has deprived the Latin American countries of the advantages of specialization and economies of scale, and owing to the protection afforded by excessive tariff duties and restrictions, a healthy form of internal competition has failed to develop, to the detriment of efficient production."[57]
- ISI was constrained by relatively small domestic markets. Moreover, a high effective protection stimulated investment in industries that produced nonessential goods, which responded to the demand of the elite, whereas the bulk of the population lacked access to essential goods.
- ISI was heavily based on importing inputs and machines to start new manufacture of finished consumer goods. The move toward higher stages of manufacture, particularly capital goods, meant that the countries following the ISI path were increasingly constrained by the lack of access to foreign exchange. This aspect of ISI led to a growing indebtedness of Latin American countries and, paradoxically, a growing dependence on the export of primary products.
- ISI was based on the import of Western technology, which created another kind of dependence. Moreover, the imported technology was capi-

tal intensive and labor saving and the new industries did not make an adequate contribution to the solution of the employment problem.[58]

A different type of critique emerged in the form of the "dependency school." Despite the heterogeneity of the dependency literature and important ideological differences among dependency writers, a common analytical framework emerged based on an uncompromising criticism of the modernization paradigm. The dependency school in the late 1960s and early 1970s made a contribution to development thinking, in the sense that it went beyond the economic bias of ECLA and proposed new lines of explanation of underdevelopment which were more sociological and political.

Box 4.1. State-Led Industrialization in Brazil

Brazil is a large country, the fourth biggest in the world in terms of area and fifth in terms of population. Economically Brazil has functioned as a mixed economy with the state—during certain periods—as an important actor. Until 1980, Brazil was among the most rapidly growing countries in the world, on a par with Japan, South Korea, and Taiwan.

From the early postwar years to the mid-1960s, Brazil implemented a state-led industrialization strategy based on import substitution, in line with the ideas of ECLA and Raúl Prebisch. Industrial growth was fostered by import controls, tariffs, and quantitative restrictions as well as overvalued exchange rates. Industry grew rapidly, and Brazil achieved a large measure of self-sufficiency through broad-based industrialization.

However, growing problems of inflation, balance of payments, and rising social tensions over inequalities led to military intervention in 1964. The new regime sought to promote industrial exports through abolishing export taxes, introducing subsidies and tax incentives, maintaining realistic exchange rates, and encouraging foreign private investment. These policies were successful in restoring "miracle growth rates" of over 11 percent per year between 1968 and 1974.

Then came the two shocks of the 1970s, following the surge of oil prices in 1973 and 1979. These put renewed pressure on the balance of payments and inflation. The government responded with policies to maintain high growth rates through the intensification of import substitution and huge infrastructure projects. Most of this was carried out by state enterprises and financed by external borrowing. Very soon Brazil was faced with huge debt-servicing problems. The adjustment to this problem in the 1980s resulted in severe declines in both living standards and GDP.[59]

Brazil's economic and social performance over the period 1950–2000 was characterized by rapid economic growth averaging almost 4 percent per annum for the first three decades, slipping to 0.7 percent over the 1980s and 1.5 percent over the 1990s. From 1950 to 1980, the share of industry in GDP increased from 24 to 37 percent in 1980 before falling to 29 percent in 2000, while agriculture over the same period declined from 27 to 10 and then to 9 percent.

Life expectancy has risen from 57 years in 1960 to 67 in 1998, while infant mortality fell from 128 to 60. Primary-school enrollments have risen from a low of 28 percent in 1950 to over 90 percent in 1980, with adult literacy reaching about 85 percent in 1999. But inequality has remained very high, and the standard of living of the poorest 60 percent has risen only slowly over the last fifty years, in spite of rapid growth.

There were two main positions within the dependency school: the reformist and the Marxist.[60] The intellectual roots of the former were in Latin American structuralism. Dependency writers such as Fernando Henrique Cardoso, Osvaldo Sunkel, Anibal Pinto, and Celso Furtado were close to ECLA and adapted the structuralist approach in the light of the crisis of ISI.[61] They criticized ECLA for not going farther and deeper in the analysis of the obstacles to the development of Latin American countries. The main advocates of the Marxist approach, who based their arguments on notions such as imperialism and overexploitation, were André Gunder Frank, Ruy Mauro Marini, Theotonio Dos Santos, and Alonso Aguilar.[62]

All the members of the dependency school rejected modernization theory in general and Rostow's stages of development in particular. The keywords were "national disintegration" for Sunkel, "dependent patterns of consumption" for Furtado, and "associated dependent development" or "development of underdevelopment" for Frank, whose approach was the most radical of the three.

On the other hand, there was a large measure of agreement about the fact that Latin American economies were brought to a state of "dependent capitalism" by their position in the international division of labor. Moreover, the failures of import-substitution strategies showed the limits of reformist efforts within the world system. The periphery had been unable to break the center-periphery exploitation process.

Thus, for the more radical dependency school, the solution was to dissociate themselves from the world market and follow new development strategies based on a self-sustaining development pattern. Samir Amin, who was one of those responsible for the term "de-linking," has a more subtle view and now says that he finds the term unfortunate because "de-linking does not mean autarky. . . . It is a strategic choice that submits external relations to the imperative of progressive internal development. It is the reverse of structural adjustment."[63]

An important weakness of the dependency approach, in all its various forms (except perhaps in Cardoso's analysis), was that it simply did not fit the facts, even of the early 1970s. When most dependency writers were advocating a stagnationist and pessimistic view of "development of underdevelopment," there were strong signs of economic growth and development in the emerging newly industrializing countries—and in Latin America and the Caribbean.[64] Dependency theory failed to provide a satisfactory explanation of the process of rapid accumulation in some countries. It became clear that capitalist development was decidedly possible, including in the so-called periphery. The dependency school rapidly lost ground around the mid-1970s in the light of the dynamism of the capitalist development of the newly industrializing countries. Thus, as Cardoso argued, history had prepared a trap for pessimists.[65]

Nevertheless, the impact of the dependency school on development thinking and practice should not be underestimated. The dependency dimension of the center-periphery relationship and the predominance of external causal factors in underdevelopment influenced the work of UNCTAD and the debate about the new international economic order (NIEO) after 1974. The NIEO was in many ways an attempt by the leaders of the South to change the rules of the game in order to overcome the structural obstacles limiting their development.

Box 4.2. Korea: From Poverty to Affluence in Four Decades

Korea is a country that achieved the rare distinction of transforming itself from rags to riches within one generation. Land reform in the late 1940s and early 1950s redistributed land to the poor peasants and landless workers. This led to what Irma Adelman later called a "redistribution before growth" strategy. Literacy campaigns raised literacy from 30 to 80 percent between 1953 and 1963. Universal primary education was reached by 1960. During the 1950s, the country relied massively on foreign aid, but economic growth remained sluggish.

Korea then started a policy of import substitution and it was accused of self-defeating protectionism. However, the actions of the leaders of the country remind us of what Friedrich List had to say about a timely switch to more liberal policies, and in the 1960s Korea shifted to export promotion without abandoning a selective import-substituting policy.

A number of aspects of Korean industrial strategy must be underlined. First, the government used public enterprises to establish or strengthen capacity in some sectors, especially capital goods and high technology. Second, the government encouraged the formation of giant conglomerates in order to achieve economies of scale, promote R and D, and pioneer cutting-edge technology. Third, there has been rela-tively little foreign private investment. Once the country had achieved industrial strength, the government began to liberalize imports and reduce some of the incentives and subsidies to the export sector, in line with the thinking of Hamilton, List, and Prebisch.

The economic and social achievements of Korea's development have been spec-tacular, thanks to an intelligent and independent policy as well as to timely changes in the emphasis of protectionism and liberalization. GDP rose at about 5 percent per annum in the 1950s to around 9 to 10 percent per annum in the next three decades, slowing to over 6 percent in the 1990s. The domestic savings rate rose from 13 per-cent in 1952 to 35 percent in the 1990s. Over the 40-year period between 1960 and 2000, Korean living standards rose from barely subsistence level to those approaching the industrial countries. From 1960 to 2000, infant mortality declined from 62 to 9, life expectancy rose from 54 to 73 years, and adult literacy rose from 71 to 98 percent.[66] Fertility has fallen from about 5 in 1950 to 1.6 in the year 2000. Moreover, the country continues to have a very even income distribution, although inequalities have risen recently.

And so the country went from aid to export promotion via import substitution: a three-stage missile that did not misfire.

Sources: Lloyd Reynolds, *Economic Growth in the Third World: 1850–1980* (New Haven: Yale University Press, 1985); World Bank, *World Development Indicators 2000* (Washington, D.C.: World Bank, 2000); UNDP, *Human Development Report 2001* (New York: Oxford University Press, 2001).

UNCTAD and the Emergence of a Unified South

The creation of UNCTAD was one of the main achievements of the UN Development Decade. It was the result of the emerging new international environment where North-South tensions were almost as serious as East-West tensions. The creation of UNCTAD stressed that the UN had a unique contri-bution to make toward the lessening of both. The world press had prophesied that the 1964 founding conference of UNCTAD would be an unqualified fail-ure. The fact that this did not happen was largely due to cooperation and coordination among developing countries. The establishment of the Group of 77 countries was the first event to herald the success of the conference.

A great deal of intellectual work went into the preparations for the found-ing conference. The papers were published in several impressive volumes, in-cluding submissions from many distinguished economists.

During the preparatory work for UNCTAD, the developing countries drafted a joint declaration emphasizing that the developing countries consider that the UNCTAD should represent an outstanding event in international cooperation conducive to the development of their economies and the integrated growth of the world as a whole. They believe that the full attainment of even the modest targets of the UN Development Decade will depend on the concrete decisions taken at this conference and on their effective implementation. The developing countries are already making, and are determined to continue to make, great efforts for the economic and social advancement through full mobilisation of domestic resources, agricultural development, industrialisation and diversification of their production and trade. However, this task can be accomplished only if those domestic efforts are supplemented and assisted by adequate international action.[67]

The conference provided a unique opportunity to make a comprehensive review of the problems of trade affecting the developing countries. The discussion and recommendations of the conference stressed the following:

- The expansion of world trade in the 1950s and early 1960s failed to benefit all countries. Indeed, the share of developing countries in world exports declined steadily from nearly one-third in 1950 to only slightly more than one-fifth in 1962.[68]
- The access of developing countries to capital goods and machinery from developed countries was limited by their low level of export earnings.
- The terms of trade of developing countries, which exported predominantly primary products, deteriorated during the period 1950–1962.
- The developing countries realized that the Development Decade objectives were hindered by the instability of international markets for primary goods and by the conditions restricting their access to the markets of developed countries.

After three weeks, the conference—held in Geneva from 23 May to 16 June 1964—recommended a series of general principles to govern international trade relations and trade policies conducive to development. But perhaps the most outstanding decision of the conference on the substantive issues was the recognition that the achievement of adequate growth targets by the developing countries was linked to a considerable extent to reaching corresponding trade and aid targets and that the developed countries had a key role to play in that process.

The conference recognized the urgent need to diversify and expand the export trade of developing countries in manufactures and semi-manufactures as a means to accelerate both economic growth and improvements in standards of living. It recommended individual and joint action by both developed and developing countries to enable the latter to increase their participation, commensurate with the needs of their development, in the growth of international trade in manufactured and semi-manufactured products. The conference adopted a number of recommendations designed to help promote industries with an export potential. Here there was a need for a preferential system. The granting of preferences to exports of manufacture products from developing countries to developed countries was extensively discussed. The case for preferences was a logical extension of the generally accepted argument for the protection of infant industries.

At the conference, member states recognized that international trade was an important instrument for economic development. The first paragraph of the final act of the conference states that "[I]n an age when scientific progress has put unprecedented abundance within man's reach, it is essential that the flows of world trade should help to eliminate the wide economic disparities among nations."[69]

However, as Sidney Dell argued about the outcome of the conference, "The extent of the change should not, of course, be exaggerated."

> Whatever the texts agreed to at UNCTAD may have contained, it certainly cannot be said that they embodied international agreement on the specific steps needed to promote development through trade. Indeed, even today, almost two generations later, the battle for better access of the exports of developing countries to the markets of industrial countries continues to rage. In some respects protectionism of industrial countries is even stronger today than it was in the 1960s.[70]

This was written in the 1980s. The same comments could be written in the first years of the twenty-first century.

UNCTAD never received the confidence and support from the industrial countries it needed to be truly effective in its ambitious aims. The policy recommendations adopted at UNCTAD were generally opposed to the laissez-faire philosophy of mainstream economic theories about international trade. In terms of power politics, developed market-economy countries did not want any compulsory measures aiming at increasing export earnings of developing countries or stabilizing primary commodity prices. The negative attitude of the rich countries was in no small measure due to the fact that Prebisch, as secretary-general of the conference, resisted the attempts of the developed countries to introduce a weighted voting system, as in the case of the Bretton Woods institutions. Very much in the same vein, Gamani Corea, who became secretary-general of UNCTAD in the 1970s, resisted UNCTAD becoming a specialized agency "because I felt that UNCTAD got its strength from the link with the General Assembly and the UN."[71]

We have been relatively brief about the origins and the early years of UNCTAD because the companion volume in this series, *The UN and Global Political Economy,* discusses these issues extensively.[72]

Concluding Observations

Some seventy low-income countries between 1960 and 1970 achieved a growth rate in line with the 5 percent annual target established for the first Development Decade, and some twenty countries achieved an annual growth rate of over 6 percent. In spite of this extraordinary success, the results of the Development Decade were generally regarded with disappointment. The basic reason was that this high rate of economic growth brought little visible improvement in the living standards of the majority of people in many developing countries.[73] In part this was because population growth was faster than anticipated. In part it was because employment and poverty reduction advanced less than anticipated.

In the Development Decade manifesto, *Proposal for Action,* development had meant "growth plus change." But there was not enough change in the quality of life of a large part of the population in developing countries. Nevertheless, as regards social trends it was observed that the gap between the advanced and the less-advanced countries was widening with respect to some indicators and narrowing with regard to others. Health was the most obvious example because it tended to improve more rapidly at the lower level of development than at higher levels. And in fact, the 1960s were marked by a dramatic improvement in the prevention of diseases, which added ten to twenty years to life expectancy in the developing countries.[74] The decade had also seen an almost universal reduction in infant mortality rates (the World Health Organization target of a 25–50 percent reduction in the decade was achieved), a general extension in life expectancy, and a rapid increase of enrollment rates in primary school. However, despite those achievements, the quality of life in many areas failed to improve during the 1960s and a growing number of people suffered from hunger, malnutrition, and lack of opportunities to earn income.

Many of the proposals of the Development Decade were unrealistic, particularly for those African countries that had just become independent. Francis Blanchard, who spent a lifetime in the International Labour Organization, fifteen years as director-general, takes a dim view of the very idea of development decades "which left too large a place to intellectual speculation."[75] Retrospectively, Hans Singer also admitted that at the beginning of the Development Decade, "We thought of Africa as more or less the same as Latin America. Africa was another Latin America to us. The poverty area was India

...and our mistake was not to foresee what happened to Africa after independence."[76]

The poor results of the Development Decade in reducing poverty and bridging the gap between poor and rich countries resulted in two major shifts in development thinking in the 1970s:

- Interest was renewed in the relationship between economic growth and income distribution. Dudley Seers, who had worked for the UN in Latin America and Africa, illustrated this shift toward a more comprehensive way to define development: "The questions to ask about a country's development are: What has been happening to poverty? What has been happening to inequality? What has been happening to unemployment? If all three of these have become less severe, then beyond doubt this has been a period of development of the country concerned. If one or two of these central problems have been growing worse, especially if all three have, it would be strange to call the result 'development' even if per capita income doubled."[77]
- Development thinking in the developing countries took a radical form with the dependency school and the idea of de-linking and a reformist form with the movement for a new international economic order.

Seen in this light, it becomes clearer why *Partners in Development* faced strong criticism in spite of its general excellence. Published in 1969, the report, also know as the Pearson Report in recognition of the role played by Lester B. Pearson as chair of the Commission on International Development, recognized that the widening gap between the rich and poor countries had become a central issue of the time. However, as a solution, it proposed that partnerships between developed and developing countries be strengthened. This was considered by the critics to be little more than an illusion. As its title, *Partners in Development,* indicated, the Pearson Report recommended actions that developed countries—the donor countries—would judge "acceptable" and "reasonable." The report also suggested a 6 percent rate of growth per year for the developing countries throughout the 1970s. But the report did not take into account the growing disappointment and disillusion in the South regarding the attitude of the North.

Among other significant insights in postwar development thinking during the decade of the 1960s, mention must be made of the idea of investments in human capital. The importance of the human factor was so overriding that success or failure of the Development Decade was seen as linked to the success or failure to carry out training activities and education programs. The basic idea was that no breakthrough would be possible unless countries rapidly increased their resources in skilled manpower.

Thus, the human dimension gained importance with the development of technical assistance in that field from the specialized agencies, EPTA, and the Special Fund. The UN contributed at that time—less in thinking than in practice—to the emergence of a more balanced view in which physical and human capital were both necessary conditions of economic development.

The annual rates of growth recorded in many developing countries during the 1960s were impressive, the productive capacity of developing countries increased significantly, their investment and saving levels recorded gains, and, what is perhaps more important, their ability to undertake wider and more complex activities rose steadily. But economic and social progress was not evenly shared among developing countries or different social groups. Indeed, in this regard, the performance of many countries was totally inadequate. Between 1960 and 1967, the developed market economies increased their total gross domestic product by 5.1 percent and their per capita gross domestic product by 3.8 percent per year; in centrally planned economies, these rates were respectively 6.7 and 5.4 percent.[78] Despite the fact that developed market economies were rapidly getting richer, the objective of the Development Decade—to increase international aid to 1 percent of their national product—was never reached.

The almost exclusive concentration of the first Development Decade on a global economic target (an increase of GNP) appeared to be warranted by considerations of two kinds: recognition of the fact that economic development was indispensable to the improvement of living conditions and, more generally, the achievement of social and human progress and the conviction that improvements in living conditions and social progress would result almost automatically from economic development.

The experience of the Development Decade showed that these two assumptions reflected only partial truths. The proposals for an international development strategy for the 1970s in the framework of the preparatory work for the Second United Nations Development Decade reflected a shift of emphasis compared to the First Development Decade.[79] The CDP argued that it was in the common interest of the nations of the world to intensify the struggle against poverty, hunger, and disease and to attain significantly higher levels of living for the poor during the Second Development Decade. The work of the CDP toward the end of the 1960s also marked the end of the assumption that economic progress was automatically followed by improved living conditions for the mass of the people. But this abandonment was only temporary; it came back as a pillar of mainstream structural adjustment in the 1980s.[80]

In its recommendations for the Second Development Decade, the CDP stressed that a fundamental objective should be to accelerate markedly the growth of GNP per capita and to make the fruits of development available to the poor in much greater measure than before. It emphasized that the ultimate purpose of development was to provide opportunities for a better life to all sections of the population. To achieve this objective, it was crucial to reduce the great inequalities in the distribution of income and wealth prevailing in developing countries, including consideration of the disparities between regions and groups. It called for new employment opportunities, greater supplies of food, and arrangements for better education and health facilities for the growing population, especially for the lower strata of society and the young.

5

The 1970s: Equity in Development

- **Employment and Basic Needs–Oriented Strategies for Development**
- **The New International Economic Order (NIEO)**
- **The Environment and Development**
- **Women, Gender, and Development**
- **Concluding Observations**

Over the 1960s, a gradual shift in development thinking took place from an almost exclusive preoccupation with growth rates to concern also with equity, poverty, and employment. This shift originated in a perception that despite the relatively favorable growth rates being achieved, there often appeared to be inadequate progress in overcoming hunger, malnutrition, and illiteracy. In particular, there was growing concern with the employment problem[1] and worsening income distribution.

When the First Development Decade drew to a close, there was an emerging convergence of views on the need for development policies to focus more specifically on employment generation and reduction of poverty and inequalities. This was consistent with the observations of Dudley Seers mentioned near the end of the previous chapter.[2]

Gunnar Myrdal, who was also preoccupied with an increasing incidence of poverty, outlined a world anti-poverty program that proposed major reforms in agriculture, education, population, and the role of the state.[3] Hans Singer drew attention to the fact that a dualistic labor structure had emerged in some countries, characterized by small numbers employed in the modern sector at relatively high wages and an increasing share of the labor force relegated to a marginal existence.[4] David Turnham marshaled impressive evidence to document the worsening employment situation in most developing countries.[5] Bagich Minhas outlined a poverty-focused approach to planning.[6]

The 1969 report of the ILO director-general was devoted to a detailed analysis of the employment and poverty problems in developing countries and the

ILO response to them in the form of the World Employment Programme.[7] His 1970 report discussed poverty and minimum living standards. As he stated:

> The reason for my concern is basically that the immense—and, in global economic terms, not altogether unsuccessful—efforts for development during the past two decades have not so far resulted in many perceptible improvements in the living standards of the majority of the world's population.[8]

The CDP issued statements in the same vein. ECOSOC came up with a resolution on the urgency of action against mass poverty and unemployment.[9] The key agencies of the UN system responded by developing policies and programs for a human-centered pattern of development. In addition to the 6 percent growth rate target and targets for flows of aid and resources, the Second Development Decade strategy (covering the 1970s) contained targets for employment, education, and health.[10] UNESCO launched a program to eradicate illiteracy and developed targets for moving to universal primary education;[11] the WHO developed a strategy of health for all and adopted the goal of eradicating smallpox;[12] and the FAO initiated the Campaign against Hunger.[13] The World Food Conference in 1974 convened by FAO strengthened the World Food Programme and led to the creation of the International Fund for Agricultural Development (IFAD).[14] The ILO established the World Employment Programme, which provided interagency advisory employment missions, a global research program, regional employment teams, and national projects.[15]

The 1970s were marked above all by a strong emphasis on equity in development:

- Equity among different socioeconomic groups
- Equity between the North and the South
- Equity between present and future generations
- Equity between men and women

These themes are discussed successively in this chapter. For each of these topics, an attempt is made to show the emergence of the issue, ideas inside and outside the UN on it, the UN's institutional and policy response, and the impact of UN work. The concluding section contains some general observations on how different interests affect the evolution of development ideas and practice.

Employment and Basic Needs–Oriented Strategies for Development

A major challenge facing the UN was how to propose strategies and policies that would directly and quickly reduce poverty and raise the living standards of the people in low-income countries. This search led to the development of new strategies that were described using the terms "employment-oriented," "basic human needs," and "redistribution from growth." While each of these approaches had its distinctive elements and differed somewhat in the emphasis placed on different development objectives and policy instruments, the strategies were and still are interrelated and have many common elements.

The new approaches resulted from collaboration among the UN agencies and between them and the academic community. The employment-oriented strategies emerged from a research network on the one hand and on the other from the reports of the comprehensive employment missions composed of academic researchers and officials from the ILO and other UN agencies and led by eminent development scholars. Between 1970 and 1976, the ILO organized comprehensive employment missions to Colombia, Sri Lanka, Kenya, Iran, the Philippines, the Dominican Republic, and Sudan and published many research reports.[16]

The redistribution with growth approach emerged from the ILO's employment mission to Kenya and was then generalized by a group that consisted of representatives from the World Bank and the Institute of Development Studies (IDS) of the University of Sussex.[17] Credit for the idea must go to Hans Singer, who conceived of the general notion in the course of the work for the Comprehensive Employment Mission to Kenya. He argued that rapid progress in poverty reduction could best be made by allocating an increasing share of the annual increment of a country's growth to investment in the credit, assets, and skills of the working poor. This would be redistribution from growth—a means to accelerate the growth of income of the poorest without reducing the income of the better-off.[18]

The contribution of the World Bank–IDS team was to generalize this strategy. So instead of always being redistribution from growth, the strategy became a variety of options combining redistribution with growth. The principal thesis was that rapid progress toward reduction of poverty and income inequalities could be made by transferring a high or increasing proportion of additions to output to enhance the credit, assets, and skills of the working poor. This could complement or substitute for measures of redistribution from current income. The resources from growth could be redistributed to the poor either from tax revenues or through other mechanisms.[19]

The basic-needs strategy was also developed in the 1970s by a number of organizations working independently of each other. The Bariloche Foundation in Argentina had developed a physical model showing that it was possible to meet the essential needs of the people at specified levels with the available resources.[20] The Dag Hammarskjöld Foundation had also brought out a report that consisted of elements of a basic-needs approach.[21] *What Now? Another Development* made the satisfaction of needs—beginning with the basic needs of the poor who constituted the world's majority—the focal point of the development process.

In the ILO, the basic-needs approach was developed as part of the preparatory work for the 1976 Tripartite World Conference on Employment, Income Distribution and Social Progress, and the International Division of Labour—often referred to as the World Employment Conference (WEC). It grew out of the ILO's earlier work on employment-oriented strategies.

The document prepared for the conference, however, went beyond purely employment concerns to outline a basic-needs approach to development.[22] The WEC endorsed this approach and adopted a wide-ranging program of action at national and international levels to achieve the objectives of remunerative and satisfying work and the meeting of essential human needs for all.[23]

These "new" development strategies encouraged a shift of emphasis in the goals of development from economic aggregates such as economic growth, savings and investment rates, and sectoral changes from agriculture to industry and services to a direct focus on the meeting of basic human needs, the generation of productive employment, and the reduction of poverty. The main problem of employment in poor countries was not seen as widespread unemployment, despite its visibility in large cities, but rather one of lack of remunerative work opportunities due to low productivity. Thus the focus of attention shifted toward the working poor and toward overworked women, who worked a double day consisting of paid employment and familial duties, in both urban and rural areas. This approach to development also highlighted that employment issues are intimately linked with overall economic and social policies and thus cannot be discussed in isolation from macroeconomic policies in such areas as government budget, trade regimes, and exchange rates. Nor can employment generation be divorced from policies on industry, agriculture, services, credit, education, training, health, wages, and labor institutions. In short, an employment strategy is tantamount to an integrated development strategy.[24]

The basic-needs approach also foresaw the need to view development policies within the broader framework of participatory processes and human rights in line with the values and criteria set out in Chapter 1:

> A basic-needs oriented policy implies the participation of the people in making the decisions [that] affect them. . . . The satisfaction of an absolute level of basic needs as so defined should be placed within a broader framework—namely the fulfilment of basic human rights.[25]

Basic-needs policies further strongly supported the need to organize poor working people and their participation in the political process. The WEC further stressed the importance of measures to improve the status of women:

> Since women constitute the group on the bottom of the ladder in many developing countries in respect of employment, poverty, education, training and status, the Conference recommends that special emphasis be placed in developing countries on promoting the status, education, development and employment of women and on integrating women into the economic and civil life of the country.[26]

The employment and basic-needs approaches did not imply a unique strategy for development. The specifics of development strategy focused on generating employment opportunities, and meeting basic needs would necessarily vary from one country to another depending on the social, economic, and political situation. Nevertheless, certain policies appeared common for a broad range of countries. It is these policies that distinguished these approaches from the earlier growth-centered strategies.

The central objective of these policies was to raise the incomes, assets, and productive potential of the vulnerable and poor groups, including the unemployed, the landless, rural workers, small farmers, nomadic groups, and workers in the informal sector.

In most developing countries, the greatest concentration of poverty was in rural areas. Thus, emphasis was put on measures to raise the incomes and productivity of small farmers, agricultural workers, and casual employees through agrarian reform, new settlements, rural works programs, stimulation of non-farm activities, and provision of government technical and social services.

In parallel, measures for the urban poor included credit and training for informal-sector workers and expansion of work opportunities through improvement in urban infrastructures (including low-cost housing) and in health and education services.

The third focus was on encouraging labor-intensive industry to meet both domestic and foreign demand. With the cumulative improvement in income distribution, the entire pattern of demand for goods and services would become more labor intensive.

A fourth feature common to growth-with-equity strategies was a restructuring of public social and economic services such as education, training, health, credit, and extension services to cater to the needs of low-income groups.

Finally, policy packages contained recommendations on international trade and resource flows designed to reinforce the thrust of a basic-needs strategy.

The new strategies foresaw an active role for the public sector not only in providing some vital social and economic services to all members of a society but also in devising programs and policies to enhance work opportunities and access to credit, land, and other assets for poverty groups. They favored reliance on markets, liberalization of trade and payments, and macroeconomic policies that promote stability and provide incentives to enterprise.

What was the impact of these employment and basic-needs strategies on actual development? The new strategies attracted growing international support in the 1970s and early 1980s. There were follow-up reports by the CDP and there were ECOSOC resolutions on mass poverty and unemployment. These strongly endorsed policies and programs for a direct attack on mass poverty and deprivation. And as we shall see later, the world conferences of the 1970s on the environment, population, women, and food gave strong support to similar policies and programs. Perhaps the strongest indicator of international support for the new approaches is in the Third Development Decade Strategy (TDDS) adopted in 1981. Unlike its two predecessors, the TDDS contained detailed social goals and wide-ranging policies and programs for promoting human development and ending destitution, as indicated in the following quotes:

> The new International Development Strategy aims at ... reducing significantly the current disparities between the developed and the developing countries, as well as the early eradication of poverty and [deprivation]. ... The ultimate aim of development is the constant improvement of the well-being of the entire population on the basis of its full participation in the process of development and a fair distribution of the benefits therefrom. ... In this perspective, economic growth, productive employment and social equity are fundamental and indivisible elements of development.[27]

The Third Development Decade Strategy then went on to set specific goals not only for the usual economic aggregates—GDP, agriculture, industry, savings, investment, exports, imports, and external resource flows—but also for employment, hunger, malnutrition, infant mortality, life expectancy, literacy, primary health care, safe water, and access to sanitation.

The employment and basic-needs strategies also had an impact on the thinking and activities of multilateral and bilateral development agencies. Some parts of the World Bank also took them seriously and did further analytical work on the conceptual and operational aspects of a basic-needs approach to development.[28]

But what happened in the real world? Unfortunately, the ringing endorsement of the new strategy in national and international declarations and programs of action found only feeble echoes at the ground level. Some countries appeared to follow at least parts of the policy packages recommended by the new development approaches.

Kenya undertook in 1974 to change its punitive policy toward the informal sector in favor of measures to promote its development. Unfortunately, the new policy was applied only sporadically. To this day, the police swoop down periodically on the makeshift structures of petty traders and other entrepreneurs, destroying their premises and confiscating their goods.

Colombia for the most part disregarded the recommendations of the ILO employment mission, but it did seek to create employment opportunities through massive investment in urban infrastructure, including housing, which was the exact opposite of the policies proposed by the ILO mission!

The Philippines attempted to shift its industrial policies from import substitution to exports of labor-intensive manufactures. But these were partial ad hoc measures. They did not amount to a comprehensive strategy for promoting employment and meeting basic human needs.

Other countries implemented major components of new strategies on their own initiative without the advice of the ILO. For example, Cuba and China undertook far-reaching agrarian reform and universal provision of social services. The newly industrializing countries such as South Korea and Taiwan carried out agrarian reform, promoted labor-intensive patterns of industrialization, and provided free and compulsory primary education.

Similarly, the Southeast Asian countries of Malaysia, Thailand, and Indonesia emulated the policies of the Asian tigers in their emphasis on labor-intensive industry and universal education. Countries such as Sri Lanka and Costa Rica implemented universal and free health care and education. In most of these countries, such policies were adopted before the new strategies came into vogue.

Box 5.1. Tanzania: Another Road to Development?

The Tanzanian development strategy aroused intense interest in the late 1960s and the 1970s, especially because of its commitment to *ujamaa*—a self-reliant, participatory, and egalitarian pattern of development. The ruling party and the state in Tanzania, under the leadership of Mwalimu Julius Nyerere, sought to articulate and implement a socialist strategy in one of the least-developed African countries.

In the early years after independence, the country chose to build upon the development policies of the 1950s. There was an emphasis on boosting agricultural production by peasant farmers, both for domestic sales and exports, with state support provided for extension services, credit, marketing, seeds, and fertilizers. Some of these services were directed through the cooperative movement, which was quite widespread in the Arusha and Western Lake provinces. At the same time, the coming of independence spurred manufacturing activity with investments by some multinationals and the Asian community that were already established in East Africa. The government also stepped up its spending on health and education.[29] The economy grew by around 5 percent per annum.

The leadership in the ruling party and the government, especially President Nyerere himself, was, however, dissatisfied with what was perceived as a relatively slow pace of development, the emerging economic inequalities, and dependence upon outside capital. In order to address these problems, the ruling party came out with a new strategy embodied in the Arusha Declaration of 1967. It committed the government to a socialist development strategy that promoted social and economic equality, mass participation, self-reliance, and satisfaction of the basic needs of the people.[30] Over the next three years, sweeping institutional changes touched every aspect of social and economic policy. The Arusha Declaration was followed in quick succession by the nationalization of banks, insurance companies, major manufacturing enterprises, plantations, large commercial concerns, and urban property.

The policies pursued in the wake of the Arusha Declaration led to a sharp reduction in income inequalities because of controls on private economic activity and compression of salary differentials in the public and private sectors. The social indicators improved steadily till 1980 but have either stagnated or declined in the subsequent period. Strong emphasis was put on adult literacy, primary education, and basic health services in the 1970s. A literacy campaign in the 1970s helped raise adult literacy from 10 percent in 1960 to 70 percent in 1980 but has remained around that level since.

In the rural sector, there were equally dramatic changes. The peasants were encouraged to move from their homesteads to *ujamaa* villages. The intention was to facilitate higher productivity through the pooling of efforts and the provision of social and economic services such as credit, marketing, extension, education, health, water supply, and transportation. It was hoped that gradually peasants would shift from individual to cooperative production and undertake joint infrastructural projects. The original intention was to persuade peasants to make the move voluntarily. As Nyerere noted in 1967, socialist communities cannot be established by compulsion. Villages are democratic polities in which democracy must operate from the start if the system is to succeed.[31]

Unfortunately, these principles were not followed in practice. Impatient at the slow pace of villagization, the party and the government ordered accelerated moves to villages. Using a mixture of incentives and compulsion, over 1 million people were moved into villages in 1971 and 10 to 11 million people between 1974 and 1976. Although village councils were established to govern the rural communities, the real power rested with the government and party bureaucrats who controlled the resources. The marketing, extension, and credit functions were transferred to state corporations. Despite these institutional upheavals, the Tanzanian economy continued to expand fairly rapidly until the early 1970s, but a good deal of this growth represented expansion of government services, and the productivity of investment began to decline rapidly.

By the early 1970s, peasant production and state enterprises covering virtually all sectors of the economy dominated the Tanzanian economy, which was increasingly controlled by regulations and directives. All imports and exports and all marketing of cash crops were handled by state enterprises. Imports were subject to controls, and foreign exchange was allocated by priority sectors. A large number of prices were fixed by government agencies. The exchange rate became increasingly overvalued. The occurrence of droughts in the mid-1970s in combination with the oil-price shock and the war with the Idi Amin regime in Uganda led to a serious economic crisis characterized by stagnant agriculture and falling exports. There were widespread shortages of all kinds of goods, even of goods of mass consumption. The parallel economy transactions were estimated at 30 percent of GDP and the foreign exchange price in the parallel market had reached a rate of over 9 times the official value.[32] The government became increasingly dependent on foreign grants and loans to finance imports and capital formation.

To conclude, the Tanzanian economy expanded fairly rapidly in the 1960s and early 1970s—in the region of 4–5 percent per annum. It slowed down sharply over the subsequent decade, resulting in declining per capita incomes. Despite considerable external support, the development strategy failed in the end to deliver rising living standards and strong participation by peasants and workers. Since the mid-1980s, the country has been obliged to pursue a program of liberalization and privatization very much along the lines of that of other countries in Africa and Latin America.

There would appear to be two basic reasons for the failure of most developing countries to adopt policies for employment promotion and poverty reduction in the 1970s. Most of the proposed measures involved a restructuring of public spending and taxation, reallocation of resources and assets, and liberalization of prices, credit, and trade that adversely affected the interests of powerful and privileged groups. Only in exceptional circumstances such as deep crisis or intense internal and external pressure do such policies stand much chance of being implemented.

The second reason was the dramatic deterioration in the external environment of developing countries in the late 1970s and the early 1980s. Some industrial countries, private creditors, and the Bretton Woods institutions brought growing pressure to bear on developing countries to adopt neoliberal policies. The Mexican debt crisis in 1982 was the turning point. As one country after another experienced balance-of-payments difficulties, these powerful groups imposed a new set of policies on them as a condition for financial support. This was the start of the new policies of stabilization and adjustment discussed in the next chapter.

Notwithstanding these setbacks, some of the core ideas associated with employment and basic-needs strategies have endured and others surfaced again in the 1990s, though often under a different garb. Among these ideas, the notion of the informal sector was especially important.

The informal sector was first popularized by the report of the ILO Employment Mission to Kenya in 1972.[33] The report showed the parallel existence of and extensive linkages between the formal and informal sectors. Official policy tended to favor the formal economy, while workers and entrepreneurs in the informal economy had to struggle against a wide variety of discriminatory and even punitive policies. Despite these handicaps, the informal economy continued to flourish and constituted an important source of employment, incomes, and livelihood for the working poor and new entrants to the labor force. The Kenya report made wide-ranging proposals to end discriminatory treatment of the sector and to promote its growth through provision of premises, credit, training, and advice on how to improve the quality of the goods produced and the marketing of those goods.

The informal economy has received a lot of attention ever since. At the same time, important initiatives such as microcredit programs have been taken at the national and international level to stimulate its expansion.[34]

The notion of a development strategy focused on the eradication of poverty, the generation of employment, and the satisfaction of basic needs came into vogue once again in the late 1990s. The failure of the policies of stabilization and adjustment to promote growth and make a dent in poverty reduction stirred renewed interest in these strategies. The series of world conferences in the 1990s also had an important influence. By the late 1990s, the Bretton Woods institutions were declaring that policies to reduce poverty and promote human development were their highest priority. The World Bank declared poverty reduction to be its central objective.[35] In 1999, the IMF established the Poverty Reduction and Growth Facility. A necessary condition for obtaining credits under this facility is the formulation of anti-poverty strategies by developing countries, active participation of the poverty groups, and "full local ownership."

It would, however, be a mistake to consider the new policies being promoted by the Bretton Woods institutions as identical to the basic-needs and employment-oriented strategies of the 1970s. The latter emphasized removing structural barriers to growth, redistributive measures such as land reform and access to training, a strong role for the public sector not only in social services but also in planning for growth, and poverty reduction. The poverty-reduction strategies promoted by the Bretton Woods institutions continue to emphasize liberalization of the economy and are generally silent on redistributive measures.

However, they recognize a greater role for the public sector in provision of social services and the direction of these services toward the poor.

The New International Economic Order (NIEO)

Employment and basic-needs strategies sought to promote equity at the national level. Although they spelled out the implications for foreign trade, investment, and assistance, their focus was on national action. In parallel, however, another significant event dominated discussions on international development in the 1970s, also aiming at equity between rich and poor countries. This was the proposal to establish a new international economic order (NIEO) made by the developing countries.[36]

The historic importance of this proposal derives from the fact that it was an authentic Third World initiative, launched at a time of probably the peak bargaining power of the poor countries in the entire postwar period. This power came from the imposition of the oil embargo by the Arab countries during the Arab-Israeli War of 1973. The oil scarcity gave the opportunity to the Organization of Petroleum Exporting Countries (OPEC) to raise oil prices fourfold in one decisive move in 1973. Although OPEC had been formed many years before, until 1973, oil was treated as any other commodity. While there was a rapid increase in oil consumption in the previous years, its real price fluctuated around a declining price trend.

The oil embargo and the OPEC action in raising oil prices represented the first assertion of economic power by a group of developing countries. Given the unique importance of oil in international trade and in the functioning of all economies, the oil shock resulted in a massive transfer of resources to OPEC countries, equivalent to some 2 percent of global GNP. For the first time, the industrial countries were deeply affected by an action taken collectively by a group of poor countries. The oil-exporting countries, in cooperation with other developing countries, quickly followed this initial victory with a broader set of demands for a restructuring of the world economy. These demands were not completely new. They had been made separately on various occasions in UN forums but without any result. It was in fact the cumulative frustration of the leaders of developing countries over the total neglect by the industrialized market countries of their demands for reform, which they had made on numerous occasions in international fora, that led them to push for an NIEO at what appeared to be an opportune time.

Unlike the other initiatives in the UN system, the NIEO was fundamentally concerned with a radical restructuring of international economic, financial, and political relations.[37] The NIEO would dominate North-South discussions in the 1970s in three different fora—the sixth and seventh special sessions of the General Assembly in New York in 1974 and 1975, the fourth session of UNCTAD in Nairobi in 1976, and the Conference on International Economic Cooperation (CIEC) in Paris in 1976–1977.

The key demands of the 1974 Programme of Action on the Establishment of an NIEO may be summarized as follows:[38]

- Increasing sovereignty over economies and natural resources
- Increasing control over the level and nature of foreign investment
- Maintaining or increasing the purchasing power of raw material and commodity exports
- Increasing access to markets of developed countries
- Reducing the cost of technology transfer
- Increasing the flow of development assistance
- Reducing the debt burden of certain developing countries
- Increasing the decision-making power of the developing countries in the UN and the Bretton Woods institutions

These eight demands implied fundamental changes. The specific proposals made to advance them consisted of the stabilization of the prices of raw materials at remunerative levels through buffer stocks and the formation of associations of commodity producers, the removal of tariff and nontariff barriers on exports from developing countries, and the reform of the international monetary system to control inflation, promote exchange-rate stability, and bring about an improved compensatory-finance facility and link between development assistance and special drawing rights. There were also proposals to establish a code of conduct for transnational enterprises and transfer of technology, set targets for the volume and terms of development assistance, increase cooperation among developing countries, and strengthen the role of the United Nations in implementing the NIEO.

The NIEO proposals were an ambitious attempt to change international power relations and bring about a redistribution of incomes and assets from industrial to developing countries. They were strongly opposed by the developed countries at the sixth special session of the General Assembly in 1974.[39] On subsequent occasions, a few of the developed countries, notably the Netherlands, Sweden, and Norway, showed flexibility on some issues such as improved access to imports from developing countries, an increase in development assistance, and a common fund for commodities. The hard-liners were led by West Germany and included the U.S., the UK, Austria, Belgium, Italy, and Japan. On the side of the developing countries, the leadership positions were taken by Algeria, Jamaica, Mexico, and Venezuela. The Middle East and the least-developed countries were less outspoken.

Despite protracted negotiations, the results for developing countries were meager. A few industrial countries introduced some improvements in the GATT Generalized System of Preferences. Agreements were negotiated for a few commodities. The Organisation for Economic Co-operation and Development (OECD) countries adopted a voluntary code of conduct on transnational enterprises. There was some increase in OPEC voting shares in the IMF and the World Bank, but this was offset by increases in the share of majorities needed for passing resolutions.

But on most of the important proposals made by the developing countries, almost nothing was done. These proposals included the reduction or cancellation of debt for the poorest countries, control on the restrictive practices of transnationals, assumption of sovereignty over their natural resources by developing countries, increase in development assistance to 0.7 percent, and the Integrated Commodity Programme.

Indeed, the very success of OPEC's action planted the seeds of the weakening of developing countries and reassertion of the power of industrial countries. It led to a huge transfer of incomes from the rich and most-developing countries to oil exporters. While some resources were mobilized for the most seriously affected countries, the vast OPEC surpluses were recycled to developing countries through the Western banking system. This laid the foundations for the severe debt crisis of the 1980s.[40]

In retrospect, it is the height of irony that the most radical appeal for national sovereignty and control over economic activities in the postwar period should have been followed by the greatest surrender of control over national policies in the 1980s. The turnaround in the development policies of most countries and in the international agenda for discussions represented a change beyond recognition. No longer did the developing countries insist on sovereignty over natural resources or nationalization of foreign enterprises. On the contrary, they bent over backward to court foreign enterprises and compete with one another to offer them more and more incentives.

However, in the end, the question must be asked how serious the developing countries were in pushing for the NIEO. Gamani Corea, the longtime secretary-general of UNCTAD, maintains that "much of the so-called agenda of the G-77 was articulated by the UN secretariat rather than by the G-77 itself."[41] And Gert Rosenthal, the executive secretary of ECLAC during the 1990s before becoming ambassador of his country, Guatemala, to the UN asserts that "a lot of countries do not take issue with the more militant G-77 positions—which they feel do not reflect their own—simply because they do not want to alienate the leadership."[42]

Box 5.2. The Brandt Report

In 1977, Robert McNamara, president of the World Bank, called upon Willy Brandt to assume the chairmanship of the Independent Commission for International Development Issues. Its mandate was "to study the grave global issues arising from the economic and social disparities of the world community" and "to suggest ways of promoting adequate solutions to the problems involved in development and in attacking absolute poverty."[43] Four principal elements were envisaged in the commission's program: first, a large-scale transfer of resources to developing countries; second, an international energy strategy; third, a global food program; and fourth, the start of major reforms in the international economic and financial system. The report also made a clear connection between armaments and poverty in developing countries. It emphasized how a worldwide disarmament process could make available considerable resources to develop those countries.

One of the recommendations of the Brandt Report was that the rich countries should increase their development assistance to 0.7 percent of their GNP by 1985 and to 1 percent in 2000. Of course, we know that these targets have not been met. The average level in the OECD countries was only 0.35 percent in 1977 and had fallen to 0.22 per cent in 2000.[44]

The Brandt Commission also stressed the need for more outward-oriented development policies once the early phase of industrialization was reached. It combined cautious support for export-promoting industrialization in the South with a series of recommendations to industrial countries to reduce protectionism and open their markets. This recommendation remained part of an unfilled international agenda until the 1990s and the establishment of the World Trade Organization (WTO).

The Brandt Report was an important contribution to a new, mature kind of cooperation based on global interdependence, policy dialogue, and reciprocity between North and South. However, the visionary proposals and warnings of the commission came at a most unfortunate moment. The report proposed a global Keynesian pact based on an increased level of development assistance from the developed countries at the same time that the neoliberal counterrevolution was taking ground in the North. The Brandt Report belonged to a time—the one of the hopes of developing countries for an NIEO—that had passed. Thus, its recommendation for a global stimulus through a twenty-year Marshall Plan was never taken seriously by the developed countries.

The North-South Summit in Cancún in 1981 that followed the publication of the report led to disappointment about the process initiated by the Brandt Commission.[45] The failure to instill new life into the North-South dialogue signaled the definitive rejection of the NIEO agenda by the major developed countries. Instead, the debt crisis and the conditionality associated with structural adjustment programs obliged developing countries themselves to bear most of the burden of adjustment with too little international support.

The Environment and Development

While basic needs and the NIEO focused on equity for the present genera-tion, the environmental dimension in development introduced issues of intergenerational equity. Environmental concerns first arose in the industrial countries, led by the U.S. They were awakened by the increasing pollution caused by industrialization and modern farming. Scientists and conservation-ists had documented the pollution of waterways, the disappearance of flora and fauna, and the emission of toxic substances and gases.[46] A related concern was the apparent shrinking of the stock of nonrenewable natural resources such as coal and minerals but also of renewable resources such as forests and wildlife.[47]

The UN played its part in bringing these issues to the attention of the world. The Secretary-General's report to the General Assembly in 1969 was entitled *Problems of the Human Environment*. Its opening sentence set the tone for the report: "For the first time in the history of mankind, there is arising a crisis of world-wide proportions involving developed and developing countries—the crisis of the human environment."[48]

The report identified most of the key issues that were subsequently to be-come part of the literature and debates on the environment. The range of environmental problems was identified—land erosion; deterioration and salin-ization of water resources; deforestation; extinction of many forms of animal and plant life; unplanned extension of urban settlements; the pollution of air, water, and land; toxic substances; noise; and congestion. The report even mentioned the increase in atmospheric carbon dioxide due to the use of fossil fuels and warned of its consequences for world weather and climate. It stated: "It is becoming apparent that if the current trends continue, the future of life on earth could be endangered."[49]

The Secretary-General's report prepared the ground for the World Con-ference on the Human Environment held in Stockholm in 1972, which resulted from a 1968 initiative by Sweden.[50] This was the first of the megaconferences that have become such a feature of conducting business at the UN. Such con-ferences were used in subsequent years to create awareness of new or emerg-ing issues, promote the study and analysis of these issues, encourage discussion and debate among all segments of the world society, and adopt declarations and action plans that specified the responsibility of all major stakeholders.

The Stockholm conference's preparatory phase was marked by "massive criticism"[51] from several industrialized countries and strong skepticism among developing countries about its relevance and utility. More than a few leaders felt that the conference could serve to derail the industrialization and modernization of their economies under the pretext of the imperative of environmental protection. In 1971, the secretary-general of the Stockholm conference, Maurice Strong, put together a panel of experts on development and the environment to explore these issues.[52]

The seminal Founex Report prepared by this panel of experts marked an important step in integrating environmental concerns with development objectives and policies.[53] It argued that the key concerns of developing countries are "the environmental problems of poverty"—unsafe drinking water, inadequate housing and shelter, illness, and natural disasters. Development was regarded as a cure for most of the environmental problems rather than their cause. The report suggested that development strategies should include targets for progressive reduction of malnutrition, disease, illiteracy, squalor, unemployment, and inequalities. There should also be targets for consumption of basic-needs products, water supply, sanitation, soil use, and land management.

The report also stressed the need for a new development strategy based on the elimination of mass poverty and the creation of a decent human environment. Some environmental problems would arise, it argued, as a consequence of industrialization. Efforts should be made to minimize these problems through planning and project appraisal. But the report warned the industrial countries not to invoke environmental concerns to reduce access to their markets. "Sweated environment" should not become an excuse for neoprotectionist trade policies.

In 1972, the World Conference on the Human Environment adopted a declaration and program of action covering a wide range of these environmental issues.[54] It stressed the need to integrate environmental objectives and policies in development plans and recommended that national institutions be created to manage the environment. The conference gave birth to the United Nations Environment Programme (UNEP) and the establishment of a voluntary fund to finance programs of environmental protection.[55] The proposal of Maurice Strong, as executive director of UNEP, to launch an inquiry into the means of satisfying basic human needs without transgressing the outer limits of the biosphere played a great role in the decision to launch the 1975 Dag Hammarskjöld Project on Another Development.[56]

The environment became a theme of growing and enduring importance in the period following the Stockholm conference. The United Nations Conference on Human Settlements (Habitat I) was held in Vancouver in 1976. Its outcome further reinforced the linkage between the environment and development:

> The improvement of the quality of life of human beings is the first and most
> important objective of every human settlement policy. These policies must fa-
> cilitate the rapid and continuous improvement in the quality of life of all people,

beginning with the satisfaction of the basic needs of food, shelter, clean water, employment, health, education, training, [and] social security . . . in a frame of freedom, dignity and social justice.[57]

The topic of the environment generated a steady stream of practical initiatives and publications over the next two decades, culminating in the 1992 Rio Conference on Environment and Development (also known as the Earth Summit) and the 2002 World Summit on Sustainable Development in Johannesburg. A companion volume published in the UNIHP series analyzes in more detail the role of the United Nations in developing and consolidating universal values and concepts of international governance in order to promote sustainable development.[58]

Major landmarks include the UN Convention on the Law of the Sea (1972), the Convention on the Prevention of Marine Pollution by Dumping of Waste and Other Matter (1972), the Basel Convention on the Control of Transboundary Movements of Hazardous Waste and Their Disposal (1989), and the Vienna Convention on the Protection of the Ozone Layer (1985). The Rio conference led to further conventions on climate change, biological diversity, and desertification. Rio also gave rise to a new funding mechanism for environmental programs—the Global Environment Facility (GEF)—which provides finance and technical assistance for projects designed to preserve biodiversity, protect forests, and improve soils.

Agenda 21, the program of action adopted at the Rio conference, was a hugely ambitious enterprise.[59] Running into 500 pages, it covered social and economic development, natural resources, fragile ecosystems, by-products of industrial production, the major stakeholders, and the means of implementation. It differed from the outcome of the Stockholm conference in the emphasis placed on citizen participation, community initiatives, and specific vulnerable groups. It also captured the spirit of the 1990s in the emphasis placed on open governance, participatory democracy, transparency, and accountability.

The UN issued various important reports that documented the degradation of environmental resources, assessed the policies under way, and made proposals for new initiatives and measures to arrest environmental deterioration. These included the UNEP report *Environmental Perspectives to the Year 2000 and Beyond;*[60] the International Union for the Conservation of Nature (IUCN) and UNEP's publication of *World Conservation Strategy;*[61] and the UNDP's *Human Development Report 1998* on consumption and human development.[62] These and other publications have contributed many new concepts, insights, and policy frameworks that have served to deepen our understanding of the extensive linkages between development and the environment. They have also shown how environmental objectives can be incorporated in development strategies and plans.

One of the most important reports was the report of the Brundtland World Commission on Environment and Development.[63] Although this report was prepared by an independent commission, it was submitted to the UN Secretary-General and the General Assembly. Maurice Strong, the secretary-general of the Stockholm conference, was a member of the commission.

The commission sought to reexamine the environment and development problems facing the world through a new analytical framework, considering them as one common challenge to be solved by collective multilateral action. It emphasized the need to reach a new era of economic growth that would be socially and environmentally sustainable. The holistic perspective adopted by the commission regarding these common concerns led logically to the proposal to create a "global agenda for change."

Among its many useful contributions were the introduction and definition of the notion of sustainable development. Sustainable development was defined as meeting the needs of the present without compromising the ability of future generations to meet their own needs. It added that the concept of sustainable development does imply limits—not absolute limits but limitations imposed by the present state of technology and social organization on environmental resources and by the ability of the biosphere to absorb the effects of human activities.

The concept of sustainability was not new.[64] But the Brundtland Commission transformed it from a purely ecological to a more socioeconomic approach in which development was to be distinguished from growth and the quality aspects of development became as important as the quantitative dimensions. The definition of sustainability developed by the Brundtland Commission greatly contributed toward public understanding of the concept and of the measures that countries need to adopt to put it into practice.

After this, and greatly encouraged by the Earth Summit in Rio in 1992, sustainable development has became an integral part of the policy discourse of many international and national organizations.[65] Although implementation lagged, a large international consensus developed about the need to design integrated development policies that include the economic, social, and environmental dimensions and to adapt the decision-making process to that new analytical framework.

Women, Gender, and Development

There are few areas where development thinking and practice have changed so radically over the past fifty years as in the rights and roles of women in development.[66] In the early postwar years, women were largely invisible in the literature on economic development. There was little analysis of how women are affected by or how they contribute to economic and social development. For all practical purposes, gender was not an issue in development policy, at least in the way most economists treated the matter. Chapter 2 showed how the classicists viewed the social and economic position of women, with John Stuart Mill an honorable exception. The neoclassical writings were essentially blind to gender.[67] It was only with the appearance of the pathbreaking book by Esther Boserup in 1970 that the role of women in development received serious treatment.[68]

Although most of the UN writings on economic development in the early postwar years were silent on the role of women, the UN played a pioneering role in highlighting the discrimination suffered by women in political and social domains. From the outset, the UN had enshrined the ideal of equality between men and women in its founding documents.[69] In the subsequent decades, the UN took up a wide range of political, social, and economic issues that are fundamental to women's equality and well-being. It deployed a variety of means to advance justice and equality for women. These have included international declarations, norms, and conventions; analytical and empirical work; conferences and meetings; and advisory work and operational activities. The collection and publication of data on the role of women in political, economic, and social affairs was especially important. These data are now available in the Women's Indicators and Statistical Database (WISTAT). As a consequence of this work, there is a vastly greater understanding of the gender dimensions of development, which is increasingly reflected in economic and social policies and programs. Providing such data on a global scale has been one of the most important contributions of the UN to changing global perceptions about women; this data often provides the information which has served as a source around which mobilization for women has been organized.

Initially, the emphasis was on ensuring legal equality for women. Article I of the Charter of the United Nations committed the organization to "promoting and encouraging respect for human rights and for fundamental freedoms for all without distinction as to race, sex, language or religion." The Commission on the Status of Women was created in 1946 to "prepare recommendations and reports to the Economic and Social Council on promoting women's rights in political, economic, civil, social and educational fields" and to make recommendations "on urgent problems requiring immediate attention in the field of women's rights."[70]

In subsequent years, the UN system sought to promote equality for women in specific areas through international norms and conventions. The adoption of such agreements was preceded by the preparation by the UN Secretariat or the specialized agencies of reports demonstrating the existence of discrimination against women in specific areas. Some of the milestones are shown in Box 5.3.[71]

Box 5.3. UN Milestones in Advancing Rights and Roles of Women

December 1946: A General Assembly resolution recommends that all member states grant women political rights equal to those granted to men.

- December 1949: The General Assembly adopts the Convention for the Suppression of the Traffic in Persons and of the Exploitation of the Prostitution of Others.
- June 1951: The ILO adopts the Convention on Equal Remuneration, incorporating the principle of equal pay for men and women for work of equal value.
- December 1952: The General Assembly adopts the Convention on the Political Rights of Women, under which member states commit themselves to allowing women to vote, stand for election, and hold public office on equal terms with men and without discrimination.
- January 1958: The ILO adopts the Discrimination (Employment and Occupation) Convention, committing member states to adopt national policies to eliminate discrimination in employment on the basis of race, color, sex, religion, political opinion, national extraction, or social origin.
- November 1962: The General Assembly adopts the Convention on Consent to Marriage, Minimum Age for Marriage and Registration of Marriage, decreeing that no marriages may take place without the consent of both parties.
- December 1966: The General Assembly adopts the International Covenant on Civil and Political Rights and the International Covenant on Economic, Social and Cultural Rights. Both conventions contain provisions specifying that all the rights therein apply equally to men and women.
- November 1967: The General Assembly approves the Declaration on the Elimination of Discrimination against Women.
- December 1974: The General Assembly adopts the Declaration on the Protection of Women and Children in Emergency and Armed Conflict, affirming that all forms of repression and cruel and inhuman treatment of women and children are criminal acts and that governments should do everything to spare women and children from the ravages of war.
- December 1976: UNIFEM, the UN Development Fund for Women, is created to provide support for projects and initiatives which promote the political, economic, and social empowerment of women throughout the developing world.
- December 1979: The General Assembly adopts the Convention on the Elimination of All Forms of Discrimination against Women.
- December 1993: The General Assembly adopts the Declaration on the Elimination of Violence against Women.
- June 1996: The ILO adopts the Convention on Home Work, which provides for minimum standards on pay and working conditions for home-based work.

Although the declarations and conventions began to have impact on the reality of women's daily lives slowly and unevenly and some countries expressed reservations about specific provisions or failed to ratify the conventions or implement their provisions, these steps provided women and advocates of women's rights with powerful ammunition. Over the years, these steps have exercised important influence on national policy and practice.

The 1979 Convention on the Elimination of All Forms of Discrimination against Women (CEDAW),[72] described as an international bill of rights for women, consolidated provisions from other instruments and declarations. It enjoined member states to adopt a legal regime providing for equality between men and women in political, social, economic, and cultural matters. It identified specific areas for action such as those relating to nationality, political rights to vote and hold office, education and training, health, employment, and social security and social security services. The convention required the state parties to ensure equal rights in the legal areas of marriage, divorce, custody of children, and property.

The UN system devoted increasing attention to the role of women in development from the early 1970s. It is interesting that it was in the ECA, the Economic Commission for Africa, that issues related to women in development began first to be a focus of the UN's work. This involved a number of pioneering ideas that were often well ahead of the thinking of other bodies. The ECA's first regional workshop focused on women in urban development. The ECA's 1967 publication on the *Status and Role of Women in East Africa*[73] documented how women were carrying the major share of the economic burden in society three years before Esther Boserup's pioneering study emerged.[74]

In the UN itself, UNIFEM,[75] the UN International Research and Training Institute for the Advancement of Women (INSTRAW),[76] and the UN Research Institute for Social Development (UNRISD) have contributed to research on women in development.[77] The ILO, through its labor standards, especially the conventions on equal pay and discrimination in work,[78] was one of the early champions of equality for men and women in employment, remuneration, and conditions of work. As part of its research work under the World Employment Programme, the ILO published numerous monographs and papers demonstrating the important role played by women workers in production, gender discrimination in work, and the undervaluation of women's contribution to the labor force and production.

With the UN Population Fund (UNFPA) in the 1980s and 1990s, the WHO developed programs directed toward defining and strengthening reproductive health services, many of which had a special focus on reducing maternal mortality rates. About the same time, UNICEF pioneered programs directed to "the girl child," a response to the growing realization that the roots of discrimination against women would be ended only with focused attention on ending gender discrimination at each stage of a child's growth and upbringing—from care and protection in the womb and in early childhood to adequate nutrition and support for girls at every stage of growth to access to education to encouragement and respect as they grow toward adulthood. All of these programs also underlined the need for social support to mothers in society in addition to ending discrimination against them as women.

Amid the numerous theoretical and empirical contributions made in publications of the UN system, three areas are touched upon here:

- Disparities in political, social, and economic domains
- Undervaluation of women's contributions
- Approaches to women's integration in development on a basis of equality

As early as 1947, the UN Secretariat organized a survey among the member states to determine the extent to which law and custom were blocking women's political, civil, social, and economic rights and educational opportunities.[79] Of the seventy-four states that responded, the survey revealed that twenty-five had not granted full political rights to their female citizens, including the right to vote or hold public office. The FAO has worked on women's access to land, credit, and extension services, while UNESCO has highlighted discrimination against women in education and culture. The WHO has contributed to the eradication of infectious diseases and improvement of nutrition and health services for women and children. Through its publications, it has also drawn attention to the special health needs of women in precarious situations.

Many UN reports prepared in the 1990s revealed the enormous disparities still persisting between men and women with regard to access to credit, ownership of property, and provision of social security. At the same time, gaps had narrowed in most fields over the past few decades. For instance, in developing countries, women's literacy increased from 54 percent of the male rate in 1970 to 74 percent in 1990, and combined female primary and secondary school enrollment increased from 67 percent of the male rate to 86 percent. Between 1970 and 1990, women's life expectancy in developing countries went up by 9 years—20 percent more than men's.[80] The total fertility rate has fallen by one-third over this period. Likewise, the share of women in parliaments and in cabinets has tended to rise in most countries. The proportion of professional, technical, managerial, and administrative posts held by women has also increased in most countries over the past three decades.

In order to evaluate progress toward gender equality, the UNDP's *Human Development Report 1995*[81] constructed two indices to supplement its Human

Development Index (HDI): the Gender-Related Human Development Index (GDI) and the Gender Empowerment Measure (GEM). GDI provides a measure of gender disparity in capabilities and choices, based on an index combining life expectancy, educational attainment, and adjusted real income. The GEM provides an index of gender disparity based on women's participation in political decision-making, their access to professional opportunities, and their earning power. In 2001, GDI estimates were made for 146 and GEM estimates were made for 64 countries.

Since 1984, the UN, in cooperation with the specialized agencies, has brought out every five years a publication on the role of women in development containing a wealth of information on trends, critical problems, and key policy issues. UNIFEM initiated a biennial publication in 2000 entitled *Progress of the World's Women*.[82] The UN's extensive range of publications has demonstrated the serious underestimation of women's contribution to national output.[83] This is due to several reasons. First, in most countries, there is underrecording in national income accounts of the work done by women in such areas as subsistence production and the informal sector. Second, the national accounts in most countries do not even attempt to capture the value added of the work done by women and girls in such activities as fetching water and fuel, processing food, manufacturing handicrafts and clothing at home, and so forth. Third, no country counts the work associated with reproduction, rearing of children, cooking, washing, and looking after the house in its national accounts. Since in most societies status and power are closely related to income earned, the underestimated, unrecorded, and unpaid work done by women adds to their invisibility and marginality.

According to the HDR 1995, women work longer hours than men in nearly all countries, but in industrial countries only 33 percent of their work is paid, whereas for men, 66 percent of their work is remunerated. In developing countries, only 34 percent of women's work is paid, compared with 75 percent of men's work. The HDR 1995, on a basis of necessarily inadequate evidence and some rather large assumptions, estimated that the value of the unpaid and underpaid work of women worldwide amounted to some $11 trillion, the equivalent of nearly half of the total measured global GDP in that year, $23 trillion.[84] Discrimination against women workers and entrepreneurs and underestimation of their economic contribution have led to inefficiency in resource allocation and hence to lower rates of economic growth.

The development approaches designed to promote women's well-being and capabilities that are advocated by the UN system and outside specialists have passed through at least three different stages. Initially, in the 1960s, the emphasis was on welfare programs and projects to promote health, nutrition, education, childcare, and spacing of children. There was little effort to address the structural dimensions of women's subordination and inequality.

The 1970s onward witnessed a shift to an approach described as WID, or women in development. The emphasis was placed on formulating projects for income-earning opportunities including skills training, credit schemes, and assistance with marketing. This involved either new projects or the addition of "women's components" to ongoing projects. Since the late 1980s, the focus has shifted again—to "engendering" the full spectrum of development policies. This reflects the understanding that all aspects of the development process have gender implications and therefore that an integrated approach encompassing micro- and macroeconomic and social and institutional policies is required to address the full range of problems faced by women and men. At the same time, there is a shift in emphasis from regarding women as passive beneficiaries or victims of the development process to their being considered as active agents of growth and transformation.[85]

Four major UN world conferences on women—the Mexico City conference in 1975, the Copenhagen conference in 1980, the Nairobi conference in 1985, and the Beijing conference in 1995—have played a vital role in mobilizing public opinion on gender issues; promoting dialogue among governments, international agencies, women's organizations, and specialists; and influencing global and national policies through declarations of principles and programs of action. Their messages have been reinforced by other world conferences convened since the Teheran International Conference on Human Rights in 1968. These conferences also reflect the evolution of thinking on gender issues. While successive conferences signal many areas of continuing concern—an indication of slow progress in implementing agreed-upon goals and policies—new themes are also introduced by each conference. An extraordinary change over the period is the growing participation in conference deliberations of women's movements, other civil society organizations, and specialists. Whereas the Mexico City conference attracted 4,000 nonofficial participants, their number rose to 30,000 at the Beijing conference.[86]

The Mexico City conference in 1975 constituted a milestone; for the first time it put together a comprehensive global and national program of action that covered all dimensions pertaining to women's well-being and development.[87] Indeed, the subsequent three women's world conferences have largely reiterated and elaborated the themes the 1975 conference put on the world agenda for the first time.

The Mexico City program of action referred to political, civil, economic, and social rights.[88] It addressed recommendations that have been echoed since on health, maternal care, child care, nutrition, family planning, literacy, education, technical and vocational training, access to credit, and access to employment and social services. It called for action to combat trafficking, prostitution, child and sexual abuse, domestic violence, and inhumane treatment of persons convicted of crime. The Copenhagen conference carried forward the Mexico City agenda with a focus on employment, health, and education. It came out with the famous, often-quoted but never fully substantiated statistics that have reverberated around the world that state that women represent 50 percent of the world adult population and 33 percent of its official labor force, that they perform nearly 66 percent of all working hours, that they receive 10 percent of the world's income, and that they own less than 1 percent of world property.[89]

As with the Mexico City conference, Copenhagen placed the theme of women's equality in the broader framework of the global economy and structural imbalances at national and international levels. Five years later, the Nairobi conference in 1985 drew upon the previous conferences and the state of women's situation to come up with a long-term plan of action—*The Nairobi Forward-Looking Strategies for the Advancement of Women.*[90] It further enlarged the scope of action by including sections on energy, the environment, and women in special and precarious situations.

Ten years later, the Beijing conference emphasized the role of civil society and the importance of empowerment and full participation of women in achieving implementation of its platform of action.[91] Women's inequality and subordination has been—and still often is—one of the central problems of our age. For the first time on a worldwide scale, the global conferences acknowledged this reality and set out an agenda of action of integrated approaches to overcoming this problem. They also established contacts and activist networks of and for women on a global scale, which played a major part in mobilizing awareness and action in many countries where previously women's issues had received little public attention.

The major effort made by the UN system over the past fifty years to highlight injustices suffered by women and their untapped potential to contribute to peace, development, and equality has already borne fruit in many areas of public and private life. But the situation still varies enormously from one region to another. While there has been undoubted progress in the reduction of gender disparities in most fields, these have persisted in varying degrees in most countries. The greatest challenge in the coming years and decades is to translate into reality the global agenda adopted at the Beijing conference. While major advances have been made at the conceptual and theoretical levels in engendering development strategies and policies, there is still a long way to go in incorporating gender concerns in the actual policies pursued by governments and other actors and institutions.

Concluding Observations

There has been a tendency within the UN system to broaden the scope and objectives of development over time. Starting with a narrow concern with economic growth and savings and investment requirements, the notion of development was broadened to include eradicating poverty, meeting basic human needs, generating employment, distributing income and wealth fairly, protecting the environment, working toward equality for women, protecting the welfare and development of children and indigenous groups, and participation in the decision-making process at all levels and respect for human rights. Development has become a multidimensional concept that includes many objectives and requires synthesis and harmonization of policies in several different domains.

The development policies promoted by the UN system have, therefore, changed over time. These changes have often been influenced by the conditions in and ideas emanating from the industrial countries. The earlier theories of growth, which emphasized modern industry, the transfer of labor from rural to urban areas, and the key role of savings and investment, were largely taken from the history of developed countries. Likewise, the shift toward liberalization and privatization followed the pursuit of similar policies in industrial countries. Perhaps only the strategies to generate employment and satisfy basic needs owe their origins to the experience and conditions in developing countries. In a different manner, of course, the proposals to establish a new international economic order were wholly a developing-country initiative— and they aroused massive opposition from the industrial countries.

Later, in Chapter 10, we consider the extent to which some of the development ideas propagated by the UN have in fact been taken up and implemented by both the poor and the rich countries as well as by the multilateral agencies. As a broad generalization, it would seem that while many policies associated with planning, industrialization, and accumulation had a considerable influence, policies to eradicate poverty and generate jobs had much less influence, at least until the late 1990s. Moreover, the UN has made numerous recommendations addressed to the industrial countries and, to some extent, to the Bretton Woods institutions. For the most part, they have been politely, or less politely, ignored.

A major part of the explanation for this pattern is provided by how the proposed policies affect powerful interests. The industrialization and growth policies were an outcome of an alliance of the political elite, the industrialists, and the urban working class. The primary losers were agricultural interests, which in most countries were largely unorganized. On the other hand, employment and basic-needs strategies generally called for redistribution of income from richer to poorer groups, agrarian reform that adversely affected the interests of large farmers and landlords, and reallocation of public spending and credit from middle classes and industrialists to low-income groups and informal-sector workers. It is not surprising that such policies received mostly lip service.

The structural adjustment policies of the 1980s and 1990s—removal or reduction of subsidies, reduction in government social services, lowering of tariff and nontariff barriers, privatization of enterprise—also trod on many powerful toes. They hurt state functionaries, industrialists, and other members of the middle class. That these policies were successfully imposed on a large number of countries shows the even greater power of industrial countries, foreign creditors, and the Bretton Woods institutions, which insisted on their adoption as a condition for releasing funds to support their balance of payments and national budgets.

The power factor once again explains the persistent failure of most industrial countries to do much to implement the UN's recommendations in successive international development strategies relating to development assistance, trade liberalization, transfer of technology, and codes of conduct for transnational enterprises. It is also for this reason that although it was formulated at a time of maximum power of oil-exporting countries, the NIEO in the end turned out to be a dead letter. It is interesting to speculate whether, now that the power of rich countries, the Bretton Woods institutions, and the UN itself is apparently united in support of poverty-reduction strategies, the governments and the elites of developing countries will implement them more seriously than they did three decades ago.

6

The 1980s: Losing Control and Marginalizing the Poorest

- **The Debt Crisis**
- **UN Proposals on Debt**
- **An Era of Economic Liberalization**
- **The Washington Consensus and UN Reactions**
- **Neoliberal Policies in the Transition Economies**
- **UN Ideas on Transition in Central and Eastern Europe**
- **The Least-Developed Countries**
- **Three International Conferences: Commitments and Performance**
- **Concluding Remarks**

The 1980s witnessed three remarkable changes for development. They marked a decisive turning point in development policies pursued by most developing countries. They constituted a watershed in the role the UN system played in generating ideas and influencing strategies for development. Finally, they witnessed a serious erosion of the authority and influence of developing countries in shaping international economic policies. Behind all these changes we find the severe economic problems encountered by the industrial countries from the mid-1970s and the policy responses they fashioned to cope with these difficulties.

This chapter first describes the forces that ushered in the global trend in favor of economic liberalization. It discusses the content of these policies as they spread rapidly through the developing world and the UN response to them. Because foreign debt played a critical role in the "lost decade" of the 1980s and the adoption of the new policies, there is, first, a discussion of the emergence of the debt problem and efforts made to deal with it. After the presentation of the "new" policies, there is discussion of how they affected the situation in two distinct groups of countries—the erstwhile centrally planned economies in Europe and the least-developed countries, mostly concentrated in sub-Saharan Africa, most of which suffered regression and marginalization in the 1980s.

The Debt Crisis

The debt crisis burst upon the world economic scene in the early 1980s. Since then, it has remained a critical issue in discussions on international economic policy. It has had a major impact on the evolution of national development strategies and policies over the period. Few developments have exerted such profound effect on economic growth, unemployment, and the poverty situation in developing countries over this period. The approach that was adopted to tackle the debt problem and the policies that were evolved to cope with it shed some light on global financial power politics and the priority accorded to development objectives. Understandably, the international financial organizations and the creditor countries and commercial banks have determined the overall approach and policies to handling the debt problem. The influence exerted by the UN system in this domain was all but negligible. Nevertheless, UNCTAD did some useful analytical work on external debt, especially in the mid-1980s, and outlined a different approach to dealing with the debt problem.[1]

While the burden of external debt has been an issue in discussions on international development from at least the 1960s, it became a major global preoccupation only in the early 1980s.[2] Even in the 1980s, the G-7 members were overwhelmingly preoccupied with threats the debt posed to their own economic well-being.[3] When these threats eased in the mid-1980s, concern with the continuing debt crisis in developing countries slipped from being a high priority of the global agenda until the late 1990s.

In developing countries, debt service as a proportion of exports of goods and services rose from less than 9 percent in 1975 to around 11–12 percent after 1980. The regional differences are quite considerable. For Latin America, the ratio rose sharply from 20 percent in 1975 to nearly 40 percent in 1982 but fell to 22 percent in 1995. For North Africa, the proportion rose from around 12 percent in 1975 to 30 percent in 1990 before falling to 20 percent in 1995. The debt-service ratio rose sharply for sub-Saharan Africa from less than 7 percent in 1975 to around 19 percent in the 1990s. For Asia as a whole, the proportion has been remarkably stable over the entire period between 5 and 8 percent, although for West Asia it has risen nearly threefold from around 3 percent in 1975 to about 9–10 percent in the 1990s.[4]

The composition of debt underwent major changes in the 1970s and 1980s. For instance, in 1971, for all developing countries, two-thirds of their medium- and long-term debt consisted of overseas development assistance (ODA) and official export credits from the OECD countries and multilateral organizations.[5] By 1979, the share of the concessional and official debt had fallen to 55 percent and that of loans from private banks had risen to one-third. Eurocurrency loans to developing countries, which were confined to a small number of middle-income countries, rose at an annual average rate of 40 to 50 percent in 1971–1975 and about 30 percent in 1975–1979.[6] However, by 1990, the share of private debt in total long-term debt to developing countries had fallen to around 18 percent.[7]

There is now widespread agreement on the factors that led to the explosive growth of debt for developing countries, especially in Latin America and Africa, in the 1970s and 1980s. The debt crisis was caused primarily by changes in the world economy that were beyond the control of the developing countries. The most important factor was the sudden and sharp slowdown in the growth of industrial countries after the first oil-price shock in 1973. For instance, output in the OECD countries expanded at an annual rate of 4.9 percent from 1960 to 1973 but only by 2.7 percent over the period 1974–1979 and 1.0 percent over 1980–1982.[8] This resulted both in a sharp reduction of demand for exports from developing countries and a decrease in primary-product prices.

At the same time, inflation in industrial countries jumped from 4.1 percent per annum over 1960 to 1973, to 9.6 percent per annum over the period from 1974 to 1982. The result was a massive deterioration in the terms of trade of non-petroleum-exporting developing countries, especially those excessively dependent upon primary-product prices. The index of the terms of trade of non-petroleum-exporting developing countries fell from 110 in 1973–1975 (1980=100) to 94 in 1981–1983 and further to 84 in 1989–1990.[9] The other external shock came in the form of a sharp rise in international interest rates following the adoption of tight money policies in the U.S. and other industrial countries. For instance, the short-term real interest rate in the U.S. rose from an annual average of 0.7 percent in 1972–1975 to 5.0 percent in 1980–1982.[10]

As for the developing countries, they had to cope not only with a sharp rise in oil prices but also with a big decline in foreign demand for their exports and in the terms of trade with the industrial countries. Given that the real international interest rates were negative in the early 1970s, it was rational for them to borrow from the commercial banks, who, flushed with OPEC deposits, were themselves bending over backward to push loans to developing countries. Furthermore, this period witnessed a marked slowdown in flows of concessional funds and official export credits from industrial countries. The international financial institutions did not increase their lending to any significant extent either. Developing countries were encouraged to borrow from commercial banks, as it was generally believed that this was a short-term recession likely to be followed by resumption of rapid growth in rich countries and hence in the demand for those developing countries' exports. Finally, the developing countries were eager to maintain the momentum of their rapid growth of the past decade and a half.

Several features characterized the dominant approach to the debt problem. First, there was an implicit assumption, especially in the early years of the debt crisis, that the cause of external debt-servicing difficulties lay with the policies of the debtor countries themselves, despite the existence of considerable literature pointing to the external approximate causes of the debt crisis.[11]

Second, it was believed that the problem was of a short-term nature. Once the appropriate policies were put in place, the debt problem would take care of itself through expansion of exports, the reduction of imports, and the resumption of capital flows. The problem was also seen in the early years of the crisis largely in financial terms, divorced from its impact on structural imbalances and medium- and long-term growth. This way of conceptualizing the debt problem led to the conclusion that the primary responsibility for economic adjustment to cope with the debt problem should rest with the debtor countries and "that rescheduling policies would need to keep debtor countries on a tight leash designed to enforce policy reforms on these countries. . . . All in all, the impression has sometimes been given that the main purpose of external financing is to encourage policy reform rather than to transfer resources."[12]

The third feature of the approach to the debt problem has been that policies have been devised largely by the "creditors' cartel" that has brought together the creditor countries, banks, and the Bretton Woods institutions. The developing countries, and the indebted countries among them, have been largely left out of policymaking. The cartel also preferred to deal with the indebted countries on an individual country basis in the London and Paris Clubs.[13] This inevitably resulted in a massive inequality in the balance of negotiating power between the creditors and the debtors. Although the Latin American countries tried on some occasions to form a common front of debtor countries, they did not get very far. It is therefore not surprising that the creditor organizations were able to impose their terms on the indebted countries.

Another feature of the approach to the debt problem has been the sharp distinction that was drawn between debt resulting from ODA flows and all other debt. While considerable flexibility has been shown with regard to the terms of ODA debt, including cancellation in various forms even in the 1970s, with regard to all other debt, it has been held that although obligations on account of interest and amortization can be postponed, they must eventually be met in full.

The policies that evolved in the 1970s and early 1980s to deal with the debt problem followed from the approach outlined above. Their essence was that in return for debt rescheduling, or cancellation in the case of ODA debt, the indebted countries must pursue a set of policies under IMF supervision that were designed to correct financial and payments imbalances. Initially these policies amounted to reduction of public spending, increase in revenue, currency devaluation and removal of price controls. Later they evolved into a broader package involving liberalization of trade and foreign exchange restrictions, deregulation of the economy, privatization, and other elements of what came to be called the Washington Consensus.

These policies were responsible in large measure for the lost decade of the 1980s. They led to stagnation or decreases in output, increases in unemployment, decreases in wages, reductions in public spending on social services, and, more generally, the aggravation of poverty which characterized the decade.[14] For several years in a row, the heavily indebted middle-income countries experienced negative resource flows. For instance, in Latin America and the Caribbean, GDP and income per capita fell respectively by 6.6 and 16 percent between 1980 and 1988. The transfer of resources shifted from an inflow of nearly $16 billion in 1978–1979 to an outflow of about $23 billion in 1987–1988, equivalent to nearly 21 percent of exports of goods and services.[15]

The debt crisis may be said to have begun officially in August 1982 when Mexico declared its inability to service its debt. Earlier in the year, Argentina had suspended payments on its $37 billion debt following its defeat in the Falkland Islands War with Britain. But it was the Mexican default that shook the financial world. Many of the major banks, especially in the U.S., were dangerously exposed to borrowers in Latin American countries. The Mexican shock led to a sudden halt in new lending by the banks. A growing number of heavily indebted countries found themselves in a position of insolvency.

The virtual cessation of private lending combined with continued stagnation in indebted countries intensified social problems in a growing number of countries. The creditor countries came under increasing pressure to modify their debt policy. A number of steps were taken to put in place a more effective approach to handling the debt problem. From 1984, the commercial banks agreed to multiyear rescheduling of debt. For instance, in 1984, Mexico obtained a four-year agreement on debt rescheduling. This was followed in 1985 by the adoption of the Baker Plan, under which, in exchange for wide-ranging economic reforms in debtor countries under IMF supervision, the commercial banks agreed to increase their lending by $20 billion over three years and the multilateral financial organizations agreed to increase their disbursements by $3 billion a year.[16] Other new ideas included debt swaps for equity and environmental and social projects and conversion of debt into "exit bonds."

While these measures helped to ease somewhat the pressure of debt payments in some countries, they failed to make a significant dent in the debt problem and restore economic growth. The next step in the evolution of debt policy was taken at the Toronto G-7 Summit in 1988, when, for the first time, the major industrial countries accepted the principle of debt relief rather than just debt rescheduling. Under the Brady Plan in 1989, the emphasis shifted to debt reduction, voluntary exchanges of old debt for new bonds, and lending by multilateral financing agencies to enable countries to buy back debts at secondary-market prices.[17] Mexico was again the first country to negotiate under the Brady Plan in 1989. Other countries followed with their own debt-relief programs. For the first time, commercial banks accepted debt forgiveness and voluntarily reduced their loans. The Brady Plan in combination with other programs helped restore the creditworthiness of a number of middle-income countries and led to a resumption of private credit flows on a significant scale in the 1990s.

For low-income countries, most of whose debt consisted of concessional loans from industrial countries and multilateral financial agencies, the traditional approach consisted of rescheduling principal and interest payments, forgiving bilateral debt, reducing commercial debt through the IDA debt reduction facility, and special programs supported by donor countries to enable them to pay their debt to the Bretton Woods institutions.[18] Although these debt-relief mechanisms alleviated the debt problem of many poor countries, they did not provide a durable solution.

The continued serious economic situation in most low-income countries led to intense pressure on the industrial countries to cancel debts, especially from the civil society organizations (NGOs), through such initiatives as Jubilee 2000 and mass demonstrations at important international gatherings.[19] This led, among other things, to the Highly Indebted Poor Countries (HIPC) Initiative,[20] which embodied three new elements. First, it widened the coverage of the types of debts that are eligible for relief to include multilateral debt. This is important for the poorest countries, since multilateral debt forms an important proportion of their total debt. Second, the initiative set an explicit target for debt sustainability and provided a commitment to the HIPCs that if traditional debt-relief mechanisms could not bring their debt to a level that is sustainable, additional action would be taken by the international community to do so. A third innovation of the HIPC Initiative was that new sources and mechanisms for financing debt relief were introduced. These include gold sales by the IMF and the setting up of the HIPC Trust Fund, to which bilateral donors may contribute to help the multilateral institutions provide debt relief.[21]

UN Proposals on Debt

In practical terms, the UN did not have much of an influence on the evolution of debt policy for developing countries. But this was not for lack of trying. The UN sought to influence policy on external debt through analytical work and specific proposals for action, the resolutions adopted by various sessions of UNCTAD and the General Assembly,[22] the programs of action adopted at world conferences, and technical assistance to strengthen the capacity of developing countries to manage debt more effectively. Within the UN system, the work on debt was done primarily in UNCTAD and the regional economic commissions.

The analysis of the debt crisis carried out by UNCTAD in the 1987 *Trade and Development Report* put the debt issue in a developmental context. It pointed out the weaknesses of the international debt strategy pursued in the 1980s, mentioning the disproportionate burden of macroeconomic and trade adjustment on debtor countries, reliance on supply-side measures to increase the flexibility of the productive structure through liberalization, and reliance on market forces while neglecting variables such as aggregate demand and investment.[23] The report argued:

> The most striking weakness of the debt strategy as implemented thus far has been the failure to conceive it within a broader strategy for accelerating growth in the world economy. The prospect of slow growth in developed market-economy countries in the period ahead casts doubts on the prospect for rapid growth in export earnings of most debtor countries. Yet rapidly expanding export earnings are fundamental to any successful debt strategy and, without them, the objectives of accelerating growth in debtor countries and achieving financial viability cannot be reconciled.[24]

The report put forward proposals for a more effective international debt strategy. It called for higher growth rates in industrial countries and an internationally agreed-upon set of guidelines.[25]

The United Nations has also developed technical cooperation programs in strengthening debt-management capacities in developing countries. In the early 1980s, UNCTAD developed an effective framework analysis for debt management and the computer-based debt-management tool known as the

Debt Management and Financial Analysis System (DMFAS). This software, which has subsequently been upgraded, is installed in fifty user countries, of which nineteen are HIPCs. The DMFAS Program has recently established an interface with the Debt Sustainability Model developed by the World Bank for debt-sustainability analysis.[26]

More recently, the UN Executive Committee on Social and Economic Affairs has evolved a UN position on the debt problem. It made a number of proposals to improve the handling of the debt problems of both middle-income countries and HIPCs.[27] For the former, the committee recommended the inclusion of contingency clauses in debt contracts that would automatically allow for an extension of maturities in times of acute financial crisis. It also stressed the importance of early and anticipatory debt restructurings and greater transparency and accountability from the private sector, national authorities, and international financial institutions.[28]

It also made a number of proposals to improve the HIPC Initiative that have since been implemented. The UNCTAD *Least Developed Countries 2000 Report* made a cogent analysis of the development and debt situation in least-developed countries (LDCs). The report considered even the latest version of the HIPC Initiative completely inadequate to meet the growth requirements of the LDCs. It argued that there is a danger that debt relief will be substituted for development assistance. In a situation of stagnant and even declining flows of ODA, not only will debt reduction not result in overall increases in resource flows for indebted countries but it will even deflect such increases from countries that have managed to avoid debt crisis. The amount of benefits is inadequate to achieve a lasting end to the debt problem. Furthermore, the whole process of debt relief is too cumbersome and slow moving, despite recent improvements. The addition of the poverty-reduction conditionality to the already formidable list of formalities will further complicate the situation. There is much uncertainty about how this new conditionality will be interpreted and what impact it might have on productive capacity and growth.[29]

An Era of Economic Liberalization

The 1980s were marked by the growing influence of neoliberal ideas in development thinking and practice as a consequence of stagflation, the crisis of the welfare states in the North, and the debt crisis and failure of some past development strategies in the South. The essence of the "new" thinking was that objectives of poverty reduction and growth are best served by relying on market forces and private enterprise and restricting the role of the state to a minimum of essential functions.[30]

Table 6.1. Long-Term Debt in Developing Countries

Region	1975	1980[1]	1990	1995
Total Debt in $ Billions				
All Developing Countries	154	424	1,042	1,354
Latin America and Caribbean	65	176	350	397
North Africa	16	47	96	95
Sub-Saharan Africa	14	40	133	141
West Asia	14	39	99	141
Other Asia and Pacific	45	104	345	568
Debt as a Percentage of GDP				
All Developing Countries	17	18	28	25
Latin America and Caribbean	18	24	32	23
North Africa	27	36	58	58
Sub-Saharan Africa	19	81	78	86
West Asia	16	8	19	21
Other Asia and Pacific	19	14	22	20
Debt Service as a Percentage of Exports				
All Developing Countries	9	12	12	11
Latin America and Caribbean	20	26	21	22
North Africa	13	16	30	20
Sub-Saharan Africa	7	9	19	19
West Asia	3	4	9	9
Other Asia and Pacific	8	8	8	7

[1]The OECD time series have been revised as of 1982 with a new database; therefore data starting in 1982 are not strictly comparable to those of previous years.

Sources: UNCTAD, Handbook of International Trade and Development Statistics (Geneva: UN, 1985 and 1995); data provided by the OECD Secretariat and published in External Debt Statistics (Paris: Organisation for Economic Co-operation and Development, 1984–).

The groundwork to the adoption of new policies was done by the theories associated with the Chicago School of economics since the late 1950s. Among the major contributors to these theories were Milton Friedman and Gary Becker.[31] An earlier inspiration to the resurgence of neoliberal doctrines was provided by Hayek's classic, *The Road to Serfdom*.[32] These theories also constituted an attack on the Keynesian economics that regard demand deficiency as the cause of unemployment and recommend intervention by the public authorities to influence aggregate demand. According to the Chicago School, markets were self-equilibrating. Government intervention in the economy was the primary cause of disturbances, and the best way to control the level of economic activity was through monetary policy. Inflation was essentially a monetary phenomenon and could be brought under control through a restrictive monetary policy.

These doctrines eulogizing the virtues of free markets and private enterprise and decrying the evils of state intervention fell on the receptive ears of the new conservative leaders who had captured power in the UK and the U.S.—Margaret Thatcher and Ronald Reagan. The new policies were also opportune because the industrial countries, after a period of unprecedented growth and prosperity from 1950 to 1974—the "Golden Age"—had run into economic difficulties resulting in stagnation and high inflation. The immediate cause of these difficulties was the fourfold rise in petroleum prices, but neoclassical economists attributed them to the growing role of the public sector, the power of trade unions, high taxation and an expensive welfare system, and other "market-distorting" institutions and policies. Led by Thatcher and Reagan, the "counterrevolution" resulted in curbs on trade unions, reduction in taxes and welfare spending, privatization of state enterprises, reduction or removal of subsidies and price controls, deregulation of key sectors of the economy, and liberalization of exchange restrictions. The central objective of macroeconomic policy became control of inflation through monetary policy and the attainment of budgetary balances.

Over a period of time, these ideas spread to other industrial countries but seldom in such extreme form. The new thinking in economic policy was also reflected in the literature on economic development. Peter Bauer, Hla Myint, and Harry Johnson were among the early critics of planning and the state role in the economy.[33] Their thesis essentially was that state taxation and marketing and industrial protection had squeezed the peasantry, blunted incentives for farmers and traders, and misallocated resources through state-sponsored industrialization based on import controls. Their lead was followed by a number of influential publications that were strongly critical of the role played by state enterprises, promotion of industrialization through protection, and restrictions on private economic activity, free trade, and payments. Among the leading critics of state-led efforts for economic growth were Bela Balassa, Ian Little, Tibor Scitovsky, Jagdish Bhagwati, Anne Krueger, and Deepak Lal.[34] They showed through empirical research that state protection of industry and allocation of resources through licensing and administrative means had seriously distorted resources, worsened income distribution and employment, provided wrong signals for investment, and led to corrupt and rent-seeking behavior by bureaucrats and industrialists. These policies thus constituted a strong obstacle to economic growth. They advocated retrenchment of state enterprises, reliance on market forces and private enterprise, and liberalization of trade and payments.

These ideas had a profound impact on the operations of the IMF and the World Bank. As an agency concerned primarily with financial stability and liberalization, the IMF has had a traditional bias in favor of macroeconomic balance, control of inflation and trade, and financial liberalization. The new doctrines reinforced these proclivities. In the 1970s, the World Bank, under Robert McNamara and his chief economic advisor Hollis Chenery, had become an increasingly articulate advocate of reducing poverty and satisfying basic needs. It should, however, be added that its rhetoric for the most part did not match up to its actions on the ground. In the 1980s, it too became a convert to neoliberal development policies.[35] This was partly through the influence of the new literature on development. But the Bretton Woods institutions were also reacting, as always, to the wishes of their powerful members—the rich countries that carry a disproportionate weight in their decision-making organs.

The emphasis the Bretton Woods institutions placed on economic liberalization was reflected in the pursuit of such policies by an increasing number of countries, first in Latin America and then in Africa and Asia. Obviously, some developing countries had, through mismanagement of their economies, also run into intractable problems of persistent inflation at galloping rates. A few suffered from stagnation and extreme distortion of their economies caused by breakdown of the market mechanism and the pervasive role of the state sector in the ownership and management of the economy. Thus, in these countries a significant constituency developed for economic reform. This consisted of technocrats as well as businesspeople, agricultural interests, conservative political parties, and sometimes even trade unions. A leading and early example of the embrace of neoliberal policies was Chile under Pinochet, which preceded the monetarist policies under Reagan and Thatcher by nearly a decade. In the 1980s and 1990s, most developing countries initiated programs of economic liberalization and adjustment under the tutelage of the Bretton Woods institutions.

Box 6.1. Chile: Pioneering Neoliberal Strategies

Chile under Pinochet was probably the first country in the world to chart the neoliberal course in the mid-1970s. Chile was followed by Mexico, Argentina, and several other Latin American countries in the 1980s. It is worth recalling that Chile embarked on these policies well before related policies were popularized by Margaret Thatcher and Ronald Reagan and before they were championed by the World Bank and the IMF as the Washington Consensus. Not only did the Pinochet regime introduce these policies but it also pursued them rigorously and consistently for seventeen years before its departure from the political scene. Furthermore, the democratically elected governments since 1990 have maintained the essentials of these policies while introducing some new dimensions concerning organization of labor and social development.

The changes brought about by the Pinochet regime affected all sectors and all aspects of economic and social policy.[36] These sweeping changes amounted to a social and economic revolution. They were designed to destroy all elements of a state-controlled economy and create the basis of a modern capitalist system. There was also a massive purge; political parties and trade unions were repressed and many leading opponents of the military coup were tortured, killed, or expelled.

In foreign trade, multiple exchange rates, import quotas, and other restrictions were done away with to be replaced by a single rate and uniform tariffs, price controls were lifted on 3,000 items, and prices and wages were left to be determined by market forces. The state-owned enterprises were sold to private investors: their numbers went down from 530 in 1973, when they covered all aspects of the economy, to 41 by 1990, when they covered copper and oil extracts, water and sanitation, transportation, and power generation.[37] The tax reform included the introduction of value-added taxes, removal of wealth taxes, and very low corporation rates. The interest rates were freed, banks were privatized, and capital markets were deregulated. Capital controls in the foreign exchange markets were lifted, though some regulation was reintroduced later.

What were the results of these radical changes in economic organization and policy? The economy has become far more export-oriented in the last twenty-five years. Although there are inevitable fluctuations, the ratio of exports to GDP has risen from around 15 percent in 1950–1952 to 18 percent in 1978–1981 to around 35 percent in the 1990s. More remarkable, and contrary to the experience of most rapidly developing countries, is that the share of manufactured exports has remained low—only 15 percent in the 1990s. The bulk of exports consist of copper, nitrate, fruit, and forestry products. This has led some observers to state that Chilean growth has happened at the expense of natural resources and the environment.

Chile is also justly famous for its social indicators, which have been well above the levels corresponding to its per capita income. Infant mortality declined sharply from 165 in 1945 to 65 by 1965 and to 20 by 1985. This success is partly the result of the Pinochet regime's policy of targeted nutrition provision to poor children and mothers. Moreover, life expectancy in Chile rose from 57 in 1960 to 67 in 1980 and 75 in 1998. Adult illiteracy in 1952 was already low at around 20 percent and fell further to 11 percent in 1970 and 5 percent by 1998. Primary-school enrollment rose from 66 percent in 1950 to complete coverage by the 1960s, and secondary-school enrollment rose from 24 percent in 1960 to 65 percent in 1980 and 80 percent in 1995. There is no gender disparity in educational enrollments. The incidence of poverty probably declined in the 1960s but rose in the 1970s and most of the 1980s. Income distribution in Chile, among the most unequal in the world, has been getting worse: the Gini coefficient of income distribution rose from 0.45 in 1968 to 0.53 in 1980 and 0.58 in 1989 before declining to 0.56 in 1994.[38]

The Washington Consensus and UN Reactions

The Washington Consensus became a shorthand expression for stabilization and structural-adjustment policies advocated by the Bretton Woods institutions and major industrial countries. The different components of the
policy package have been well summarized in a UN document.[39] The earlier
IMF analysis of economic problems focused on excessive government spending, overvaluation of currencies, quantitative controls over imports, and negative real interest rates. The recommended policies included cuts in government
spending and "getting the prices right"; that is, in line with market forces.

The Washington Consensus added three new elements.[40] Apart from bal-
ancing budgets and correcting prices, the policy package included the liberalization of trade, payments, and foreign investment; privatization; and
regulation of domestic markets. Trade liberalization involved the removal of
quantitative restrictions on imports, reduction in tariffs, imposition of a uniform rate of tariffs, and free trade. Liberalization of foreign investment meant
nondiscriminatory treatment of domestic and foreign enterprises. The Bretton
Woods institutions and the G-7 further stipulated the return of nationalized
enterprises to private hands, closure of state enterprises that did not turn a
profit, and transfer of public firms to private hands. The domestic-market
deregulation agenda included the establishment of free markets for goods,
labor, and finance. In the 1990s, two new elements were added to secure political support for the package: the imposition of local government ownership of the program and introduction of social safety nets.

What role did the UN play during this period when the ideas it had been
promoting—the employment and basic-needs strategies and the NIEO—
which were incorporated in the Third Development Decade Strategy adopted
by the General Assembly in 1980,[41] were summarily swept off the global and
national agenda? There is no doubt that the Bretton Woods institutions seized
the initiative in setting global and national development policies. The UN
found itself largely marginalized, unable to come forward with a new agenda
that offered the prospect of coping with the new problems while preserving
the social and human development goals it had been advocating. Its role became largely reactive. To the extent that it played a constructive role, it was to
point out the negative social and growth consequences of the policy package
prescribed by the IMF and the World Bank.

Each of the major specialized agencies—the ILO, the WHO, UNESCO, and
the FAO—and the regional commissions in Africa and Latin America published reports drawing attention to some undesirable consequences of stabilization and structural-adjustment policies.[42] UNCTAD usually provided the

intellectual leadership in matters related to international economic policies and development. But its role was increasingly restricted by the pressure some industrial countries put on it not to duplicate the work of the international financial organizations. It was asked to focus its work on practical programs to expand trade and reduce poverty. Indeed, at one stage efforts were made to close down the agency.[43]

In the end, the advocacy and analytical work by UNICEF had the greatest impact and played an important role in influencing international opinion and persuading the Bretton Woods institutions to pay greater attention to poverty and human development dimensions when devising structural-adjustment programs. Two UN research institutes—WIDER (World Institute for Development Economics Research) and UNRISD—also brought out publications that critiqued these programs from different perspectives.

The *State of the World's Children* report issued by UNICEF started calling for "a broader approach to the adjustment process" in 1984,[44] building on an earlier study, *The Impact of World Recession on Children.*[45] Both studies provided evidence of the negative impact of stabilization and adjustment policies on growth, income distribution, incidence of poverty, and child welfare in a large number of countries. UNICEF's 1987 study, *Adjustment with a Human Face,* proposed alternative approaches with more expansive macroeconomic policies; more selective and targeted policies in the fields of taxation, government spending, foreign exchange, and credit; improvements in the efficiency and equity of the social sector by restructuring public spending; instituting compensatory programs such as public-works employment schemes and targeted nutritional interventions; and monitoring of human welfare and living standards, health, and nutrition.[46] The phrase "adjustment with a human face" accurately described the proposed approach.[47]

The WIDER project, which included eighteen country studies, "focused on whether alternative policy packages could have been devised in particular country situations which would contribute to desirable adjustment and growth goals ... at a lower social cost than that incurred by the country packages that were in fact negotiated."[48] The study concluded that there is no unified theory or policy to facilitate solutions to problems of stabilization and adjustment. A variety of policies involving a combination of different approaches seem to have worked well, depending on the peculiarities of the countries concerned. The WIDER study agreed with UNICEF findings on negative social and growth effects of the orthodox policies. It emphasized the structural roots of poverty, was skeptical of the prominent role accorded to price mechanisms in promoting adjustment and growth, and suggested the need for more realistic macroeconomic and financial analysis based on institutional and real-life assumptions.

The UNRISD studies addressed such issues as the impact of crisis and adjustment on social structures and organizations, the struggles waged by different social groups to defend their economic interests, and the effect of economic and social changes on the balance of political forces, the nature and power of the state, and shifts in power between national and foreign economic and political interests.[49] These studies showed that the pursuit of stabilization and adjustment policies weakened popular institutions such as unions and cooperatives, impoverished significant sections of the working and middle classes, strengthened the influence and power of foreign investors and creditors and of domestic groups linked to the international economy, and decreased the power, reach, and capacity of the state. A vital part of national decision making on social and economic policies was effectively transferred to foreign creditors, both private and official. The studies also analyzed the survival strategies of vulnerable groups and the links between the economic crisis and intensification of ethnic and religious tensions, crime, violence, and prostitution.[50]

Neoliberal Policies in the Transition Economies[51]

The collapse of communism in Europe and the Soviet Union provided new opportunities to extend neoliberal policies to a vast region that had hitherto been the home of central planning. The focus of this book is the contribution made by the UN system to development ideas and practice in the postwar period in poor countries. This section devoted to the experience of the European and Soviet centrally planned economies may thus appear as a digression from the main theme of the book. However, it is of interest to examine the UN's role in the evolution of development strategies in the former communist countries in the 1990s.

The experience of European communist countries presents several points of interest to developing countries. First of all, it constituted an alternative development strategy to the classical capitalist pattern of growth. The Soviet Union and the Eastern European countries were economically among the most backward countries in Europe prior to their communist revolutions.[52] Communism was looked upon not only as a system designed to end exploitation and promote social justice but also a system that would usher in a period of rapid growth and material prosperity. The Soviet experience in the interwar period was considered by many to demonstrate that, despite hostility from the capitalist world, a backward country could make rapid strides in industrialization and avoid unemployment and depression. In the postwar period, too, for nearly three decades, the communist countries in Europe attained higher growth rates of material production than their Western counterparts.

Centrally planned economies were thus considered an attractive model by many developing countries. A few of them, such as China, Vietnam, North Korea, and Cuba, themselves experienced communist revolutions. Several countries in Africa, such as Angola, Mozambique, and Ethiopia, adopted many features of a communist state and economy. A much larger number of countries throughout the developing world were deeply influenced by some political, economic, and social aspects of communism. Among these the most important were a one-party state, nationalization and public ownership of important enterprises, a strategy for accelerated industrialization, development planning, and universal provision of social services. The European communist states also served as alternative or additional sources of financial and technical assistance and markets for exports of primary products. Furthermore, in international negotiations on trade, aid, investment, and restructuring of the world economic system, the presence of the communist bloc strengthened the bargaining position of developing countries, as the Western and the Soviet blocs vied with each other to gain their allegiance and support.

The communist development model as pioneered by the Soviet Union was characterized by some unique features. Politically, it consisted of a one-party state where all power was monopolized by a single party and centralized in the executive committee of the Communist Party. All other parties and civil-society institutions were declared illegal. Mass organizations such as trade unions, peasant associations, and women's and youth groups were created but were strictly controlled by the Communist Party. Thus, civil and political liberties enshrined in the Universal Declaration of Human Rights were denied to the people living in orthodox communist states. Even when these countries launched a series of economic reforms in the 1970s and 1980s, there was no loosening of restrictions on freedom of speech and association.

Economically, the communist model was characterized by state ownership of most productive assets. After the triumph of communism, the state steadily expanded its property and capital base, expropriating private factories, machinery, and buildings. In practically all cases, this was done without compensation, in accordance with the Marxist doctrine of "expropriating the expropriators." The scope of the private sector varied from one country to another.

Another feature of the communist model was its emphasis on rapid industrialization. Following the Soviet model, most countries attempted to pursue an "integrated industrialization strategy," giving priority to heavy industry and infrastructure. In the consumer-goods sector, priority was given to essential goods and consumer durables lagged behind. The state used its power to fix prices and wages at levels that would generate a high proportion of surplus from the national output. Thus, all communist countries achieved extremely high rates of accumulation. Trade was controlled to meet shortages and dispose of surpluses. As part of the reforms attempted since the 1960s, a greater role was given to a "socialist division of labor," and trade among the socialist countries and with the outside world became steadily more important.

Socially, the communist model ensured a state of continuous full employment. Indeed, work was obligatory for everyone. The extensive phase of growth first pulled in male labor from the countryside and then relied increasingly upon high rates of female participation. The levels of productivity were relatively low. The state provided free education and health services to the entire population. The working population also benefited from cheap housing, pensions, maternity leave, kindergartens for children, family and disability benefits, and so forth. Wages were fixed to ensure that they were adequate to meet the essential needs of the family for food, clothing, transport, heating, and similar items. The standard of living was distinctly lower than in the Western countries, but there was a high degree of income and consumption equality.[53]

Box 6.2. The Cuban Strategy for Equality and Development

Cuba is a typical example, along with North Korea, of a country that has maintained its socialist system despite several economic and political crises and an extremely hostile international environment. Prior to the revolution of 1959, Cuba shared the economic and social features of other Latin American countries, reflected mainly in massive economic and social inequalities.

The revolution resulted in profound political, social, and economic changes. Most of the private property was expropriated. The markets were replaced by administrative methods of allocating resources and a rationing system established to ensure an equitable distribution of food and other resources. By 1968, most of the productive assets had been nationalized and had become state property. Dramatic improvements in the skill profile of the labor force, in the physical infrastructure (roads, transport, irrigation), and in machinery and equipment were introduced. The socialist countries, particularly the USSR, offered secure trade markets, stable and remunerative prices for exports, and considerable financial and technical assistance.

The abandonment of the careful calculation of benefits derived from the alternative use of resources, and material incentives, together with the administrative allocation of resources, led to increasing production problems, resulting in a severe economic crisis in the late 1960s. The annual rate of growth was 1.5 percent in 1961–1970, below the 2 percent growth in population.[54] The economic difficulties in the 1960s were exacerbated by a massive outflow of professional and managerial personnel and the imposition of an economic boycott by the United States, necessitating major reorientation in trade and capital flows and a substantial buildup in defense spending. These problems prompted a series of economic reforms designed to strengthen economic accounting and provide material incentives to enterprises and workers. These reforms contributed to a major boost in the average rate of economic growth to 6.7 percent in 1970–1981 and about 7 percent in 1980–1985.[55]

Cuba again entered a period of stagnation in the second half of the 1980s. The poor prices for sugar in the free markets and declining growth in the socialist and developed-market economies contributed to the reversal in economic performance. The economic crisis greatly intensified after the collapse of communism in Europe and the breakup of the Soviet Union. There was a virtual cessation of assistance from the socialist countries, including the cessation of the supply of petroleum at subsidized prices. Nor was Cuba able to sell its products to the former socialist countries at prices above the world market. The GDP declined by 37 percent, according to official sources; other sources estimate the decline to be between 29 percent and 58 percent.[56] It is, however, noteworthy that right through the economic crisis the government managed to avoid a reduction in resources allocated to education and health and succeeded in increasing them for social security, despite a fall in state revenue of 20 percent between 1990 and 1995.

Despite its authoritarian regime and poor growth performance, the Cuban experience is remarkable for its social achievements and great improvement in the living standards of the majority of the population. The social indicators point to major improvements in living standards in the first two decades after the revolution. Illiteracy was reduced sharply from around 24 percent in 1959 to around 4 percent in 1961 as a result of a massive literacy campaign. Life expectancy rose from 62 years in 1960 to 73.4 in 1980–1985 and to 74.4 in 1990–1993.[57] This was possible because of massive income and wealth redistribution brought about by such means as agrarian reform, nationalization of most productive enterprises, the reduction of inequality in remuneration, free health and education services, a rationing system that facilitated access to food and other essential goods at low cost to every individual, and relatively low prices for transport, housing, and electricity. Nevertheless, inequalities will almost certainly have risen since the late 1980s because of unequal access to earnings in dollars in different sectors and occupations.

Communism in Europe was suddenly and quickly swept away in the early 1990s. It was followed by attempts to restore some version of the capitalist system as it had developed in the Western world. The reversal from communism to capitalism was historically unprecedented.

A full explanation of the collapse of the communist system must go beyond economic factors to probe the changing global strategic situation, the burden of military spending, and, not least, the revolt against restrictions on people's civil and political liberties. The big difference in the living standards between the communist and Western countries in the 1980s became more visible with the growing contacts between the two systems and the steady opening of the former communist countries to the outside world. The role of the Soviet Union and its leadership under Mikhail Gorbachev were central factors in permitting the collapse of communism in Eastern and Central Europe.

The breakup of the communist political and socioeconomic system and its replacement by different varieties of capitalist systems was followed in practically all countries by draconian decreases in production, employment, and public social spending. Between 1989 and 1993, real GDP fell by 15 percent in the five countries in Central Europe, 32 percent in Southeast European states, 42 in Baltic states, and 30 percent in the former Soviet republics. By 1999, ten years into the transition, only the Central European countries had exceeded earlier GDP levels—by 9 percent, a growth of less than 2 percent per year. In the Commonwealth of Independent States (CIS), output levels were 55 percent below those in 1989, in Southeast European transition economies by 30 percent, and in the Baltic states by 35 percent. Total employment in the former communist countries was down by 15 to 20 percent.[58]

Economic collapse had the most severe consequences for people. The number living in poverty rose more than eightfold between 1988 and 1994—from 14 million to 119 million.[59]

UN Ideas on Transition in Central and Eastern Europe

What role, if any, did the UN system play in the transformation of the former communist states into the transition economies of the 1990s? The answer is very little. This was not for lack of ideas. The UN had definite and clear-cut views on the historically unique process of transformation from communism to capitalism. But for a number of reasons, UN advice made little impact on the policies pursued in these countries. The central role among the outside parties was played by the Bretton Woods institutions and Western governments and economists. This is somewhat surprising, given the fact that in the postwar period the UN agencies were among the few multilateral organizations open to full membership to the communist states. The UN system provided a forum for discussions, exchange of experience, and participation by the communist countries in its technical cooperation work and operational activities. One of its regional commissions—the Economic Commission for Europe—included both the Western and the communist states. For decades, its annual reports contained analysis of social and economic development in the communist countries. It thus had considerable staff expertise relating to centrally planned economies. It also played an important role in doing technical work and developing norms and agreements in such areas as transportation, the environment, and energy.

Most of the former centrally planned economies opted for an approach to transition that has been called variously "the big bang," "shock therapy," or "one leap." This approach was strongly advocated by the Bretton Woods institutions and Western advisory groups and economists.[60] It was also supported by some political parties and economists in the transition economies.[61]

The new approach reflected the neoliberal ideas associated with Washington Consensus—the dominant ideology in the 1980s on economic policy and development strategies. It advocated rapid and simultaneous action on many fronts—freeing prices, removing subsidies, opening up the economies to external trade and investment, removing exchange controls, achieving budgetary equilibrium, privatizing enterprises, closing unprofitable companies, and reducing social spending. This approach was considered economically and politically superior to other alternatives. Economically, it consisted of a series of mutually supporting policies that would quickly put the economies on a path of rapid growth after the inevitable but short-lived recession. Politically, it would make reversal to communism virtually impossible by destroying its central pillars.

In contrast, the ECE's *Economic Survey of Europe* argued for a different and more gradual approach to transition.[62] The ECE's views were articulated in its series of annual reports, starting in the 1989/1990 *Economic Survey of Europe.*[63] Priority in the reform process, argued the ECE, should be given to the creation of the legal, financial, and institutional framework that was essential for the operation of a competitive market economy. A substantial amount of technical assistance from Western sources should be channeled to institution-building. The liberalization of prices and trade should proceed at a more gradual pace, as was done in Western Europe after World War II. The ECE also proposed the creation of a currency payments union, citing the precedent of the European Payments Union. It further suggested the continuation and strengthening of a free trade area among the former centrally planned countries as a step in the direction of greater opening to the outside world.

On privatization, the ECE recommended a gradualist approach, starting with legal and institutional reform and beginning with small enterprises. It warned of the risk of "hijacking" public assets and property by privileged groups—the "risk that social assets would be sold off at prices that would imply large transfers of wealth either to old managers and to former members of the *nomenklatura* or to newcomers from the west."[64] The ECE advocated a Marshall Plan for the former centrally planned countries with a focus on technical assistance for building the legal and institutional foundations of a capitalist system and stressed the need for proper sequencing, as opposed to a "big bang" or "one-leap" approach to transforming the economic system.

Nevertheless, the policies advocated by the Bretton Woods institutions and Western advisors carried the day. There were many reasons for this outcome. The most important undoubtedly was the fact that these institutions and Western countries controlled the bulk of the resources needed for programs of reform and transformation. In contrast, the ECE and the UN generally could at best provide technical assistance. Another important reason was that the new governments that came to power in many of these countries were profoundly anti-communist and wished to move as rapidly as possible to the Western capitalist systems they so admired. Their perceptions of the changes needed were often similar to those of the Bretton Woods institutions. At the same time, the Western countries as well as the postcommunist regimes regarded the ECE with suspicion as a remnant of the old system. Indeed, the ECE itself recommended that another institution take the responsibility for technical work and coordinating assistance to these countries![65]

The social, economic, and political costs of the policies followed in these countries in the transition phase were heavy. These consisted not only of abrupt decreases in production and employment, destruction of social security systems, and a sharp rise in poverty but often also of wars and violence and an increase in crime and corruption. No one will ever know for certain whether these costs could have been avoided and whether a more orderly transition to democracy and capitalism might have taken place under a different set of policies such as those proposed by the ECE. It is, however, pertinent to note that the gradual and more carefully sequenced approach to economic reform in China and Vietnam yielded dramatically different results and much more positive outcomes for social and economic development.

Box 6.3. From Socialism to Transition with Chinese Characteristics

China was the first country in the developing world to adopt a socialist economy. In 1949, when the communists came to power, the economy was devastated. The communist government's first priority was to restore production and curb inflation. By 1953, the economy had recovered and was growing rapidly. The Party initially adopted a gradualist approach to socialization. Landlords were dispossessed and the land distributed to the landless and poor peasants. The first steps in the socialization of agriculture consisted of mutual-aid teams and the pooling of some resources in cooperatives. The year 1955 marked a watershed. The collectivization of agriculture was accelerated and commerce and industry were nationalized. By 1959, the socialization of the economy was largely completed; state-owned industry, commerce, and agriculture were organized through communes and production brigades and teams.

In 1958–1960, the Great Leap Forward represented an effort to give maximum autonomy to provinces and counties and to push production and investment to their limits. The experiment ended in a disaster with a famine that is estimated to have killed more than 30 million people. This was followed by recentralization of planning and resource allocation. The Cultural Revolution after 1966 represented another massive effort to destroy the dominance of bureaucracy and industrial managers and to shift power to peasants and the working class. The destruction wrought by this upheaval constituted a major setback to production and living standards.[66]

There was a major reorientation of Chinese development strategy in the years following Mao's death in 1976. The reformers began with the decollectivization of agriculture. Gradually the production teams and brigades gave way to a household-responsibility system under which families became de facto tenants with long leases. Farmers were given greater freedom to choose and market their crops. Prices of agricultural products were raised significantly over the 1976–1983 period. All of this contributed to a sharp increase in rural incomes and agricultural output.

The reform was extended in the 1980s to all sectors of the economy. Private small enterprises were allowed in manufacturing, commerce, and services. Foreign private capital was welcomed with various incentives, initially only in large cities and special export zones but later extended to other parts of the country. Imports were liberalized, foreign exchange regulations were simplified, and a new banking system was created that separated the central bank from commercial banks. There was a shift to export-oriented industrialization. Greater autonomy was given to provinces and localities in revenue collection and spending. Most important, a process of price reform began in 1985 that over the next decade freed most of the products from price control.

The post-reform period witnessed stupendous growth and a sharp reduction in poverty in the first decade, but the improvement in social indicators has not kept pace with the tempo of the economy. The strategy of development pursued by China over the past two decades shares many characteristics with the export-oriented industrialization strategies of the "Old Tigers," but the sheer size of the country and the key role still played by state enterprises set it apart from them. Thus, by the end of the 1990s, the economy was driven by market forces, the share of private production had risen sharply, direct foreign investment had become important, and manufactured exports had increased dramatically. China's importance as a trading nation and its conversion to the market system was recognized by its admission to the World Trade Organization in 2001.

While China's growth performance has been outstanding, especially over the past two decades, its social achievements were more impressive over the first three decades. The living standards of the poorer sections of the Chinese population rose substantially in the early years after the revolution—the result of increased production and access to food (due to land redistribution), consumption of other essential commodities that were rationed, and the rapid expansion of literacy, primary health care, and basic education. In particular, women and girls experienced a major improvement in their status and welfare. The commune system provided a minimum of social security and assured access to food, health care, shelter, and schooling. It is not surprising that China's social indicators around the 1970s were way above the levels that corresponded to its per capita income. Although social indicators have continued to show improvements, the big improvement was made between the 1950s and 1970s. The rate of progress has shown a distinct decline in the period of economic reform.[67]

The Least-Developed Countries

The UN's work on development in the 1950s tended for the most part to focus on Latin American and the larger Asian and Middle Eastern countries. Most of the Asian and Arab countries became independent during this period. Although there was significant diversity in the structure and level of development among different groups of countries—for example, per capita income in West Asia in 1950 was double that of Latin America and nearly ten times that of South and East Asia[68]—a good deal of the analysis on economic problems and strategies treated underdeveloped countries as a homogeneous unit.

As many African countries attained independence in the 1960s, there was greater appreciation of the specific problems of underdevelopment they faced, which was reinforced by the establishment of the ECA and the Institut Africain de Développement Economique et de Planification (IDEP) in Dakar. Despite this new understanding of Africa's problems, much of the professional work in the UN continued to revolve around the threefold classification of developed-market, socialist centrally planned, and developing countries.

This tendency was reinforced by the establishment of the Group of 77 (G-77) on the occasion of the first UNCTAD in 1964.[69] Although the G-77 attempted to incorporate the concerns and priorities of all its regional groups, many of its proposals on trade, foreign investment, transnational corporations, and transfer of technology, for instance, were inevitably of greater interest to the more advanced among the developing countries.

Nevertheless, the UN showed a special sensitivity to the problems its economically weakest members faced. As early as the 1950s, the UN published three reports on the economies and development problems of African colonies.[70] At the first UNCTAD session in 1964, attention was given to the "less developed among the developing countries." The first resolution on the least-developed countries was adopted at UNCTAD II in 1968.[71] The Second UN

Development Decade contained special measures in favor of LDCs. Two expert groups were set up by UNCTAD in 1969 and 1971 to examine the special features of the economies of LDCs, analyze the constraints to rapid growth, and sketch the elements of a development strategy embodying national and international measures.[72] The CDP was asked to suggest criteria for the identification of LDCs.[73] Based on this work and that carried out by UNCTAD, the General Assembly approved the list of the LDCs in 1971. The criteria suggested by the CDP included per capita GDP of $100 or less per annum (in 1968 dollars), a share of manufacturing in GDP of 10 percent or less, and adult literacy of 20 percent or less. However, the criteria for identification were updated and others were added over the years.

Twenty-four countries were on the original list of the least-developed countries in 1971.[74] In subsequent years, countries were added, and by 1998, the LDCs consisted of forty-nine countries with a population of 614 million, accounting for about just over 10 percent of the population of the world and just over 13 percent of the population of developing countries. Botswana was the only country that had graduated out of the list of the LDCs.

Overall, the economic performance and social indicators of the least-developed countries have lagged well behind those of other developing countries over the past two decades. Thus, while the per capita GDP in the LDCs in 1980 was 30.5 percent of that in all developing countries, it had fallen to 22.8 percent by 1998. Population growth in other developing countries slowed down from 2.3 percent per annum over 1960–1970 to 1.7 during 1990–1997. In the LDCs, it rose from 2.4 to 2.6 over the same period.

The presence of the LDCs as a distinct group is now well established institutionally in the UN system—though not formally in that of the Bretton Woods institutions.[75] UNCTAD has created a department devoted to work on issues of interest to the LDCs. A committee of UNCTAD entitled the Inter-Governmental Group on the Least Developed Countries has been meeting regularly since 1975 to discuss their problems, review progress made, and identify emerging critical issues. UNCTAD also publishes an annual report on the LDCs. The WTO has set up a working party on the LDCs. It has evolved a special technical assistance program to help them in their work relating to multilateral trade agreements and negotiations relating to the adhesion to the WTO of nonmembers among them. Specialized UN agencies recognize the LDC category and are devoting an increasing proportion of their resources to assist them.

The experience of the LDCs with regard to trade, development assistance, and foreign investment has been quite disappointing since the 1980s. Their share of world exports, already very low at 0.4 percent, has declined further. The LDCs, in contrast to other developing countries, have relied heavily upon concessional resource flows. In 1985, concessional loans and grants accounted for over 96 percent of all financial flows to the LDCs. This share had declined to over 84 percent by 1998. For all developing countries, the corresponding figures were 71 and 26 percent. Over the period 1985–1998, total financial flows to all developing countries in current dollars rose from over $45 billion to $191 billion. The bulk of this increase came from nonconcessional, mostly private, resource flows that jumped from $13 billion in 1985 to $141 billion in 1998.[76]

The situation had also deteriorated on the debt front. The total external debt nearly doubled between 1985 and 1998, rising from $71.3 to $138.7 billion. As a proportion of the GDP of the LDCs, external debt rose from 61 to 85 percent. On the other hand, thanks in part to debt-service rescheduling and accumulated arrears, the burden of debt service decreased somewhat over the period from $4.546 billion in 1985 to $4.162 billion in 1998. As a proportion of exports of goods and services, the debt-service ratio halved from 30 to 15 percent. This appears to have been the only point of relief in an otherwise extremely dismal picture of the external economic relations of the LDCs.[77]

Since 1981, three UN world conferences have been held to deal specifically with the problems faced by the LDCs and the measures that can be taken at national and global levels to accelerate their progress and integration into the global economy. The 1981 conference in Paris was followed by a second in Paris in 1990 and a third in Brussels in 2001.

Three International Conferences: Commitments and Performance

The growing gap between the economic and social performance of the LDCs and the other developing countries became a matter of increasing concern to the international community after the 1970s. This concern was reflected in the three major international conferences on the LDCs held since 1981. These conferences brought together UN member states, international and regional agencies, the business community, and voluntary development and humanitarian organizations. Their purpose was to agree on a comprehensive and integrated set of measures for accelerated development and more beneficial integration of the LDCs into the world economy. The LDCs and the donor community assumed joint commitment and responsibility in carrying out these measures. Notwithstanding, the outcome in terms of strengthening international support and accelerating social and economic development in the LDCs has been bitterly disappointing. The fragmentation of the Third World has proceeded apace. Most LDCs are increasingly marginalized in the world community, they experience declining living standards, and they suffer disproportionately from natural disasters and violent conflicts.

Many of these countries have made valiant efforts to undertake economic reforms under the tutelage of the World Bank, the IMF, and the regional development agencies. But, as argued cogently by UNCTAD in its 2000 report on the least-developed countries, these reforms have often not addressed the core problems in these countries.[78] They have far too often consisted of standard packages of economic liberalization, privatization, and deregulation that the Bretton Woods institutions have crafted for all developing and transition economies. And for the most part, the donor community has failed to live up to its commitments in the fields of trade, aid, technology, and other areas.

The 1981 conference on the LDCs was preceded by intensive work in UNCTAD on the problems of the LDCs, priority areas for assistance, and an action plan. The fifth session of UNCTAD in Manila in June 1979 proposed a comprehensive and substantially expanded program in two phases: an Immediate Action Program (IAP; 1979–1981) and a Substantial New Program of Action (SNPA).[79] It also proposed the convening of an international conference to finalize, adopt, and support the SNPA. The General Assembly decided in 1979 to act upon this recommendation.

The 1981 conference adopted a comprehensive plan of action to accelerate economic and social development in the twenty-one LDCs at the time.[80] The objective of the SNPA was to "transform their economies toward self-sustained development and enable them to provide at least internationally accepted minimum standards of nutrition, health, transport and communications, housing and education, as well as job opportunities, to all their citizens, and particularly to the rural and urban poor."[81] It proposed as targets an annual growth rate in the 1980s of 7.2 percent per annum. The SNPA set out policy measures and projects relating to agriculture and the production of food, human resources and social development, industry, and the environment.

These measures were to be accompanied by a supportive international environment. The conference proposed that 0.15 percent of GDP in rich countries should be allocated to the LDCs, which would double development assistance to them by 1985 compared with 1975–1980. The conference also accepted proposals relating to commodity agreements, liberalization of market access for LDC exports, debt relief, and transfer of technology on easier terms.

The 1990 conference was held under the shadow of a deepening crisis in the LDCs, which was affecting many other countries in Africa, Latin America, and Asia. It followed the onset of the debt crisis and the widespread adoption of stabilization and structural-adjustment policies initiated by the Bretton Woods institutions with support from bilateral donors. The conference was preceded by the preparation of development programs by each of the LDCs with the help, where necessary, of multilateral agencies and the convening of regional conferences. Its outcome was contained in the Paris Declaration and the conference's program of action.[82] As in the 1981 conference, the program of action covered all areas and sectors, including food production and security, rural development, human resource development, industry, transport, and communications as well as international dimensions.

On macroeconomic policy, the conference recommended that the LDCs take into account market signals while aiming at accelerating long-term growth and show concern for the most vulnerable groups of the population.[83] Much stress was laid on partnership between the LDCs and the international community. Reflecting the new themes of the time, the conference stressed respect for human rights, women's equality, observance of the rule of law, and promotion of transparency and accountability.

On international measures, the rich countries took an extremely cautious attitude. On bilateral debt, the LDCs were asked to negotiate at the Paris Club. On debt owed to multilateral financial agencies, they were invited to pay attention to alleviating the burden of their debt. Similarly, on access to market for the LDCs' exports, the conference stressed that special attention should be given to LDC needs within the framework of the Uruguay Round.[84] On development assistance, it did not prove possible to achieve any agreement on a target—a regression from the 1981 SNPA. Donor countries were invited to choose among four options on development assistance. Those who had reached 0.20 percent of GDP in assistance to the LDCs would seek to reach a higher figure. Those in the 0.15 percent range were asked to increase it to 0.20 percent. Others would attempt to reach the 0.15 percent target. In the event, the share of ODA to the LDCs fell over the 1990s in eighteen Development Assistance Committee (DAC) countries and rose in only four. In 1990, eight donors exceeded the 0.15 percent target. By 2000, it was only five—and on average, DAC net ODA to the LDCs had fallen from 0.09 to 0.05 percent of gross national income.[85]

As seen above, most LDCs continued to lag behind the progress made by other developing countries in the 1990s, thereby further intensifying their marginalization in the world economy. No significant initiatives were taken in the fields of trade or technology transfer—indeed, the tightening of law on international property rights often made the situation much worse. In development assistance, there was a steady deterioration from the achievements of the 1980s. The share of aid to the LDCs fell from 0.09 percent of the GDP of rich countries in 1990 to 0.05 percent in 1998.[86] It was only in the area of debt relief that the introduction of the HIPCs held the promise of significant progress. But the positive effects of this relief for the group as a whole were greatly offset by declining development assistance and deteriorating terms of trade in most years in the 1990s. While the international environment moved against them, the LDCs themselves made a major effort to follow the policy prescriptions laid down by the Bretton Woods institutions. As stated by Rubens Ricupero, the secretary-general of UNCTAD:

> The record of the 1990s shows that there has been an accelerating process of economic liberalization in many LDCs. In fact 33 out of the 48 LDCs have undertaken policy reforms under the IMF-financed Structural Adjustment Facility (SAF) or Enhanced Structural Adjustment Facility (ESAF) since 1988. . . . As a consequence of these reforms, the policy environment in many LDCs changed significantly in the 1990s. IMF data actually show that trade liberalization has proceeded further in the LDCs than in other developing countries. In 1999, for 43 LDCs for which data are available, 37 per cent had average import tariff rates of below 20 per cent coupled with no or minor non-tariff barriers, while amongst the 78 other developing countries in the sample, only 23 per cent had this degree of openness. . . . Similarly, UNCTAD data for the late 1990s show that, in a sample of 45 LDCs, only 9 maintain strict controls on remittances of dividends and profits and capital repatriation. Twenty-seven LDCs have adopted a free regime, guaranteeing such transfers, whilst nine have a relatively free regime.[87]

It was against this background of the deteriorating situation in the LDCs that the General Assembly approved the holding of the Third International Conference on the Least Developed Countries in Brussels in May 2001. The preparatory process included forty-five country plans of action, regional conferences, and two preparatory conferences in New York. The outcome of the conference consisted of the Declaration of Brussels and a program of action.[88] As with the 1991 conference, the Brussels conference reviewed the progress made in the LDCs over the past ten years, evaluated the implementation of agreed-upon measures by the LDCs and the international community, and proposed targets, policies, and programs for the period 2001–2010.

While there was much common ground between the two conferences, the 2001 conference differed from LDCII in Paris in 1990 in at least four respects. First, there was a much stronger sense of partnership and mutual responsibility in 2001 than there had been ten years earlier. Second, the representation and participation of civil-society, business, women's, and youth groups were more vigorous. Third, the program of action was more comprehensive and far more detailed than it had been in 1991. It spelled out in considerable detail the policy and program commitments made by the LDCs and the international community. Fourth, the industrial countries went much farther than before in committing themselves to specific measures to help accelerate the development of the LDCs.

The program of action took an integrated and comprehensive view of development, drawing upon the results of the series of world conferences of the 1990s, and proposed a vast array of national and international measures in all areas affecting human well-being and economic development. These measures emphasized a people-centered development approach, good governance at national and international levels, gender equality, health, education, development of a skilled labor force, development of the physical infrastructure, development of business enterprises, technology, energy, agriculture, food, industry, trade, the environment and natural disasters, mobilization of domestic resources, debt, foreign aid, investment, and the promotion of exports.

The developed countries went farther and were more specific in their commitments than they had been at the 1990 Paris meeting. They recommitted themselves to the development-assistance targets agreed upon in Paris, and a number of countries announced increases in their aid programs. The OECD unveiled its initiative to untie aid to the LDCs after 2002. The developed countries made a commitment to provide adequate resources for the speedy and full implementation of the enhanced HIPC Initiative and to make rapid progress toward full cancellation of outstanding official bilateral debt.[89]

In the field of trade, the European Union agreed to extend duty-free quota-free treatment to all LDC products except arms.[90] It also announced a multilateral initiative to forego exporting below market prices in relation to the LDCs. Several countries also announced increases in technical assistance in the areas of export promotion, trade negotiations, and accession to the WTO. The conference also agreed to make the process of WTO accession less onerous and more tailored to the specific economic conditions of the LDCs. A number of measures were announced by developed countries, the business sector, and multilateral agencies to promote investment, develop enterprises, and strengthen technological capabilities.[91] The extent to which these and other commitments will be implemented in the coming years remains to be seen.

Concluding Remarks

The continuing deprivation and marginalization of the LDCs, especially in sub-Saharan Africa, has become one of the most important, if not the most important, issue on the international agenda for development. The UN can take credit for recognizing it as an important issue for international discussions and action as far back as the late 1960s. In that sense, the UN was surely "ahead of the curve." This recognition was followed by a whole series of measures to keep the problems of the LDCs before the world community and to fashion a comprehensive strategy that included national and international measures to promote the economic and social progress of these nations. The fact that these efforts have not generally been successful is in some considerable measure due to the failure of the developed countries to live up to their commitments with regard to development assistance, debt relief, trade, and related areas. The terms of trade have also been quite unfavorable for the LDCs over most of the years in the past two decades. While political instability, civil conflicts, mismanagement, and corruption in some LDCs have no doubt constituted serious obstacles to progress, in the 1990s, the LDCs on the whole have had a better record of economic reform than other developing countries, especially with regard to liberalization of prices, marketing, trade, and payments—though weaker regulatory capacity may have caused problems with implementation.

In its 2000 report, UNCTAD challenged the adequacy of the reform agenda that was largely fashioned by the Bretton Woods institutions to come to grips with the problems confronted by LDC countries. It criticized as major obstacles to sustained growth and development the exclusive focus on economic liberalization and structural adjustment, the inadequacy and uncertainty of aid flows, the poor quality and coordination of delivery of aid, the scale of debt relief, and the erosion of government capacity. It is best to quote the critique of these policies from the UNCTAD report:

> [T]he policies currently recommended have serious design shortcomings in the context of LDC-type economies. These go beyond the past insufficient attention to social issues. In short, they have neglected the impact of structural constraints, lack of social and economic infrastructure, weakness of market development, the thinness of the entrepreneurial class, and low private sector production capabilities.[92]

The UNCTAD report went on to underline the consequences of this devastating critique.

> The sustainability of economic growth stemming from these reforms is questionable in most countries. . . . The lack of coordination among the activities of various aid agencies and the failure to integrate their projects into domestic economic and managerial structures have undermined the sustainability of aid projects. . . . [T]he fragmented aid delivery system, administered by multiple donors, has profoundly disrupted the resource allocation mechanisms in these countries, with serious negative consequences for economic management, the overall efficiency of resource use, and economic growth in general. . . . Aid effectiveness has also been undermined by the external debt burden. This has reduced public and private investment within recipient countries, and also had negative effects on the allocation and use of aid by the international creditor-donor community.[93]

Moreover, the prospects for expecting major change from the special efforts on debt relief were questioned:

> Current expectations regarding the implementation of the enhanced HIPC Initiative are unrealistic. The scale of debt relief will prove insufficient to ensure debt sustainability in the medium term unless external conditions are very favourable and economic performance under policy reform somehow improves; moreover, the magnitude of debt relief, and its manner of delivery, will not have major direct effect on poverty reduction, although it does provide a vehicle for promoting the adoption of pro-poor policies within poor countries.[94]

UNCTAD set out an alternative strategy for sustainable development in the LDCs, constructed from its analysis of the weaknesses in the existing system. The main elements of the UNCTAD alternative approach included:

- Need to strengthen productive capacities and international competitiveness and promote diversification out of the narrowly specialized primary product economies.
- Greater reliance on markets and private initiative along with measures to overcome shortcomings of markets, institutions and infrastructure.
- Need to support domestic reform efforts by adequate external finance. External resources would need to be more than doubled for sub-Saharan Africa to achieve the goal of reducing poverty by half by 2015.
- Increased aid flows must be accompanied by efforts by both the LDCs and their development partners to enhance aid effectiveness. The implementation of partnership based on genuine national ownership is vital for success in development. This requires that countries themselves must establish comprehensive and coherent budgets and medium-term expenditure plans with necessary transparency, accountability and realism.
- Need for deeper, faster and broader debt relief based on lower thresholds for judging debt sustainability, more realistic forecasts of economic growth, exports and imports.
- Need to exploit the potential for increasing the positive synergies between international policies towards LDCs in the domains of aid, debt reduction, international trade and the promotion of private capital flows.[95]

We cannot conclude this chapter in a better way than to repeat what the respected Canadian development economist Gerry Helleiner said: "The neo-liberal thrust was a reaction to previous over-reliance on the state and the direction of the reaction was appropriate. But it was overdone. The legacy of the neo-liberal thrust of the 1980's will be close to zero. They moved things back in the right direction but greatly overshot."[96]

7

The 1990s: Rediscovering a Human Vision

- **The Development Context**
- **Human Rights and Development**
- **National and Global Governance**
- **Human Development: A New Integrating Framework?**
- **The Impact of World Conferences**
- **Concluding Observations**

For development, the 1990s were years of backlash, adjustment, and public relations. Some efforts were made to rein in the extremes of policy prescriptions of the 1980s and strike a balance with the concerns and approaches that had dominated development policy in the preceding decades. There was a strong and widespread upsurge of interest in human rights and good governance. The UN made an effort to regain some of its lost authority as a leading force in development, primarily by convening a series of international conferences on some of the most critical social and economic problems facing the peoples of the world. In 1992, the Secretary-General published *An Agenda for Peace*[1] and three years later *An Agenda for Development.*[2]

This chapter addresses human rights and good governance. It considers the links between human rights and development, the emerging issues relating to governance, and efforts made in the UN system to provide a unifying framework through its work on human development. The chapter concludes with an assessment of the contribution made by the UN world conferences in building a blueprint for goals, strategies, and policies for global social and economic development in the first decade of the twenty-first century.

The Development Context

The context for UN initiatives in the 1990s was set by three major developments—the end of the Cold War, the upsurge of globalization, and reaction to the lost decade of the 1980s, which had exacerbated the problems of poverty in most countries of the developing world. Each of these had direct repercussions for development policy.

The collapse of the communist states in Europe dealt serious blows to what remained of development doctrines that emphasized the role of central planning, nonprice mechanisms for resource allocation, and state ownership of enterprises. The obvious failures of central planning in the former Soviet Union boosted the neoliberal agenda of the Washington Consensus.[3] Second, the end of the Cold War further eroded the declining influence of the developing countries, as the great powers no longer felt the need to court their support. Among other consequences, this reinforced the decline in development assistance, belying the hopes of those who expected that some dividends from the disarmament process would flow into development assistance. On the positive side, interest in issues of human rights and democracy revived.

The acceleration in globalization was in part the intensification of trends that had been under way in the preceding decades. But the revolution in information technology and communications and striking advances in capital mobility, trade liberalization, and internationalization of production made it a qualitatively different phenomenon. Globalization represented an opportunity to increase the pace of social and economic progress in some countries and a threat of marginalization in others. Over the 1990s, inequalities between the richest and poorest countries—and between the world's richest and poorest peoples—soared, creating gaps between the fortunate minority and the deprived majority which were both gargantuan and grotesque.[4] Measures to deal with these gaps were not even on the agenda, but growing awareness spurred renewed efforts to deal with world poverty.

The lost decade of the 1980s was a major setback to development not only in Latin America but also in Africa and the Middle East. The list of adversely affected countries was further lengthened in the 1990s by catastrophic economic and social trends in most of the former centrally planned countries in Europe and the Soviet Union. Increasing impoverishment and deprivation raised serious doubts about the efficacy of neoliberal policies to promote broad-based growth.[5] There was a renewal of interest in strategies for poverty reduction and human development that led to a series of world conferences in the 1990s dealing with the welfare and development of children, the environment, human rights, population, social development, equality for women, habitat, and nutrition.

These conferences went farther than those of the 1970s in forging the links between their various themes and development. They also sought a synthesis between neoliberal ideas and poverty-reduction strategies. Thus, the declarations of principle and programs of action adopted at these conferences gave

Box 7.1. Ghana

The development experience of Ghana over the past fifty years is a dramatic story. Ghana boasts of many firsts in sub-Saharan Africa. The first to achieve independence, the first to embark on a state-led industrialization strategy, among the first to declare a one-party state, and probably the first to totally reverse past policies in favor of liberalization and privatization. Politically, the country has been through four republics, a one-party socialist state, four military coups d'etat, two brief civilian administrations, and two decades of authoritarian rule, ending up with a plural democratic system since 1992.

Economically, Ghana in the 1950s was among the most advanced in Africa, with abundant natural resources, an educated elite, and an enterprising peasantry. It entered the 1980s with one of the most disastrous economic performances in Africa, but since embarking on reforms has been held up once again, at least for a decade or so, as a model for other African countries.

In 1983, the second administration of Jerry Rawlings undertook wide-ranging economic reforms with the support of the World Bank, the IMF, and donor countries. Over the next seventeen years, the government, led by Rawlings (first as military ruler and after 1992 as elected president), persisted with reforms in all aspects of social and economic policy. A major element of the reform program was divestiture of state enterprises. During 1989–1992, a total of fifty-two out of 350 state enterprises were divested, twenty-six of which were liquidated because they had negative value. Between 1983 and 1999, 149 enterprises were liquidated or sold off or entered into partnership with other firms. Most of the enterprises sold were small and medium-sized, and the majority were sold to Ghanaian nationals.[6]

In 1986, to offset the adverse social impact of stabilization and adjustment policies, especially staff retrenchment and measures to recover the costs of health and education, the government introduced the much-talked-about Programme of Action to Mitigate the Social Costs of Adjustment (PAMSCAD), which amounted to $84 million over a two-year period.[7] The program was only partially successful.

The reform program was underpinned by a major expansion of external finance from the Bretton Woods institutions and the donor community. Although in many areas, reform remains incomplete and there have been reversals of steps already taken, on the whole, the program over the past seventeen years represents a decisive break with the policies pursued between 1961 and 1983. Ghana's GDP expanded by 5.1 percent between 1983 (a drought year) and 1990. It has grown by 4.3 percent per annum in the 1990s—a big reversal of the trends since the 1960s.[8] The incidence of poverty is estimated to have declined from 36 percent in 1991/1992 to 29 in 1998/1999.[9] But with regard to social indicators, there is no evidence of any marked improvement in the post-reform years. Per capita income in 2000 was still below the 1960 level.

prominence to appropriate macroeconomic policies, reliance on markets, and the role of private enterprise, foreign investment, and trade liberalization. But they also emphasized the universal provision of social services, the restructuring of public taxation and spending, employment-creation schemes, allocation of credit to low-income groups, agrarian reform, programs for small farmers and informal-sector workers, promotion of children's welfare and development, and empowerment of women and indigenous groups. The conferences adopted a series of goals and targets in the areas of their concern.

Many of the most basic of these goals dealing with poverty, human development, and gender equality were reiterated in the OECD Declaration on Development Assistance[10] adopted in 1996. Its importance was that for the first time the rich countries committed themselves in their own club to precise quantitative goals in the domain of social development. The UNDP Human Development Office contributed a key paper that had a marked influence on the declaration adopted by the ministers from the OECD countries.[11] The Millennium Declaration adopted by the heads of state and government of UN member states in September 2000 reiterated some of these goals.[12]

Human Rights and Development

As we have often emphasized, the UN, from the outset, placed respect for human rights at the core of its concerns. The Universal Declaration of Human Rights is one of the most inspiring international documents of the twentieth century. It has played a fundamental role in influencing thinking at the global and national levels in the domains of politics, economics, and social policy. Since the adoption of the declaration more than fifty years ago, the UN has undertaken a great deal of work to further elaborate the content of human rights, to develop a variety of instruments to influence legislation and practice human rights at the national level, and to create institutions and procedures within the system to encourage the implementation of such instruments.[13]

A mention of the principal human rights instruments brings out the scope and range of the UN work in this area. The Universal Declaration of Human Rights was adopted by the General Assembly in 1948[14] along with the Convention on the Prevention and Punishment of the Crime of Genocide.[15] The following year saw the adoption of the Convention for the Suppression of the Traffic in Persons and of the Exploitation of the Prostitution of Others.[16] The year 1951 saw the adoption of the Convention on the Status of Refugees.[17] From an early period, the UN has been much concerned about the deprivations suffered by women and children. The Convention on the Political Rights of Women was adopted in 1952[18] and the Convention on Consent to Marriage, Minimum

Age for Marriage and Registration of Marriages was adopted in 1962.[19] A land-
mark instrument in this regard was the Convention on the Elimination of All
Forms of Discrimination against Women in 1979.[20] The 1959 Declaration of the
Rights of the Child was followed by a convention in 1989.[21]

In 1966, the General Assembly adopted the International Covenants on
Civil and Political Rights and Economic, Social and Cultural Rights.[22] These
covenants "constitute the most extensive corpus of international . . . law on
the subject, both in terms of the areas . . . and in terms of their geographical
scope."[23] Other important conventions adopted by the General Assembly include the International Convention on the Elimination of All Forms of Racial
Discrimination (1965),[24] the Convention against Torture and Other Cruel,
Inhuman or Degrading Treatment or Punishment (1984),[25] and the International Convention on the Suppression and Punishment of the Crime of Apart-
heid (1973).[26] Instruments have also been adopted to promote the rights of
minorities,[27] indigenous people,[28] and migrant workers.[29]

After ten years of discussion, the Declaration on the Right to Development
was adopted by the General Assembly in 1986.[30] A working group within the
Centre for Human Rights of the UN Office of the High Commissioner for
Human Rights has been meeting to discuss the next steps to give weight to the
declaration.[31] While some progress has been made, because of the nature of
the topic, it has not yet been possible to reach agreement on the formulation
of policies and programs that need to be implemented and the respective
rights and responsibilities of different parties.[32]

While the UN can boast of an impressive body of work to promote human
rights on a global basis, much less discussion has taken place on the relationship of human rights to its work on social and economic development. In general, work on human rights and on development has proceeded on parallel
paths with few meeting points. At first sight, this seems paradoxical because the
UN work on human rights has covered social, political, economic, and cultural
domains. Indeed, the very first and the most famous document on the subject—the Universal Declaration of Human Rights—provides a comprehensive
and integrated treatment of all kinds of human rights. It treats them as indivis-
ible and inalienable. The Covenant on Civil and Political Rights and the Covenant on Economic, Social, and Cultural Rights further elaborate rights in these
domains. Any work on implementation of the major human rights conventions immediately leads to a consideration of legal instruments, institutions,
and policies to promote these rights whether they relate to children, women,
minorities, migrants, or the general public. Indeed, any artificial distinctions
between different types of rights and legal action and development policies disappear in the context of the concrete reality of daily life.

The separation of the two approaches can be explained to some extent by the disciplinary biases of economists and lawyers; the professions of economics and law have been dominant in the discussions on development and human rights, respectively. For instance, the early work on development in the UN focused largely on how to raise savings and investment and improve technology and productivity. While the general objectives of development were always mentioned, as was the importance of an enabling environment, little attempt was made to link them to the UN instruments on human rights. Although the subsequent approaches based on employment and meeting basic human needs specified objectives in terms that could have been lifted from the Universal Declaration and the two covenants, few analysts made the connection between them. Indeed, the discussions on development objectives and policies were conducted almost totally separate from the human rights vocabulary. The shift in development strategy toward neoliberal policies only tended to increase this distance because these discussions were couched in even more technical and narrow terminology.

Similar isolationist trends characterized the discussion on human rights. This isolation became even more pronounced with the growing divergence between the adherents of civil and political rights and adherents of social, economic, and cultural rights. This divergence coalesced around the ideological divides of the Cold War and, to some extent, differing North-South priorities. The outcome was a long period of stagnation when the discussions on the two great themes went their separate ways.

It is only recently, assisted by the end of the Cold War, that serious discussions have taken place on the interdependence of different types of human rights and between advocates of development and advocates of human rights. The world conferences of the 1990s have attempted within their declarations and programs of action to bring together the two strands of thinking. The Vienna Conference on Human Rights sought to forge links between human rights and development when it stated that "the existence of widespread extreme poverty inhibits the full and effective enjoyment of human rights."[33]

One of the first analytical discussions of these interrelationships in the UN context took place in the UNDP's 2000 report on human rights and human development.[34] The ILO director-general's conceptualization of decent work is also an attempt to fuse the agency's long-standing concerns with development and workers' rights into a unifying framework.[35]

The concept of decent work includes fundamental rights of workers, remunerative employment, social security, and social dialogue. Thus, it links development objectives such as adequate and remunerative work opportunities and security against the risks of unemployment, sickness, and old age with the civil and political rights of freedom of association, nondiscrimination in work, and freedom from forced labor. In the words of the ILO's director-general: "The primary goal of the ILO today is to promote opportunities for women and men to obtain decent and productive work, in conditions of freedom, equity, security and human dignity."[36]

The links between the two themes—human rights and development—are self-evident and multiple. Just to mention the most important ones, many development objectives such as health, education, nutrition, safe drinking water, sanitation, and work have been incorporated in major human rights instruments such as the Universal Declaration and the two covenants. Further, in many situations the "development rights" of the type mentioned above and the "classical rights" are mutually supportive and reinforcing.

Better health and education enable people to benefit from civil and political rights. These rights in turn help in the struggle to obtain social and economic rights. Expressing it negatively, denial of basic freedoms and equality before the law is at the root of many violent conflicts that threaten all hopes of realizing economic and social rights. Likewise, illiteracy, malnutrition, and disease impede the realization of civil and political rights. More generally, there is now growing recognition that the rights of freedom of speech, association, and religion and equality before law are crucial components of an enabling framework and constitute the core of good governance. These in turn are increasingly considered to be central to broad-based growth and poverty reduction.

Box 7.2. Sri Lanka: Combining Social Progress with Economic Liberalization

Despite a prolonged civil war, Sri Lanka is one of the very few developing countries to have maintained a plural democratic system with respect for fundamental human rights and an independent judiciary over the past fifty years. It was among the first countries in the developing world, and the first in South Asia, to implement measures of economic liberalization. It has been fairly successful in its effort to combine stabilization and adjustment with preservation of key social programs and policies. It has achieved moderate but not outstanding rates of economic growth over the past fifty years.

Sri Lanka has from the 1950s been a leader in the field of social development. Its indicators of infant mortality, life expectancy, literacy, and schooling have been among the best in the developing world. There has been a political consensus among the parties to maintain free education and health services. The share of resources devoted to education and health has fluctuated around 4 to 6 percent of GDP for most of the postwar period, with lower percentages in the 1990s, in part because of increased defense costs over the past two decades. Life expectancy rose from 55.6 in 1950 to 65.6 in 1970 and 72.5 in 1990. Infant mortality halved from 141 in 1945 to 71 in 1953. This was described by the WHO as the sharpest drop in mortality ever recorded. Infant mortality fell further to 57 in 1960, 34 in 1980, and 16 in 1998. Adult literacy, already high at 58 percent in 1945, rose to 77 in 1960, 83 in 1980, and 87 in 1995, and disparities in literacy rates by gender are small. There has been nearly universal primary schooling since the late 1960s.[37]

Sri Lanka has had a relatively even income distribution. The degree of equality improved further in the 1960s: the share of national income that went to the poorest 40 percent rose from 15 percent in 1963 to 19 percent in 1970, while that of the top 10 percent declined from 41 to 30 percent.[38] Income inequality worsened after the adoption of measures of economic liberalization. While starvation and destitution have been wiped out in Sri Lanka for quite some time, poverty has remained at relatively high levels. It has been estimated that the incidence of poverty fluctuated between 25 and 30 percent for the period 1970 to 1985.[39] The World Bank estimates that the proportion of households living below the poverty line fell from 31 percent in 1985/1986 to 20 percent in 1990/1991 but rose to 25 percent in 1995/1996.[40]

Sri Lanka carried out major economic reforms starting in 1977, but these have been spread out over an extended period. Despite the escalation of costs associated with civil war, the country has been fairly successful in maintaining the universality of its health and education services. The economic reforms have attracted more foreign resources and have lifted the growth rate from around 3.1 percent per annum in the preceding two decades to over 5 percent in the post-reform period. But poverty has declined at a relatively slow pace and still affects every fourth or fifth family in the country.

The UNDP's Human Development Report (HDR) presents a subtle analysis of the relationship between human development and human rights, drawing directly on the work of Amartya Sen. Since both human development and human rights seek to "[guarantee] the basic freedoms that people have reason to value—the ideas of human development and those of human rights are linked in a compatible and complementary way."[41] Human rights represent claims on other people or institutions. This aspect of human rights adds a dimension to the human development approach, namely that others have duties to facilitate and enhance human development. It also brings with it the notion of accountability of the international community and governments for achievement of human development goals.

Furthermore, "individual [human] rights express the limits on the losses that individuals can permissibly be allowed to bear, even in the promotion of noble social goals."[42] In other words, outcomes are not independent of the means used to attain them. On the other side, the human development approach introduces the idea of scarcity of resources, the need to establish priorities, and sequencing of achievement in the promotion of human rights. Furthermore, "by adding the perspective of change and progress in conceptual and practical reasoning about human rights, human development can help to deepen the understanding and broaden the usefulness of the human rights approach."[43]

National and Global Governance

The 1990s also witnessed a heightening of concern with what are now called issues of governance. The term refers to a variety of themes such as human rights, rule of law, corruption, multiparty democracy, transparency, accountability, institutional development, and people's participation. The concern with good governance was stimulated by the end of the Cold War and the explosion of ethnic, religious, and regional conflicts in a large number of developing countries. The growth and strengthening of civil-society institutions have also been important contributory factors, as has been the increasing realization that governance issues are central to economic and social progress. Their importance in international thinking is reflected in the documents issued by the world conferences in the 1990s and in the official statements of bilateral donors and the Bretton Woods institutions. The UN has dealt with these issues mostly in the context of human rights. But a number of agencies, including the UNDP and the UN Secretariat, have developed practical programs to assist with improvements in governance.[44]

The governance issues are not confined to the national level. The developing countries and civil-society organizations have for decades demanded major reforms in global institutions and mechanisms for decision making. The call for an NIEO in the 1970s was their most ambitious attempt to change global governance in a more equitable way. In 1994, an independent Commission on Global Governance explored a major set of challenges and made wide-ranging proposals for reform relating to world institutions in the domains of security, politics, the economy, development, and the environment.[45] Numerous studies and reports have been prepared touching on various aspects of global governance.[46]

Global governance is much bigger than the reform of the UN system or even of the Bretton Woods institutions, although it is obviously related to it. Former UN Secretary-General Boutros Boutros-Ghali maintains that "we must prepare a third generation type of international organizations; the first was

Box 7.3. The Commission on Global Governance

Early on, Willy Brandt saw the importance of political action regarding global governance to face major challenges that could be met only through coordinated multilateral action. He took the initiative, in January 1990, to bring together the members who had served on the North-South Commission (the Brandt Commission), the Independent Commission on Disarmament and Security Issues (the Palme Commission), the World Commission on Environment and Development (the Brundtland Commission), and the South Commission (chaired by Julius Nyerere).

At the end of that meeting, the participants asked Ingvar Carlsson (then prime minister of Sweden), Shridath Ramphal (then Commonwealth secretary-general), and Jan Pronk (then minister for development co-operation of the Netherlands) to prepare a report on global cooperation on issues requiring multilateral action.

This was followed up by the Stockholm Initiative on Global Security and Governance,[47] which proposed that an international commission be set up to explore the opportunities created by the end of the Cold War to build a more effective system of world security and governance. Ingvar Carlsson and Shridath Ramphal were invited to co-chair the commission. In April 1992, the co-chairs met with UN Secretary-General Boutros-Ghali to explain the purpose of the commission. He commended the initiative and assured them of his support.

The commission published its report in January 1995—at the start of the UN's fiftieth-anniversary year—calling it *Our Global Neighborhood:* a signal, they thought, of the kind of world that globalization and technological change were creating. It saw that title as a reasonable description of a physical reality. However, they were under no illusion that the neighborhood was wholly benign or that it was cohesive, integrated, or secure; what it reflected was the reality of a human community. But they saw that title as embodying an aspiration that a neighborhood could evolve in worthier ways—a fulfillment to which global governance had much to contribute.[48] The title *Our Global Neighborhood* echoed the new conventional wisdom that people now live in a global and interdependent world.

The report called for a shift in the vision of global governance to include civil-society organizations, transnational corporations, academia, and the mass media. It made clear that global governance was not global government. For the commission, governance was "the sum of the many ways individuals and institutions, public and private, manage their common affairs. It is a continuing process through which conflicting [and] diverse interests may be accommodated and co-operative action may be taken."[49]

the League of Nations, the second the United Nations; the third must include, next to governments, the non-state actors."[50] Hence, the challenge goes far beyond the streamlining of multilateral institutions. The speed and pattern of globalization, the existence of massive inequalities and widespread poverty, the explosive growth of world civil-society movements, the trends toward region-alization, the emphasis on democracy, participation, and accountability—these and other important developments have far-reaching implications for issues of global governance. No doubt they will figure prominently on the interna-tional agenda in the coming years and decades.

Human Development: A New Integrating Framework?

The world conferences of the 1990s provided a rough blueprint of the ac-tion needed at national and global levels to realize the universally agreed-upon social, economic, and political objectives. They did not and could not attempt to come out with new theories of development that synthesized dif-ferent approaches and perspectives.

A notable contribution in this regard was made by the series of Human Development Reports (HDRs) published annually by the UNDP beginning in 1990. While in some respects these reports simply helped to revive interest in the ideas associated with the basic-needs and employment-oriented ap-proaches to development of the 1970s and ideas of choice and identity which had long preoccupied sociologists, in at least four areas they helped advance thinking on development issues. First, the human development approach de-veloped a pioneering framework that integrated different development con-cerns and objectives. At the heart of this framework lay the notion of human capabilities, developed by Amartya Sen, which is in turn related to Sen's con-cept of "functionings" in different domains of human life and action. The basic purpose of development is to enhance human choices and the human capabilities to undertake activities which people have reason to value. Thus, development policies, Sen argued, should be dedicated to enhancing people's capabilities through improved nutrition, better health, literacy, training, and civil and political rights. These ideas of welfare, choice, capabilities, and functionings introduced new and important theoretical foundations to many familiar development objectives and policies.[51]

The second major contribution made by the HDRs was the construction of a simple measure to evaluate human development in different areas and countries. The HDR index—a composite of indicators of life expectancy, edu-cation, and income per capita—provided an alternative measure of social and economic progress and soon attracted widespread attention.[52] The index was extended to measure performance in other areas such as gender inequality, gender empowerment, and human poverty. This new framework helped generate both popular and professional interest in the ideas of human development. By the year 2002, over 120 countries had used the methodology to produce more than 400 human development reports focused on their own countries.

Third, as seen above, the human development reports integrated human rights and development objectives and strategy more clearly than even before. Human rights brought to human development concerns with duties and accountability as well as the tradition of legal tools and institutions. "Rights also lend moral legitimacy and the principle of social justice to the objectives of human development."[53] In turn, human development brings value added to the concepts of human rights: a dynamic long-term perspective to fulfilling them; attention to the socioeconomic context in which they can be realized; and the tools of human development which provide for systematic assessment of economic and institutional constraints as well as the policies and resource needs required to overcome those constraints.

The fourth contribution made by the HDRs was an analysis of the impact of different strategies and policies on human development. This work showed that human development and economic growth performance could vary significantly: some countries at low levels of economic development had high human development indices while some with high per capita GDPs had relatively low indices of human development. This naturally led to an exploration of the impact of different patterns of growth and economic and social policies on human development. The HDRs also attempted to analyze policies in many other areas from a human development perspective. These areas included trade, aid, foreign investment, the environment, technology, gender, and human rights. Although widely distributed, the HDRs apparently did not penetrate the bastions of international financial power. For instance, Jacques Polak, who spent a lifetime in the IMF, had this to say: "The Human Development Report is not put on the agenda of the Executive Board of the IMF. I doubt many people in this building have even looked at it. I don't think it is generally distributed even."[54]

The Impact of World Conferences

The world conferences were invented by the UN system in the 1970s. They fell into disuse in the 1980s but were revived in a big way in the 1990s with the convening of no less than ten world conferences on a wide variety of themes.[55] Four of these were summits that attracted growing numbers of heads of state and government—71 at the World Summit in 1990, 147 at the Millennium Summit in 2000.

A great deal of debate and controversy has surrounded these conferences and summits. Critics often dismiss them as extravagant and wasteful jamborees that provide social gatherings for the development elite in some of the world's most attractive cities along with opportunities for shopping and sight-seeing expeditions. According to these jaundiced views, the conferences achieved little or nothing either in terms of generating new ideas or in promoting adoption of sound policies by governments and international agencies. In contrast, proponents of the conferences emphasize their role as building blocks for integrated social and economic strategies at national and global levels. They give them much credit for raising political and media awareness of new global problems and influencing policy and action from the grassroots to the planetary level. What is the truth? Have the conferences incubated new ideas and triggered policy changes or have they been grand talking shops of no practical consequence? This section seeks to provide elements of a response to these questions through addressing three issues: contribution to ideas, mobilization of opinion and pressures for change, and impact on policy and action.

The impetus to convene world conferences generally came from the need to propagate and elaborate relatively new dimensions of development thinking, such as protection of the environment or the achievement of equality for women, or to respond to familiar but persistent problems, such as unemployment, hunger, shelter, population expansion, and the well-being of children. In the former case, the issues were generally raised first by the work of the specialists. For example, the concern with the environment was stimulated by the work of such authors as Rachel Carson and Donella Meadows.[56] On women's equality, there was a long tradition of feminist writing but not much on the role of women in development; Esther Boserup's work was a milestone.[57] Many other persistent world problems have received continuing attention in the literature and in policy since the early postwar years. The world conferences were designed to renew attention to these problems and to prompt national and international measures for addressing them.

While the world conferences may not have generated completely new ideas, they contributed in various ways to the evolution and adaptation of ideas to the situation in developing countries. For instance, the Founex meeting in 1971 did much to illuminate the relationship between the environment and development. Likewise, the series of world conferences on women, beginning in Mexico City, went a long way in translating feminist concerns that reflected conditions in industrial countries to the reality of women in poor countries.

The world conferences also stimulated original research on important themes by scholars, international agencies, and civil-society groups. Furthermore, the preparatory process of the world conferences, which involved numerous workshops and seminars from the local to the global levels with participants drawn from many different sectors, generated new ideas and approaches that were followed up in further research. More important was the worldwide propagation of new ideas and new approaches. It is no exaggeration to say that these conferences put new issues, such as the environment, gender inequality, and children's well-being, on the world agenda. They enhanced awareness of the gravity of old problems, such as poverty, unemployment, malnutrition, illiteracy, ill health, and population expansion, and of the measures that need to be taken to tackle them. The sharing of success stories that provide detailed examples of how countries have successfully handled these problems is especially important.

The world conferences of the 1990s were particularly effective in mobilizing and energizing civil society. The conferences evoked active participation of constituencies as diverse as women, ethnic groups, corporations, churches, unions, farmers' associations, local authorities, youth and professional groups, and voluntary development agencies.

It is not possible to assess adequately the impact of the world conferences on global and national policies and programs. The declarations and programs of action adopted by the delegates by their very nature represent aspirations and ideal policy packages rather than politically feasible action programs for the near future. They gloss over vested interests and the political and administrative obstacles to their implementation. Little attempt is made to establish priorities. Often the programs of action represent little more than a wish list, and these lists can run into scores of pages! Despite these qualifications, it is possible to indicate the ways in which the world conference outcomes have impacted national and global policies and programs.

At the international level, the recommendations made at the conferences have helped shape the plans of action and spending priorities of international agencies, voluntary organizations, and bilateral donors. Some conferences resulted in the creation of new institutions that played an important role in realizing the programs of action. The Stockholm conference led to the creation of UNEP[58]—the first global agency charged with monitoring and protecting the environment. The Mexico conference gave rise to INSTRAW[59] and UNIFEM[60] to promote research about and training of women and funding of projects. The World Food Conference in 1974 gave birth to IFAD (International Fund for Agricultural Development) and the World Food Council, designed respectively to raise more funds to increase food production and reduce rural poverty and coordinate policies on food security, world food stocks, and aid.[61]

The Vienna Conference on Human Rights in 1993 also had an important institutional impact.[62] It resulted in the creation of the post of the high commissioner for human rights to give greater visibility and prestige to the work on human rights. The conferences have also sought to stimulate policy changes through promoting global norms, conventions, and treaties. The World Summit for Children in 1990 led to accelerated ratification of the Convention on the Rights of the Child and the preparation of some 150 national plans of action. The Rio conference in 1992 spawned several international treaties for controlling toxic substances, preserving biodiversity, and preventing the spread of deserts.

The world conferences have also influenced domestic policies through a wide variety of national channels. The preparatory process, which involves meetings, workshops, and organization of country papers, stimulates interest in the issues, encourages research, and provokes debate about policy options. It facilitates the participation of diverse constituencies with contending views in the drawing up of policy and program priorities. The conference outcomes often lead to the establishment of new national programs and agencies. For instance, by the end of the United Nations Decade for Women in 1985, 127 member states had reported the creation of some form of national machinery to deal with the promotion of policy, research, and programs aimed at women's advancement and participation in development.[63]

In a different field, in 1974 when the first World Conference on Population was held in Bucharest, only twenty-seven countries had explicit population policies. In 1994, more than 100 countries had such policies and most countries provided support for family planning. The Stockholm conference was followed up by the creation of ministries or departments of the environment, thus embedding it into governmental structures. The World Summit on Social Development stimulated new programs and policies to reduce poverty and generate employment. The national responses to world conferences naturally vary from one country to another, but some countries have taken them seriously enough to reorient their approaches and policies in major areas. Vietnam provides an example of one such country.

Box 7.4. Vietnam's Response to World Conferences

The Vietnamese government has responded strongly to the programs of action adopted by the series of world conferences organized by the UN in the 1990s.[64] Some of the important initiatives taken by the government are listed below and on the next page.

World Summit for Children: the first country in Asia to ratify the Convention on the Rights of the Child and draw up national and regional plans of action for children (1991–2000).
World Conference on Education for All: adopted a National Program of Action and is well on the way to meeting most of the goals.

Conference on Environment and Development: adopted a National Plan for Environment and Sustainable Development; in 1993 established a National Environmental Agency and promulgated a National Law on Environmental Protection.

International Conference on Women: developed a National Plan of Action for the Advancement of Women as well as plans of action for every ministry and province.

International Conference on Population and Development: developed a National Reproductive Health Strategy; revised its population policy and plan of action; adopted a program of action for the Youth Union.

World Summit for Social Development: adopted a National Program for Hunger Eradication and Poverty Reduction.

World Food Summit: drew up a National Program for Food Security; established a National Program on Integrated Pest Management.

International Conference on Nutrition: established a National Plan for Nutrition.

The Secretary-General's report for the Millennium Summit built in part upon the results of the earlier conferences. It made proposals designed to reduce poverty, promote gender equality, protect the environment, remove trade barriers on exports from poor countries, reduce the debt burden, increase development assistance, cut the incidence of HIV/AIDS, and strengthen the UN system.[65]

The Secretary-General also proposed new initiatives relating to creating a volunteer corps to help spread the use of new technology in developing countries; establishing a Health Inter-Network to provide online access to up-to-date medical information; setting up a quick response to disasters; and creating a global policy network to combat youth unemployment. The summit participants endorsed most of these proposals and committed themselves to eight goals—seven of which are social targets to be achieved by 2015 relating to the eradication of extreme poverty, universal primary schooling, reduction of child mortality, promotion of environmental sustainability, reversal of the spread of HIV/AIDS, improvement in maternal health, and reduction in gender disparities. The eighth is a commitment to a global partnership in support of the goals.[66]

It is clear from the foregoing that we agree with Gert Rosenthal, who said, "One of the things the UN does best is to impact on public awareness through either global conferences or reports or just the repetition of certain topics."[67]

Concluding Observations

The last two decades of the twentieth century witnessed a wave of economic liberalization and privatization through the world. All categories of developing countries and the transition economies have sought in varying degrees to overhaul their economic and social policies. But as the 1990s drew to a close, there was a growing realization that the new policies, even when fully implemented, had not delivered on their promise of rapid growth and poverty reduction. Most Latin American, African, and transition economies were still caught in a "low or negative growth equilibrium" characterized by stagnant or declining living standards for the majority of the people. It is now accepted by most specialists and development agencies that the pendulum has swung too far in one direction. Efforts were made in the late 1990s to evolve more balanced approaches that emphasized a stronger role by the government and more vigorous policies to tackle unemployment and poverty.

In the 1980s and 1990s, the UN system was largely overshadowed by the Bretton Woods institutions, which took the leadership in developing policy ideas and action programs. It has been subjected to increased pressure from some industrial countries to conform to the dominant orthodox ideas in its technical work and advice. This has undoubtedly had a dampening effect on the integrity and originality of work done by the UN agencies.

However, the UN has played an important role as a critic of some of the policies propagated by the international financial organizations and the orthodox economists. The UN critique of stabilization and adjustment policies contributed to growing skepticism about their effectiveness. On the debt issue, UN ideas were largely ignored but have found favor in recent years. On the consequences of globalization, the validity of the more balanced and comprehensive analyses done by the UN agencies is gaining increasing acceptance. In the 1990s, the UN took the leadership in attempting to synthesize the human development and human rights approaches. The world conferences played a role in developing more balanced and synthetic approaches to development policy. The Bretton Woods institutions have taken on board many of the ideas generated or propagated by the UN system such as employment- and anti-poverty–oriented strategies, human development, human rights, gender equality, and environmental protection. But in some cases, this has only amounted to window dressing. Quite often the core of World Bank and IMF approaches remain unaltered.

It became clear that if the UN system was to play an innovative and pathbreaking role in drawing attention to emerging social and economic problems and helping to design effective responses—as it did in the first three decades of its existence—it would need to regain its autonomy and capacity for original and courageous research. But this also meant that there would need to be strong centers within the system where independent analysis, research, and reflection on development issues could take place.[68]

8

Building the Human Foundations

- **Population**
- **UN Shifts in Population Thinking and Policy**
- **The Slow Awakening**
- **Women's Empowerment, Safe Motherhood, and Reproductive Health**
- **Nutrition**
- **Health**
- **Education**
- **Culture and Development**
- **Concluding Observations**

The human dimensions of development have been central in the mandates of the specialized agencies from the beginning. The WHO's constitution, for example, states, "The enjoyment of the highest attainable standard of health is one of the fundamental rights of every human being without distinction of race, religion, political, economic or social condition."[1]

UNESCO has over its lifetime emphasized the multifaceted right to education contained in the Universal Declaration of Human Rights. Three articles in the declaration spelled out "the right to education," the need for education to be "directed to the full development of the human personality and to the strengthening of respect for human rights and fundamental freedoms," and the principle that "parents have a prior right to choose the kind of education that shall be given to their children."[2]

Many other examples could be given, such as the Declaration of Philadelphia attached to the ILO constitution.[3] More interesting is the way these early human commitments were carried forward and elaborated during later decades. For example, the Convention on the Elimination of All Forms of Discrimination against Women (CEDAW),[4] which was adopted in 1979, and the Convention on the Rights of the Child (CRC),[5] which was adopted in 1989, both enlarged considerably the rights of women and children and elaborated in detail what each set of rights should consist of. Equally significant, the CRC specified the international obligations of state parties to the convention "to promote and encourage international co-operation with a view to achieving progressively the full realisation of the right [to health and education with particular attention to] ... the needs of developing countries."[6] In other words, the rights of children were no longer just a national matter but also an international obligation.

Skeptics might ask what the recognition of human rights has brought to education, health, and the other human dimensions of development. Surely, by their very definition, issues of education and health are already focused directly on matters of human concern. What more does their acknowledgement as human rights contribute? There are at least five answers. First, by incorporating them as human rights, the UN gives these rights a universal international legitimacy that is applicable to all persons on the planet. Second, their international recognition as rights underlines the obligations of all state parties to ensure that these rights are fulfilled. Third, emphasizing rights directs particular attention and gives priority to meeting the needs of marginalized groups who are not yet enjoying these rights, as opposed to improving the standards of education and health in general. Fourth, legal redress is made possible; any who are deprived of them can demand that their rights be fulfilled. Fifth, their recognition as rights asserts that the meeting of these needs is an end in itself, not merely instrumental to the fulfillment of other objectives.

The recognition of many of the human dimensions of development as rights does not mean that measures to implement them were from the beginning fully incorporated in programs of action. There were many delays and failures in translating formal recognition into full action.

Having said this, overall advance during the last fifty years has been extraordinary and, over the long period of human existence, unprecedented. Life expectancy in the world as a whole has increased by an average of nineteen years from 1950 to 2000, more than in any 50-year period of history. The increase has been most dramatic in the developing countries. In the industrial countries and in Eastern Europe and the former Soviet Union, it increased by only about ten years.[7] In developing countries, there has been an enormous and unprecedented increase in the number and proportion of persons who are literate, from about one-third in 1950 to well over three-quarters in 2000.[8] The numbers educated to primary, secondary, and higher levels has increased by multiples, in parallel with other human improvements as judged by a wide range of other human indicators. The UN and its various agencies have played a significant and sometimes a leading role in these advances, typically by setting regional and international goals and guidelines and often, in poorer countries, by providing technical, financial, and other forms of practical support for translating goals and guidelines into national action.

This chapter elaborates the record of UN contributions in the main areas directly affecting human well-being; namely, population, nutrition, health, education, and culture.

Population

> Population must be balanced against resources or civilisation will perish.
> —Julian Huxley, director-general of UNESCO, 1948[9]

In 1945, when the UN was founded, the population of the world numbered just under 2.5 billion. The population of developing countries formed some 70 percent of the total, about 1.7 billion, with China numbering nearly 550 million and India about 350 million, the two largest countries together constituting more than one-third of total world population. At the time, the industrial countries accounted for almost one-fifth of world population and Eastern Europe and the Soviet Union accounted for just over one-tenth.

Fifty-five years later, in 2000, global population had more than doubled to slightly over 6 billion. The population increase over these years had been by far the largest and most rapid in human history. It had taken until the early nineteenth century to reach the first billion of the world's human population. It took some 125 years, from about 1800 to the late 1920s, to add the second billion. It reached the third billion in 1960, the fourth in 1974 and the fifth in 1987. To add the sixth billion took barely twelve years.

Equally important, the shares of the world population have changed. That of developing countries has grown—to almost 80 percent in 2000. The share of Eastern Europe and the CIS countries has slipped to 7 percent and that of the developed countries to some 14 percent. China and India now account for nearly two-fifths of total world population. The shares of sub-Saharan Africa and Latin America have also expanded.

There are also many more older people in all regions of the world. The number of total persons over 65 has increased from barely 100 million in 1955 to about 400 million in 2000 and is projected to be over 800 million by 2025. The share of seniors over 65 in global population will have risen from 5 percent to 7 percent to a projected 10 percent by 2025. In parallel, the proportion of the world's population under 20 has decreased—from 45 percent in 1955 to under 40 percent in 2000, and it is projected to become 32 percent in 2025—from nearly one-half to under one-third in three-quarters of a century.[10]

Though some have commented that "no social phenomenon has attracted more attention in the past half century than the 'population explosion,'"[11] the truth is that for the first two decades of the UN's life, population growth was not treated as a major policy issue. The UN set up a Population Commission in 1946 to study and advise ECOSOC on population changes, including migration, and their effects on economic and social conditions. Its first tasks were concerned with making population projections for the different regions of the world.[12]

A major volume, *The Determinants and Consequences of Population Trends*, was published in 1953.[13] This presented projections for the growth of world population and included estimations for world population in the year 2000 ranging from 3.3 to 3.8 billion.[14] The UN had projected in 1951 that world population would increase from 2.4 billion to between 2.9 and 3.6 billion in 1980 and 3.3 to 4.7 billion in 2000.[15] This makes clear the considerable uncertainties at the time in terms of analysis and projections. Not surprisingly, levels of population and rates of population growth were initially seen as features to study and note but not ones to cause general alarm or require urgent action.

Indeed, outside the UN, and especially among the developed countries that had played the main role in setting up the UN, there was more worry about declining population. As Richard Symonds and Michael Carder put it, as far as attitudes to populations were concerned, the most striking feature of the late nineteenth and early twentieth century was the eclipse of Malthusian ideas.[16]

In the developing countries, little was known of the demographic situation during the first decade of the UN's existence. The one big exception was India, where a series of censuses since 1881 had long created awareness and concern about population growth.[17] During the 1950s, in large part as a result of the work of the UN's Population Division, there was a gradual awakening to the fact that world population was growing at an unprecedented rate. It is now estimated that the rate of population growth in developing countries accelerated during this period from around 1 percent to over 2 percent per annum. But policy discussion in the UN at the time was limited, "hampered by the prejudices and passions which the [population] question aroused."[18]

This reluctance to take on policy discussion of population issues is hardly surprising. A generation earlier there had been attempts to raise population issues in the League of Nations.[19] One notable example was the proposal for a world conference on population made by Margaret Sanger, the pioneering birth control advocate. She argued for a conference, outside the League but with the League attending, which would bring together experts in economics, sociology, demography, and biology to discuss population problems and recommend solutions. Various neo-Malthusian groups had actively lobbied and some resolutions were drafted, but attempts to have population growth treated as a serious problem failed. When attention was given to two closely related matters—birth control and international migration—controversy boiled over, especially about the issue of birth control. In many countries in the 1920s and 1930s, "the dissemination of information about contraception or abortion was suppressed under the laws relating to obscenity."[20]

UN Shifts in Population Thinking and Policy

In spite of this slow beginning, the UN over its lifetime has given strong and increasing attention to population issues, moving from caution and reticence to advocacy and support on a global scale. Five stages can be identified:

- 1950–1960s: gradual awakening to population growth, which was increasing from 1 to 2 percent per year.
- 1968: recognition of the rights of parents to determine the number and spacing of their children.
- 1974: mobilization of world opinion at the first UN World Conference on Population in Bucharest, which introduced links between population and development.
- 1980s: promotion of country-level integration of population measures into comprehensive social and economic plans.
- 1994: shifting of emphasis at the Cairo Conference on Population and Development from fertility reduction to women's equality and empowerment, safe motherhood, and reproductive health and a range of other actions such as reducing child mortality and expanding education for girls.[21]

This important evolution of ideas, policy, and action resulted from a continual interaction between the international and national within the UN and with agencies and governments outside. There was also an interesting but less-emphasized interplay—though with something of a time lag—between the calls for action to slow population growth and increasing signs of success, shown most clearly by the way fertility and population growth rates have been falling. After rising from 1 to 2 percent per annum over the 1950s and 1960s, the world rate of population growth reached a peak of 2.1 percent in the late 1960s and thereafter has been in decline.[22] At the time of writing, world population is growing at an annual rate of just over 1.2 percent.[23]

Though this decrease has represented some measure of success, a decline in the rate of population growth has not, of course, meant any immediate decrease in the year-by-year additions to total world population. Moreover, life expectancy has been rising, more than at first expected. The combined result is that world population has increased from 4 billion in 1974 to 5 billion in 1987 and 6 billion in 2000.

The Slow Awakening

The awakening to the unprecedented rate of population growth took place at different paces in different places. The early awareness in India rapidly spread to other countries in Asia. In 1966, ESCAP (then ECAFE) was able to organize a meeting on the management of family planning. Within two or three years, several Asian countries had identified rapid population growth as a basic constraint to the achievement of their development goals and had initiated family planning programs as one means of curtailing rapid rates of demographic increase. By 1974, at the time of the first UN World Conference on Population in Bucharest, seventeen Asian countries had population policies and almost all had family planning programs. "In general, Asian countries have had the least problems in legitimizing family planning as a means of achieving a smaller family size and consequently lower fertility rates."[24] In part because of this, fertility rates fell more rapidly than in other developing-country regions— and today they are the lowest in the developing world.[25]

At the other end of the spectrum were most of the sub-Saharan African countries, whose governments were largely unaware of their population situations or unwilling to recognize the difficulties presented by very rapid rates of population growth. Many had not conducted a complete census since gaining independence and thus had no firm evidence of the pressures being exerted by high fertility, high mortality, and imbalances in population distribution.

Falling someplace between these two extremes were the countries of Latin America and the Caribbean and those of the Middle East and North Africa. Though census-taking in Latin America had long been established, governments were often cautious about intervening because of the influence of the Catholic church and other traditional institutions. In the Middle East, only Egypt and Tunisia had family planning programs.[26]

In 1968, at the International Conference on Human Rights in Teheran, governments agreed for the first time that "parents have a basic human right to determine freely and responsibly the number and spacing of their children."[27] That year, the UN Secretary-General had given a lead at ECOSOC, where he stated that "on the strength of a historic General Assembly resolution the UN can now embark upon a bolder and more effective program of action [on issues of population]."[28]

Barely six years later, at Bucharest in 1974, it was recommended that all governments, regardless of their demographic goals, should "respect and ensure ... the right of persons to determine in a free, informed and responsible manner, the number and spacing of their children."[29] The family planning programs of many countries in the 1970s developed a strong emphasis on fertility control, often encouraged by the U.S. and other donors. Some of these became highly controversial, such as the national family planning program in India and the one-child family policy in China. Donors' views varied, sometimes encouraging and strongly supporting vigorous programs of family planning, sometimes stressing the need for choice and human rights, sometimes doing both at once. The attitude of the U.S. administration had experienced a conversion toward family planning in the mid-1960s, but it subsequently underwent a major reversal—from strong support in the 1970s to strong antagonism in the 1980s.[30]

The World Conference on Population emphasized the strong links between population and development, stating that "the basis for an effective solution of population problems is, above all, socio-economic transformation."[31] The significance of the Bucharest conference must be seen against the long and tortuous efforts of different parts of the UN to develop a clear and strong policy toward family planning. As early as 1946, at the International Health Conference, the Polish delegation had suggested that the WHO's functions should include the important subject of population problems, but the conference resolved that overall, population issues should be the responsibility of the United Nations.[32] In their 1959 report, the UN Population Commission stated, "It is not the task of the Population Commission to suggest policies that any Government of any Member State should pursue."[33] At the time, several members of the commission disputed the very existence of a population explosion.

However, beginning with ECOSOC resolutions in 1964 and 1965 and a General Assembly resolution in 1966,[34] a dramatic change occurred toward population activities in the UN. By 1968, the WHO, UNICEF, UNESCO, the ILO, and the FAO had all agreed on new policies to provide support to developing countries on population matters. But the policies of different countries still varied widely. Bucharest provided the global push for and brought UN legitimacy to more active international lobbying. At the Bucharest conference, countries were encouraged to establish population policies, which in many parts of the world were still controversial. The World Population Plan of Action, which was adopted at the conference, suggested that countries develop population policies that were integrated into comprehensive social and economic plans.[35] The Bucharest conference also encouraged countries to establish a high-level unit to deal with population issues within their national administrative structures. Less than ten years later, by 1983, about 70 percent of the countries who had participated in the Bucharest conference had established such units. The UN's review and appraisal of developments in population policy reported steady incremental progress but no breakthroughs.[36]

UN support and action was already being channeled through the UN Fund for Population Activities (UNFPA), which had been established by the Secretary-General in 1967 as the Trust Fund for Population Activities and two years later made part of the UNDP. After the Bucharest conference, UNFPA was available to help countries prepare national plans of action.

Perhaps even more important, a range of new contraceptives became available with the contraceptive pill and other devices in the decade of the 1960s. These made it possible for women and men to have control of their fertility with more reliability than ever before. Along with this, attitudes and cultural mores started to change enormously in most parts of the world.

Women's Empowerment, Safe Motherhood, and Reproductive Health

In 1994, at the International Conference on Population and Development in Cairo, the emphasis on the right to choose was widely publicized, strongly promoted, and firmly established. The declaration and plan of action of the conference also contained strong commitments to empowerment of women and gender equality; improvements in maternal and reproductive health, especially safe motherhood; and actions to reduce child mortality. The emphasis on human rights and on these three specific areas of action was so strong in Cairo that the conference has sometimes been described as if it was the first time that human rights in matters of population were emphasized in the UN, or at least the first time that these rights were given priority over fertility control. This is not true. At the same time, it is important to recognize that the Cairo conference represented an important step forward in these respects. More clearly than ever before, the focus and operational emphasis for policymakers was shifted to empowerment, reproductive health, and the reduction of child mortality.[37]

Nutrition

The idea of international action to improve world nutrition dates from the League of Nations and the 1930s. The Yugoslav delegates suggested that the Health Section of the League should prepare a report on the food position of

representative countries of the world. After visiting and assessing the situation in a number of countries, a pioneering report, "Nutrition and Public
Health," was prepared in 1935. It showed an acute food shortage in the poor
countries, but no action was taken.[38]

Some, however, pressed for more to be done. The World Monetary and Economic Conference was held in London in June 1933 to seek solutions to the
world recession. At the conference, Stanley Bruce, prime minister of Australia
in the 1920s and at that time high commissioner for Australia to London, challenged the conventional wisdom that declining commodity prices should be
countered by cutbacks in production. He warned that if the best that could be
done for a poverty-stricken world was to restrict the production of food and
other necessities of life, the Western political and economic system was headed
for disaster.[39] In 1935, Bruce proposed that the League of Nations explore what
might be done to mobilize cooperation for a world food plan based on human
needs. Two years later, the final report of the League's Mixed Committee on
Nutrition, *The Relation of Nutrition to Health, Agriculture and Economic Policy,*
was published.[40] The *New York Times* called it a best-seller.

The beginning of the war delayed action, but the issues were not forgotten.
In 1943, Franklin D. Roosevelt called a conference on world food problems at
Hot Springs in Virginia. This conference laid the foundations for the FAO but
envisaged the new organization as having a more limited mandate—collecting
statistics on food production and distribution, promoting research, and providing technical assistance.[41]

But the more ambitious vision would not entirely go away. John Boyd Orr, a
distinguished food and nutrition scientist and longtime supporter of the need
for a world food plan, was elected the first director-general of the FAO. He was
chosen, he later claimed, on the strength of a passionate speech he made at the
conference in Quebec in October 1945 which was called to launch the FAO.[42]
But in spite of Boyd Orr's convictions and support from many governments,
the idea of a world food plan or world food policy was to become one of the
paths not taken. A conference in Copenhagen was organized for September
1946, at which the director-general outlined his proposal for a world food board.[43]
This was strongly supported by food-deficit countries, by the food-exporting
countries, and initially, apparently, by the American delegation. Only Britain
was opposed. But by April 1947, the U.S. and Britain were united in opposition
and the plan was killed. John Boyd Orr resigned and handed over his responsibilities to a successor in 1948. He was awarded the Nobel Peace Prize in 1949,
international recognition of his leadership and vision.

A quarter of a century later, the UN would return, at least in rhetoric, to
the goal of ending hunger and malnutrition on a global scale. But even though

the grand vision was off the global agenda, action to develop food aid as an additional dimension of multilateral assistance was under way. The World Food Programme was created in 1961 to use food aid for the support of economic and social development, emergency relief, and the promotion of world food security.[44]

Then a decade or so later, in 1974, the vision of eradicating hunger and malnutrition returned, set out at the World Food Conference. The convening of the conference had been the proposal of the U.S. secretary of state, Henry Kissinger, who was concerned about the instability and unpredictability of world food stocks and the world food situation. But whatever his motivation, he presented the challenge in human terms in his much-quoted words: "Within a decade, no child will go to bed hungry. . . . [N]o family will fear for its next day's bread."[45]

The Universal Declaration on the Eradication of Hunger and Malnutrition with which the conference concluded embodied a range of solemn commitments, including the eradication of hunger as a common objective of all countries.[46] The focus of action was kept firmly on national plans and programs but recognized the responsibility of developed countries to help developing countries. Not everyone agreed with the proposal to establish a world food authority. Instead, a World Food Council was created; it met at the ministerial level and reported to the UN General Assembly.[47] The council existed for a difficult two decades; it produced some good reports but had little impact. In 1996, the council was abolished—more precisely, its functions were taken over by the FAO—in response to pressures for the UN to make savings in its budget and rationalize its structure.[48]

The third occasion for the big push on ending hunger in the world came in 1996 at the World Food Summit, which was convened by the FAO in the aftermath of the plethora of global summits and world conferences of the 1990s. Representatives of 186 countries gathered at FAO headquarters in Rome and agreed with the goal of halving the number of people "living in food insecurity" by the year 2015. The summit mandated the establishment of FIVIMS— the Food Insecurity and Vulnerability and Mapping Systems program, which now tracks progress toward the goal.[49] By 1995–1997, the estimated number of undernourished people had declined from 830–840 million in 1990–1992 to some 790 million, which represented a beginning and some progress but was too slow to achieve the goal without clear acceleration in the rate of progress to 2015.[50]

Over the UN's life, a number of coordinating initiatives have been taken to ensure a multidisciplinary perspective and operational collaboration. One of the earliest efforts was the creation of the Protein Advisory Group in 1955,[51] bringing together the FAO, the WHO, and UNICEF, initially to provide UNICEF with nutritional advice to guide their programs. The focus on protein accorded with scientific thinking of the time, which stressed the protein gap as the critical food deficiency that was thought to underlie kwashiorkor and other serious forms of child malnutrition.

By the 1970s, it had become clear that the focus on the protein gap was vastly exaggerated, if not seriously misguided. The true nutrition problem was a general calorie shortage, better described as protein-energy malnutrition. In parallel, it was recognized that the most serious nutritional problems were those of children under the age of five. For these very young children, with their relatively small needs for food intake, health and sanitation were the critical issues and basic health problems such as diarrhea and acute respiratory infections and diseases such as measles were the main threats.

In the 1980s, to explain the interacting set of causes and factors that influenced malnutrition and to provide a frame for action, UNICEF[52] devised the conceptual framework shown below as Figure 8.1. The lower section of the diagram indicates the basic determinants—the resources available to a country (or a region or a community), the political and economic structure influencing the availability and distribution and use of these resources, and the nature of family and community structures and control. These are all broad factors, as indeed they must be. They set the frame within which the underlying determinants all take effect in three main areas of action: 1) household food security; 2) health services and the healthy environment; and 3) the care and attention provided by mothers, fathers, and other family and community members. These factors all feed into dietary intake and health as the immediate determinants of nutrition of young children—and, indeed, the nutritional status of the rest of the population.

Over the last decade or so, this conceptual framework has been widely used in and outside the UN. It makes clear that nutrition is not the simple outcome of a linear chain of inputs but the result of many interacting factors—health, sanitation, diet, household income, and adequate breastfeeding. Indeed, shortage of food in the household is not the main cause of malnutrition of young children. The conceptual framework has the great virtue of setting out the causes of malnutrition in a systematic and logical hierarchy, which, at the same time, can be used to indicate where effort needs to be applied to improve the nutritional situation in any particular country. In other words, it is highly operational. Though it draws on much research and thinking in the nutritional community at large, it is a clear example of a UN group producing an intellectual synthesis of fundamental significance and widespread importance.

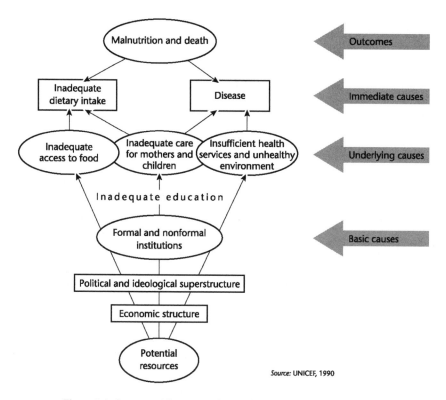

Figure 8.1 Conceptual Framework for the Causes of Malnutrition in Society

The UN has taken the lead in producing the statistics needed to assess nutritional problems and progress. In 1975, only four developing countries had systematic and comprehensive data on nutritional status within the country at large. The UN work drew on statistical inputs from many parts of the organization but most especially from the nutritional work and analysis of the FAO, the WHO, and UNICEF. The findings of the data have been important and in some ways unexpected. The data in Table 10.7 show significant improvements from 1980 to 2000 in both the proportions and the numbers of malnourished children worldwide. The proportion of preschool children who are underweight has fallen worldwide from 37 to 24 percent and the numbers have fallen from 175 million to under 140 million. The proportion of preschool children who are stunted—who have low weight for their height—fell over the same period from 47 to 29 percent and the numbers from 220 million to 165 million. These were important and in many ways unexpected advances during the 1980s, a period often described as a lost decade for development because of the severe economic difficulties of poor nations, especially in sub-Saharan Africa and Latin America. Only in Eastern and Western Africa did the proportion of children who were underweight sharply rise rather than decline. Though this worsening nutrition is a matter of the greatest concern, this decline needs to be set in the context of the remarkable improvements elsewhere in the world.

The benefits of iodizing salt had been known since the 1920s. But only when taken up by the UN in the 1980s did applications of these programs go to scale, reaching a high proportion of the affected population in these countries. The idea of mass action is now accepted and by the year 2000, some two-thirds of edible salt in the world is now iodized.

Progress with Vitamin A supplementation has also been impressive. Here the idea initially came from non-UN research—especially the work of Professor Al Sommer[53]—who showed that Vitamin A supplementation not only prevented blindness but could reduce child mortality by almost one-quarter in areas where there was a risk of Vitamin A deficiency, a condition that is estimated to affect more than one in five of all children in the world.[54] Promotion and application of supplementation on a mass scale owed much to the UN, notably to the WHO and UNICEF. By the year 2000, more than forty countries were reaching the large majority of their children with a least one high-dose Vitamin A supplement early in their lives, achieving 80 percent coverage in the least-developed countries—a major advance on the situation in the mid-1990s. UNICEF estimated that about 1 million child deaths were prevented by this means during 1998–2000.[55]

The central importance of early nutrition in the womb and in the first two years of childhood has emerged over the last decade. Epidemiological evidence from both developing and industrialized countries now suggests a link between fetal undernutrition and increased risk of various adult chronic diseases much later in life—notably hypertension, diabetes, coronary heart disease, and cancer. This link has fundamental implications for nutritional strategy and for related issues of human rights, especially those pertaining to the rights of women and children, girls in particular. Nutritional deficiency and neglect, leading to severe malnutrition in the womb and in early childhood, have consequences over a person's whole life. If the person is a girl, the impact often extends to her children and possibly her grandchildren. These multigenerational consequences greatly reinforce the need for attention to nutrition and prevention of malnutrition among women and mothers. To ignore this is a double violation of human rights—of women themselves and of the next one or two generations of their children.

Health

The detached and cold-blooded approach of the economic theorist is well captured in the definition of health as "both an intermediate commodity that affects production and a final commodity that affects utility directly."[56] The tardy awakening to health as a factor in development among mainstream development agencies is indicated by the fact that only in 1979 under Robert McNamara did the World Bank create a Health Department and decide to fund stand-alone health projects in addition to health components in other projects.[57] As the bank's historians comment, "[T]he full embrace of health and education as productive investments was germinating under cover of the basic needs proposal of the late 1970s, but its official recognition came at the close of the McNamara period, most publicly in the 1980 World Development Report." They comment revealingly "that pure welfare spending, or income transfer with no convincingly 'productive' outcome—a category that through the 1970s included primary education and health—was also frowned upon."[58]

The United Nations had no such conceptual or operational difficulties. The WHO was from 1948 one of the UN's major institutions, and health was therefore a continuing and active concern. Moreover, the UN's concern with development was multidisciplinary and was organizationally, if not always conceptually, influenced by the perspectives and approaches of many professionals, not just economists. This said, the WHO for its first forty years was, by its own admission, too neglectful of the socioeconomic dimensions of health. The WHO's organizational culture has been dominated by scientists, doctors, and medical experts.[59] "Up to 1978, the biomedical model of health systems predominated and the health sector was confused with the medical sector."[60]

The change came with the adoption of primary health care in 1978 and the goal of achieving health for all by the year 2000. The drive toward primary health care was a joint initiative of WHO and UNICEF and drew on the thinking and experience of both organizations.

Over the years, the WHO, with other partners in the UN, has led the way in four major areas of ideas and thinking on health:

- Health as a human right
- Global action to reduce and eradicate communicable disease
- Primary health care and health for all
- Research, statistics, and epidemiological analysis

The Universal Declaration of Human Rights in 1948 stated that "everyone has the right to a standard of living adequate for the health and well being of himself and of his family."[61] In the same year, the WHO's constitution elaborated the point: "The enjoyment of the highest attainable standard of health is one of the fundamental rights of every human being without distinction of race, religion, political, economic or social condition."[62]

Health in the WHO's perspective has embodied mental as well as physical health. Both are critical for an individual's cognitive and emotional and physical capacity, the elements that make possible a full life for an individual in the community. Health for a full life needs a broad interpretation.

Box 8.1. International Action for Health

In spite of long awareness that disease could spread across national borders, international action to tackle public health across national borders was slow in coming. Cholera overran Europe in 1830, but it was only in 1851 that the first International Sanitary Conference was held in Paris.[63] This conference failed to produce agreement on an international sanitary convention. Indeed, it took another forty years before an International Sanitation Convention was adopted on 30 January 1892 during the Seventh International Sanitary Conference in Venice, and that was restricted to cholera.[64] R. N. Cooper argues that these long delays were the result of failure to achieve consensus on the scientific causes of the problems and the international actions that could deal with them effectively.

After the convention was adopted, international organization soon followed. In 1902, the International Sanitary Bureau was created in Washington, D.C.—renamed the Pan American Sanitary Bureau in 1923 and later still the Pan American Health Organization, which exists today. In Paris, L'Office International d'Hygiene Publique (OIHP) was set up in 1907, with a permanent secretariat and a permanent committee of senior public health officials of member governments. Its function was to provide to participating governments general information on public health, especially infectious diseases. Progress was made on the control of the main infectious diseases, including yellow fever, cholera, malaria, and tuberculosis. Activities also covered food safety, hospital-building, school health, industrial hygiene, and biological standardization.

When the League of Nations was created in 1919, it had many responsibilities, one of which was international action to prevent and control disease. There was a proposal to transform the OIHP into the health organization of the League, but this never happened. Instead, the Health Organization of the League was set up in Geneva in parallel with the OIHP. However, the weekly epidemiological bulletin of the OIHP was incorporated into the weekly epidemiological record of the League. Today, the OIHP weekly record is published by the WHO.

In 1945, the founding UN conference held in San Francisco unanimously approved the setting up of a new, autonomous international health organization. The health of all peoples was considered to be fundamental to the attainment of peace and security in the world. A year later, an international health conference approved the constitution of the WHO, to be run by three bodies: a world health assembly, an executive board, and a secretariat.[65] The first World Health Assembly was held in 1948; the assembly had forty-eight members at its opening and fifty-five when the meeting closed a month later. This assembly also established a regional structure for the WHO—Africa, the Americas, Eastern Mediterranean, Europe, Southeast Asia, and the Western Pacific.

Source: WHO, *The World Health Report 1998* (Geneva: WHO, 1998), 9–20.

Initially, WHO focused on the strengthening of national health services. But in the 1950s, the WHO moved from traditional concerns with international quarantine and epidemiological intelligence to a radically new and fundamentally different approach: global eradication. In the earlier years of the century, yellow fever had been eliminated from Central America, and malaria, from much of Europe. At first in the 1950s, WHO developed two major objectives: to eradicate malaria and to eradicate smallpox.

The goal was subsequently modified from eradication to control, using a variety of actions adapted to the specifics of each environment. But notwithstanding some progress in the 1970s and 1980s, the malarial situation worsened after this. At the turn of the twenty-first century, there were 300 to 500 million new clinical cases of malaria each year, with some 1.5 to 2.7 million people dying annually of the disease. Ninety percent of the deaths occur in sub-Saharan Africa.[66]

In contrast, smallpox eradication became one of the early and great successes of the United Nations—though not until after heated and tortuous debate in the World Health Assembly and some two decades of struggle and pioneering action. The WHO's first director-general made an unsuccessful attempt to persuade the World Health Assembly to undertake a program of smallpox eradication in 1953. Five years later, a Soviet delegate persuaded the WHO to accept responsibility for a global program, but only minimal funds were allocated. One reason was that WHO was preoccupied with the malaria eradication program, but in addition, many were skeptical about the feasibility of smallpox eradication, especially in Africa. Only in 1967 was the program intensified and coordinated efforts of an unprecedented nature started on a worldwide scale. At first, mass vaccination campaigns were launched in thirty countries where smallpox was endemic. These campaigns gave way in the 1970s to a "surveillance containment strategy," under which flying squad teams immediately went to vaccinate all contacts wherever a possible case was discovered. By 1975, the number of countries where the disease could still be found had fallen to three: India, Bangladesh, and Ethiopia. The last case was finally reported in Somalia in 1977, carried by nomads from Ethiopia. The WHO declared the disease extinct in 1980.

The costs and benefits, though often quoted, are worth summarizing again because of their impressive demonstration of the benefits of coordinated international programs. The total cost to achieve smallpox eradication was officially estimated to be about $300 million, of which one-third came from international sources and two-thirds from the afflicted countries. The world now saves at least $2 billion each year by avoiding the need to purchase smallpox vaccine, support vaccine administration, or apply international health regulations and related costs.

The eradication of smallpox was dramatic—but it was not the only success of mass action. Between 1950 and 1965, 46 million patients in forty-nine countries were successfully treated with penicillin against yaws, a tropical disease which affects the skin and bones. Yaws is no longer a significant problem in most of the world. The global threat of plague has declined in the last four decades, largely due to antibiotics, insecticides, and other control measures. Control programs against onchocerciasis were started in West Africa in 1974 and have recently been expanded to cover some twenty other African countries. An onchocerciasis elimination program was started in six Latin American countries in 1991.

Two other efforts of global eradication are under way. Though eradication has not yet been realized, major advances have been achieved. These are the eradication of polio and of dracunculiasis—guinea worm. Over the last decade, the WHO and UNICEF have led efforts that have reduced the number of cases of guinea worm from well over 600,000 in 1990 to 75,000 in 1997.[67]

In 1978, jointly with UNICEF, the WHO developed a major new initiative, primary health care.[68] Launched at the International Conference on Primary Health Care in Alma Ata, it was recognized from the beginning to require multisectoral action, community involvement, and appropriate technology. Three years later, a Global Strategy of Health for All by the Year 2000 was adopted by the World Health Assembly and the UN General Assembly. Together they represented a fundamentally new approach to health care that had the goal of ensuring health for all.[69]

Primary health care was defined as "essential health care based on practical, scientifically sound and socially acceptable methods ... made universally accessible to individuals and families, at a cost they can afford."[70] It was to be guided by several key principles: access for all to basic health care, a more equitable distribution of health resources, a participatory approach at the local level, and the objective of attaining a level of health for all people of the world sufficient to permit them to lead socially and economically productive lives.

From the heart of what is perhaps the most technical of the specialized agencies, the creation and adoption of the primary health care initiative was a triumph. It was not so much a triumph of medico-scientific discovery as of bold rethinking, born of a recognition of the limits of the biomedical solutions in tackling the basic health problems of the mass of humankind. Though adapted to the realities of poor countries, many recognized that its challenge and messages applied also in the much richer circumstances of industrialized countries.

Probably more than any other UN specialized agency, the WHO has, in addition, reviewed, overseen, and undertaken a mass of technical work, resulting in authoritative guidance on many issues and the implementation of many new approaches to health problems and solutions.

Education

Education is one of the major sectors of national activity in all countries, usually absorbing from 5 to 8 percent of national income and 10 to 25 percent of public expenditure.[71] Education has from the beginning been one of the most important areas of UN concern. UNESCO has had the central responsibility, but other UN bodies such as UNICEF, the UNFPA, the WFP, the ILO, the WHO, and the FAO have also had important roles and made important contributions.

Given the dominant role of nations in meeting the educational needs of their people, what has the UN contributed? From the beginning, education was recognized in the UN to be a "multi-faceted right." The Universal Declaration on Human Rights declared education to be the right of everyone; it also declared that "education shall be free, at least in the elementary and fundamental stages," that "elementary education shall be compulsory," that technical and professional education shall be made "generally available" and that higher education shall be "equally accessible to all on the basis of merit."[72] In a world where, at that time, 42 percent of people in Latin America, 63 percent in Asia, and 84 percent in Africa were estimated to be illiterate, these were extraordinary, bold, and forward-looking declarations.[73] It is difficult to imagine similar statements being made today in a similar context—and if they were to be made in the halls of the UN today, one can guess at the range of dismissive comments that would be directed toward those supporters who were so foolishly pressing for such an unrealistic resolution.

Within the UN this multifaceted right has been reaffirmed many times. Eight years after the Universal Declaration, the right was elaborated further in articles of the International Covenant on Economic, Social and Cultural Rights (1966), which called for education to be directed to the full development of the human personality and stated that it should acknowledge and foster the sense of dignity of all humans. It also recognized that education should "strengthen the respect for human rights and fundamental freedoms." The covenant went on to state that "education shall enable all persons to partici- pate effectively in a free society, promote understanding, tolerance and friend- ship among all nations and all racial, ethnic or religious groups, and further the activities of the United Nations for the maintenance of peace."[74]

Implementation has been extraordinary. Over the fifty years since the Uni- versal Declaration, primary-school enrollments have grown worldwide from some 200 million to over 650 million, well over a threefold increase. Enroll- ments in Africa have increased more than tenfold, in Latin America and the Caribbean nearly six times, and in Asia nearly five times (Table 10.6). This far exceeds the experience of industrial countries over any comparable period.

Notwithstanding this enormous expansion, the right of everyone to educa- tion is still far from being achieved. Worldwide, about 115 million primary- school–age children were estimated to be out of school in 1999.[75] Primary-school enrollment ratios at the end of the century ranged from 55 percent in sub- Saharan Africa, 70 percent in South Asia, 84 percent in North Africa and the Middle East, and 92 percent in Latin America and the Caribbean to 97 percent in Southeast Asia. In terms of gender, female enrollments had expanded faster than male enrollments, but even so, only in Latin America was the female enroll- ment ratio as high as for males. On average in developing countries, 79 percent of girls were enrolled compared to 85 percent of boys.[76] Primary-school atten- dance rates were lower for girls than for boys, as were primary-school comple- tion rates and secondary-school entrance and enrollment ratios.

UNESCO and other agencies of the UN played a major role around 1960 in devising ideas for education planning and providing support to encourage and assist the process in many developing countries. Conferences were orga- nized in every region of the developing world that took stock of the educa- tional situation and recent trends and related these to education goals for 1980. The conferences explored what it would take to provide universal and free primary education within two decades. They also examined what should be ambitious but realistic targets for the expansion of secondary education; they looked at the balance between general education and specialist educa- tion that focuses on providing technical and professional skills; and they asked what should be the goals for higher education and the balances within it. Common to all these conferences was a focus on the long-term goals for 1980 and a more immediate short-term plan that was usually focused on the first five years post-conference.

The conferences did much to translate the general objectives for education as set out in the Universal Declaration into the differing contexts of the main regions of the developing world. This was the period when postcolonial ambitions and hopes ran freely. Because the conferences assembled ministers of education from most countries of each region and representatives of most of the donor countries, the participants at the conference were able to do significant work to hammer out the specific details that would enable rapidly expanding education systems to fulfill the goals of universal coverage.

What progress was made? By comparison with all previous trends, expansion over the following 1960s and 1970s was extraordinary, though education for all was achieved only in Eastern Asia and Oceania. In South Asia and sub-Saharan Africa, expansion was very rapid but not sufficient to deliver education for all in the context of school-age populations that were growing more rapidly than was at first realized.

For those tempted to be skeptical about plans and goals, it is worth underlining the situation in sub-Saharan Africa. As mentioned, population data was weak around the 1960s in many countries. Thus, the population projections for educational expansion in Africa underlying the Addis Ababa Plan[77] of 1961 were also unavoidably weak. Nevertheless, ambitious goals were set for all levels of education to be attained within twenty years. By 1980, expansion of secondary and higher education enrollments had exceeded the targets set in the Addis Ababa Plan. Primary-school enrollments had broadly expanded in line with the original targets, but population had considerably exceeded the early projections. The result was that in spite of very rapid expansion of enrollments at all levels in sub-Saharan Africa, faster than in all other regions, enrollment ratios in 1980 were behind the target, especially at the primary-school level.[78]

All this took place about a decade before the World Bank started lending for primary education as part of the important changes brought about by McNamara in the early 1970s. As the World Bank history explains, these changes as applied to education began in 1968 with a sober, cautiously worded report by Ed Mason, who wrote the first World Bank history with Robert Asher, that argued for a gradual broadening of support from secondary, vocational, and technical education to primary and university education. The argument was presented entirely in terms of productivity, with "no reference to equity, poverty or non-economic educational objectives."[79] Even in 1970, after the World Bank Board had considered the new policy proposals, the proposed engagement with primary education was to be limited to experimental and demonstration projects. There was no reference to equity or poverty.[80] Once again, the UN had led the way in vision, in planning, and to a modest extent, in support.

Over the 1980s and 1990s, the increase in debt, the decline in export earnings, and the adoption of adjustment programs with cutbacks in health and education (often made under heavy pressure from the World Bank and the IMF) meant that primary schooling in most countries in Africa declined both in quality and quantity. Enrollment ratios, and often total enrollments, fell. Typically, primary schools struggled on with few if any books and with teachers who were paid sporadically if at all. Compared with the vision of two decades earlier, the national and international neglect of the rights of all children to education in the 1980s and 1990s was a tragedy and a disgrace.

The question remains about what the UN contributed to ideas on education planning. The 1950s and 1960s were in fact pioneering times for ideas, research, and policymaking in matters relating to education and what today is called human resource development. Among economists and planners, new initiatives to calculate the benefits of education were under way, and research on the sources of growth was shifting ideas on capital investment from physical to human capital. In the early 1960s, UNESCO published a massive bibliography of the burgeoning literature of books, articles, and research papers on the economics of education.

But neither UNESCO nor other organizations of the UN directly contributed much to this new thinking. Much of the new thought, of course, was developed in universities and research institutes and tended to focus on the costs and benefits of education and the emerging methodology for calculating rates of return to education. Though more than a thousand books and articles were published on the economics of education over the decade of the 1960s, the extent to which these contributed to policymaking on education in the Third World is debatable. In most developing countries, especially those that were newly independent, expansion of education was a political imperative. Showing that a nation's investment in education would be worthwhile economically added little to the debate or to the technical discussion. To show that rates of return were often higher for primary than for secondary or university education also carried little weight. Most political leaders sought expansion at all three levels of education. The donor community largely agreed. The World Bank, the main international institution that might have been expected to be influenced by rate-of-return calculations, had not yet made the decision to lend to education.

Surprisingly, it was the Organisation for Economic Co-operation and Development (OECD) which first developed a systematic methodology for education and manpower planning. In its Mediterranean Regional Project, the OECD undertook a number of country studies in the Mediterranean region and in a number of developing countries, including Argentina and Peru. The country studies followed a pragmatic methodology to analyze the education and training situation mostly at secondary and higher education levels. In addition, with the assistance of Jan Tinbergen, the OECD developed a methodology that created quantitative planning models to assess educational requirements for economic development.[81]

By the mid-1960s, UNESCO had set up IIEP, the International Institute of Education Planning. This somewhat restored UNESCO's serious involvement in planning methodology and analysis of education in relation to development.

In 1950, two years after the Universal Declaration was adopted, the UN General Assembly called upon UNESCO to report on "measures for suppressing illiteracy which could be applied . . . in Non-Self-Governing Territories, and to communicate annually to the United Nations an account of these measures."[82] As with population, the early statistical work of the UN—this time with UNESCO's compilations of estimates of illiteracy—did much to raise awareness of the scale of the worldwide challenge. From these estimates, it emerged that in around half the countries of the world, half or more of the adult population could not read or write. Most of these countries were in Asia and Africa. In Latin America, the situation was somewhat better, though in Brazil and in some of the smaller countries, more than half of all adults were thought to be illiterate. UNESCO's estimates also suggested that the number of illiterates was growing.

Ideas on how to tackle the backlog of illiteracy fell into three approaches: (1) national campaigns against illiteracy, building on the models of the USSR and of Mexico; (2) smaller-scale programs of functional literacy; and (3) reliance on the school system to achieve slow reduction of adult illiteracy as the school-age generation grew and replaced adults in the labor market and in other adult roles.

The third approach was generally rejected as being too slow, though in practice it was the approach followed in many countries.

The first approach was followed in a number of countries, most notably those that, like Cuba, China, and later Nicaragua, could build their literacy campaign on the enthusiasm and mobilization of revolutionary fervor. In these cases, the literacy campaigns reached out to most of the country's illiterates. A number of other countries—Algeria, Brazil, Colombia, Guatemala, Guinea, Indonesia, Jamaica, Peru, Thailand, Tanzania, and Zambia—mounted literacy campaigns. But without the revolutionary rhetoric and organization, the campaigns generally achieved much smaller coverage. However, in a number of countries, many hundreds of thousands achieved literacy, as in Tanzania in the 1970s.

The functional-literacy approach became a major effort of UNESCO in the late 1960s. The starting point was motivation: "people are not 'made' literate," proponents of this approach contended, but "make themselves literate when they have the motivation and incentives to do so."[83] This led to putting the emphasis on achieving functional literacy, with the view that the focus of the literacy efforts should be on meeting learning needs. Thus, country-level literacy activities were to take the form of work-oriented training that was closely integrated with socioeconomic development. These principles were embodied in the Experimental World Literacy Programme (EWLP) focused on literacy linked to learning by doing.

The program was agreed to at the World Congress of Ministers of Education in 1965 and was launched by UNESCO and the UNDP in 1966. It became the largest-ever internationally sponsored program that was specifically focused on eradicating adult illiteracy. Eleven countries participated—Algeria, Ecuador, Ethiopia, Guinea, India, Iran, Madagascar, Mali, Sudan, Syria, and Tanzania. A total of nearly a quarter of a million adults were enrolled in the various national EWLP projects. It was, in retrospect, an expensive failure. The program never took off, and the hopes of developing a breakthrough never succeeded. The differences between the various projects ended up being much greater than the similarities and "the whole idea of a World Campaign to eradicate illiteracy fizzled out and has never since been revived."[84]

Thus, efforts to stimulate worldwide action on adult illiteracy must be judged a failure. Rates of illiteracy dropped slowly in all regions of the world, but the number of illiterates continued to rise until it peaked at just under 900 million in the late 1980s.[85] Even the recent slow decline in the global total of illiterates is somewhat misleading. It is largely the result of the dramatic decline in the number of illiterates in China. In South Asia, sub-Saharan Africa, and even in the Arab states, the number of illiterates continues to rise, in spite of sometimes-large increases in enrollments.

Inequality and class differences have been at the heart of education from the early days of formal schooling. Indeed, some have portrayed educational systems as above all else systems for maintaining and legitimizing differences of class and other social divisions. However, over time the educational imbalances have been reduced in practically all countries. This is most clearly shown by considering the changes at the university level over the last fifty years.

In 1950, more than half the countries of the world had fewer than 1,000 students enrolled at university or other institutions at the tertiary level, and probably half of these countries had no institution of higher learning at all. Only nine countries—China, India, the U.S., the UK, and five other industrial countries—had more than 100,000 enrolled at this level. Fifty years later, an extraordinary transformation had taken place. Virtually all countries had at least one institution of tertiary-level education, sixty-eight countries had more than 100,000 students, and twenty-one countries had more than a million, including nine developing countries.

At the tertiary level, worldwide enrollments of women amounted to 47 percent of the total of 88 million enrolled, compared with 32 percent in 1950. In both the developed and transition countries, female enrollments accounted for more than half—52 percent in the developed countries and 54 percent in transition countries. In developing countries, the proportion was 40 percent, about double that of 1950.[86]

In the first two decades, quantitative educational expansion was the dominant concern in development. Though UNESCO never lost sight of the broader aims and purposes of education—notably education for peace, human rights, and democracy—the divisions of the Cold War made each of these values matters of intense debate rather than the subjects of simple progress.

In the early 1970s, a more fundamental rethinking of education emerged, the result of a report commissioned by UNESCO entitled *Learning to Be*. This report of the International Commission on the Development of Education (Faure Commission, 1971–1972) set forth a vision of "the Learning Society" built on the concept of lifelong education in which "every individual is in a position to keep learning throughout his [or her] life."[87] There was a double message in this vision. First, learning should be a more continuous and open process, supported by many institutions of society, including those outside the system of formal education and schooling. Second, further publicly financed linear expansion of the formal school and education system was no longer viable. Beyond the period of compulsory education, further education had to be a shared partnership with responsibility for financing and other support shared between governments, employers, and the students themselves.

If one asks what are the original and special contributions of the UN to matters affecting the curriculum, one must surely answer with its emphasis on education for peace, human rights, and democracy. Even this emphasis was weak during the early years of the Cold War, in spite of the references in Article 13 of the 1966 International Covenant on Economic, Social and Cultural Rights. But in 1974, an international recommendation was adopted by the General Conference of UNESCO that declared that education should be infused with the aims of the UN Charter and the Universal Declaration of Human Rights.[88] The declaration went back to Article 26 of the Universal Declaration, which referred to education being directed to "the strengthening of respect for human rights and fundamental freedoms. It shall promote understanding, tolerance and friendship among all nations, racial or religious groups, and shall further the activities of the United Nations for the maintenance of peace."

In 1994, ministers of education meeting at the forty-fourth session of the International Conference on Education updated this commitment with a focus on democracy.[89]

Culture and Development

Culture has been one of the great areas of neglect in mainstream thinking about development policy. Both inside and outside the UN, economists and others who articulated the mainstream literature of economic development did so with few words about culture, except for the earliest phases of misunderstanding, when "cultural factors and tradition" were brought in to explain why development lagged in "under-developed countries." For example, it was argued that plantation workers and others in many rural communities showed little interest in the hard work of development.[90]

Awareness and sensitivity to different cultures and traditions has always been a critical part of international relations, and for this reason, the UN from the beginning recognized culture as part of its mandate and concerns. The UN Charter states that "the United Nations shall promote . . . international cultural and educational co-operation,"[91] and the Universal Declaration of Human Rights says that each person is entitled to realize his or her "economic, social and cultural rights, indispensable for his [or her] dignity and the free development of his [or her] personality." The Universal Declaration later states that "everyone has the right freely to participate in the cultural life of their community, to enjoy the arts and to share in scientific advancement and its benefits."[92]

In spite of this early, if partial, recognition of the importance of culture, "cultural concerns were absent from development planning for a very long time."[93] As late as the year 2000, UNESCO could state in its *World Culture Report* that while "areas like education or science can call on decades of statistics and debates to provide a clear state of the art, the field of culture is only now creating the art. The basic concepts, analytical methods and indicators are only now being constructed."[94]

Some people believe that this early neglect of culture had a major impact on the way societies developed. As Lourdes Arizpe has put it:

> One cannot help exploring the idea that it was the neglect of the cultural dimensions in economic models in the early post-War period which fuelled the outburst of anti-establishment phenomena of the sixties. The civil rights movements brought to the fore the deep racist-cultural divisions which underlay the economic prosperity of the period in the United States. The revolt against the invisibility of the "feminine mystique" and the sexual politics brought women into the cultural front. The rejection of the "one-dimensional man" of economic determinacy and bureaucratic uniformity galvanized student movements in many countries. Not only were cultural, spiritual, artistic and solidarity dimensions left out, but there was no institutional means to express dissatisfaction, despair or rejection of such a soulless development."[95]

Of course, beyond the charmed and self-regarding circle of economists and other professionals in the mainstream of economic development policy, anthropologists, sociologists, political scientists, and many of the critics of colonialist imposition wrote much about culture. In his early life, Jomo Kenyatta, later president of Kenya, produced a pioneering anthropological study called *Facing Mount Kenya.*[96] The arrogant disregard of Indian culture was one of Gandhi's major criticisms of the colonial system.[97] In his influential study of five poor Mexican families, Oscar Lewis gave central importance to the richness and power of the sub-culture of poverty.[98] But in the economic mainstream of development thinking in the UN, these writers were most often treated as voices from the past or from the side. Development policy remained focused on the economic mechanisms of what was largely seen as a unidimensional economic process.

Why was this so—in the UN, of all places, which prided itself on being an international, multidisciplinary, and multicultural organization? A major reason was that anthropologists, sociologists, and other noneconomists were largely excluded from the circle of UN policymaking, leaving them more often in the role of critics rather than participants in decision-making activities. A second reason was that anthropology, especially Western anthropology, was for many years deeply divided about whether accelerated development was even desirable. Many anthropologists were opposed to its purposeful pursuit.[99]

Furthermore, academics and nonacademics from industrial countries overwhelmingly dominated the profession of development studies. As Lourdes Arizpe has put it, "Culture, as studied by anthropology since the end of the 19th century, has been explained as the concept derived from the growing need of the West to find order in its increasing knowledge of immensely varied human life-ways. As cultures, in the plural, became part of the larger whole of the globalized world, relations between them have grown more unsettled."[100]

Other reasons for the neglect of cultural issues are related to the confusions and difficulties in defining culture and the role it plays in all societies. Anthropologists "searching for order in the immensely varied human ways of life" gave one meaning—a meaning derived from their own efforts to construct an intellectual order from culture. But there was a more restricted and often more elitist meaning of culture—the search for meaning and quality in the world of art and intellect. The first is sometimes seen as "the culture of people," the second as "the culture of the elite or of culture, as defined by the elite."[101] The two meanings were important; both fit the mandate of UNESCO and both were much confused in the early days.

But today, in the world of globalization, there is a further complication. Development and the media exert a strong impact on cultural representations and people's own sense of identity. Thus, power and wealth influence representation and people's own cognitive, ethical, and socializing functionings.[102] Though this process can sometimes work for greater harmony and understanding, often it plays on stereotypes and divides traditional cleavages between people of distinct cultures even further, exacerbating inequalities and the unevenness of development.

Notwithstanding these differences and difficulties, some parts of the UN emphasized culture as a core element of development and policy from their earliest days. The UNESCO constitution focused on culture as a shield against "war . . . in the minds of men"[103] and paid particular attention to education. Stephen Spender, the British poet and critic who helped organize UNESCO's first conference, asked, "Can a world organization such as UNESCO contribute to aiding development in education, science and culture around the world [in order to provide] the certainty of peace?"[104] This was no light or easy question. There was deep awareness at the time of the fact that Germany, a "nation which had most highly held aloft the values of 'Kultur' had [also] perpetrated the most deliberate planned genocide against its own and other citizens in the name of racial and religious identity."[105]

UNESCO also focused on cultural development, exploring what it could do for "the arts, the heritage and the life of the mind," especially the intellectual mind. "Culture as heritage, culture as creativity" as Raj Isar puts it. The French, with their own strong and long experience of making and implementing cultural policy, played a formative role, pressing for UNESCO to increase the budget and give more attention to cultural policy, which they saw as public action in the cultural field.[106]

Several initiatives on culture were taken by UNESCO and accorded considerable attention and resources. The protection of cultural heritage developed as a major activity after 1959, when Egypt and Sudan issued an urgent request to UNESCO to provide help with the safeguarding of the sites and monuments of Nubia. The historic temple complex of Abu Simbel was threatened with submersion by the lake that was being created as part of the construction of the Aswan Dam. UNESCO appealed to "governments, institutions, public and private foundations and all persons of goodwill" to provide financial and technical support. Thus was established a new idea—the new principle and concept under which such exceptional world treasures "could be seen as belonging to the cultural heritage of humanity and were therefore of concern to the entire international community."[107] On this principle, UNESCO built the World Cultural Heritage Program, which was later expanded to incorporate nature sites of great importance.[108]

A number of conventions, recommendations, and charters were adopted to back up the principle of a common cultural heritage. These covered the protection of cultural property in situations of armed conflict; the protection and restoration of monuments and sites; measures to prohibit and prevent illicit import, export, and transfer of ownership of cultural property; and the Convention concerning the Protection of the World Cultural and Natural Heritage, better known as the World Heritage Convention.[109]

These important measures were all agreed upon in the years between 1954 and the 1970s. It was not until 1989 that the same concern was turned to safeguarding traditional culture and folklore, and it was nearly a decade after that before a system was implemented for the institutional recognition of the "oral and immaterial heritage of humanity."[110] Whereas the Western paradigm turns all things into objects—for example, "knowledge," "life forms," or "commerce" —traditional communities tend to regard all things as processes—for example, "knowing," "coming to know," or "living."[111]

In relation to culture of the people, UNESCO took somewhat longer to get action under way. In 1963, UNESCO produced one of its early publications, *Social Change and Economic Development.*[112] This explored how to take account of "cultural readjustment" in economic development programs. It was an attempt to respond to "the problem" of resistance to "technical improvement in communities governed by principles which run counter to such improvements." Its author, Jean Meynaud, recognized that the evidence for such problems often reflected hasty analysis, and sometimes racial prejudice, leading to charges of apathy among industrial workers and to more general complaints about the attitudes of workers. He stressed that this problem had become a live issue as a consequence of the desire for independence in countries and the eagerness for development. The publication recommended "the study of cultural models" to help situate the individual in his or her social context, since "it is largely through the imitation of such models that attitudes become established and are handed on."[113]

In 1969, UNESCO embarked on a program to help governments formulate cultural policy that linked culture to the fulfillment of personality and to economic and social development.[114] From the beginning, the role of government was controversial. The U.S. argued against central governments having the right to set policy on the grounds that this would force states and the private sector to adopt concepts regarding culture that were suitable to their aims, resulting in a pluralistic approach. The U.S. position was based on diversity, not plurality, in cultural policy.[115]

A further effort was made in 1982 with the first World Conference on Cultural Policies in Mexico City.[116] The very title of the conference—Mondiacult—was apparently chosen to signify the broadest possible perspective on culture. The conference themes ranged over "the whole complex of distinctive spiritual, material, intellectual and emotional features that characterize a society or social group." They included "not only the arts and letters, but also modes of life, the fundamental rights of the human being, value systems, traditions and beliefs."[117] The Mondiacult Declaration, with which the conference concluded, stated: "Balanced development can only be insured by making cultural factors an integral part of the strategies designed to achieve it; consequently, these strategies should always be devised in the light of the historical, social and cultural context of each society."[118]

After such lofty but vague generalities, it is a mercy to move to something more precise and substantive. As part of a World Decade for Cultural Development (1988 to 1997), an Independent World Commission on Culture and Development was established jointly by the UN and UNESCO that was chaired by Javier Pèrez de Cuèllar, the former Secretary-General.[119] Its pioneering report, *Our Creative Diversity,* was published in 1995.[120]

This report made some important and elegantly expressed contributions to ideas on culture and development. Under its opening statement, "Development divorced from its human or cultural context is growth without a soul,"[121] the report elaborated what it argued was a new approach. The commission advanced the view that far from culture being merely an instrument that helped or hindered the process of economic development, economic development is part of a people's culture.[122] Culture was central, not economic development.

This realization led to a more profound and positive view of culture and development. The commission argued that culture was the fountain of progress and creativity and that, in its full meaning, development encompasses cultural growth. Here the commission drew on ideas of human development, with which some of its members were already closely associated,[123] as the very essence of human development is a process of broadening choices and strengthening human capabilities. Cultural growth and cultural diversity add to the choices available and give richness, depth, and subtlety to human capabilities. As the commission put it, development is "a process that enhances the effective freedom of the people involved to pursue whatever they have reason to value."[124]

Our Creative Diversity tackled the problem that faces all liberal philosophies which emphasize enlarging choices as the essence of the good life and the good social system. Are there some choices—in this case some cultural traditions—which must be excluded? For example, should traditions involving discrimination against women or religious beliefs involving prejudice or superiority toward other groups be excluded? In a world where social and racial prejudice and religious fanaticism have become familiar and at times have led to the extremes of ethnic cleansing and genocide, these issues take on an immediate relevance and urgency. The World Commission on Culture and Development argued that "[u]niversalism is the fundamental principle of a global ethics."[125] Its report saw the development of international standards of human rights as helping to define this global ethic, with democracy and protection of minorities as important principles and as conditions for social stability and peace. The commission also included the important principle of protecting future generations by sustaining the environment and keeping other options open for future generations.

All of these ideas reinforce ideas of the culture of peace—"a process by which positive attitudes to peace, democracy and tolerance are forged through education and knowledge about different cultures."[126] Just as the founders of the United Nations dreamed of peace, so the World Commission on Culture and Development had a bold vision for the future that was built on the widest possible democratic mobilization of people.

Nonetheless, the influence of the media and the power and influence of those who control it raise most serious questions about whether this promise can be realized. Global television and much of the movie industry is dominated by a small number of producers, almost all of whom are based in the industrial countries. The world trade in goods with cultural content—printed matter; literature; music; the visual arts, both cinema and photographic; and radio and television equipment—almost tripled between 1980 and 1991, from $67 to $200 billion.[127] Hollywood has 70 percent of the film market in Europe, 83 percent in Latin America, and 50 percent in Japan.[128] From the viewpoint of cultural diversity, the challenge is not only the economic domination of the global market or even the shrinking of the numbers of national producers of film or television. It is rather how countries can avoid the spread of global consumer culture and cultural homogenization in ways which keep space open for their own cultural activities and their own strong cultural identities. If development is to have a soul in the twenty-first century, this challenge must remain high on the global agenda.

Box 8.2. Dag Hammarskjöld: The Core of Art and Culture to His Life as Secretary-General

In modern international politics—aiming toward that world of order which now more than ever seems to be the only alternative to disruption and disaster—we have to approach our task in the spirit which animates the modern artist. We have to tackle our problems without the armour of inherited convictions or set formulas, but only with our bare hands and all the honesty we can muster. And we have to do so with an unbreakable will to master the inert matter of patterns created by history and sociological conditions.[129]

The following passages are excerpted from Brian Urquhart, "Dag Hammarskjöld: A Leader in the Field of Culture," *Development Dialogue* 1 (2001): 15–16.

One of the most impressive and unusual features of Dag Hammarskjöld's way of life was the integration of all his interests and pursuits into one scheme of activity. Literature, music, the visual arts and nature were both his recreation and an important and sustaining part of his routine. As Barbara Hepworth (distinguished sculptor and friend of the Secretary General), put it, "Dag Hammarskjold had a pure and exact perception of aesthetic principles, as exact as it was over ethic and moral principles. I believe they were, to him, one and the same thing."

Even at his most critical periods, Hammarskjold made a point of finding time for his literary and artistic interests. Just before and during the period of the Congo crisis, which absorbed absolutely all the time and energy of the rest of us, he translated into Swedish Perse's *Chronique* and Djuna Barnes' extremely difficult play, *The Antiphon,* which premiered in Stockholm, published an article on Mount Everest with his own superb photographs, and kept up a correspondence with Barbara Hepworth. Hammarskjold also started on a translation of Martin Buber's *Ich und Du,* which he was actually working on during his fatal last flight. He evaded answering a journalist who asked him how he found time for all this extra-curricular activity. The point, I think, is that, for Hammarskjold, it was not extra-curricular. It was very much a part of a perfectly balanced curriculum.

Hammarskjold instituted the tradition of annual concerts on UN Day—concerts which had the largest worldwide broadcast audience in history. He devoted a great deal of time and attention to the programs and other details of these concerts and was extraordinarily knowledgeable about music.

Hammarskjold regarded as completely private the essential part of his life devoted to the arts. None of us at the time had any idea of the extent and variety of it. Nor did we know much of his love of nature, and the walks he delighted in, whether around Brewster in New York, where he had a weekend house, or along the shore in Skane, or in the mountains of Lapland. His beautiful photographs are a lasting witness to his love of nature.

Box 8.3. To Convey the Spirit of Professionalism and Cultural Sensitivity among UN Interpreters[130]

Without interpreters and translators, the United Nations would have been a Tower of Babel. Simultaneous interpretation is an art, just as much as is political negotiation. To reach international agreement, diplomats must find the right words, the right tone, and the right emphasis in order to convey a message and then recast it as advances are made toward agreement. But what good will this do if an interpreter is not there to convey exactly the right words, the right tone, the right emphasis—in sum, to convey the spirit of such a negotiation? Interpreters cannot forsake meaning while searching for the right word, and they must think and act fast to convey meaning as accurately and rapidly as possible. This is why interpreters need special skills—both a fluent knowledge of other languages and a deep understanding of other cultures.

Many of the early UN interpreters were trained for interpretation at the Nuremberg trials by Colonel Dostert. All came from multicultural backgrounds. Extending such simultaneous translation to the United Nations, however, drew great skepticism early on from delegates. It was argued that consecutive translation, which had been used in the League of Nations, allowed greater accuracy in rhetorical expression in speeches and would be lost in simultaneous translation. Even so, at its plenary meeting on 1 February 1946, the UN General Assembly recommended that "the Secretary General [make] thorough [enquiries] into the question of the installation of telephonic systems of interpretation."[131]

Once installed, the system became indispensable. Interpretation was extended to six languages: English, French, Spanish, Chinese, Russian, and Arabic. More than just literal translations were required of interpreters.

At the height of the Cold War, interpreters had to deal with both oratory and ideological combat.[132] Since the 1970s they have also had to become experts on many technical subjects—science and technology, the environment, outer space, women, and population. In the 1990s, political and diplomatic eloquence has changed toward more practical issues and greater recourse to well-built arguments. Pressure on interpreters has also increased because reporters use their interpretations immediately for media dissemination even before the corresponding official documents are published.

Interpreters always strive to be professionally neutral in their work. When they formed a professional association, the main item in the codes of ethics was the code of secrecy and discretion. Yet as they themselves describe their craft, it is human communication they are conveying.

The United Nations will always be a multilateral and, hence, a multilingual organization that will always be in need of interpreters. And to carry on with ever-more complex and global negotiations, the subtle skills of interpreters will always be needed to convey the right spirit of seeking international intercultural agreements.

Concluding Observations

The UN has been closely related to promotion of improvements in the human condition from its very beginning in 1945—indeed, considerably before, if one takes account of the work of the ILO on working conditions, the Pan American Health Organization's work on health in Latin America, and the work of the League of Nations on issues of population and nutrition.

But with the UN's creation, improvements in the human condition were recognized to be a basic function of the organization—in Article 55 of the Charter—and rights to health, education, and certain other basic aspects of well-being were specifically recognized in the Universal Declaration and in the mandates of the UN agencies concerned with health and education.

In the key areas of population, nutrition, health, and education the UN has made substantial contributions—both in formulating ideas and in providing leadership for national and international policymakers. Because over most of this period the UN's international role in these areas has not been challenged, the UN must be credited with at least some of the considerable and often remarkable progress which has been achieved in all these areas and in all regions of the world. Moreover, as judged by the basic statistics of life expectancy, reductions in child mortality, nutrition, and access to education, the gaps between the richest and the poorest countries have narrowed during the life of the United Nations. This contrasts sharply with the widening gaps in income between the richest and the poorest countries.

However, this praiseworthy record is not without important areas where questions must be raised. Though the UN became active in promoting concern with population policy beginning in the 1970s, one must ask whether this concern might have emerged earlier or advocacy on the issue might have been more effective. Though fertility rates have fallen rapidly, often more rapidly than at first anticipated, global population has grown at unprecedented rates and is still projected to increase by a further 50 percent before leveling off soon after the middle of the twenty-first century.[133]

Health and education raise different issues. In both these key sectors, the UN called for rapid advances in the early years, much earlier than was done in the Bretton Woods institutions. However, progress often slipped badly in the lost decade of the 1980s, especially in sub-Saharan Africa, Latin America, and the Caribbean. This was in large part because of the rising economic problems of debt, terms-of-trade declines, and declining aid. But it was also due to the failure of adjustment policies to give priority to protecting the human situations of the population in the countries concerned. The UN could have done more to argue for a different and more human approach to adjustment.

Finally, culture. Here the record shows that apart from minor exceptions, most of the UN has neglected the cultural dimensions of development, at least until the last decade of the twentieth century. Following the World Commission on Culture and Development in the late 1990s, UNESCO issued some innovative reports.[134] But the area remains one where much more awareness and sensitivity is required.

Notwithstanding these weaknesses, the long experience of the UN in all these critical areas provides a solid foundation of ideas and institutional strength on which the UN can build. The paradigm of human development provides a new rationale for strengthening human capabilities as the foundation for human development in all countries. The priorities accorded to poverty reduction and the Millennium Development Goals reinforce this need, and the specialized organizations and funds of the UN have a leading role to play in this endeavor.

9

Structural and Sectoral Change

- **Agricultural Development**
- **World Food Security and the Right to Food**
- **The WFP**
- **IFAD**
- **Industrial Development**
- **Disarmament and Development**

In the first decades of the UN, the essence of development was thought to be changes in the economic and social structures of underdeveloped countries. Underdeveloped countries were those in which almost all the population was poor and rural, depended on agriculture for its livelihood, and spent a very high proportion of its income, in cash or kind, on food. Industrial production in most underdeveloped countries at the time was small, both absolutely and as a share of the country's total production. Exports of primary products to earn foreign exchange to buy imports from industrial countries was the main way to obtain industrial goods. These characteristics of underdeveloped countries reflected both the legacy of colonial dependence and the main economic challenge which underdeveloped countries, especially newly independent ones, needed to face. The moves to independence were the political background to this process in many countries, as was the process of nation-building and the replacement of colonial officials by a national administration. But these political and administrative changes were mostly treated as parallel to the process of development planning and action—not part of an integral process of development.

In parallel, the UN was developing as a multifaceted body, reflecting the many international concerns of its member states. As the UN grew—and over time, it grew with increasing intensity and complexity—the Secretariat and the various agencies and organizations of the UN found themselves having to relate to an increasing number of areas and issues which were found to form part of development policy and strategy. In agriculture and the rural sector, these included land reform, natural resources, soil fertility, food safety, pastoralism, rural technologies, small-scale markets, fertilizers, regulations for international trade in food and commodities, and pricing, not to mention equivalent aspects of fisheries and forestry. In the same way, the UN found itself needing to relate to a myriad of issues in industry, urban development, the promotion and regulation of services, science and technology for development, international shipping and aviation, telecommunications and postal services, intellectual property rights, and public administration. Later, the UN would also be asked to take on more specific problems of development—drug control, money-laundering, crime prevention, and the environmental consequences of economic growth and development.

It would take too much space and be tiresomely detailed to describe and analyze all these involvements. Rather, this chapter will concentrate on three areas of structural and sectoral change where the UN has made important contributions: agricultural and rural development, industrial development, and disarmament and development.

Agricultural Development

When the UN was created, most poor people lived in rural areas and depended on agriculture, directly or indirectly, for their livelihoods. This is still true today in most low-income countries. In the urban areas, then as today, the poorest people spend a high proportion of their limited incomes on foodstuffs. Thus, the capacity of the agricultural sector to produce low-priced food of good nutritional quality matters to the health and welfare of the whole population. Even this last assertion must be qualified, as will be seen later, by the fact that poor peasants, who are often very poor and suffering hunger themselves, need to sell their crops at adequate prices in order to escape their poverty.

These realities point to the seven basic ways in which the agricultural sector can contribute to a people-centered process of development: by serving as a source of food production, by generating income in cash or kind, by creating formal and informal employment, by earning foreign exchange for the country through exports, by producing inputs for other sectors, by serving as a source of labor for the urban sector, and, finally, by acting as an employment safety net for poor urban dwellers. The first three and the last two of these help individual households directly. All of them contribute to development in the economy at large. And all seven have an international dimension, linking local impacts and concerns to international policy and action.

An American businessman, David Lubin, first saw the need for international action in support of agriculture and took the early initiatives, some fifty years before the founding of the UN and of FAO. Lubin, a businessman-turned-farmer, had personally experienced the problems of agriculture during depression in the late nineteenth century—yet another example of global initiatives arising from a sense of national crisis in the more advanced countries. This experience led David Lubin to the conclusion that

> the modern economy was a battleground between conflicting interests: agriculture was at a great disadvantage in comparison with industry, commerce and finance because farmers were not effectively organized. However, it was not enough to organize at the national level: trade played such a major role in price-setting that only an international organization could satisfactorily defend farmers' interests. Farmers in different nations, he urged, had less to fear from each other than from exploitation and speculation in their own countries.[1]

Lubin found no support for his ideas in the United States, so he sought allies in Europe. Rebuffed in London and Paris, he eventually obtained help from Italy's king, Victor Emmanuel III. This led to an international conference convened by the Italian government in 1905, which established the IIA—the International Institute of Agriculture.[2] Though differing in many ways from the international chamber of agriculture that he had envisaged, the origin of the IIA clearly was Lubin.

The IIA started operations in 1908 as an intergovernmental technical body that was concerned with collecting information and statistics and formulating proposals to governments regarding measures to protect the common interests of farmers and improve the conditions of farmers. The IIA later developed the first system for the worldwide collection of agricultural statistics[3] and in 1929–1930 organized the first World Census of Agriculture.[4] The IIA had already pioneered several other firsts in the 1920s—the first International Convention on Locust Control (1920), the first International Wheat Conference (1927), and the first International Convention on Plant Protection (1929).

There was a second strand of international concern linked to agriculture. The pioneering work of the League of Nations on the problems of nutrition had revealed widespread malnutrition in the most-advanced countries that was linked to the unemployment and poverty brought by the Great Depression of the 1930s. Yet there were serious contradictions in the ideas and policy recommendations that sought to address the problem. Agriculture was in serious worldwide difficulties, and wheat imports of the industrialized countries had fallen drastically. Farmers thus had growing surpluses, leading economists to argue for cutbacks in production. Nutritionists, in contrast, were advocating increased consumption.

The founders of the FAO brought vision and strong convictions to their work when they decided to establish a permanent organization in the field of food and agriculture.[5] The FAO's broad mandate was strongly influenced by three founding luminaries in science and nutrition—John Boyd Orr, Frank McDougall, and André Mayer, who described the purpose as bringing about "a marriage between health and agriculture." The FAO's mission was "to adapt the production and distribution of food to the needs of humanity and to ensure a sufficient and balanced diet for all by attacking the very root cause of hunger: poverty."[6]

The Early Vision: Food for All and the Ending of Malnutrition

The goals of food for all and the ending of malnutrition on a global scale were driving passions of the founders of the FAO. The preamble of the FAO's constitution referred to the nations that accepted the constitution as "being determined to promote the common welfare . . . for the purposes of raising [the] levels of nutrition and standards of living of the peoples under their respective jurisdictions,"[7] to which was added in 1965 "and ensuring humanity's freedom from hunger."[8]

But controversy started immediately. We mentioned in the previous chapter the rejection of the World Food Plan proposed by FAO's director-general, John Boyd Orr, in 1946. Three years later, the proposal to establish an "international commodity clearing house" was rejected by the FAO conference.[9] In 1954, FAO's Principles of Surplus (Food) Disposal were formulated, a Consultative Sub-Committee on Surplus Disposal was set up in Washington,[10] and the Agricultural Trade Development and Assistance Act was passed, which institutionalized U.S. food aid. But in 1958, four years later, the FAO's proposal to establish an international emergency food aid reserve was not approved.[11]

This was not the last time proposals for action to implement a humanitarian plan to end hunger and malnutrition would be developed with vision and idealism, only to fall prey to cynicism and short-term self-interest. Some might argue that the rejection was not of the vision but of the means proposed to achieve it—a global policy, a global plan, a world food board, and various world institutions to implement and monitor policy. Lord John Boyd Orr, the FAO's first director-general, summarized with some bitterness his view of the causes of British opposition to a world food policy:

> England's wealth had been created by the import of cheap food and raw material produced by natives with wages so low that they lived in abysmal poverty, and paid for by expensive industrial products. The suggestion of a "new deal" for the native producers, beginning with a fair price for the food Britain imported, seemed to threaten English economic prosperity.[12]

Boyd Orr was not making ideological points; he was thinking back to the 1930s, when Britain's Conservative Party had offered support for a world food plan based on human needs. Boyd Orr also believed that the U.S. position was explained by the departure of Franklin Roosevelt, the growth of the influence of big business in U.S. politics, and the reluctance of the U.S. to support any scheme in which it would have to put up half the cost.[13]

Edouard Saouma, the FAO's sixth director-general (1975–1993), summarized the battle as between the specialists who believed that the FAO should have an active and dynamic role and the representatives of the political powers, "who preached prudence bordering on total opposition to change"—especially when the proposals "did not square with the political views and commercial interests of the powerful developed nations that were the first signatories of the Constitution."[14]

Once these proposals were rejected, the FAO's work for the first two decades was confined to technical assistance. In the much-quoted words of Boyd Orr, "The people ask for bread and we give them pamphlets."[15] When people claim today that the UN writes too many reports and spends too little time in action, it is worth remembering that it was the developed-country powers of the time that insisted on this priority, at least for the FAO.

Nonetheless, the FAO's technical assistance made some important contributions and grew rapidly. In 1947, the United Nations Relief and Rehabilitation Administration (UNRRA) transferred $1.1 million to the FAO for technical assistance—just over one-tenth of the FAO's regular budget in those days. By 1956–1957, the FAO's technical assistance budget was more than the regular budget and over half of the FAO's total annual expenditure. By 1980–1981 it was more than thirty times its size twenty-five years earlier and formed over two-thirds of the FAO's total expenditure.[16] Professional staff in the field or in country or regional offices also grew rapidly and soon accounted for nearly two-thirds of total staff[17]—though both numbers and proportions had fallen by 1995 as a result of economies and cutbacks.[18]

Mobilizing Global Awareness

The delivery of advice in the form of pamphlets and technical assistance was not all. Under an initiative of Dr. B. R. Sen, the FAO's fourth director-general—and the first from a developing country—the organization launched in 1960 the Freedom from Hunger Campaign (FFHC) to arouse public awareness on a global scale and stimulate concrete action and participation. Promoting the idea that "one man's hunger and want is everyman's hunger and want," the FFHC brought into prominence the role NGOs could play. Sen's passionate insistence also led to a revision of the FAO constitution to include in the preamble the words "ensuring humanity's freedom from hunger."[19]

Another development was the creation in 1965 of the FAO/Industry Cooperative Programme, operated under a trust fund to which participating industries contributed.[20] The FFHC continued for at least two decades. In 1979, the conference of the FAO instituted World Food Day,[21] to be celebrated on 16 October, in order to inspire thought, resolution, and action regarding food and agriculture and to stimulate new commitments to agriculture and the rural sector.

Some might judge that these efforts to mobilize public awareness and commitment were of little value. This would be a mistake. Over the years, such efforts by the UN have had a substantive practical impact by energizing NGOs and mobilizing public support more directly. Even if it cannot be quantified, support for the goals of poverty reduction, for development, for aid, and for relief in times of drought and humanitarian disasters owes much to the steady buildup of awareness and informed public opinion through such programs.

From the earliest days, the FAO undertook surveys and issued reports outlining and analyzing the current knowledge of the world's food problems. The first survey was published in 1946, less than nine months after the organization's founding meeting in Quebec.[22] It covered seventy countries, whose population accounted for about 90 percent of the world population. The survey's principal finding was that in regions with over half the world population, food supplies provided an average of less than 2,250 calories per capita daily.[23] It proposed nutritional targets and calculated the country-by-country increases in production and consumption that would be needed to attain them.[24] Despite various methodological weaknesses, the survey was a pioneering attempt to analyze the world food and nutrition situation.

A second survey was published in 1952 and four more were published after that—in 1963, 1977, 1985, and 1999. Though the quality of the data in many countries improved somewhat and various improvements were made in the methodology, the weakness remained that all the surveys were based on the food balance-sheet method. Essentially, this meant that the calculations made in each country were of all forms of food produced and estimates were made of how much of this food was available for domestic human consumption. As a final step, these totals were converted into estimated equivalents in calories. These caloric totals were then divided by adult population equivalents, taking account of the age composition of the population, reference body weight, estimated average physical activity, and mean environmental temperature. The final result became an estimate of average calorie consumption per person for each country.

In spite of the sophistication of the various adjustments, the fact remains that the final result is an estimated average of calorie consumption per person over the calendar year for each country. It is not surprising that the methodology has given rise to severe criticisms, an underlying rumble of controversy that every so often reached a crescendo of criticism, questioning whether the whole effort produced information of any real meaning or value. More meaningful data has often been demanded: statistical information on actual consumption from sample surveys that take account of variations in consumption by different income groups or different regional groups in different parts of a country. The need to focus on seasonal variations over the year has been emphasized and, more directly, the need to focus on the nutritional status of different groups of each country's population. The response of the FAO has been that some estimate of total world food supply in relation to total world population is needed, especially in relation to how the country averages compare between countries and over time. For all their weaknesses and conceptual difficulties, the calorie averages are used and help, the organization argues, to identify countries where food production presents problems and needs action.

Box 9.1. The Codex Alimentarius

The Assyrians, the Egyptians, and the Romans were already concerned with codifying rules to protect food consumers. This tradition was pursued throughout the Middle Ages and modern times. In 1950, a joint FAO/WHO Expert Committee on Nutrition noted: "Food regulations in different countries are often conflicting and contradictory. . . . New legislation not based on scientific knowledge is often introduced, and little account may be taken of nutritional principles in formulating regulations."[25] This legislation has implications for trade and health. The ECE focused on the trade dimension in developing its common standards for perishable foodstuffs, which are mainly used by importers and wholesalers. The FAO contributed to the building of international norms for safety in food production, food preparation, and food trade. In 1961, a major step was the establishment in the FAO, with the cooperation of the WHO, the ECE, the OECD, and ECOSOC, of the Codex Alimentarius Europaeus, a comprehensive international system of food standards.[26] The Codex Alimentarius has remained a centerpiece of the FAO's contributions to international standard-setting.[27]

Though in many respects it was pioneering, the Codex Alimentarius can be criticized on three major counts. First, by aiming at general international standards, the norms may at times be set at too high a level to be within the practical capacities of poorer countries. When basic human safety is at risk, the case for high standards is difficult to argue against. A second argument is that the Codex has been too influenced by the commercial interests of multinational corporations and rich-country producers. In such cases, norms can lead to standards which favor large-scale production methods that are more matched to the capacities of big corporations and large farmers than to those of small-scale farmers. Third, both arguments have taken on more relevance in recent years with the growth of global trade and greater concerns with food safety in the industrial countries.

In addition to the Codex, the FAO developed norms and standards in other areas. In 1983, the International Undertaking on Plant Genetic Resources was adopted by the FAO Conference, "based on the universally accepted principle that plant genetic resources are a heritage of mankind and consequently should be available without restriction."[28] The objective was to make sure that all the resources involved are surveyed, well stored, evaluated, and made available to breeders and researchers.[29] There were, of course, major disagreements,

> on the definition of the plant genetic resources to be covered and therefore to constitute a freely accessible international heritage. Most of the developed countries wanted to consider only wild and cultivated species and varieties, whereas the developing countries wanted a much wider coverage encompassing all species representing or capable of representing in the future, an economic or social benefit, particularly for agriculture. The latter interpretation prevailed but it gave rise to reservations on the part of several industrialized countries.[30]

The debate did not end there. A Commission on Plant Genetic Resources was set up to monitor the development of international arrangements.[31] A particular focus was on the rights of farmers, who for generations have conserved and improved plant genetic resources. By 1989, it was clarified that the expression "free access" did not mean "access free of charge" and that "common heritage of humanity" was in fact a principle subordinate to that of the sovereignty of nations. Nonetheless, by 1992 at the International Conference on Environment and Development, the Earth Summit in Rio de Janeiro, the early ideas and principles of the undertaking were drawn upon to become the Convention on Biological Diversity.[32]

Initially, the Codex was more concerned with tropical products. When developing countries started to produce "temperate food products" for industrialized-country markets, the risk grew that competing norms produced by the ECE and the Codex would trigger trade disputes. Protracted negotiations will soon result in the inclusion of ECE norms in the Codex.

World Food Security and the Right to Food

Postwar surpluses of food began to emerge around 1952–1953. As in the 1930s and at Roosevelt's 1943 conference on world food production at Hot Springs, Virginia, the topic engendered heated debate. The 1953 FAO Conference stated unequivocally that the main remedy for surpluses was to be found in "courageous policies for increasing consumption."[33] This led to the preparation of FAO's Guiding Lines and Principles of Surplus Disposal, drawn up by the FAO Committee on Commodity Problems. At the core of these voluntary principles were the twin objectives to avoid disruption to regular trade and to discourage food production in countries receiving the surpluses. Initially, the surpluses were mainly from the United States. Within a few years, interest grew in the possibilities of a multilateral scheme, building on a proposal in a 1956 FAO staff paper for a World Food Capital Fund, which at the time had not been accepted.[34]

In 1974, the World Food Conference was convened in completely different circumstances.[35] By this date, food crises affected the lives of millions in Africa, Asia, and Eastern Europe. Shortfalls in production and inadequate food reserves had resulted in the trebling of grain prices. The conference agreed on ways to improve food production, storage facilities at the local or national level, research, and land and water use at the country level. It also drew attention to the need for policies and structures that would benefit landless laborers and small farmers, and agricultural policies that were fully integrated into national development strategies. But the conference failed to deal adequately with international constraints on food exports from developing countries and on other issues of the international food trade. Moreover, almost no progress has been made since then.

Food trade is an important way of easing national food shortfalls. It is a good mechanism when there are only weak national mechanisms to adjust to fluctuations in national production. In spite of these good arguments, an international agreement on reserve stocks was rejected in 1974. Moreover, the negotiations on the wheat trade which did get under way failed in 1979. In the 1980s and 1990s, while food exports from developing countries continued to meet innumerable obstacles in developed countries, strong pressures from the Bretton Woods institutions, GATT (WTO), and the industrialized countries were successfully exercised on the developing countries to liberalize food imports. While this practice certainly helped provide cheap food to urban people, its effects often increased poverty and hunger in rural areas, where the majority of the poor lived. Liberalization of trade imposes international prices on the national markets of developing countries, but in agriculture, these prices have little economic significance because food exports from developed countries are so heavily subsidized. Poor peasants are thus exposed to unfair competition and are obliged to sell increasing amounts of their production to maintain their incomes. Often they end up without adequate means to provide for their family.

Such analysis, though well established in academic and NGO documents as well as in some FAO papers, was not discussed at the World Food Summits in 1996 and 2002.[36] Trade issues were left to the WTO. The division of interrelated issues between different organizations with different concerns and rationales deprives the United Nations of the ability to promote appropriate comprehensive policies.

Within the UN system proper, the necessary complementary approaches are sometimes better coordinated. The right to food is a case in point. It is implicit in the 1948 Universal Declaration of Human Rights[37] and explicit in Article 11 of the 1966 International Covenant on Economic, Social and Cultural Rights[38] (as a result of a direct intervention by Dr. B. R. Sen, then director-general of the FAO), but it remained, like many other economic and social rights, more of a declaration than a guideline for urgent action until the World Food Summit in 1996. Though the 1996 summit was not able to reach an agreement to call for the development of a code of conduct on the right to adequate food, its plan of action invited the high commissioner for human rights "to better define the rights related to food in Article 11 of the Covenant."[39] This led to the 1999 General Comment 12 on the Right to Adequate Food[40] and at the 2002 summit to the decision to elaborate voluntary guidelines related to the implementation of the right to adequate food.[41] Though the definitions of the right to adequate food, food security, and food sovereignty appear to be clear (see Box 9.2), debate has continued on the relative emphasis to be put on availability of food versus generating sufficient income to buy food and on the margin of maneuver of the state in implementing the right to adequate food.

Box 9.2. The Right to Food: Food Security and Food Sovereignty

The right to adequate food is defined as the right of every man, woman, and child, alone and in community with others, to have physical and economic access at all times to adequate food or the means to procure it in ways that are consistent with human dignity. The definition used by General Comment 12 highlights the access to an income base of each individual either through access to productive resources (land, fish, seeds, etc.) or through work, or, if not possible, through adequate transfers.

Food security was defined by the World Food Summit in 1996: "Food security exists when all people, at all times, have physical and economic access to sufficient, safe and nutritious food to meet their dietaries needs and food preferences for an active and healthy life."[42] Food security and the right to adequate food both emphasize the right of individuals or households to access to income or food-producing resources in dignity.

The concept of "food sovereignty" has been promoted in recent years by alliances of small farmers' organizations, landless peasants, and indigenous communities. Food sovereignty means that countries have the right to decide how to supply themselves with food products without outside economic or political interference.

> **Box 9.3. The World Food Council**
>
> Created in 1974 by the General Assembly, following a resolution of the 1974 World Food Conference,[43] the World Food Council acted as a global ministerial forum on food and agricultural issues until it was abolished in 1996 following the World Food Summit of the same year and an intergovernmental review.
>
> The 1974 World Food Conference had made clear that the elimination of the scourge of hunger should take place through integrated actions in different national and international sectors. The WFC had also assigned responsibilities to existing UN agencies. The WFC was established to ensure coordinated follow-up and monitor progress.
>
> In a succession of innovative and sometimes outspoken reports, the WFC made recommendations for more integrated food policies, encouraged greater food self-reliance, and encouraged the liberalization of trade in agricultural products. It also organized training for policymakers.
>
> Constrained by the obligation to reach unanimous agreement and without any direct authority over other UN agencies, the WFC became an obvious candidate for abolition in the mid-1990s, when the UN came under heavy pressure from governments obsessed with cutting costs in the UN.

The WFP

By the end of the 1950s, influential voices in the U.S. were calling for a multilateral food aid facility. How the UN World Food Programme (WFP) developed has been described in Chapter 4 and in more detail and with great care by John Shaw.[44]

With positive support from the U.S., the WFP was created[45] as an "expanded program of surplus food utilization," but it soon evolved to become the food-aid arm of the UN focused both on disaster relief and development and on pioneering new ways to support poor people in poor countries, especially through food for work and food for schoolchildren.

A major part of the WFP's contribution has been in developing ideas which have enabled it to become an international system to provide food supplies and to pioneer methods to use those supplies in ways which are efficient and which avoid disincentives to local food producers, especially small-scale farmers. Hans Singer identifies five areas where WFP ideas and mechanisms have been pioneering:

1. Building a mechanism for food aid to become multilateral.
2. Establishing a policy framework for food aid, both for development and for emergency relief.

3. Developing a project approach for food aid.
4. Becoming a principal international channel for food aid and institutionally becoming a natural coordinator of food aid globally and within countries.
5. Developing roles for food aid in the continuum between disaster relief and development.[46]

IFAD

The International Fund for Agricultural Development (IFAD) was a child of the 1974 World Food Conference, which decided to set up a new multilateral financial institution with a mandate to combat hunger and rural poverty and focus on the poorest rural communities.[47] Its structure and mandate contained several innovations. Its board was trilateral—initially one-third of the members were from developing recipient countries, one-third from the oil-exporting donor countries, and one-third from the developed countries—and it was the first UN funding agency with a governing body on which developing countries were in the majority. Funding was also split between oil-producing and industrial countries, at least initially. Finally, IFAD's innovative spirit is well shown by the fact that it is the only UN funding body in which the clients are formally defined not as governments but as the poorest people.

Over the more than twenty-five years of its life, IFAD has been a pioneer in identifying and supporting a number of innovative programs and projects,[48] most notably microcredit schemes in the late 1970s, well before other UN agencies and most donors recognized the important potential of these programs for helping the poorest people in many parts of the world.

From the earliest phases of the UN and its specialized agencies, direct action to end poverty was recognized as a central focus of UN work in the agricultural and rural sectors, probably more so than in economic planning in general. Much of this focus stemmed from concern about malnutrition and the ideas and thinking of the founders of the UN and the FAO, who recognized poverty as the major cause of malnutrition. At the World Food Conference in 1974, this focus was sharpened further, challenged by the experience of development in the 1950s and 1960s, which had made only too clear the limitations of approaches which focused only on economic growth and production. With the creation of IFAD in 1978, a UN agency existed with the sole function of targeting assistance to the rural poor.[49]

In relation to World Bank funding or private-sector flows, IFAD remained small. But from the beginning it was innovative, struggling to be fast-moving and to maintain a clear focus on the poorest people. From the start of its operations in 1978 until 2000, IFAD supported nearly 600 projects with over $7 billion, which with other donor grants and domestic contributions added up to about $27 billion.[50]

Over the years, IFAD's approach to poverty reduction evolved. IFAD was one of the first of the UN agencies to involve poor people in defining priorities and in designing and implementing highly participatory projects that respond to the basic needs of rural women as well as men. It was the first international donor to make loans to the Grameen Bank in Bangladesh (in the late 1970s), thereby demonstrating confidence that loans to the poor were bankable; it was remarkable at the time for such recognition to come from an international funding agency. IFAD has also pioneered cooperation with NGOs as stakeholders from the beginning and involved them in the final negotiations concerning projects. Between 80 and 90 percent of all ongoing IFAD projects target women specifically.[51]

Drawing on its field experience, IFAD also issued some pioneering documents on the nature of rural poverty and policies to accelerate the reduction of such poverty.[52] From an early stage, IFAD recognized and emphasized that a focus on production and growth alone would not be sufficient to reduce poverty. It stressed the need for parallel actions in many other areas, such as improving the allocation and distribution of water and direct action for disadvantaged groups such as ethnic minorities, hill people, and those living in semi-arid regions.[53]

Box 9.4. Nigeria: Oil Wealth but at a Price

Nigeria is the largest country in Africa by population, with over 110 million people accounting for about one-fifth of the population in sub-Saharan Africa. It has been blessed with agricultural and enormous mineral resources. Nevertheless, through most of the time since independence, these resources have been used wastefully and have been looted for personal enrichment. Transparency International has repeatedly assessed Nigeria as the most corrupt country in the world.[54] Its development experience over the last fifty years demonstrates that resources alone are not enough to assure development. Indeed, easy access to very large resources, as with the agricultural and mineral resources in Nigeria, may derail the development process.

In the 1950s, Nigeria's economy grew by over 4 percent per annum, propelled largely by the growth of agricultural exports. During that period, incentives were provided to stimulate industrial production. After independence, more deliberate measures were taken to step up the pace of industrialization and to increase the national share in the nonagricultural sectors.[55]

The civil war of 1969–1970 led to the imposition of exchange controls, licensing of imports, and price controls on selected products. Most of these mechanisms were retained after the war as tools of economic planning. Thus, allocation of foreign exchange for imports of capital equipment and intermediate goods was used to promote industrialization and the granting of subsidized credit from banks. While in the 1950s and early 1960s incentives were directed to foreign investors, later efforts were made to enhance Nigerian control and participation in the industrial sector.

In the early 1970s, Nigeria's economic base shifted from agriculture to minerals. Oil became the major determinant of the pace and pattern of growth in the 1970s. Oil production led directly to higher export earnings and to swollen government revenues. Because of waste and corruption, this development had momentous consequences for the economic structure and for the living standards of the people.

After the slump in oil prices in the 1980s, an attempt was made between 1986 and 1990 to liberalize the economy by reducing price controls and trade and foreign exchange restrictions and increasing real interest rates. The reform effort was abandoned in 1990 with a reversion to earlier policies of trade and foreign exchange restrictions, price controls, and administrative allocation of credit and foreign exchange.

No account of the Nigerian development experience would be complete without reference to horrendous mismanagement and misappropriation of resources by the military, civil-service, political, and business elite.[56] While such things are a common occurrence in many countries, they assumed dimensions in Nigeria that have rarely been paralleled elsewhere. The oil revenues were spent on prestige projects, wasteful capital investment, and payments to groups and individuals to buy political support or were stolen outright for personal use. The elite gave kickbacks on contracts, collected rents on allocation of scarce foreign exchange and goods, and gave away state enterprises at throwaway prices to acquire resources. The misappropriation of resources reached monumental proportions during the regime of General Sani Abacha from 1993 to 1998.

Despite the rapid growth of the economy in the 1960s and 1970s, the living standards of the majority of the people did not improve significantly. According to one study, average private consumption was *lower* by around 30 percent by the mid-1980s than it was in the early 1950s. Although the human development index in Nigeria shows a slow and small increase since 1975, real income today is less than it was in the 1960s.[57]

The Nigerian experience shows in a dramatic manner the importance of governance for social and economic development. Although the country is blessed with abundant agricultural and mineral resources, the living standards of Nigerians declined over the past two decades—largely the consequence of political instability, massive corruption, and mismanagement of resources. Lack of democratic control and accountability has been at the heart of the failure of the Nigerian development effort.

Box 9.5. Taiwan

Taiwan has been among the three or four most successful economies in the post-war period. Its GDP per capita (in constant 1990 dollars) rose elevenfold from $1,080 in 1953 to $11,590 in 1992, a stupendous rate of economic growth. Its exports increased even more, from $180 million (constant 1990 dollars) in 1950 to $82 billion in 1992,[58] and the standard of living of the Taiwanese people improved rapidly. Employment expanded at a brisk pace, and by the late 1960s, the surplus labor was fully absorbed. Wages rose sharply thereafter. Its social indicators rose rapidly and its already low levels of inequality improved further between the 1950s and the 1970s. The Taiwanese experience is thus of profound interest to students of Third World development. Despite some divergences among specialists on Taiwan, there is a broad measure of agreement on the key strategies pursued by the country to reach such extraordinary results.

In the 1950s, Taiwan was a major recipient of U.S. aid, which amounted to over 2 percent of its GDP. It followed a policy of substitution of imported industrial goods, using a variety of tools such as import licensing, quantitative restrictions, and overvalued and multiple exchange rates to promote domestic industrial output.

Taiwan embarked upon a policy of export promotion only in the early 1960s. Among the steps taken to stimulate exports were the establishment of a uniform and realistic exchange rate, subsidies, a reduction in protection, duty-free importation of machinery and raw materials, export insurance, marketing support, and research and development.

Agroindustry and textiles were the basis of Taiwan's early industrial development. For many years the government combined policies of export promotion with protection of domestic agriculture and industry.[59] But at the same time, industrial enterprises were subjected to heavy pressure to develop products that met international standards. The state also used a variety of other means to promote technological upgrading of industry. Only in the 1980s, when the Taiwanese industry had reached international standards, was the trade regime progressively liberalized.

Another feature of industry in Taiwan was the predominance of small and medium enterprises. At the same time, the state sought to capture some of the benefits of large-scale production through special research and development institutes and the industrial district form of economic organization.

In less than fifty years, Taiwan has been transformed from a poor to an affluent country. Its economic structure, state of technology, living standards, and social indicators resemble those of industrial countries. It has become an important capital exporter. Its potential for continued rapid economic growth remains high. It weathered well the 1997–1998 crisis that convulsed East and Southeast Asia. It has shown that it is possible to attain high levels of industrialization through small- and medium-sized enterprises.

Industrial Development

The birth of UNIDO, the United Nations Industrial Development Organization, was "a child of the pill," the result of a single act by a potent "parent" that was long guarded against but consummated on one occasion when defenses were down. The General Assembly had proposed its creation several times, but it was always opposed by the industrial countries.[60] Then in 1966, for a short period and without informing the UK, the French, or other major industrial countries, the U.S. switched positions.[61] With support from such a powerful player, the deed was done. The General Assembly approved the creation of an institution that had long been resisted.

The background to the shift of the U.S. position shows once again the importance of personalities and leadership. The son of the former president Franklin Roosevelt was a member of the U.S. delegation to the General Assembly. Apparently he asked why the UN had no organization for industry akin to the FAO for agriculture, which led to President Johnson's approval of the change in U.S. policy.[62]

Industrial development had already been identified in the (First) Development Decade as a fast-moving sector. Manufacturing output in the developing countries—it was estimated—would need to rise by at least 130 percent over the decade if the 5 percent growth target was to be achieved.[63] To assist this process, the UN established in 1961 the Centre for Industrial Development[64]—the CID—which in 1965 and 1966 organized a series of regional industrialization symposia.[65]

With the creation of UNIDO in 1966, the CID was discontinued and the stage was set for more ambitious plans. Ibrahim Helmi Abdel-Rahman of Egypt was appointed as the first executive director. An International Symposium on Industrial Development was held in Athens in 1967, which approved UNIDO's mission.[66] UNIDO's role was to act as the central coordinating body for industrial activities within the UN system and to promote industrial development and cooperation at global, regional, national, and sectoral levels.

Within five years, developing countries were pressing for UNIDO to be transformed into a specialized agency with a wider scope, more resources, and full financial and administrative autonomy.[67] This, not surprisingly, was opposed by the industrialized countries until 1979, when a constitution establishing UNIDO as a specialized agency was adopted,[68] on condition that it would only enter into force when it had gathered eighty ratifications. This finally happened in 1985.

Because of its difficult birth, in its early years UNIDO kept a low profile on matters of industrial policy. Did every state have to have an industrial policy?

Should governments decide if a line of production should be pursued, or should they leave it to the market to allocate resources to the most promising activities? Already in the 1960s, there was strong opposition to industrial policies based on import-substitution strategies, which had experienced mixed success in Latin America. Shy of trying to compare different industrial policies, UNIDO fought import substitution, picking winners, or even discussing the efficiency of various instruments for implementing such choices. Thus, UNIDO failed to help governments that, nevertheless, were conducting such policies.

Even though UNIDO failed to enlighten governments on industrial policies, it assisted countries in their dialogue with enterprises in two ways. First, it published information on equipment performance and cost for different industrial activities, which helped governments in their negotiations with investors or equipment sellers. Second, it organized fairs where governments or national enterprises presented their projects to interested foreign entrepreneurs. Organizing competition between potential investors strengthened the bargaining power of participating countries.

The big developments occurred in Lima, at the Second General Conference of UNIDO in 1975, in the preparation of which François Legay, then director of the UNIDO Industrial Policy and Programming Division, played a key role. Three major ideas were agreed on and made part of UNIDO's philosophy, strategy, and plan of action. These were:

1. The promotion of industry should be part of a purposeful development strategy—as opposed to the outcome of a total laissez-faire market approach.

2. As part of global structural change, the share of industry in developing countries should be increased from 7 percent in 1970 to 25 percent by the year 2000.

3. Industrial cooperation should be the key mechanism of industrial acceleration, based on strengthened cooperation between the North and the South, between developing countries (South-South cooperation), and sectorally between firms. Cooperation and support from other parts of the UN were envisaged, notably in matters of trade with UNCTAD and where public finance was involved with the World Bank.[69]

The idea of a world strategy for accelerated industrialization became a focus of UNIDO's work from about 1973, accelerated in part by calls for a new international economic order. A paragraph on industrialization was included in the NIEO resolution passed by the General Assembly in 1974.[70] By the time of the Lima conference in March 1975, a draft World Strategy for Industrialization had been produced by the UNIDO secretariat.[71]

A quarter of a century later, the Lima Declaration appears very much to be a child of its time. With the big swings to neoliberal economic policies in the

1980s, nationally and internationally, the idea of purposeful industrial strategy seems mistaken and dirigiste. Yet it must be recalled that in the 1970s, even the OECD governments were concerned with policies to combat "deindustrialization." Their own industrial bases were being eroded by imports from developing countries, and in response, they were trying to "pick the winners," seeking to identify the new areas of industrial production and technology into which they should encourage their own industries to move through incentives, technological support, and other policies. In the event, such strategies often proved magnificently unsuccessful, but at the time, they were seen as rational policymaking. In this respect, the Lima Declaration would today be judged far behind the curve of the free-market orthodoxies about to burst on the scene in the early 1980s—but so also would much industrial-country strategy of that era.

It is difficult to dismiss the third element of the Lima strategy, industrial cooperation, so lightly. There were many strings to this bow—a system of consultations including both public and private sectors, a commission for international development law, an international industrial technology institute, an international center for joint acquisition of technology, an international center to examine patents, a system for resolving industrial conflicts, an investment promotion center, a research center, and, established in 1977, an Industrial Development Fund. The latter was to be funded by voluntary contributions and was designed to make possible rapid and flexible responses by UNIDO to requests for technical assistance.[72]

At the time of the 1974 Lima conference, the Lima target—which said that the share of industrial output in developing countries should reach 25 percent of total world industrial output by the year 2000—aroused skepticism and a great deal of scorn. Even UNIDO's own publication, *Industry 2000— New Perspectives,* admitted that "the Lima target may be difficult to reach, since its growth and market access requirements are of such enormous magnitudes that they may not be forthcoming without drastic political changes"— though it admitted that Jan Tinbergen and Hans Singer had expressed the opposite view.[73] Despite the criticisms of naysayers, the Lima target has been nearly achieved. The share of developing countries in total world industrial output in 2000 was 21 percent.[74]

Despite this success, progress in dealing with the underlying concerns about the growing economic divide has been both limited and different from what was hoped for or envisaged. Certainly the industrialized countries still dominate global finance and global technology, they still provide the largest (and fastest-growing) market for exports from developing countries, and they still serve as the source of most direct foreign investment.

The big difference, however, is *within* the developing world. UNIDO's identification of the major concerns took place within a global view which postu-
lated a sharp divide between developed and developing countries. Since 1975,
the economic divide has grown between the developing countries—with the
poorest and least-developed countries falling ever-farther behind while a group
of more dynamic and increasingly better-off countries are clearly moving
ahead. The latter group has included China and some of the leading Southeast Asian countries—the Republic of Korea, Indonesia, Malaysia, Singapore,
Thailand, and Hong Kong—and a few other developing countries such as
Botswana, Chile, and Mauritius.[75] Because of the inclusion of China, this group
represents over one-quarter of the world's population; it also represents over
one-third of all developing countries. In contrast, the population of the 49
least-developed countries represents over one-tenth of the world population's
and one-seventh of the developing nations.[76]

Over the 1980s and 1990s, UNIDO moved into other areas of policy. An
increasing focus was put on small- and medium-scale industries and attention was paid to such areas as cleaner and energy-efficient industrialization.
Support for industrial development in Africa was made a priority. The role of
women in industrial development became a special focus of research, evaluation studies directed to women's entrepreneurship, opportunities for women's
advancement in industry, and studies and action related to technology and
women in industry.

Notwithstanding these contributions, UNIDO became a target for abolition in the movement for UN reform in the mid-1990s. The report of the
Commission on Global Governance argued that realities had changed. UNIDO,
they said,

> was set up when industrialization was just beginning in most developing coun-
> tries. Governments were expected to be the prime movers in accelerating in-
> dustrial development at a time when most of them lacked the technical and
> managerial capacities to perform that task. . . . By now, however, all but the
> least developed and smallest have established a wide range of industries, accu-
> mulating considerable experience both in industrial promotion and negotia-
> tion with TNCs [transnational corporations]. . . . If a case can be made for the
> retention of UNCTAD and UNIDO in some form, it will have to rest on the
> need to provide substantial support to the least developed and smallest coun-
> tries in trade and industrial production.[77]

Notwithstanding this clear recommendation by a group that included members from developing and transition countries as well as industrial countries,[78]
the proposal to abolish UNIDO was soundly defeated in the General Assembly.
The evidence presented above suggests that the UN still has a major role to play

in supporting industrial development both in the least-developed countries and in a number of other developing countries where development is lagging because of the weakness and failures of industry.

Disarmament and Development

Global military spending was enormous. By 1984, a General Assembly resolution had declared that military spending had "acquired a staggering magnitude" both in industrial and in developing countries. Moreover, after increasing in many countries over the previous half-century, the global trend in military expenditures in 1984 was accelerating, "in dramatic contrast to the sombre state of the global economy."[79]

In spite of reductions since the end of the Cold War, military spending in many countries throughout the world is still very high, both as the sum of financial expenditure and resources used and as a proportion of GNP. At a time when a clear priority of the development challenge in most developing countries is to raise the rate of savings and investment, more than 4 percent of GNP is still being allocated to the military in some twenty developing countries. Only some ten developing countries devote less than 1 percent of their GNP to the military.[80]

Compared to the relative neglect elsewhere, the UN has over the whole period displayed a sustained preoccupation with disarmament and development. Proposals for disarmament and for actions linking disarmament with development were made in the 1950s and continued over much of the period afterward. In 1978 and 1982, the UN General Assembly held two special sessions devoted to disarmament and development and an international conference on the same theme in 1987.[81] Over the years, the UN issued a number of reports on disarmament and development, including the pioneering Thorsson Report in 1982 on *The Relationship between Disarmament and Development,*[82] for which Wassily Leontief, the Nobel Prize–winning economist, prepared one of the background papers. Under the auspices of the UN, a panel of thirteen eminent personalities, including two Nobel Prize winners, issued a joint declaration in 1986 that treated disarmament, development, and security as a "triad of peace."

All this, once again, is in sharp contrast to the World Bank and the IMF. As the World Bank historians commented:

> Arms reduction . . . plainly is sensitive as well as political and was typically avoided by the Bank until—in the aftermath of the cold war—the presidents of the Bank, first Conable, then Preston, joined Managing Director Camdessus

of the Fund, in making borrowers' allocations to defense a matter of greater Bank-Fund concern. The initial strategy was to deal with the issue indirectly, with the Fund specifying ceilings on total public expenditure and the Bank promoting floors on social expenditures, thereby encouraging borrowing governments to squeeze defense expenditures. The Bank, as part of its observation of borrowers' fiscal policies in the context of adjustment lending, became engaged in closer reviews of public spending programs from the mid-1980s onwards. This entailed attention to the transparency of expenditure accounting, including that for defense.[83]

Some of the main UN proposals are summarized in Box 9.6. Most of these were initiated by governments; only limited analytical work on disarmament and development was undertaken in the early years by the UN Secretariat. One Secretariat report in 1962, entitled *The Economic and Social Consequences of Disarmament*, argued the case for allocating "an appropriate proportion" of financial resources released from disarmament to international aid in order to prevent all of the resources being allocated to domestic purposes in industrial countries.[84]

The action proposals for the UN Development Decades included references to the potential contribution from disarmament to development. The (First) Development Decade explored what could happen if governments devoted a portion of their disarmament savings to an international fund to assist development and reconstruction in underdeveloped countries.[85] These proposals estimated that an "acceleration of growth of aggregate incomes in developing countries from perhaps $3^1/_2$ to 5 percent would require no more than the diversion of about 10 percent of the savings resulting from a reduction in armament expenditures by one-half."[86] Though this is a striking conclusion, the result is less surprising given the fact that at that time spending on armaments was about equal to the aggregate of national incomes of all underdeveloped countries and about ten times the net capital formation of those nations.

Subsequently, the UN issued a number of reports on disarmament and development.[87] By the end of the 1970s, the topic had moved up the agenda of international debate, though probably more for international effect and debate than for serious action among the major military powers and many other governments.

In 1982, the United Nations undertook a study "to investigate systematically and in depth the range of relationships between the prospects for balanced and sustainable global economic and social development on the one hand and disarmament on the other through the reallocations of real resources." The Thorsson Report that resulted brought together disarmament and development and security, though the latter to a lesser extent.[88]

Box 9.6. Disarmament and Development

In 1955, France made the first proposal within the UN for a link between disarmament and development. Participating states would agree to reduce their military spending each year by a certain agreed-upon percentage, which would increase year by year. Reductions would be monitored following a common definition of military spending and standardized nomenclature for military budget items. The resources released would be paid into an international fund, 25 percent of which would be allocated to development. The rest would be left at the disposal of the government concerned.

In the following year, the Soviet Union proposed a variant that was further developed two years later. The UN Special Fund, which had already been under consideration for several years as a key component of international development strategy, should be financed through reductions in military budgets. The military budgets of the Soviet Union, the U.S., the UK, and France were to be cut by 10 to 15 percent and part of the savings would be used for development assistance.

In 1964, Brazil called for a fund to finance industrial conversion and economic development. This fund would be allocated at least at 20 percent of the global value of reductions in military budgets.

In 1973, the General Assembly adopted a resolution calling for a 10 percent one-time reduction in the military budgets of the five permanent members of the Security Council. Under this resolution, 10 percent of the sum thus saved would be allocated for social and economic development in developing countries. The resolution called on other states to join in.

In 1978, at the first Special Session on Disarmament, several proposals were made for a link between disarmament and development. Senegal called for a 5 percent tax on armaments, which would be paid to the UN for use in development. France proposed the establishment of an international disarmament fund for development. Romania proposed that military budgets be first frozen, then gradually reduced. In the first stage, military budgets were to be cut by at least 10 percent; half the amounts released would be transferred to the UN for development support of countries with per capita income of less than $200 per year.

In 1980, the UN Institute for Disarmament Research (UNIDIR) was established within the United Nations Institute for Training and Research (UNITAR), and in 1982 it was established as a separate institute. It was given the mandate to "carry out research for the purpose of assisting ongoing disarmament negotiation, stimulating initiatives for new negotiation and providing general insight in to the problems involved."

Source: UN Department of International Economic and Social Affairs, *1985 Report on the World Social Situation* (New York: UN, 1985), 20–21.

The Thorsson Report criticized many of the previous UN studies, claiming that they had been excessively cautious about exploring the relationship between disarmament and development and too fearful, for "normative reasons," about declaring too close a relationship between disarmament and development.

After reviewing a great deal of evidence and analyzing it more carefully than most earlier studies, the Thorsson Report threw caution to the wind and concluded that "the investigation suggests very strongly that the world can either continue to pursue the arms race with characteristic vigour or move consciously and with deliberate speed toward a more stable and balanced social and economic development. It cannot do both."[89]

The report summarized evidence that suggested a strongly negative relationship between the arms race and economic growth and development:

- In the poorer countries, increases in military spending as a share of GDP are associated with reductions in the rate of economic growth.

- For an arms-importing developing country, the price paid for the equipment represents only an initial cost entailing substantial economic and political liabilities which go far beyond its subsequent operation and maintenance.

- Not many newly independent countries have succeeded in evolving an indigenous military sector. For a majority of developing countries, ambitious arms-production programs are likely to overburden their industrial and manpower bases, while the almost inevitable dependence on imported technology may largely negate the effects of self-reliance advocated by many developing countries as the critical reason for the domestic manufacture of arms.[90]

The Thorsson Report also summarized the broader picture regarding security, disarmament, and development in developing countries. It noted that almost all studies show evidence of a triangular relationship between disarmament, security, and development in the military spending of developing countries.[91] Three types of insecurity were identified: adversarial relationships with neighbors, insurgency and the threat of secession by hostile groups, and an adverse strategic environment of the conflicting interests of the major powers that do not reflect the national security concerns of the developing countries themselves.

The Thorsson Report drew on the work of Leontief to prepare alternative scenarios of the global economy until the year 2000: a baseline scenario which assumed continuation of the share of military outlays in GNPs; an accelerated arms race which envisaged a doubling of the share of military outlays in GNP by the year 2000; and a "disarmament scenario" under which military spending by the U.S. and the Soviet Union would fall by one-third by 1990 and by a further third over the 1990s. For all the other regions, the report projected that military spending would decline by one-quarter by 1990 and by a further fifth over the 1990s. The study concluded that even modest resources released through disarmament could make a significant contribution to global economic prospects.[92]

This study was presented in 1982, a year before President Reagan would speak of "the aggressive impulses of an evil empire"[93] and seven years before the fall of the Berlin Wall. Though considered wildly optimistic and visionary at the time, the UN disarmament scenario and its projections emerge as being nearer the actual situation in 2000 than the other two projections. With the winding down of the Cold War, global military spending peaked in 1987 and by the mid-1990s had fallen by one-third. By the end of the 1990s, military spending was rising again and, at the time of writing, decisions have been taken which will lead to a rapid increase in U.S. military spending.

In the event, however, the reductions in military spending from 1987 to 1995 were to have very different consequences from those envisaged in the Thorsson Report and in most of the other prospective analyses of the "peace dividend." Most of the UN studies and most proposals for a peace dividend had assumed that reductions in military spending would lead to reallocations of this spending into nonmilitary, peaceful uses.

What occurred in the United States and in many other countries over the 1990s was a reduction of military spending combined with parallel reductions in government spending. This has led many to argue that there was no peace dividend. The analysis of Professor Lawrence Klein, another Nobel laureate economist who contributed to the UN's work in this area, suggests otherwise. Far from accepting the popular view that there has been no peace dividend, Klein has argued that the reductions in military spending have resulted in major reductions in government deficits and interest rates over the 1990s. These reductions, according to Klein's interpretation, were major forces behind the U.S. economic expansion of the 1990s, helping to make it the longest-lasting expansion in U.S. history.[94] This expansion in turn has had a positive impact on the global economy; the U.S. has served as "the locomotive of the world economy" in a way that has brought actual and potential benefits to the poorest and lowest-income countries. This overall argument in favor of the positive effects of reductions in military expansion is not negated by the fact that the benefits to the poorest and lowest-income countries were often offset by the mixed signals of the Bretton Woods institutions and by the disruptive effects of local conflicts encouraged by the arms trade.

A final contribution of the UN to the analysis of disarmament and development has been in the elaboration of the concept of human security. This concept was first put forward in the HDR of 1994[95] and enlarged further in the HDR of 1999.[96] Human security is defined as involving a shift from the protection of geographic borders by military means to a protection of people from a range of dangers, such as terrorism, urban crime, drug wars, and gender violence. The threats to human security go beyond physical violence to the human consequences of environmental degradation, the risks of HIV/AIDS and other diseases, and the human repercussions of financial collapse on a major scale. Broadening the concept of security in this way raises basic questions about the level of military spending in relation to the diversity of threats faced by a country's whole population. Perhaps more important, it stimulates questions about underspending on actions outside the military which might be more effective than the military in tackling the other causes of human insecurity. These would include spending on the police force, judges and courts, community action, health services, and a broad range of social and economic measures to tackle unemployment and environmental deterioration.

Part III. Outcomes and the Future

10

The Record of Performance

- **Economic Growth and Development**
- **Human Development**
- **The Contributions of the UN**
- **UN Goals and Development Performance**
- **Country Action and Alternative Strategies**
- **Concluding Observations**

As has become clear from previous chapters, the process of development in the poorer countries over the last half-century has been unprecedented—in terms of economic expansion, human development, the advancement of human rights, and poverty reduction. In the long record of human history, there have never been changes on such a scale, let alone in only half a century. Moreover, taken as a whole, the rate of change in economic growth, lengthening life expectancy, reducing child mortality, expanding education, and reducing the numbers and proportions in poverty exceeds considerably the speed of advance attained in the industrial countries in the nineteenth century or the early years of the twentieth.

Everyone should be impressed by this record. At the same time, there is not the slightest room for complacency. By historical standards, the story is one of extraordinary advance. But in relation to the possibilities that have been opened by new technologies and by the soaring wealth in the world as a whole, the record is much diminished. There have been missed opportunities on the grand scale, major failures to live up to expectations, and failures to fulfill commitments clearly made. Worse still, though the lives of the poor have seen significant improvements in at least some respects in most countries, the better-off sections of the population in both richer and poorer countries have generally enjoyed the bigger benefits, absolutely and relatively, especially during the last two decades. The richer countries have also pulled ahead economically, and the gaps have widened in terms of absolute income between the richer countries and almost all others. Between the richest and the poorest countries, the gaps have also widened in relative terms.

Economic Growth and Development

All this can now be quantified—the result of worldwide improvements in the availability of economic and social data, much of which has been stimulated by fifty-five years of statistical work by the United Nations.[1] From 1950 to 2000, GDP expanded in real terms by 5 percent per year, five times its estimated growth of 1 percent per year for the years between 1900 and 1950.[2] In developing countries, the increase in growth rates per capita was even greater: income per capita grew by 0.3 percent per year in the first half of the twentieth century and by 2.9 percent per year in the second half—an astounding tenfold increase, a truly gigantic leap.

In spite of this remarkable economic progress, there were many negative items on the balance sheet, especially over the last two decades of the twentieth century. The advances made by developing countries over this period were neither steady nor well balanced, either temporally or geographically. The 1960s saw the fastest growth in the postwar period at about 6 percent per year, but the rate of growth slackened to less than 4 percent in the 1980s—barely 1 percent per capita. Latin America and the Caribbean region grew rapidly in the

Table 10.1. Growth of Gross World Product by Decade, 1951–2000

Region	Growth of Gross World Product (percent)				
	1951–1960	1961–1970	1971–1980	1981–1990	1991–2000[1]
World	4.7	5.3	3.7	3.0	2.4
Developed Market Economies	4.3	4.9	3.1	2.8	2.3
Economies in Transition	6.3	6.5	5.0	2.3	−3.8
Developing countries	5.3	6.0	5.1	3.8	4.9
Latin America	5.5	5.8	5.4	1.5	2.7
North Africa	5.3	11.0	4.1	2.3	3.4
Sub-Saharan Africa	4.0	4.5	2.4	1.4	2.8
West Asia	5.2	8.0	4.7	−0.6	3.3
South and East Asia	4.2	5.2	6.2	6.4	4.7
Mediterranean	6.4	6.1	5.0	2.4	1.5
China	8.2	4.7	5.9	8.8	8.8

[1]Estimates.

Source: Development Policy Analysis Division of the United Nations Secretariat, based on Statistics Division of the United Nations, National Accounts Statistics, and other national and international sources.

first three decades but also experienced a sharp slowdown in the last two. The Middle East and North Africa followed a similar course, as did sub-Saharan Africa, where the decline started in the late 1970s. In contrast, the South Asian region saw its growth accelerate around 1980, from around 3.5 percent per year in the first three decades to nearly 6 percent in the last two. The Southeast and East Asian countries have grown at extremely rapid rates throughout the period. China experienced the most rapid growth over the entire period with an average in excess of 8 percent per year, except for the 1960s and 1970s.

As a result, the structure of the global economy has changed considerably. The share of developing countries in total world production has almost doubled over the period, rising from 16 percent to 28 percent, with a particularly sharp jump in the 1990s. Half of this increase has been due to China, whose share in world production has risen between 1950 and 2000 from under 2 to well over 8 percent. India's share has also increased from about 1.5 to about 4 percent.[3] The situation in the developing world at the end of the century looks quite different once China and India are included. The Asian continent—West Asia, South Asia, and Southeast Asia—now accounts for about one-fifth of world output and over two-thirds of the output of developing countries. If the Asian countries can maintain these rapid rates of economic expansion over the next two decades, there will be extremely important implications for the growth of the developing world as a whole; there will be major reductions in poverty in the region where the great majority of the world's poor presently live.

In contrast, sub-Saharan Africa is the one Third World region to have suffered a decline in its share of world production; it has shrunk from 2.3 to 1.6 percent over the 50-year period.

Income per capita has grown most rapidly in China over the period 1950–2000, rising thirteenfold, followed by East, Southeast, and South Asia (and the developed-market economies). At the other extreme, per capita income in sub-Saharan Africa has been on a declining trend over the past three decades, falling by one-third. It was 10 percent less in 2000 than it was in 1960—a stark measure of its catastrophic economic performance since the 1970s. The Middle East and North Africa and Latin America also experienced declines in per capita incomes in the 1980s.

Income gaps between the developing and industrial countries have been of major interest to the UN, especially during the first two or three decades of its existence. The absolute gap between average income per capita in the rich countries and average income per capita in the poor countries has widened enormously over the half-century, rising from some $3,800 in 1950 to almost $14,000 in 2000 (in constant 1980 prices). In contrast, the relative gap has

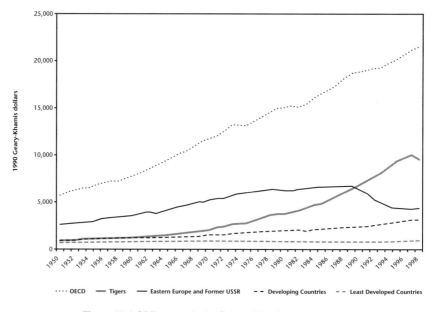

Figure 10.1 GDP per capita by Selected Regions, 1950–1998

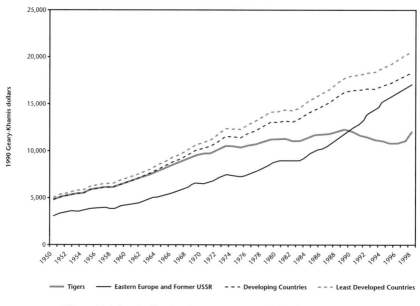

Figure 10.2 Gap in Absolute Income between OECD Countries and
Other Selected Regions, 1950–1998

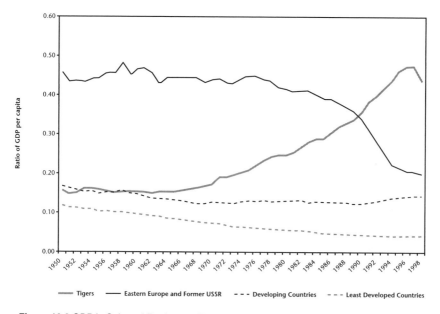

Figure 10.3 GDP in Selected Regions as Percentage of OECD Average Income, 1950–1998

fluctuated within a fairly narrow margin of thirteen and fifteen; the per capita income in the rich countries was fourteen times the level of that of the poor countries in 1950, rising to fifteen in 1970 and falling to thirteen in 2000. But, again, the weight of China and India is considerable and the picture is very different if these two countries are excluded.

Indeed, the slight reduction in the relative gap in real incomes between developed and developing countries has largely been due to the superior performance of China and East Asia. In 1950, income per capita in the rich countries was forty-three times that of China. By 2000, it had fallen to less than twelve times. For sub-Saharan Africa, in contrast, the relative gap has grown from less than nineteen in 1950 to over thirty-three in 2000. Overall, as the World Bank has reported, the gap between the world's richest twenty countries and the poorest twenty doubled to thirty-seven in the last three decades of the twentieth century.[4]

Paradoxically, over this period, concern with inequality, both nationally and internationally, has slipped from the agenda. For the first three decades of the UN, the need to narrow global gaps was an important part of development debate. After calls for a new international economic order were effectively removed from the international agenda in the late 1970s, talk about narrowing global gaps also disappeared from UN deliberations, at least from polite UN diplomatic discussion.

Nonetheless, outside the UN, one eminent historian commented that by the end of the twentieth century, the gap in wealth and health had become "the greatest single problem and danger facing the world of the third Millennium. The only worry that comes close is environmental deterioration and the two are intimately connected, indeed are one."[5]

Human Development

Human advance in almost all parts of the world over the last half-century has also been impressive by historical standards, in many respects more so than economic advance. It is worth recalling the headlines. Life expectancy in developing countries added on average 18 years of life between the mid-1950s and the end of the century, an increase of more than 40 percent. In China, the increase was 29 years, from 41 years in the mid-1950s to 71 years in about 2000, an increase of more than two-thirds.[6] These are extraordinary changes that have major implications for the pattern of life of both children and adults. A major part of this change can be accounted for by the sharp reductions of child mortality rates, but it also indicates the expectation of a lengthening of life of those in adult years. There were also important increases of life expectancy in all other countries, though not as much relatively. In industrial countries over the same period, life expectancy increased by about 10 years, from 68 to 78 years.

This lengthening of life has added to global population, though not as much as the large additions over the last half-century in the numbers of children born and surviving each year. Total population has expanded as shown.

Table 10.3 shows the increases of life expectancy, the decreases in infant mortality, and the extraordinary increases in the proportion of people surviving to 60 or older. In the early years of the UN, only a small minority of the population in developing countries could expect to survive to later years. To-

Table 10.2. World Population 1950–2000 (actual) and 2025–2050 (projected) in Billions

	Actual			Projected	
Region	1950	1975	2000	2025	2050
More Developed	0.8	1.0	1.2	1.2	1.2
Less Developed	1.5	2.7	4.2	5.5	6.3
Least Developed	0.2	0.3	0.7	1.2	1.8
Total	**2.5**	**4.1**	**6.1**	**7.9**	**9.3**

Source: United Nations Department of Economic and Social Affairs, Population Division, *World Population Ageing, 1950–2050* (New York: United Nations, 2002).

Table 10.3. Life Expectancy and Infant and Child Mortality, 1955, 1975, 1995, and 2025 (projected)

	1955	1975	1995	2025 (projected)
World Average				
Life Expectancy (years)	48	59	65	73
Infant Mortality Rate (per 1,000 births)	148	90	59	29
Percentage of World's Population Living in Countries With:				
Life Expectancy above 60 Years	32	60	86	96
Infant Mortality Rate below 50 (per 1,000 births)	19	30	60	94
Child Mortality Rate below 70 (per 1,000 births)	30	53	64	94

Source: WHO, World Health Report 1998 (Geneva: WHO, 1998), 39.

day, a clear majority does so—though the tragedy of HIV/AIDS horribly blights the prospects of survival for an increasing number of people, especially in sub-Sahara Africa.

Fertility is falling, as shown in Table 10.4, much faster than was earlier predicted. Fertility has declined to the point where in over fifty countries, fertility is today below reproduction rates. Almost half of the world's population live in countries in this situation, and by 2025, that figure is projected to be over three-quarters.

Adult literacy has also expanded dramatically. Less than one-quarter of the population in the low-income countries of the world were literate in 1950. Nearly two-thirds were literate at the end of the century. In middle-income countries, the increase in literacy has been almost as impressive—from 48

Table 10.4. World Fertility Rates, 1955, 1975, 1995, and 2025 (projected)

	1955	1975	1995	2025 (projected)
World Fertility Rates[1]	5.0	4.2	2.9	2.3
Percentage of World's Population Living in Countries with Fertility below Replacement Level[2]	0.1	21	45	76

[1]The world fertility rate is the fertility rate for all women of childbearing age.
[2]Percentage of world population in countries with fertility rates below 2.1.

Source: WHO, World Health Report 1998 (Geneva: WHO, 1998), 119–120.

percent to 86 percent. This shift in the balance of literate persons in the world has far-reaching consequences for access to information and public awareness. As one commentator has put it, literacy in 1950 was mostly the prerogative of people living in industrial countries. By the end of the century, the literate population in developing countries outnumbered those in the industrial world by about 4 to 1.

Dramatic quantitative expansion has been the characteristic of education at all levels.[7] Enrollments in primary education increased rapidly in all regions of the world, to the point where now only a small minority, mostly in sub-Saharan Africa and South Asia, do not start basic education. Secondary education has expanded much faster than primary, though in most developing countries less than half of school-age children complete secondary education. The most dramatic changes have occurred at the tertiary level. In 1950, university and other tertiary-level students in the industrial countries outnumbered such students in developing countries almost 3 to 1. By 2000, students at these levels in developing countries outnumbered those in industrial countries.

Nutrition is another important area of real advance, as indicated in Table 10.7. Both the numbers and the proportions of malnourished children fell over the last two decades of the twentieth century—most dramatically in Asia and Latin America and the Caribbean. Africa was the exception to this advance, where, in East, West, and Southern Africa, rates of malnutrition grew over the last two decades.

In this brief recital of human advance, it is easy to miss the historical significance. Just over a century ago, in the early days of industrialization, the now-

Table 10.5. Adult Illiteracy Rates by Region, 1950–2000 (estimated percent of persons aged 15 and above)[1]

Year	World Total	Developing Countries	Least-Developed Countries	Developed Countries
1950	44 [2]	63	83 [3]	9
1970	37	52	73	6
1980	31	42	66	3
1990	25	33	58	2
2000	21	26	50	1

[1]Where estimates were presented as a range, the midpoint has been rounded and shown here.
[2]Excluding USSR.
[3]Sub-Saharan Africa.

Sources: 1950 estimates from UNESCO, *Basic Facts and Figures: International Statistics Relating to Education, Culture, and Mass Communication* (Paris: UNESCO, 1958); UNESCO, *Statistical Yearbook 1999* (Paris: UNESCO Publishing & Bernan Press, 1999), 11–17.

Table 10.6. Primary-School Enrollments by Region, 1950–1997 (millions)

	1950	1960	1970	1980	1990	1997
World Total	206	342	411	542	597	668
Africa	9	19	33	62	81	100
Asia/Oceania[1]	84	183	253	339	367	410
Europe	75	79	55	52	49	46
Latin America/Caribbean	15	27	44	65	76	85
North America	24	34	26	23	25	27

[1]For 1950 and 1960, the figures for Europe include data for the former USSR. For later dates, the figures for Europe include data for the Russian Federation, while the figures for Asia/Oceania include data for the Central Asian countries which were part of the former USSR.

Source: UNESCO, *World Education Report 2000* (Paris: UNESCO Publishing, 2000), 41.

developed countries had child mortality rates of 150 to 200, indeed sometimes 300.[8] It took almost 100 years, until the 1940s, before these rates fell to about 70.[9] As late as 1950, developing countries still had on average infant mortality rates around 200, equivalent to those in the early years of industrialization in

Table 10.7. Malnutrition: Number and Prevalence of Underweight[1] Children in Developing Countries (total and regional totals, 1980–2000)

	1980	1985	1990	1995	2000
Underweight for Age (millions)					
All Developing Countries	176	176	177	160	150
Africa	22	26	30	34	38
Asia	146	143	141	121	108
Latin America and Caribbean	7	7	6	4	3

	1980	1985	1990	1995	2000
Underweight for Age (percentage of schoolchildren)					
All Developing Countries	37	35	32	29	27
Eastern Africa	25	28	30	33	36
Western Africa	30	32	33	35	37
North Africa	18	16	16	15	14
Southeast Asia (including China)	44	40	36	33	29
South Asia (including India)	58	55	51	47	44
Latin America and Caribbean	14	12	10	8	6

[1]Underweight is defined by the National Center for Health Statistics (NCHS)/WHO international standards. See source for details.

Source: Administrative Committee on Co-ordination/Sub-Committee on Nutrition, International Food Policy Research Institute, *Nutrition throughout the Life Cycle: 4th Report on the World Nutrition Situation* (Geneva: ACC/SCN and IFPRI, 2000), 1.

developed countries. But in developing countries, infant mortality rates fell to 160 in 1960 and to just over 60 in 2000. Thus, the transition in infant mortality rates from about 200 to about 70 per 1,000, which took the developed countries almost 100 years, was accomplished in developing countries in barely forty to fifty years.

These human advances, of course, reflect in part the impact of science and technology, progress in public health, and improvements in access to safe water and sanitation. But the advances also reflect growing awareness of human rights and demands that they be fulfilled. Advances in human rights have also been rapid and impressive. In 1900, for example, in no country of the world did all women have the vote. By 2000, there were few countries in the world where female suffrage was not a reality.[10] The same is true of the ratification of the main instruments of human rights, where there was widespread and severe neglect until the 1950s, the final years of the colonial era. Although progress was slow at first, there was a surge of ratifications in developing countries over the last two decades of the twentieth century. By 2000, three-quarters or more of countries had ratified at least five of the six major international instruments of human rights.[11]

Again, there are, of course, important negatives to this balance sheet. Ratification of the instruments of human rights is not the same as implementation of these rights. Progress in terms of human advance has generally been less, often much less, in the least-developed countries, with periods of setback, especially in times of war and during the major economic declines, for so many countries during the 1980s and 1990s. Eric Hobsbawm wrote that the century ended "not with a celebration of this unparalleled and marvelous progress, but in a mood of uneasiness." He attributed this not only to the fact that the twentieth century was the most murderous century of which we have record but also to the unparalleled scale of the human catastrophes it produced, from the greatest famines in history to systematic genocide.[12]

Measured by life expectancy, literacy, and access to basic schooling, some of the most basic indicators of human welfare, the human gaps between the poorest and the richest countries, have also been narrowing, absolutely and relatively. This is exactly the opposite of what has happened with respect to measures of basic economic progress, where the gaps have been widening absolutely and, for the extremes, relatively as well.

The Contributions of the UN

What part of the positive achievements can be attributed to the UN? This is a difficult question to answer for a number of reasons. The UN writes and recommends, it sets goals and objectives, it may even provide direct support to individual countries. But ultimately governments and communities, leaders and ordinary people, farmers and craftsmen, companies and enterprises take action. The UN can do little more than promote priorities for action, help monitor, and provide modest levels of technical and financial support. Moreover, such support is not large. Though the UN is the world's largest international provider of grant aid, the $5 billion it allocates each year adds up to much less than one-thousandth of the annual income of the developing world and well under a quarter of 1 percent of the earnings from exports of developing countries.

In spite of all this, in the economic and social arena, the UN appears to have made a difference, especially in its contributions to ideas on development. As the introductory chapter of our first volume, *Ahead of the Curve*, set out, ideas can influence events in several ways: by changing the ways issues and priorities are viewed, by helping to frame agendas for action, by serving as a focus for mobilization of support (or opposition), and by becoming embodied in an institution which serves as a source of ongoing influence. Over the years, the UN has contributed ideas that have made a difference in all four ways. The record also shows that the UN has helped fashion and frame ideas—by serving as a fount, a forum, a focus, and a funnel—sometimes, indeed, with a fanfare and occasionally with a funeral—to bury an idea no longer wanted! The first two of these roles have been identified in many of the chapters. The function of the UN as a focus and a funnel are more clearly related to priority-setting and to identification of goals. The fanfare relates especially to the advocacy roles of the UN, which at times have been strong and forthright. Perhaps the biggest example of the funeral was in the later 1970s when the UN participated in debates which led to giving up the struggle for an NIEO, paving the way for what became for much of Africa, Latin America, and the least-developed countries a decade of debt, adjustment, and lost development.

UN Goals and Development Performance

One of the more particular ways the United Nations has tried to bring its ideas and influence to bear on national and international action is by setting goals. Some of these were set as specific targets, others as benchmarks by which to judge performance. Typically, global goals have been provided as guidelines or benchmarks, with specific recognition that individual countries will need to set their own goals. Sometimes goals and targets have operated in all these ways.

Any suggestion that there is a simple and direct link between recommendations in the halls of the United Nations and subsequent and immediate actions throughout the world would be contrary to the way national and international policies are made and carried out. Many other forces are at work. Policy and action mostly reflect national influences and interests, though for developing countries, especially smaller and poorer ones, international policy factors usually exert a substantial pressure, especially when these affect available resources and the options open for action. But even in this respect, the UN has, for the last few decades at least, been only one among several players, and its economic clout has usually been weak compared with that of the Bretton Woods institutions and the larger donors, who are often among the dominant political powers.

Judged by the goals and targets it has set, the UN has exercised considerable influence over the years, perhaps more than is often realized. This is especially true for countries where the UN and its agencies have had field staff and resources. And in any case, the economic and social goals and targets agreed by the UN can be used as benchmarks by which to judge the performance of developing countries, whether or not individual countries formally adopted the targets as specific national goals.

Table 10.8 presents a summary of the more than fifty goals and objectives agreed to in various bodies of the UN over the period 1960–2000. The goal and objectives cover economic growth, increases in life expectancy, reductions in child and maternal mortality, improvements in health, access to safe water and sanitation, access to education and reduction in illiteracy, and reductions in hunger and malnutrition. In order to make possible a clearer assessment of results, Table 10.8 includes only those goals and objectives which were defined in time-bound and quantitative terms. The goals cover a wide variety of areas, so they have been grouped both by the four decades to which they referred and by four categories relating to:

- Acceleration of economic growth
- Improvements in human welfare
- Moves to sustainable and equitable development
- Support for these efforts by the expansion of aid

Table 10.8 shows the goal and the date when it was first adopted; key elements of the goal; the target date for the goal, if any; and the results achieved. Where it is possible, achievements are shown in relation to the number of countries achieving, or nearly achieving, the goal as well as the proportion of the global population included in the countries achieving the goal. The table thus provides an indication of how development performance in key areas over four decades matches up to the goals and benchmarks set by the UN.

Table 10.8. UN Economic and Social Goals, Target Dates, and Results Achieved, 1960–2000

GOAL		TARGET DATE	RESULTS ACHIEVED

FIRST DEVELOPMENT DECADE (1961–1970)

Rate of Economic Growth (1961)[1]	Developing countries (DCs) to increase growth rates to a minimum of 5% with each country setting its own target.	1970	50 DCs (accounting for about half of total DC population) exceeded the goal. GNP growth rate of DCs averaged 5.5% for 1961–1970.

SECOND DEVELOPMENT DECADE (1971–1980)

Rate of Economic Growth (1970)[2]	GNP growth rate of DCs should average at least 6%; GNP per capita growth rate of DCs should average about 3.5%.	1970s	35 DCs (with about one-fifth of the DC population) exceeded the target of 6% growth. The annual GDP growth of DCs averaged 5.6% in 1971–1980.
Increase in DC Share of World Manufacturing Production (1975)	DCs to achieve 25% share of total world manufacturing.	2000	DC share of world manufacturing rose from about 11% in 1975 to about 22% in 2000.

THIRD DEVELOPMENT DECADE (1981–1990)

Rate of Economic Growth (1980)[3]	The average annual GDP growth rate of DCs as a whole should be 7%, and in the early part of the decade as close as possible to this rate.	1980s	15 DCs (with about 30% of the DC population) exceeded the 7% GDP growth rate for the decade. The overall growth in DCs averaged 4% annually during the 1980s, while per capita growth was 1.9%.
Increase in Economic Growth of LDCs (1981)	7.2% increase in the GDP to double national income of LDCs in a decade.	1990	3 LDCs (with 0.6% of the LDC population) achieved the growth target. The average annual growth rate for all LDCs was 2.3% 1980–1990.
Structure of Production in LDCs (1981)	4% annual increase in agricultural production in the least developed countries and 9% annual increase in manufacturing output.	1990	7 LDCs achieved the agricultural production goal. The annual average growth rate for the LDCs as a whole was 1.7% in 1980–1990. The manufacturing growth rate was 2% with 5 LDCs surpassing the 9% goal.
Official Development Assistance to the LDCs (1981)	ODA to LDCs should be 0.15% of the GNP of the donor countries.	***	8 Development Assistance Committee (DAC) countries allocated more than 0.15% of their GNI[4] to LDCs in 1990. The total for DAC was 0.09%.

Table 10.8. (continued)

	GOAL	TARGET DATE	RESULTS ACHIEVED
FOURTH DEVELOPMENT DECADE[5] (1991–2000)			
Rate of Economic Growth (1990)	DCs to sustain GNP growth rate of 7%. Growth objectives to vary by country.	2000	7 DCs (with about 27% of the population) of all DCs and transition countries achieved the average annual growth of 7% for the 1990s. The annual average growth rate for DCs as a whole for 1990–1999 was 4.7%.
ECONOMIC GOALS			
Official Development Assistance to LDCs (1990)	Donor countries to reach 0.15% of their GNP as ODA to LDCs.	1995	5 out of 20 DAC countries exceeded the 0.15% goal in 1995.
	Donor countries to reach 0.20% of their GNP as ODA to LDCs.	2000	5 DAC countries achieved the goal in 2000. DAC average in 2000 was 0.05% of their GNIs, down from 0.09% in 1990.
International Development Assistance (1960)[6]	Flow of international assistance and capital to reach 1% of GNP of the developed countries.[7]	As soon as possible	Total flow of resources from the DAC countries in 1970 was 0.79% of the GNP. ODA was 0.34% of the GNP.
Financial Resource Transfers to DCs (1970)[8]	Actual disbursements to be 1% of the GNP of each developed country at minimum.	1975	9 out of 17 DAC countries surpassed the goal in 1975. Total flow from the DAC countries in 1972 was 0.78% of the GNP and 1.17% of the GNP in 1975. By 1980, total flow had fallen to 1.04% with 11 of the DAC countries exceeding the goal.
	Each developed country to provide a minimum net amount of 0.7% of its GNP as ODA to the DCs.	Mid-Decade	Average net ODA from the 17 DAC countries was 0.36% of GNP in 1975. Only Sweden (0.82%) and the Netherlands (0.75%) exceeded the goal. By 1980, DAC countries' ODA was 0.38% of GDP with Norway and the Netherlands also exceeding the goal.
Official Development Assistance (1980)	ODA by all developed countries should reach, and where possible surpass, the agreed-upon international target of 0.7% of its GNP.	1985	Net ODA fell to 0.33% of GNP in 1990 with only 4 DAC countries exceeding the 0.7% target.
	The target of 1% should be reached.	As soon as possible	

Table 10.8. (continued)

	GOAL	TARGET DATE	RESULTS ACHIEVED
KEY HUMAN GOALS			
Life Expectancy (1980)	Life expectancy in all countries should reach 60 as a minimum.	2000	In 2000, at-birth life expectancy of 60 was achieved by 124 of the 173 countries. The overall life expectancy rate was 67 years globally and 65 years on average in the DCs. In the LDCs, however, the overall life expectancy at birth was 52 years, and it was only 49 in the sub-Saharan region.
Infant Mortality Rate (IMR) (1980)	In the poorest countries, infant mortality should be reduced to less than 120 per 1,000 live births; in all other countries, it should be no larger than 50 per 1,000 live births.	2000	At least 138 DCs had reached the goal and only 12 had not by the year 2000. Global IMR was 57 per 1,000, while in DCs it was 63. The sub-Saharan region fared worst with an IMR of 106 per 1,000 live births.
Infant Mortality Rate (IMR) (1990)	Reduce IMR by one-third or to 50 per 1,000 live births, whichever is less.	1990s	IMR in the DCs declined from 70 in 1990 to 63 per 1,000 live births in 2000.
Under-Five Mortality Rate (U5MR) (1990)	Reduce U5MR by one-third or to 70 per 1,000 live births, whichever is less.		The U5MR in the DCs declined from 103 in 1990 to 91 per 1,000 live births in 2000.
Low Birth Weight (LBW) (1990)	Reduce LBW (2.5 kg or less) to less than 10%.	2000	57 DCs had LBW levels below 10% in 2000. Currently 14% of world's children are born underweight (18 million a year), 15% in both DCs and LDCs. South Asia, where 25% of children are born underweight, accounts for nearly half of all low-weight births.
Reduction of Maternal Mortality Rate (1990)	Reduce maternal mortality rate by half between 1990 and the year 2000.	2000	World MMR average in 2000 was down to 400 from 430 per 100,000 in 1990. Approximately half of the cases occur in Sub-Saharan Africa where the MMR was 1,100 deaths per 100,000 live births in 1995 resulting in a 1 in 13 lifetime chance of dying in pregnancy or childbirth.
Reproductive Health Care (1990)	Access by all pregnant women to prenatal care, trained attendants during childbirth and referral facilities for high-risk pregnancies and obstetric emergencies.	***	In 2000, 70% of women in the world and 65% of the women in the DCs received antenatal care. Delivery care coverage in Sub-Saharan Africa was 37% and 29% in South Asia.

Table 10.8. (continued)

	GOAL	TARGET DATE	RESULTS ACHIEVED
Malnutrition (1990)	Reduce severe and moderate malnutrition by half among children under the age of 5.	1990s	5 countries achieved the goal and 13 additional countries reduced malnutrition at least by a quarter. Overall underweight prevalence declined from 32% in 1990 to 28% in 2000.

HUNGER and MALNUTRITION

	GOAL	TARGET DATE	RESULTS ACHIEVED
Hunger and Malnutrition (1974)	"All governments should accept the removal of the source of hunger and malnutrition . . . as the objective of the international community as a whole."	In a decade	The number of malnourished (underweight) children in DCs in 1980–1988 was 150 million.
Hunger and Malnutrition (1980)	"Hunger and malnutrition must be eliminated."	"As soon as possible and certainly by the end of this century."	During the 1990s malnutrition declined by 17% in DCs. In Africa; however, the estimated number of undernourished *rose* by 27 million during the 1990s.
Famine (1990)	"The elimination of starvation and death caused by famine."	During 1990s	

KEY HEALTH GOALS

	GOAL	TARGET DATE	RESULTS ACHIEVED
Eradication of Smallpox (1967)[9]	Eradicate smallpox worldwide.	Within 10 years	The last smallpox case occurred in Somalia in October 1977. On 8 May 1980, the World Health Assembly declared[10] that smallpox eradication had been achieved.
Universal Child Immunization[11] (1977)[12]	Immunize 80% of the DC's children before their first birthday.	By the end of 1990	The proportion of 1-year-old children immunized against measles in the world was 74% in 1990 and the coverage for the combined three-dose vaccine against diphtheria, pertussis, and tetanus was 73%, up from approximately 5% in the 1970s.
Polio (1988)[13]	Eradicate poliomyelitis worldwide.	2000	Polio was reduced by 99% in the 1990s. "By the end of 2001, wild poliovirus was endemic in just 10 countries."[14]
Polio (1990)	Eradicate poliomyelitis worldwide.	2000	

Table 10.8. (continued)

	GOAL	TARGET DATE	RESULTS ACHIEVED
Immunization (1990)	90% immunization coverage of one-year-olds.	2000	The proportion of one-year-old children immunized against measles in the world fell from 74% in 1990 to 72% in 1999. While the rates increased from 71% to 87% in Latin America and the Caribbean, they fell from 55% to 46% in Sub-Saharan Africa and 88% to 85% in East Asia/Pacific.
Measles (1990)	Reduce measles deaths by 95% and reduce measles cases by 90% compared to pre-immunization levels.	1995	Worldwide reported measles incidence declined by 40% between 1990 and 1999.
Reduction of Diarrhea Deaths (1990)	Reduce deaths due to diarrhea in children under the age five by half and reduce diarrhea incidence rate by one-fourth.	2000	The goal was achieved globally according to WHO estimates.
Iron Deficiency Anaemia (1990)	"Reduction of iron deficiency anaemia in women by one third of the 1990 levels."	2000	"Available evidence shows little change during the 1990s in the prevalence of anemia among pregnant women."[15]
Iodine Deficiency Disorders (IDD) (1990)	Virtual elimination of IDD.	2000	Approximately 70% of households in the DCs were using iodized salt in 2000, compared to less than 20% at the beginning of the decade.
Vitamin A Deficiency (1990)	"Virtual elimination of vitamin A deficiency and its consequences, including blindness."	2000	More than 40 countries are reaching the large majority of their children (over 70%) with at least one high-dose vitamin A supplement a year. The DCs (excluding China) as a whole achieved 50% coverage and the LDCs 80% coverage in 1999.
Breastfeeding (1990)	"Empowerment of all women to breastfeed their children exclusively for four to six months and to continue breastfeeding, with complimentary food, well into the second year."	2000	Exclusive breastfeeding rates increased by 10% over the decade, but only about half of all infants are exclusively breastfed for the first four months of life. In 1995–2000, 46% of infants in DCs and 37% in the LDC were exclusively breastfed.

Table 10.8. (continued)

	GOAL	TARGET DATE	RESULTS ACHIEVED
Acute Respiratory Infections (ARI) (1990)	Reduce by one-third of deaths due to ARI in children under five.	***	63% of children with ARI in urban areas and 51% in rural areas are taken to a health provider in the DCs.

CLEAN WATER and SANITATION

	GOAL	TARGET DATE	RESULTS ACHIEVED
Water and Sanitation (1980)	Safe water and adequate sanitary facilities should be made available to all in rural and urban areas.	1990	Estimated drinking-water supply coverage was 95% in urban areas and 66% in rural areas in 1990. The figures for sanitation were 82% in urban areas and 35% in rural areas.
Safe Drinking Water (1990)	"Universal access to safe drinking water."	2000	Global coverage increased from 77% in 1990 to 82% in 2000. The biggest increase occurred in South Asia where coverage increased from 72% in 1990 to 85% in 2000. Sub-Saharan Africa has the lowest regional average of 57%, up from 53% a decade earlier. However, 42% of the 1.1 billion people without access live in East Asia/ Pacific that has the regional average of 71%.
Sanitation (1990)	"Universal access to sanitary means of excreta disposal."	2000	Global sanitation coverage increased from 51% in 1990 to 61% in 2000. In sub-Saharan Africa, coverage declined from 54% to 53%.
Guinea-Worm Disease (1990)	Eliminate the guinea-worm disease (dracunculiasis).	2000	The number of reported cases has declined 88% from 1990 to 2000. 73% of the cases in 2000 were reported in the Sudan.

KEY EDUCATIONAL GOALS

	GOAL	TARGET DATE	RESULTS ACHIEVED
Education in Asia and the Far East (1960)	Universal, free, and compulsory primary education of at least seven years' duration for all children in Asia.	1980	The average percentage of students enrolled in first grade who completed primary school over 1975–1982 was 63 percent; average net enrollment ratio in 1980 was 86%.
Expansion of Education in Africa (1961)	Increasing primary-school enrollment for the continent as a whole from 40% to 51%[16] and secondary-school enrollment from 3% to 9%.	1966	In 1965, only 12 out of 45 DCs in Africa had more than 51% of the relevant age group enrolled in primary-level education. 20 countries exceeded 9% enrollment in the secondary level.

Table 10.8. (continued)

GOAL		TARGET DATE	RESULTS ACHIEVED
	Universal, compulsory, and free primary-school enrollment, 23% secondary-school attendance, and 2% attendance at higher educational institutions.	1980	The gross enrollment ratio in primary education in Africa in 1980 was 80%, gross enrollment ratio in secondary education was 22% and in tertiary education 3.7%.
Education in Latin America (1962)	Completion of six years of primary education by all children in both rural and urban areas.	1970	The average for grade 1 enrollment completing primary school for the countries with data available was 55% in 1975–1982 and the average net enrollment for the same countries in 1980 was 85%.
	Eradicate illiteracy among persons over 15 years of age.		26% of the population over age 15 were illiterate in Latin America and the Caribbean in 1970.
Universal Campaign Against Illiteracy (1963)[17]	Reduce illiteracy by two-thirds, or 350 million, of the estimated 500 million illiterate adults in Africa, Asia, and Latin America.	Within a 10-year period	Data for 1963 is unavailable, but estimates for 1960 was as follows: Africa, 81.5; Latin America, 33.9; East Asia, 42.4; South Asia, 67.8.[18]
Illiteracy (1990)	"Reduction of the adult illiteracy rate to at least half its 1990 level with emphasis on female literacy."	2000	Adult illiteracy worldwide lowered from 25% in 1990 to 20% in 2000. In 2000, 47% of world's illiterates were in South Asia.
Primary Education (1980)	"Closest possible realization of universal primary enrolment."	2000	The global enrollment increased from 80% in 1990 to 82% in 1999.
Primary Education (1990)	Universal access to basic education and completion of primary education by at least 80% of children of primary-school age.	2000	

*** = Date not specifically provided in the resolution.

This table draws on Richard Jolly, "Global Goals—The UN Experience," a paper prepared for the *Human Development Report 2003*. The year the goal was adopted by the UN is given in brackets by or below the goal.

Notes:

[1] General Assembly resolution 1710 (XVI), 19 December 1961.

[2] General Assembly resolution 2626, 24 October 1970.

[3] General Assembly resolution 35/56 and Annex, A/35/592/Add. 1, 5 December 1980.

[4] GNI (gross national income), developed for the 1993 System of National Accounts as an improved measure of GNP.

[5] "International Development Strategy for the Fourth United Nations Development Decade," General Assembly resolution A/RES/45/199, 21 December 1990.

[6] General Assembly resolution 1522 (XV), 15 December 1960.

Table 10.8. (continued)

[7]This target was modified in 1964 at the first session of UNCTAD, when the 1% ratio was applied to the more advanced countries individually. In the second session of UNCTAD in 1968, the term "national income" was replaced by "gross national product," *World Economic Survey 1969–1970,* 161.

[8]General Assembly resolution 2626 (XXV), 24 October 1970, para. 42.

[9]The Intensified Smallpox Eradication Programme was launched in January 1967 at the request of the Twentieth World Health Assembly, resolution WHA20.15

[10]After the Global Commission on Smallpox had concluded that smallpox had been eradicated on 9 December 1979.

[11]The programme was originally initiated in 1974 in order to protect children from poliomyelitis, measles, diphtheria, whooping cough, tetanus, and tuberculosis. See "Expanded Programme on Immunization" at http://www.childinfo.org/eddb/immuni/epi.htm.

[12]*"Expanded Programme on Immunization, EPI," World Health Assembly resolution WHA30.53, 19 May 1977.*

[13]Forty-first World Health Assembly, World Health Assembly resolution 41/1988/REC/1, 13 May 1988.

[14]WHO, *Global Polio Eradication Initiative Summary Report of 2001* (Geneva: WHO, 2002), 1.

[15]Percent total enrollment ratio will be the outcome of annual increase of 5% of the beginning school-age group.

[16]UNICEF, *The State of the World's Children 2002* (New York, UNICEF, 2002).

[17]"Universal Campaign Against Literacy," General Assembly resolution 1937 (XVIII), 11 December 1963. Previously adopted by the General Conference of UNESCO, UNESCO resolution 1.2531, 12 December 1962.

[18]UNESCO, *Statistical Yearbook 1968* (Paris: UNESCO, 1968).

Goals, key elements and target dates were compiled by Merja Jutila from the following sources:

ECLA, "Provisional Report of the Conference on Education and Economic and Social Development in Latin America," 15 January 1963.

"International Development Strategy for the Third United Nations Development Decade," GA resolution 35/56 and annex, A/35/592/Add. 1, 5 December 1980.

"International Development Strategy for the Fourth United Nations Development Decade," GA resolution A/RES/45/199, 21 December 1990.

UN, *Report of the Second United Nations Conference on the Least Developed Countries: Paris, 3–14 September 1990* (New York: United Nations, 1991).

UN, *Report of the World Food Conference, Rome, 5–16 November 1974* (New York: UN, 1975).

UNICEF, *The State of the World's Children 1991* (Oxford: Oxford University Press, 1991).

UNCTAD, "Outline for a Substantial New Programme of Action for the 1980s for the Least Developed Countries," UNCTAD document TD/240, 13 February 1979.

UNCTAD, "Substantial New Programme of Action for the 1980s for the Least Developed Countries," United Nations Conference on the Least Developed Countries in Paris, 1–14 September 1981, UNCTAD document A/CONF.104/7, 22 May 1981.

UNESCO, "Plan for the Provision of Universal, Compulsory and Free Primary Education," meeting of UNESCO Asian Member States, Karachi, January 1960. In *Report on the Regional Meeting of Representatives of Asian Member States on Primary and Compulsory Education,* UNESCO document UNESCO/ED/173 Paris, 29 February 1960.

UNESCO, *Report of Meeting of Ministers of Education of Asian Member States Participating in the Karachi Plan, Tokyo, 2–11 April 1962.* Available online at http://www.unesco.org/education/pdf/TOKYO2_E.PDF.

UNESCO and ECA, "Outline of a Plan for African Educational Development," in *Final Report: Conference of African States on the Development of Education in Africa, Addis Ababa, 15–25 May 1961,* UNESCO document UNESCO/ED/180, available online at http://unesdoc.unesco.org/images/0007/000774/077416e.pdf.

UNIDO, "Lima Declaration and Plan of Action on Industrial Development and Co-operation," General Conference of UNIDO, Lima, 12–26 March 1975, UNIDO document ID/CONF.3/31, 9 May 1975.

Table 10.8. (continued)

Results have been found in or calculated from data in the following sources:

F. Fenner and D. A. Henderson, *Smallpox and Its Eradication* (Geneva: WHO, 1988).

OECD Development Assistance Committee, *Development Co-operation 1981, 1982* (Paris: OECD, November 1981 and November 1982).

OECD, *Development Co-operation Report 1996, 2001* (Paris: OECD, January 1997 and April 2002).

Report of the Secretary-General, *Implementation of the United Nations Millennium Declaration,* UN A/57/270, 31 July 2002.

Report of the Secretary-General, *We the Children: End-Decade Review of the Follow-Up to the World Summit for Children,* A/S-27/3, 4 May 2001.

UNCTAD, *The Least Developed Countries Report 2002* (UN: New York and Geneva, 2002).

UNCTAD, *Paris Declaration and Programme for Action for the Least Developed Countries for the 1990s.* (UN: New York, 1992).

UNCTAD, "Substantial New Programme of Action for the 1980s for the Least Developed Countries," United Nations Conference on the Least Developed Countries, Paris, 1–14 September 1981, UNCTAD document A/CONF.104/7, 22 May 1981.

UN Department of International Economic and Social Affairs, *World Economic Survey 1969–1970* (New York: United Nations, 1971).

UN Department of International Economic and Social Affairs, *World Economic Survey 1972* (New York: United Nations, 1973).

UN Department of International Economic and Social Affairs, *World Economic Survey 1981–1982* (New York: United Nations, 1982).

UN Department of International Economic and Social Affairs Statistical Office, *1981 Statistical Yearbook* (New York: United Nations, 1983).

UNDP, *Human Development Report 1990, 2002* (New York and Oxford: Oxford University Press, 1990, 2002).

UNESCO, *Statistical Yearbook 1999* (Paris: UNESCO Publishing, Bernan Press, 1999).

United Nations Foundation, "Promoting Children's Health and Well-being." Available online at http://www.unfoundation.org/media_center/publications/pdf/Immunization_One_Pager_02.pdf.

UNICEF, The *State of the World's Children 1985, 1991* (New York: Oxford University Press, 1985, 1991).

UNICEF, The *State of the World's Children 2001, 2002* (New York: UNICEF, 2001, 2002).

UNICEF, "Progress since the World Summit for Children: A Statistical Review" (New York: UNICEF, 2001). Available online at http://www.unicef.org/publications/pub_wethechildren_stats_en.pdf.

UNIDO Asia-Pacific Regional Forum, "Opening statement of the Director-General," Bangkok, Thailand, 23 September 1999. Available online at http://www.unido.org/en/doc/4003

World Bank, *World Development Indicators 2000, 2002* (Washington, D.C.: World Bank, March 2000, April 2002). Some statistical tables also acquired from the World Bank directly via e-mail.

WHO, *Global Polio Eradication Initiative Summary Report of 2001* (WHO, 2002).

WHO/UNICEF/WSSCC, *Global Water Supply and Sanitation Assessment 2000 Report* (Geneva: WHO, 2002).

Acceleration of economic growth: This has been a focus of each of the development decades. Here success has decreased over time. During the (First) Development Decade, over the 1960s, some fifty underdeveloped countries achieved or exceeded the goal of accelerating economic growth to reach a rate of 5 percent by 1970. This goal was also exceeded by the average growth of all developing countries taken together.

In the Second Development Decade, the UN goal for economic growth was increased to 6 percent per annum and some thirty-five developing countries reached or exceeded it, while the average of all developing countries over the decade was 5.6 percent. But differences in performance grew and the accumulation of debt, the world recession, and swinging adjustment policies slowed growth substantially in the Third and Fourth Development Decades.

In the Third Development Decade, only fifteen countries achieved the target growth rate of 7 percent, but as China was one, over one-quarter of the population of developing countries was involved in this achievement. In the Fourth Development Decade, over the 1990s, only seven developing countries achieved the 7 percent goal, though again, as China was one of them, more than one-quarter of the Third World population was involved.

Not withstanding these successes, progress in achieving the goals set for accelerating economic growth slipped badly over time. Average growth for all developing countries over the last two decades of the twentieth century was 4 percent in the 1980s and 4.7 percent in the 1990s. The result was that per capita growth, on average, was considerably below 2 percent over the 1980s and barely this figure in the 1990s.

Most serious of all have been the failures of economic growth in the least-developed countries. In 1981, the UN set the ambitious goal of doubling incomes in these countries in a decade, which was modest enough in terms of need but unrealistic in terms of the performance required. The goal implied an annual rate of growth of 7.2 percent. Only two least-developed countries achieved the goal in the 1980s. The average economic growth rate of the least-developed countries was only 2.3 percent in the 1980s and 3.7 percent over the 1990s, meaning that average GNP per capita *declined* in the Third Development Decade and increased at a rate of a little above 1 percent per annum over the Fourth Development Decade.[13]

The result has been that the gaps between the industrial countries and the bulk of developing countries have widened over the last two decades, both relatively and absolutely. In the case of the forty-nine least-developed countries, the gaps have widened even further. As the World Bank put it in 2002, "Income inequality is rising. Average income in the wealthiest 20 countries is 37 times that in the poorest 20 countries—twice the ratio in 1970."[14]

Goals for human advance: Performance with respect to human goals has been considerably better. As indicated earlier in this chapter, and as Table 10.8 made clear, most developing countries have made impressive advances in life expectancy and infant and child mortality, many along lines encouraged by the development goals. Life expectancy had been increased to 60 years in 124 of some 173 developing and transition countries by the year 2000. Some 138 developing countries had by the same year reduced their infant mortality rate to below 120 per 1,000, and only twelve countries had failed to achieve this goal.

Seven major goals for improving the health and welfare of children and women were set in 1990 at the World Summit for Children, along with another seventeen supporting goals.[15] With the strong support of UNICEF and other UN agencies such as the WHO and the UNFPA, some 150 countries then prepared national plans of action devising strategies to implement these goals. Throughout the decade, UNICEF worked to encourage country-by-country implementation and monitoring and in 2001 undertook a major review of achievements.[16] The results are included in Table 10.8 under key human goals.

Over 100 countries reduced mortality by one-fifth over the 1990s and some 63 by one-third or more. Considering that 100 years earlier, in 1900, only one country in the world (Norway) had an infant mortality rate less than 100 per 1,000, this is impressive progress, especially in the light of the economic difficulties of the last two decades and of the rising and disastrous spread of HIV/AIDS, particularly in sub-Saharan Africa. Significant improvements in nutrition and birth weight were also achieved, though mostly in Asia and Latin America, and except for five countries, by much less than the goal which called for a halving of severe and moderate child malnutrition over the 1990s. In sub-Saharan Africa, malnutrition often increased and the number of undernourished Africans rose over the decade. Unfortunately, and in sharp contrast, no part of the developing world recorded much success in reducing maternal mortality rates.

Impressive advances were also achieved in other goals for health—for immunization against communicable diseases, control of diarrhea, and actions to tackle micronutrient deficiencies, the hidden hungers whose abolition can do much to improve child intelligence and bodily growth and reduce infant and child mortality. By the year 2000, 70 percent of households were using iodized salt compared with 20 percent at the time of the World Summit for Children in 1990. Vitamin A supplements—a major step to eliminating blindness from Vitamin A deficiency—were also being provided to some 50 percent of children in developing countries and some 80 percent in the least-developed countries. Deaths caused by neonatal tetanus had declined by 50 percent and polio by 99 percent. Efforts to eliminate polio by the end of

2001 had made such progress that it was endemic in only ten countries, an extraordinary advance on the situation ten or twenty years earlier. The number of cases of polio had fallen by 99 percent from 1988.[17]

The increase in safe drinking-water resources and sanitation also made considerable progress, especially in the 1980s, which had been named the UN decade of drinking water and sanitation.[18] Access to safe water more than doubled over the 1980s, and access to basic sanitation increased by some two and half times. Moreover, great advances were made in identifying better, low-cost technologies suitable for making rapid progress in rural and peri-urban areas, laying the foundations for further progress in the 1990s. Although progress in the 1990s was not as fast, coverage increased in all regions except in sub-Saharan Africa. Impressive progress was also made in related areas such as reducing guinea worm disease, where cases fell over the 1990s by 88 percent, to the point where in 2000, the disease was endemic in only fourteen countries, all of which are in Africa.[19]

Education: Expansion of education was first adopted as a major international goal in the 1950s and 1960s, when UNESCO held a series of major regional conferences to set goals for expansion of all levels of education. As indicated earlier, over the 1960s and 1970s, education expanded very rapidly at the primary level and even more rapidly at secondary and tertiary levels. Notwithstanding this accelerated progress, the goals of achieving universal primary education by 1980[20] were not achieved in more than half of the developing countries, partly because population in many countries rose more rapidly than had been earlier projected but also because factors affecting the ability and willingness of boys and girls from poorer families to attend and stay in school for the whole course had been widely ignored. The result was that by the year 2000, some 115 million children of primary-school age were still not enrolled in school and the number of adult illiterates, which at last was beginning to fall, still amounted to 20 percent of the adult population in developing countries.[21]

Education is a subtle and multifaceted endeavor. Over the years, increased attention has been given to indicators beyond basic enrollments and to some of the qualitative dimensions that are less easy to measure: primary-school completion rates, gender equality at different levels of schooling, equitable access to appropriate learning and life skills, and others. Efforts are currently being made by UNESCO to assess progress toward the goals of Education for All,[22] which are judged by three more elaborated quantitative indices: levels of primary-level net enrollment; levels of adult literacy; and gender parity in primary-level gross enrollment ratios, which is analyzed using trends over the 1990s in relation to the goals for the year 2015. By this test, eighty-three

countries, which account for almost one-third of the population of developing countries, had achieved the three goals by 2000 or had a good chance of
doing so by or before 2015; another forty-three countries with over one-third
of the developing-country population had made substantial progress in the
1990s but would miss at least one goal by 2015; and some twenty-eight countries which account for about one-quarter of the developing-country population are in serious risk of not achieving any of the three goals without making
major changes.[23]

International Development Assistance: If there is one category of goals which
countries have largely failed to implement, it is the failure of developed countries to fulfill the 0.7 percent commitment to provide aid (overseas development assistance, or ODA) in the quantities and on the terms which the goals
required.

All but four of the twenty-four or so donor countries have not only fallen
short of the goal by considerable amounts but over the 1990s allowed aid in
total and as a percentage of developed-country GNP to decline—from 0.33
percent in 1990 to 0.22 in 2000. Moreover, the proportion of ODA going to
the poorest and least-developed countries has slipped or fallen short of the
goals set in the 1990s conference on the least-developed countries.[24]

In contrast, four developed countries—Denmark, the Netherlands, Norway,
and Sweden—have achieved the goal. Moreover, these countries have consistently maintained the goal since the late 1970s and in most years well exceeded
it. They are also the ones which have followed the UN guidelines in allocating
reasonable shares of their assistance to the least-developed countries.

It must be emphasized, of course, that often it is not the lack of aid but
other failures which account for the major obstacles faced by developing countries, especially the poorest and the least developed—decreases in commodity
prices, the accumulation of debt, an ever-changing agenda of aid conditionalities, and a profusion of reporting requirements.

Country Action and Alternative Strategies

But the developing countries must themselves share much of the blame for
development failures and weaknesses—just as they deserve the lion's share of
the credit for the development successes over the last half-century. Country-by-
country experience reveals a great diversity in performance and achievements.
Some countries have been spectacular successes—such as Korea (Box 4.2), Taiwan, Malaysia, Mauritius, Botswana, and Tunisia. China (Box 6.3) seems poised
at this juncture to emulate if not to exceed their performance. Others, such as
India (Box 3.1) and Sri Lanka (Box 7.2), have achieved moderate but solid

progress, both social and economic. Brazil (Box 4.1) has had strong but uneven progress, while Chile (Box 6.1) and Ghana (Box 7.1) have accomplished sharp breaks from their previous development strategies and pioneered far-reaching economic reforms with positive outcomes. Despite an adverse and sharply deteriorating external environment, Cuba (Box 6.2) has sought with some success to sustain its remarkable social achievements but has experienced severely declining living standards over the past decade. Likewise, Nigeria (Box 9.4) and Tanzania (Box 5.1) have encountered serious economic and social setbacks over the past two to three decades.

These countries have by no means simply followed UN advice, nor have they followed the same development strategies over the years. Most countries have been subject to a diversity of national and international ideas and influences and adopted an eclectic mix of policies that has evolved over time and strongly reflects local interests and pressures. Development thinking has also changed, as have national and international ideologies.

One can broadly identify four major types of development strategies, based on the dominant set of policies pursued by different countries:

- State-led industrialization based on import substitution
- Socialist organization of the economy
- Export-oriented industrialization
- Neoliberal economic policies

Over the half-century since the UN was founded, there has been a general shift from the first two types of strategy toward the last two. Worldwide there has been a shift from state controls and a loosening of public ownership toward more reliance on the market. Reforms emphasizing greater roles for the market and for the private sector have often improved incentives and the allocation of resources, sometimes—but by no means always—also contributing to faster growth. The contribution of these reforms to poverty reduction, human development, and a more equitable distribution of income has been much less certain.

Even with regard to growth, the majority of developing countries, especially those in Latin America and Africa, did much better during the period 1950–1980 than over the following two decades. This does not imply that greater state control of the economy was responsible for faster growth in the earlier period, though planning and state controls were certainly not the total failure that commentators sometimes suggest. But the record leaves no doubt that export-oriented industrialization "East Asia style" has generated superior growth and equity effects than purely inward-looking industrialization.[25]

While there has been a general move toward reliance on the market and on the private sector, the origin, extent, and patterns of reform show considerable variation. One common factor has been the triggering of reforms by economic crisis or political change in the governing regime. Both these elements were present in South Korea, Chile, Brazil, and Ghana, where the reform process was initiated by military, authoritarian regimes. In Sri Lanka, the election of a conservative party led to policy reforms. On the other hand, in countries as diverse as India, Taiwan, China, and Tanzania, the ruling parties initiated economic reform. Over the 1980s and 1990s, adjustment policies promoted by the Bretton Woods institutions have been a mechanism for promoting policies of the Washington Consensus.

In Korea and Taiwan, major structural changes, most notably land reform, preceded the reorientation of economic policies, thus laying the basis for an equitable pattern of growth. In China, similar results were achieved by an egalitarian distribution of land under the household responsibility system. In Chile, in contrast, the undoing of agrarian reform and creation of unequal relations between workers and employers were integral parts of the reform process. In India, Sri Lanka, Brazil, Tanzania, and Ghana, reforms were grafted onto the existing social and economic structures.

Everywhere trade liberalization and the removal or easing of quantitative restrictions and price controls constituted the first step in the reform process, often accompanied by devaluation of national currency, interest rate increases, and curbs on public spending. Reforms of financial institutions and divestiture of state enterprises came later and were embraced only partially and by some countries. Chile, and to a lesser extent Ghana, promoted privatization more actively. Elsewhere it has been a slow and gradual process.

Four of the countries considered—Sri Lanka, Chile, Cuba, and China—had relatively advanced social indicators by 1960. Taiwan and Korea also made rapid progress with literacy, schooling, infant mortality, and life expectancy. The social performance for other countries was either average (Ghana and Tanzania) or below average (India and Brazil) in relation to their per capita incomes. The relative lead of the early pioneers has declined either because social progress could not keep pace with extremely rapid economic growth or because of relative neglect of social development in reform programs.

Concluding Observations

The picture that emerges of progress and performance in the developing world is mixed and complex. Over the period 1950–2000, the developing countries achieved economic and social progress that was without precedent in history. But regional economic divergence grew over the last two or three decades. There was a marked slowdown in economic growth in Latin America and the Caribbean after 1980 and sub-Saharan Africa after the 1970s. In contrast, South Asia, India in particular, experienced a sharp acceleration in its growth rate over the last two decades of the twentieth century. East and Southeast Asia continued their impressive progress for most of the period. The outstanding feature of the last two decades was China's spectacular growth.

The most serious development setback has been the disastrous economic performance of sub-Saharan Africa over the past three decades. Likewise, the slowdown in Latin America after 1980 is disturbing and perplexing.

These developments set fundamental challenges for the future—for international policy and action and for rethinking the strategies so far pursued in these two regions.

What can one conclude from the UN's efforts to influence the rate and pattern of economic growth and the human situation in developing countries?

First, for a considerable number of developing countries, the UN has exercised considerable influence, especially but not only in setting goals and benchmarks, notably in the social sectors. Many of these objectives in a considerable number of developing countries have been largely or considerably achieved.

Second, success has been greater in those sectors where the UN agencies had field staff and programs and where it was able to back up ideas and goals with catalytic support. The eradication of smallpox and the near-elimination of polio and guinea worm are clear examples. If the UN had not provided leadership, coordination, and support, these actions would not have been embarked upon, let alone brought to such a positive outcome. The UN has also provided catalytic support that has had a real impact in other areas of human advance—notably in the reductions of infant and child mortality in the 1980s and 1990s, even in Latin America and sub-Saharan Africa during two decades when these regions were experiencing a lost decade for economic development.

Third, in other areas—such as the expansion of education in the 1960s and 1970s and the expansion of access to drinking water and basic sanitation in the 1980s and 1990s, the UN has exercised a worldwide influence through its advocacy and the catalytic support provided by some of its specialized agencies and funds.

Fourth, notwithstanding these positive outcomes, the results have been patchy, uneven, and, for many countries, generally slower than the ambitious goals set by the international community in the halls of the UN. For this, the blame must be shared. It would be both a big mistake and extremely superficial to blame all the failures on the UN—or on the countries that have failed to follow up adequately on the goals and commitments to which they had agreed. But these are the extremes and between them are many examples where countries have striven to improve development and in many cases have achieved positive results—but without the full success envisaged when the goals were set by the international community.

Here an important caveat must be entered. For the most part, the Bretton Woods institutions have not supported the UN goals. Instead, they have focused on a narrower set of economic objectives. Over the 1980s and the 1990s, the objectives of the Bretton Woods institutions were mostly those now described as the Washington Consensus—economic adjustment, reducing imbalances in the current accounts, cutting public spending, lowering inflation, increasing privatization, and reducing debt. These goals were economic goals in the sense of means to economic ends, in contrast to the goals of human advance and poverty reduction which formed the major goals of the UN since the 1980s. Moreover, the World Bank and the IMF had the resources and the economic clout to back up their goals and objectives with negotiations to press countries to adopt and implement the goals. Yet, in spite of all this, many of the Bretton Woods goals have not been achieved. One can only wonder what might have happened if the UN had been given the resources, a lead position at the country level, and strong donor support to pursue their more human and humane goals.

11

UN Contributions and Missed Opportunities

- **The Main Contributions of the UN to Development Thinking and Practice**
- **Omissions and Missed Opportunities**
- **Concluding Remarks**

We have almost come to the end of this volume. Before drawing lessons for the future, let us review where we stand. The contributions of the UN must be neither understated nor overstated. The UN has been an intellectual pioneer in issues of economic and social development, much more than is often recognized. At the same time, there have often been omissions and distortions in its work, as we will try to bring out at the end of this chapter, using the privilege of hindsight to focus on those omissions which we feel have been the most serious. And because this volume is concerned with action and achievements as well as ideas, we also draw attention to some of the cases when the ideas of the UN have been right, but not seriously applied, and one or two cases when the UN was wrong and the ideas it promoted have been neglected or rejected.

All this, in principle, could be traced through in painstaking detail, giving attention to ideas and actions country by country over the whole period of the UN's existence. This is beyond our capacity. We hope that a number of individual countries will document the record of the UN in supporting and influencing their national development. A few countries are already embarking on some part of this important story.[1] But in this chapter we give an overview, focusing on the main ideas and attempting to show how they affected the thinking and patterns of development in the main blocs of developing or transition countries.

The Main Contributions of the UN to Development Thinking and Practice

There can be little doubt that the three greatest intellectual contributions of the United Nations have been human rights on a global scale, purposeful development of developing countries, and ideas for ways to improve economic relations between richer and poorer countries, which initially focused on improving the terms of trade. Over its first three decades, the UN produced many ideas about economic growth and development that focused on national development and living standards but which—if implemented—would have substantively diminished the income gap between rich and poor countries.

These early ideas were taken much farther in subsequent decades and broadened into other fields. All were areas where important work was proceeding outside the UN, but in many of these cases, the activities by or within the UN made the major and sometimes the largest contribution. A number of the key architects of the early ideas—Arthur Lewis, Nicholas Kaldor, Richard Stone, Benjamin Higgins, Albert Hirschman—had close links with the UN and for varying periods worked as UN consultants although their main employment was outside the UN. The UN also had a number of distinguished economists working as full-time staff members: Raúl Prebisch, Gunnar Myrdal, James Meade, Hans Singer, and Dudley Seers.

Table 11.1 gives an overview of the main areas where the UN made contributions to thinking on development. The specifics of these ideas have been elaborated in earlier chapters and will not be repeated here. Rather, the summary below attempts to note which were the areas where the UN contributions seem to have been most pioneering in terms of ideas and which were the areas where UN contributions seem to have had most impact on action.

The UN's most important contributions have been in the areas of human rights and the human dimensions of development, as indicated in Table 11.1. Human rights was the focus of the earliest contributions but further elaboration and implementation of those rights rapidly became points of Cold War controversy. This began to change after the First World Conference on Women in 1975 and the adoption of CEDAW, the Convention on the Elimination of All Forms of Discrimination against Women in 1979. Gradually over the 1980s, the awareness of rights and of CEDAW in particular grew internationally. The women's movement in developing countries grew in strength, helped by CEDAW and often building on the inspiration and networks established in the international conferences, although the potential of these movements was often constrained by the priorities of structural adjustment. In the 1990s, the Convention on the Rights of the Child was influential in drawing more attention to children's issues, especially concerns about gender inequality and the needs of young girls (the question of the "girl child").

In the first two decades of the UN, its contributions to development were mostly in what were seen as mainstream areas of economic development. UN employees made pioneering analyses of trade and aid during the late 1940s

Table 11.1. An Overview of UN Contributions to Development

Areas of Contribution to Ideas and Thinking	Impact on Action				
	1950s	1960s	1970s	1980s	1990s
Human Rights	limited	limited	limited	widespread	widespread
Development Goals and Objectives					
Economic	widespread	limited	limited	limited	negligible
Human and Social		minimal	minimal	widespread	widespread
Population			minimal	minimal	minimal
National Development Policies and Planning					
Development Planning		widespread	widespread	limited	limited
Industrialization		minimal	minimal	minimal	minimal
Agriculture and Rural Development		minimal	minimal	minimal	minimal
International Cooperation for Development					
Development Assistance		limited	limited	limited	limited
Foreign Debt and Development				limited	limited
Special Needs of LDCs				negligible	negligible
Trade Inequalities and Trade Policy	limited	limited	limited	limited	limited
Disarmament and Development		minimal	minimal	minimal/limited	limited
Transnational Enterprises			limited	limited	negligible
Technology Transfer	minimal	minimal	minimal	minimal	minimal
Environment and Development			limited	widespread	widespread
Transition in Transition Countries					minimal
Equity in Development					
Empowering Women		limited	limited	widespread	widespread
Children in Development		minimal	minimal	widespread	widespread
Greater Global Equity	negligible	negligible	negligible		
Human Development					widespread

Key

■ widespread impact on action   ■ limited impact on action   ■ minimal impact on action   ▢ negligible impact on action and 1950s, in part because the Bretton Woods institutions at the time were still preoccupied with problems of European reconstruction. The UN could take the lead on development issues and it did so, though often UN ideas stirred up more opposition than support in the industrial countries. The UN's contributions in thinking about trade and the need for concessional finance—aid—for developing countries were an important intellectual contribution, as was the UN's work in the 1960s on the Development Decade. In the 1970s, the issues of employment strategy in developing countries, basic needs, and redistribution with growth (the latter developed jointly with the World Bank) maintained the UN's intellectual lead.

By the 1980s and 1990s, the UN's contributions to ideas and thinking on economic growth and development had diminished. Both the World Bank and the IMF had grown rapidly in size and resources and increasingly had the support of the donor community. In contrast, and in part as a consequence, the UN was challenged to demonstrate its relevance and capacity for development. Even so, in the areas of environment, health, gender, children, and population, the UN made important and pioneering contributions to the development agenda. But in the narrower field of economic strategy and policy, the UN was largely sidelined. Its role, when it had the courage to speak out, became that of a critic of economic orthodoxy, in particular on the issues of debt, the special problems of the least-developed countries, and alternatives to structural adjustment. On trade and codes of conduct for transnational corporations, the UN was distinctly soft-spoken, especially after the Centre for Transnational Corporations was closed as a separate institution, though UNCTAD (which took over its functions) continued to issue important reports which gave analytical alternatives to mainstream orthodoxy.

Human Rights

The UN believed that development was the responsibility of all nations; this was the first time in human history this point of view had been advanced. The UN Charter speaks of the need to employ "international machinery for the promotion of the economic and social advancement of all peoples."[2] Article 28 of the UN Declaration of Human Rights states: "Everyone is entitled to a social and international order in which the rights and freedoms set forth in this Declaration can be fully realized." In subsequent years, the UN acted as the central international forum for the discussion and negotiation of practically all major initiatives for development.

Following the adoption of the Universal Declaration in 1948, the UN embarked on a more specific review of rights and obligations for many other groups of people and areas of action. Its deliberations gave rise to numerous resolutions and conventions that further elaborated and expanded the international regime of human rights. In parallel, conventions were adopted by many of the UN specialized agencies, particularly by the ILO on labor standards. Over the last fifty years, the UN system has evolved a comprehensive regime of international law designed to foster freedom, security, and dignity and to promote minimum standards of living for all peoples and individuals. These ideas stood in sharp contrast to most of the writing on development outside the UN, where the approaches of economists, sociologists, anthropologists, and professional and technical experts such as engineers and city planners mostly ignored issues of human rights, at least until very recently.

The UN has also contributed more than other international institutions—or the academic world of development economists—to the broadening of the notion of development. The founding documents of the UN system enjoined the member states and the international organizations to work for the achievement of civil, political, social, economic, and cultural rights of all human beings. In subsequent decades, the notion of development was expanded to include issues of employment, the reduction of poverty, fairer distribution of the benefits of growth, participation in decision-making at different levels, equality of men and women, child development, social justice, and environmental sustainability.

Development Goals and National Strategies

While the emphasis on industry tended to overshadow the agricultural sector in the early UN reports on employment and economic growth in developing countries, the issue of commodity-price stabilization dominated discussions of international policy in UN forums for several decades. There was also awareness of the importance of tenure reform and equitable land distribution among the landless and marginal peasants for economic growth and poverty reduction, as witnessed by the reports prepared by the UN on land reform in the 1950s.

Land reform was also linked with the FAO's Freedom from Hunger Campaign of the 1960s. Land reform was to recur periodically along with the theme of food security. The ILO conducted important work on agrarian reform in the late 1970s and 1980s.[3] The FAO organized the World Conference on Agrarian Reform and Rural Development in 1979, which adopted a wide-ranging program of action designed to bring about tenancy and land reform, increase food production, generate employment, reduce rural poverty, and promote organizations of rural workers and peasants.[4]

IFAD dedicated itself to providing credit and technical assistance for projects designed to enhance income and employment opportunities for the landless and poor farmers. In its programs, it emphasized participatory approaches to rural development. It also supported microcredit schemes and nutrition programs for rural women.

Development planning was popular among policymakers, academics, and donor agencies in the 1950s and 1960s. The UN, in part responding to the desire of its developing-country members, made a number of contributions to planning methodologies and the adoption of those methodologies in the member states. The decision to declare the 1960s the First Development Decade was in itself an exercise in global planning. To prepare for the decade, the UN Secretariat and the specialized agencies engaged in projections of output, savings, investment, trade, and other economic variables in different parts of the world. Such projections, crude as they were, enabled the Development Decade strategy to propose targets for output and capital flows to developing countries.[5] Subsequent Development Decade strategies for international development were based on more sophisticated models. In addition to economic targets, goals included reducing hunger, malnutrition, and infant mortality and increasing life expectancy, literacy, school enrollment, and other dimensions of human development.[6]

In support of these exercises, the UN system made increasing efforts to collect and standardize data from countries around the world. The UN Committee for Development Planning, which consisted of eminent development specialists, was set up in 1966 and was charged with the responsibility of conducting studies to facilitate planning and to prepare papers for ECOSOC and the General Assembly on major global and national policy issues. The UN also set up planning and training institutes in the four developing regions.

Around 1980, planning began to be attacked and disillusion began to set in, the result of a number of forces: longer-term approaches were undercut by the short-term pressures of debt and adjustment, which were reinforced by the orthodox thought of the Bretton Woods institutions, ideological pressures from monetary theorists, and political shifts to the right under Reagan and Thatcher. National planning was dethroned and replaced by annual budgeting or short-term emergency planning to cope with problems of liquidity, debt, stabilization, and adjustment. Only a small number of countries continued to prepare five-year development plans, and often these plans lacked the authority that planning had carried in earlier decades.

At the time of writing, it is difficult to avoid the conclusion that this has been a regressive development. Whatever its defects, development planning compelled the top policymakers and social and economic groups to make a careful assessment of the major and longer-term problems faced by a country. Countries were forced to prioritize objectives, establish targets, and to work out policy implications of targets and goals in relation to resources, investment, savings, trade, foreign aid, and sectoral areas.

Development Assistance, ODA, and Debt Relief

Foreign aid to accelerate economic growth in poor countries was an area where the UN made unique contributions in the 1940s and 1950s. These contributions were detailed and specific and, over the first few decades of the UN's existence, provided the rationale which led to the formulation of quantitative goals for ODA, which with elaboration and some modifications still remain some four decades after they were first adopted.

Developing a rationale for development assistance was itself a major contribution. This was first presented in a systematic way in the 1951 UN report on *Measures for the Economic Development of Underdeveloped Countries* (though development assistance had been a recommendation of an ECOSOC subcommission in 1947).[7] The report analyzed the situation of most poor countries with limited ability to save, no access to capital markets, and few opportunities which would prove attractive to foreign investors (a situation that was neglected three or four decades later, in the heyday of promotion of global private flows as the preferred alternative to development aid). The 1951 report clearly recognized that a significant acceleration in the growth rates of the poor countries would require substantial inflows of capital at concessional rates of interest.

This inflow provided the theoretical arguments for the creation of a UN agency to provide grants and soft loans to developing countries—a role that the World Bank was unwilling to play at that time. Indeed, this proposal led to prolonged and acrimonious debate in the General Assembly and ECOSOC for seven or eight years, resulting finally in the creation of the IDA and the IFC in the World Bank and the Special Fund in the United Nations.

Eventually, development assistance became accepted as an indispensable component of international development strategies; this realization helped lay the foundations for the dramatic success of accelerated development in at least a few countries, most notably South Korea and Taiwan. The UN played the central role in developing targets for aid.

The idea of technical assistance came from the UN; it was first broached by the UN Sub-Commission on Economic Development in its first report in 1947.[8] It rapidly gathered momentum when President Truman proposed in his inaugural address in January 1949 that the UN system launch an expanded program of technical assistance, which became EPTA.

In contrast, the servicing of foreign debt emerged as a major problem for many developing countries in the late 1970s and early 1980s. This problem has continued to bedevil the economic prospects of many such countries over subsequent years. The overall approach to and policies for handling the debt problem have been determined by the international financial organizations, the creditor countries, and commercial banks. While it is not a direct party to debt negotiations, the UN has had a stake in the outcome of such negotiations in view of the massive impact the servicing of debt has had on economic growth, poverty, unemployment, and social services in heavily indebted countries.

The UN's role has been that of critic and advocate for change in the area of debt strategy. UNCTAD's work on external debt criticized the dominant features of the international debt strategy pursued in the 1980s. These included a disproportionate burden of macroeconomic and trade adjustment on debtor countries, an excessive reliance on supply-side and trade-liberalization measures to generate export earnings, and neglect of aggregate demand and investment. The result was a sharp decline in growth rates and squeezing of the living standards of the people to generate surpluses to service the debt. The thrust of UNCTAD's analysis and policy proposals was to set the debt problem within a broader strategy for accelerating growth in the world economy.

The Special Needs of the Least-Developed Countries

The UN's decision to identify the problems of the least-developed countries as a special case and develop specific proposals in response to their needs was more original and positive. From the 1960s, the UN has shown a special sensitivity to the problems faced by its economically weakest members. The first resolution on the least-developed countries was adopted in 1968[9] and the Second Development Decade Strategy contained special measures in favor of LDCs.[10] The majority of these countries were located in sub-Saharan Africa. The UN developed internationally agreed-upon criteria to identify LDCs, which currently number forty-nine countries with over 10 percent of the world population.

Over the last two decades of the twentieth century, UNCTAD produced a number of pioneering studies on and developed comprehensive proposals to deal with the special problems faced by this group of countries. In 1981, 1990, and 2001, the UN organized three international conferences to consider these problems and adopt comprehensive programs of action that included both national and international measures. The UN agencies are devoting an increasing proportion of their resources to promoting the development of these countries. The industrial countries have sometimes taken special measures in favor of these countries with regard to trade and debt relief, among other things. In contrast, the World Bank has always avoided formal recognition of this group of countries.

Trade Policy for Development

Perhaps the most important theoretical work of the UN concerned the importance of trade for development. It identified both fluctuating and deteriorating prices for primary products as the central trade problem of developing countries. This theory emerged at a time when almost all the developing countries depended upon primary-product exports to generate foreign exchange earnings. The Singer-Prebisch thesis, developed at the UN, maintained that primary-product prices were subject to secular deterioration in relation to prices of manufactured goods.

The debate over the long-term decline in the terms of trade subsequently had a checkered history. The UN's early work argued that the terms of trade showed a long-run secular tendency to move against the developing countries. Initially this theory was violently attacked in the light of short-term movements to the contrary during the Korean War. Today the thesis is generally accepted as a true reflection of the world situation.

The creation of UNCTAD in 1964 gave a powerful impulse to international efforts to develop and secure agreements on reforms in trade policies. The subsequent years were to witness numerous efforts to develop similar arrangements to stabilize commodity prices, culminating in the Integrated Commodity Programme proposed by UNCTAD in the 1970s.

Despite successes over limited periods for individual commodity agreements, such as for sugar, coffee, wheat, tea, and cocoa, hardly any commodity agreements negotiated under the UN auspices have succeeded in stabilizing prices over extended periods. The developed countries have at best been lukewarm about efforts to stabilize prices at the international level. Although a Common Fund for Commodities was created in the 1970s, it lacked the political support and financial resources it needed to make much of an impact on commodity prices.

The most successful scheme to stabilize and raise prices for a primary product was developed outside the UN framework in the form of OPEC. Other schemes to control prices of steel, coal, and diamonds have also been operated either by developed countries or by cartels of corporations. Nevertheless, the UN ideas on commodity-price stabilization have had limited success in the form of compensatory financing schemes operated by the IMF and the Stabex scheme established by the European Union for the associated developing countries under the Lomé Treaty.[11]

Thus, for the most part, the ideas the UN has promoted for establishing large-scale and durable arrangements to stabilize commodity prices have lacked political support. This failure has had serious consequences for hundreds of millions of people in developing countries. The last two decades in particular have seen new lows in real prices for many commodities, which have devastated the economies of many poor countries, especially the least developed among them. As if this was not damaging enough, over most of this period the industrial countries have spent several hundred billion dollars each year subsidizing agricultural prices for farmers and agricultural interests in their own countries.[12]

The UN has also sought to promote and diversify developing-country exports by reducing trade barriers in developed countries. The studies carried out by UNCTAD demonstrated that developing-country exports to rich countries attracted higher duties and more quantitative restrictions than products predominantly exported by industrial countries. This was the case, for instance, with competing agricultural products; almost all industrial countries operated some sort of price- or income-support policies for their farmers. The same was true with many manufactured and processed goods, especially textiles, toys, and leather goods. The successive trade rounds negotiated under the General Agreement on Tariffs and Trade (GATT) did little to bring down the barriers on these sensitive products.[13]

Disarmament and Development

Few scholars have given much attention to the issue of disarmament and its implications for development. It is to the credit of the UN that as early as the 1950s it linked disarmament and development, both in analysis and in policy recommendations. In the 1950s, a number of countries, including France and the USSR, made specific proposals to reduce expenditures for armaments and channel part of the proceeds to development. The First Development Decade strategy calculated the effects of transferring funds released by disarmament on development in poor countries. The 1982 Thorsson Report focused on the "relationships between the prospects for balanced and sustainable global economic and social development on the one hand and disarmament on the other."[14] Through in-depth analysis, the report demonstrated the negative impact on growth of expenditures on armaments and the beneficial effects of disarmament under alternative scenarios of the global economy until the year 2000.

When reductions in armaments expenditures on a significant scale did take place in the 1990s, there was no redirection of public spending in the industrial countries toward a global peace dividend and little increase in development assistance. Indeed, there were serious reductions in spending on aid. The reductions in military spending were mostly taken in the form of reduced budget deficits and reduced taxes. This encouraged the widespread belief that there was no peace dividend. In contrast, Lawrence Klein, one of the Nobel Prize–winning economists who has often contributed to the UN, argued that there had been a form of peace dividend, though not as originally envisaged. The reductions in government deficits and the lowering of interest rates played a major part in stimulating the long boom of sustained economic growth in the U.S. in the 1990s. This in turn had expansionary effects on the economies of many developing countries. In addition, developing countries experienced a form of the peace dividend as originally envisaged. In some eighty or so developing countries, military spending was reduced during the 1990s, and in a number of cases this reduction was accompanied by increases in the share of resources going to education and health.[15]

Environment and Sustainable Development

As with gender and children, the environment is another area where there has been a sea change in global opinion since the early days of the UN. While equal rights for women figured prominently in UN founding documents, even though they were largely ignored in practice, the issue of the environment was not on the UN radar screen in the first decade of its existence.

In the past two decades, the issues of environmental protection and sustainable development have become central to global and national policy-making. The UN system deserves much credit for putting these issues on the global agenda in a way that has generated strong support among political leaders, grassroots activists, and members of civil-society institutions.

The first major event in the UN's work on the environment was the presentation of the Secretary-General's report on *Problems of the Human Environment* to the General Assembly in 1969.[16] It touched on practically all the environmental issues, including global warming. The report prepared the ground for the 1972 Stockholm World Conference on the Human Environment, which played a critical role in highlighting the environment as a global issue.

The 1971 Founex Report was another pioneering intellectual contribution of the UN. It linked problems of poverty—unsafe drinking water, inadequate housing and shelter, ill health, and natural disasters—with the environment. This opened the way for linking environment with development and for development to be seen as a cure for many environmental problems rather than their cause. The report underlined the importance of integrating environmental concerns and action with development objectives and policies.[17]

The Stockholm conference led to the creation of UNEP, the first international agency to concern itself exclusively with the protection and improvement of the natural environment. Over the years, UNEP, along with the IUCN, the WWF, and major research institutes, has made a critical contribution by highlighting emerging threats to the environment and by documenting alarming environmental issues such as the deterioration in soil conditions, rapidly increasing rates of deforestation and desertification, loss of flora and fauna species, declining biodiversity, increased levels of pollution and toxic substances, and global warming. These agencies have also played a vital role in creating national machinery for dealing with the environment problems.

The Earth Summit of 1992 in Rio and the International Conference on Sustainable Development in Johannesburg in 2002 were further milestones in the international efforts to promote and mobilize concern for the environment. These went well beyond the Stockholm conference in linking the environment with broader issues of social and economic development. They also gave further impetus to the negotiation of treaties to protect the environment that cover such diverse issues as toxic waste, protection of the ozone layer, climate change, biological diversity, and desertification. The Rio conference also gave rise to a new funding mechanism for environmental programs—the Global Environment Facility (GEF)—which provides finance and technical assistance for projects designed to preserve biodiversity, protect forests, and improve soils. There is still much controversy and reluctance to provide resources on anything like the scale estimated to be necessary. But there can be little doubt that without the UN's leadership, environmental policy and action globally and in many countries would never have achieved the high profile they currently command.

Structural Change in the Transition Countries

Another important contribution is related to the transition of the centrally planned economies into capitalist market countries. The UN's ideas on this issue marked a strong contrast with the mainstream orthodoxy of the time. Most of the former centrally planned countries opted for a rapid transition that has been called variously "the big bang," "shock therapy," or "one leap." This approach, which was a product of the neoliberal ideas that were dominant in the 1980s, advocated rapid and simultaneous action on many fronts—freeing prices, opening up the economies to external trade and investment, removing exchange controls, privatizing state enterprises, and reducing subsidies and social spending. This strategy was strongly promoted by the Bretton Woods institutions and most Western countries and their advisors.

The implementation of this strategy resulted in catastrophic declines in production, employment, and incomes and a massive increase in poverty. While one can never know for sure how much more effective an alternative strategy might have been, such a strategy was in fact quietly promoted by the UN Economic Commission for Europe from 1989. Their thinking was less an ideological contrast with orthodoxy than the result of an understanding of and expertise about the centrally planned economies that had been built over the previous forty years. Instead of a big bang, the ECE recommended a gradualist approach for transition to capitalism, starting with legal and institutional reform. It warned of the risk that privileged groups would "hijack" public assets and property.[18]

Equity in Development Strategies

Perhaps the greatest contribution of the UN system to development was in shifting the thrust of strategies from an almost exclusive emphasis on increasing economic growth rates to a preoccupation with improving living standards and reducing the numbers of people in destitute and vulnerable groups.

Throughout the 1960s, the UN's message was "growth plus change." By the end of the 1960s, it was clear that despite the achievement of rapid rates of economic growth, progress in reducing poverty and generating employment opportunities was far from sufficient. The World Employment Program launched by the ILO in 1969 did much to clarify the nature of the employment problem in poor countries and to outline strategies for rapid expansion of income-earning opportunities for the unemployed and the working poor. This phase of the UN's work had a major impact on development thinking, both in the academic world and among policymakers.

The ILO also sought to promote labor-intensive industry, emphasizing the positive role of the informal sector, another intellectual contribution of the UN. The basic-needs strategy combined all these issues into a coherent strategy put forward at the World Employment Conference organized by the ILO in 1976. The conference foresaw the need to view development policies within the broader framework of participatory processes and human rights.

These ideas about employment and basic-needs strategies were pushed aside in the 1980s by the pressure to adopt stabilization and structural-adjustment policies associated with the Washington Consensus. In macroeconomic matters, the UN's role became reactive, as the neoliberal doctrines came to dominate the development literature and policies in industrial and developing countries. The ECA and the ILO both argued for broader approaches. The most prominent critique of the new orthodoxy came from UNICEF. Based on fresh empirical evidence, its publication *Adjustment with a Human Face* criticized the deflationary effect of stabilization and adjustment policies; decreased spending on health, nutrition, and education; and the disproportionate burden imposed on women, children, and other vulnerable groups.

Equality for Women

Development thinking has changed radically over the past fifty years with respect to the roles and rights of women in development. In the early postwar years, women were largely invisible in development literature. Fifty years later, there is widespread recognition of the relevance of gender to all aspects of development policy. In some respects, the early silence on the gender dimensions of development is quite astonishing, for the key UN documents repeatedly stressed the universality of the ideal of equality, and in the 1950s and 1960s the UN system passed a series of resolutions and conventions to uphold the political rights of women. Nonetheless, it was only in 1975 at the World Conference on Women in Mexico City that, for the first time, a comprehensive program of action was put forward that covered all aspects pertaining to women's well-being and development, both globally and nationally. This was a milestone. The three succeeding world conferences contributed further to raising awareness of women's issues, assessing the progress that had been made in implementing programs of action, and drawing attention to new areas of concern.

The UN's work on gender and the role and leadership of women in development has helped change the perception of the entire development process. Growing awareness of the many roles women fulfill within and outside the market economy has broadened the development agenda; many dimensions of human life, community and human relationships, and social change that were previously ignored or bypassed in the conventional discourse and practice of development are now the focus of attention. Women have all along been involved in this broad range of activities, as indeed have men. But the recognition of the need to empower women and create more space for them in leadership roles in national and international life has helped open up a new understanding of what development should be about. At the same time, the failure to achieve equality for women in many countries over many years, often over many centuries, has created new awareness of the nature and roots of discrimination for many other groups and in many societies around the world.

Human Development

Human development, in its widest sense, has been at the heart of UN efforts for economic and social progress over most of the past half-century. The creation of a network of specialized agencies to address vital human needs, staffed by professionals with expertise in many noneconomic disciplines, has contributed to the UN's broad intellectual and operational focus in matters of human development. In various ways and with considerable contrasts, human concerns have been at the heart of the work of the UN's specialized agencies—the ILO, the WHO, UNESCO, the FAO, and UNIDO—as well as its funding agencies—the UNDP, UNICEF, the UNFPA, the WFP, and IFAD as well as others such as the UN High Commissioner for Refugees and the UN High Commissioner for Human Rights. The direct involvement of many of the staff of these agencies with work in developing countries, especially the posting of staff in field offices, has reinforced a strong focus on human needs throughout the UN system. The UN's focus on humanity and its needs stands in contrast to the more economic and financial preoccupations of the international financial organizations.

In its first decade, the UN made pioneering contributions to thinking about population issues. Initially, the organization focused on gathering and analyzing data and making population projections, which led to the pathbreaking conclusion that population in developing countries was increasing at a much higher rate than at first was realized and at a much higher rate than in the first half of the twentieth century. Gradually, this work led to issues of population policy, though not without controversy over the political and religious sensitivities it raised. The turning point was the UN mission to India, which was sent at India's own request, to advise the country on population planning. Continuing in Asia and then extending gradually to Latin America, the Middle East, and Africa, population and family planning became a well-established part of the UN's approach to overall planning well before the concept was generally accepted. Beginning in 1974, the world population conferences from Bucharest to Cairo played a central role in spreading information and knowledge, promoting discussion on the economic and social impact of population growth, and debating the merits of alternative approaches to population policy and planning.

Over these years, the UN agencies also did much useful work and led or stimulated pioneering work on the incidence, causes, and consequences of malnutrition, especially for women and children. Over the last two decades, nutrition surveys have been encouraged and supported by the WHO, UNICEF, and the FAO, with the result that data on nutritional status is available for well over 100 countries and data on nutritional trends is now available for some seventy countries, compared to only a handful in 1975.[19] More recently, a system has been put in place by the FAO to monitor progress toward the goal of ending hunger.

Considerable progress has also been made, largely through the efforts of the WHO, to reduce or eliminate the menace of infectious diseases. The eradication of smallpox, which was achieved by 1977, was the biggest success. However, major advances have also been made toward the eradication of polio and guinea worm; both of these efforts, at the time of writing, will likely be successful. After a promising start with the control and eradication of malaria, the disease came back with a vengeance, as has tuberculosis.

The WHO and UNICEF made a significant intellectual advance in 1978 in developing the concept of primary health care, which had a widespread impact on thinking about the priorities and organization of health care, including in industrial countries. Three years later, the WHO formulated a Global Strategy of Health for All by the Year 2000, which was adopted by the World Health Assembly and the General Assembly. Although basic health care for all is not yet a reality globally and in some countries there have been reversals, a steadily increasing proportion of the world's population is beginning to enjoy some elements of the right to health.

Along with health, education figured in the founding documents of the UN as a basic human right. The UN system, with UNESCO in the lead, did much to mobilize governments and public opinion to expand educational enrollments at all levels; this strategy enjoyed considerable success in the 1960s and 1970s. UNESCO also launched a campaign to eradicate illiteracy in the 1960s, but this was much less successful. Pilot projects in a number of countries that focused on the functional literacy approach did not prove successful and were abandoned. More than fifty years after the proclamation of education as a basic human right, the failure to eradicate illiteracy must be counted among the major failures of member states and the international community.

The formulation of human development as a paradigm of development thinking and strategy was a major intellectual contribution. This has been embodied in the series of Human Development Reports issued by UNDP beginning in 1990. The human development paradigm has had a major impact on development thinking in many countries of the world as well as on the development profession and in university courses.[20] The intellectual boldness and development insights of Mahbub ul Haq and the theoretical and philosophical strength of Amartya Sen were responsible for this achievement. The result has been an annual publication that offers an analysis of central issues of development from a human development perspective. The HDR developed a more rigorous definition of human development, explored its key components, carried the analysis into new areas such as human security, and brought fresh perspectives to well-established fields such as economic growth, poverty, consumption, globalization, governance, and human rights.

The human development approach represents a conceptual and fundamental advance from earlier approaches—"investment in human resources" in the 1960s, "basic needs" in the late 1970s, and the important but more casual promotion of "human development as a development priority" in the 1980s. Building on Sen's work,[21] the human development report defined human development as "the broadening of choices and the strengthening of human capabilities." It thus adopted a philosophically liberal approach to freedom of choice and at the same time recognized the need for a national and international agenda of purposeful actions to strengthen human capabilities. It also moved outside the utilitarian traditions of neoclassical economics. The approach and the policies it recommended included principles of participation in decision making, human empowerment, gender equity, and the avoidance of extremes of economic inequality within and between nations. Four indices of human development were also developed and used for ranking countries in terms of their standing in human development: gender development, gender empowerment, human poverty, and deprivation. These indices were used to contrast the human development agenda and its priorities with those of development policy based on neoclassical economic analysis and the orthodoxy of the Washington Consensus.[22]

By the end of the 1990s, the Human Development Report had achieved a worldwide impact. Some 400 national human development reports had been prepared in more than 120 countries.[23] Though it did not replace more conventional economic analysis in the Bretton Woods institutions, the human development approach attracted widespread attention, both politically and in the media.

Omissions and Missed Opportunities

"Omission" is used here in the sense of areas that are important but that were too long neglected by the United Nations. In other words, even if the UN eventually turned to such areas at a given point in time, the attention it gave to these issues was too little and too late. AIDS, narcotics, international migration, and the debt burden of the poor countries are cases in point. There is also the even more serious case of areas that should have been tackled but have not to this day received the attention they deserve. Alternatives to the Washington Consensus under its various guises, actions to control the excesses of free trade and capital movements, policies and strategies to strengthen development institutions and legal frameworks, policies and strategies to strengthen property rights, and policies and strategies to control corruption would come under this heading. The key question is how far these omissions have diminished the contributions of the United Nations to the theoretical and practical aspects of economic, financial, and social policies.

Alternatives to the Washington Consensus

One of the most serious omissions was the absence of any systemwide response of the UN to the sea change in economic policies that took place around 1980. There is no doubt that increased levels of debt, budget deficits, inflation, and inefficiency, all reinforced by weak demand in many countries as a result of the worldwide recession, required action. But the policies of stabilization and structural adjustment as promoted by the IMF and the World Bank in the 1980s were narrow strategies that in the early years at least spared little room for human-focused actions.

The lack of a strong reaction by the United Nations can be explained by several factors. Elements of the strategies implemented until the end of the 1970s were deficient and had survived their usefulness. The neoliberal approach of the Washington Consensus has the strength of strong theoretical foundations that are sufficient to underpin analysis of a wide range of economic and financial issues. The analysis feeds empirical conclusions of considerable generality. In contrast, alternative approaches often seem to be less rigorous and to be arguing their case by appealing to issues and concerns that fall outside the neoliberal paradigm, a strategy that was far from easy. Examples of such issues are noneconomic factors and values—extramarket concerns that include intrahousehold income distribution, gender inequalities, the human concerns of the aged, and the socialization of young children. In short, alternatives have tended to be more microeconomic and social, to include many more noneconomic variables, and to concentrate on human values and concerns that focus on human freedoms and capabilities.

The basic-needs approach of the 1970s was a first approximation of an alternative approach to economic and social development, but this was a pragmatic approach rather than one focused on theoretical fundamentals—and its policy implications were soon displaced by what were argued to be the urgent priorities of adjustment in the context of debt and recession. The human development paradigm is a second and more comprehensive contribution. The UN had to wait until the 1990s to see that happen, among others in the shape of the human development approach. Weighing the balance of strengths and weaknesses of alternative paradigms is not an easy task.

Global Gaps in Income, Wealth, and Power

Another major omission that is related to the discussion of national and international development strategies is the neglect of the widening global income gaps. A chapter was devoted to this issue in *Ahead of the Curve*.[24] Although there may be disagreement about the exact size of the gap in global income, there is no doubt that the per capita income differences between the richest and the poorest nations have increased. The same is true of the gap between the income of the poorest 10 percent of the world's people and that of the richest 10 percent. In the early years of the UN and until the 1970s, these widening gaps were treated as a matter of international concern and policy. In our view, this concern needs to be rediscovered and policies need to be developed if global income gaps are to be kept under control. This means that the macrolevel framework mentioned earlier must contain an elaborated international sub-model whose main components are international trade, agricultural subsidies, international investments, development assistance, human rights, and freedom. Very little work has been done in this respect, within the United Nations or outside of it. This is an important omission.

International Debt

The issue of creating policies to tackle the international debt burden is yet another example where the United Nations has left the field open to the Bretton Woods institutions. In the 1980s, the commercial banks called the shots; in the 1990s, the World Bank and the IMF dominated the field. UNCTAD called for more action and undertook some important analyses, but for the most part the United Nations looked on from the sidelines. The so-called HIPC Initiative came from the World Bank. It was, and still is, a slow-moving and heavily bureaucratic process with many conditionalities and endless safeguards against "moral hazards." At every stage of the process, heavily indebted poor countries must produce documents and policy statements to convince creditors that the forgiven portion of the debt will indeed go to education, health, and other expenditures that invest in human resources, combat poverty, and boost economic growth.

The HIPC countries have had to make payments on their international debt by eating into their education and health resources. In other words, they have had to meet their international obligations by sacrificing their future. The HIPC Initiative way to solve this issue has been to forgive part of the debt to the extent that the remaining part is sustainable for the country concerned. "Sustainable" in this instance means that the remaining part of the debt can be served without eating into the future of the country. But the question that remains is How can the country concerned convince the creditors that the forgiven portion will indeed be spent on productive and social investments rather than on "frivolous" matters? The World Bank believes that this can be done only with a long and tortuous paper trail. The United Nations should long ago have come up with a convincing alternative and mobilized support for it.

The Excesses of Free Trade and Free Capital Movements

What is even more surprising is that the United Nations has not been able to make a convincing case against the excesses of free trade and capital movements.[25] As shown in Chapter 2, Alexander Hamilton and Friedrich List elaborated an intelligent defense of temporary protectionist measures for countries that want to industrialize and are faced with competitors at a higher level of economic and technological development. In such a case, free trade would tend to wipe out the feeble beginnings of industrial development of the weaker country. Raúl Prebisch and the ECLA made an analogous case in the 1950s. Since then, the United Nations has remained silent on this score with some notable but timid exceptions, for example coming from UNCTAD. Paradoxically, the most articulate attack on "premature" free trade has come from within the World Bank. Indeed, in several of his public addresses,[26] the chief economist and senior vice president in 1998, Joseph Stiglitz, has set out the negative economic consequences of premature free trade, for example in the case of the countries in transition. The price he paid for his professionalism was to give up his job in late 1999. However, he received the Nobel Prize in 2001.

Corruption

A veil of timidity has hidden the issue of corruption from view for a very long time. Occasional references were made during the early years, including some references in the report on *Measures for the Economic Development of Underdeveloped Countries.*[27] But these received little analysis and follow-up action. If the veil has finally been lifted, it is due first to the end of the Cold War and second to the fine work of a non-governmental organization—Transparency International. The United Nations, including the World Bank and the IMF, were nowhere to be seen for all these years.[28] Corruption is now classified under the rubric of good governance and its seems that the pendulum has swung from one extreme to the other, from virtually total neglect of corruption to almost endless preoccupation with it.

Narcotics

An organized effort has been undertaken by the United Nations in the field of narcotics. Indeed, there exists within the UN system a small but well-managed narcotics branch in Vienna. At times, bureaucratic politics and infighting have destroyed much of the effort invested in the fight against both the use and production of drugs. And the UN's staff and resources have always been tiny in comparison with those involved in the production and trade of drugs, even those within anti-drug administrations, and in the anti-drug efforts of the main importing countries. It was only in the late 1980s that UNRISD launched a major project on the political, social, and economic consequences of the production, commerce, and consumption of narcotic products. The project resulted in a series of national synthesis studies.[29] Even so, one thing has been made abundantly clear by the UN as a whole—namely, that the emphasis must be the fight against demand rather than supply. Say's Law, which says that supply creates its own demand, is reversed in this case. With narcotics, demand creates its own supply.

International Migration

In the case of the International Organization of Migration (IOM), the situation has been different. The organization has been working steadily on rather routine operations. It has failed in general to face up to the challenge of the (free) movement of people in a globalizing economy, in contrast to the way the Bretton Woods institutions have been facing up to the challenge of free capital and trade movements. Obviously, this is a tall order, but imaginative forward-looking initiatives are essential in this case. The IOM has been too timid, managing the status quo in name only because it has been turning more and more into a chaotic series of responses to the number of immigrants, legal and "illegal"; issues related to migration are now being regarded as problems in many developed countries.

Without going as far as to maintain that there must be free movements of all factors of production (and there are good grounds for reservations about free trade and capital movements), there must be some symmetry in the treatment of these factors. This is, of course, a terribly complex problem. At the same time, it must be acknowledged that the evolving status quo cannot go on unchecked. The dividing lines between the rich and poor areas of the world (the Rio Grande, the Mediterranean, the Adriatic, etc.) are becoming high-pressure regions where small explosions occur every day. The United Nations has no plan to prevent the big blowup that is bound to come.

HIV/AIDS

Finally, a word about HIV/AIDS. After a promising start, the WHO threw away the initiatives it had taken in this most threatening of diseases because of interagency rivalry and bureaucratic incompetence—to put it mildly—at the top. All through the 1990s—while the number of infected persons multiplied rapidly—actions by the United Nations failed to rise to the scale of the challenge. The world had to wait till the mid-1990s before a multi-agency initiative, UNAIDS, was set up,[30] and it had to wait until the beginning of the twenty-first century to see the Secretary-General launch a bold initiative, the Global Fund for HIV/AIDS.[31] This marks an omission if ever there was one—although it could also be called a missed opportunity of the first order.

New International Economic Order

Missed opportunities is a rubric that also covers those instances where ideas were advanced that could have made a major contribution to development theory and practice but little or no action was taken—or a diverting set of actions was taken instead. In the case of the NIEO, after an avalanche of words and skirmishes, no action was taken. The approach proposed by the United Nations for policies to be pursued by Eastern European countries and the former Soviet Union was rejected in favor of a very different approach. In the case of the urban explosion, we end up somewhere between these two alternatives.

The opportunity to shape the NIEO in the 1970s was probably the most important missed opportunity. The first OPEC price hike of October 1973 was a shot that misfired. The increase in oil prices represented a transfer of about 2 percent of global GNP to the oil-exporting countries (many of whom were members of OPEC) from the oil-importing countries. Instead of sharing their immense increase in income with the poorest countries, OPEC members accumulated their fortunes in Western banks, an action that resulted in the international debt crisis of the 1980s. In the meantime, the increased bargaining power of the G-77 triggered demands for a new international economic order, spearheaded by the Algeria of Houari B. Boumedienne and the Mexico of Luis E. Echeverría. The debate that followed was in a real sense a first debate about what we would now call international or global governance. The asymmetric power relationships between North and South had resulted, more and more visibly, in income and other inequalities, unequal exchange situations and access to markets, excesses of certain transnational corporations, limited access to technologies, and so forth. The G-77 countries were under the illusion that the OPEC coup had been strong and violent enough for this power relationship to change permanently in their favor.

But what could and should have become a major move of Third World diplomacy—backed up by solid and reasonable proposals to improve the international economic situation and the underlying relationship in relative strength between the rich and the poor countries—became a shouting match based on frequently excessive and unrealistic demands. Although the overenthusiastic attitude of the G-77 is understandable, it remains a tragedy that this opportunity to obtain a fundamental shift in global governance was missed. The rich countries, who were initially on the defensive, played for time, making their economies less energy intensive in the process, and the price of oil in real terms less than fifteen years afterward (in spite of a second price hike in 1979) was at the same level as before October 1973.

The goal of a different and more equitable international order disappeared over the horizon. It is probably true to say that the United Nations proper was rather impotent in this instance, given the drive of the developing member countries and the strong reaction of the industrial countries (what we called "the second United Nations" in *Ahead of the Curve*).[32] However, the chance to create a new international economic order remains one of the major missed opportunities; an alternative might have changed fundamentally the situation and prospects of the developing countries.

Concluding Remarks

Ideas are like inventions. Some are launched and never picked up. They disappear, apparently without trace. Some ideas are picked up and then discarded. They also disappear, although they sometimes leave a visible trace, albeit with little impact. And then there are ideas whose time has come, often old ideas in a new disguise. This is where the discussion in Chapter 2 was so useful. In the field of development theory, there are only a few truly large and original ideas besides those that came to the fore in the 160 years between 1776 and 1936.

In his masterpiece, Fernand Braudel convincingly shows that the industrial revolution in England of the early nineteenth century had many antecedents or "pre-revolutions," as he calls them. Alexandrian Egypt was one such case; Europe from the eleventh to the thirteenth century was another; the age of Agricola and Leonardo da Vinci was a revolution in embryo; and one can speak of a first British industrial revolution between 1560 and 1640.[33] In all these cases, something (a spark) was missing and they add up to a sort of typology of failure or missed opportunity. So it goes with ideas. For them to be successful, they must come as a spark that enlightens the environment. In other words, ideas are nothing in a vacuum; a culture must exist to receive them. One of the elements in such a culture must be generosity and the free circulation of ideas instead of trying to suppress them or to keep them for oneself. The last sentence of Braudel's three-volume work is significant in this respect: "Just as a country at the center of a world-economy can hardly be expected to give up its privileges at international level, how can one hope that the dominant groups who combine capital and state power, and who are assured of international support, will agree to play the game and hand over to someone else."[34]

12

Lessons for the Future: Development Thinking and the UN's Future

- **Maintaining a UN Environment in Which Creative Thinking and Policy Analysis Can Flourish**
- **Priorities for Development in the Twenty-First Century**
- **Priorities for Development Ideas and Analysis in the UN**
- **Toward a New and More Flexible Concept of Development**
- **Priorities for UN Ideas and Thinking about the Global Economy**
- **The Statistical Needs for Improving Management of the Global Economy**
- **Improving Implementation**
- **Conclusions**

What has become clear, we hope, is that the United Nations has done an enormous amount of pioneering and creative work in helping to shape development thinking and practice. In the early period—during the late 1940s and early 1950s—the organization dominated the development scene, particularly with macrolevel policies. Influential reports and contributions were written by some outstanding experts, including several future Nobel laureates. When later the Bretton Woods institutions took over from the UN at the international level of strategic economic thinking—around 1980—the UN was sidelined, but this did not mean that the organization vanished in all areas of development strategy and decision taking. It is true that in the main areas of economic strategy, the UN in the 1980s was largely silent—or was moved to protest. But by the 1990s, the UN had returned once again to make distinct and pioneering contributions. It did so through the global conferences, its new vitality in promoting human rights, the paradigm of human development, and organizing an unprecedented millennium consensus in defining global goals for poverty reduction and mobilizing commitments in support of those goals.

In this final chapter, we turn to the future. What lessons can we draw from the record of the UN's past that can help improve its contributions in the years ahead? What are the new issues, where should the focus be, what policies and actions are needed to maximize its impact? And what can be done to improve the UN's record of implementation?

We will concentrate on the UN's role in development matters, especially—but not only—those which concern the developing countries. After all, developing countries constitute 80 percent of the world's population today, 85 percent if the transition countries are included.[1] Developed countries contain only about one in six of the world's population. By 2015, this will be one in eight; by 2050, probably one in ten.

In total contrast to their population numbers, developed countries dominate the global economy and global debate. They account for nearly 80 percent of world GNP—and control even more. The powerful pull of developed-country markets and institutions dominates technological research and development, accounting for some 85 percent of the world's research and development expenditure and over 90 percent of the new patents issued.[2] The relative lack of research, technology, and information directly focused on the needs and problems of developing countries is a most serious deficiency and imbalance. How long can this imbalance continue?

These deficiencies and imbalances underline the importance of the UN as a fount of ideas, as a forum for debate, and as a catalyst for change on issues that are neglected or given too little priority in the world at large. This need for change is made more urgent by two further imbalances, each of which is likely to become more extreme in the years ahead unless purposeful action is taken.

First, in today's rapidly globalizing world markets, private-sector research and technological development is overwhelmingly led by profit-seeking commercial enterprises, mostly by multinational corporations of huge wealth and power. There is an urgent need to create mechanisms for research and technological development to respond to a broader range of human priorities, especially for people in poorer countries.

Second, in today's global economy, international structures of governance, with their rules, norms, procedures, and institutions, are of ever-increasing importance for the functioning of the global economy. Growing levels of global inequality are in large part the result of these structures.[3]

These problems are manmade. Most are the result of national action and international negotiation, especially in recent years. In both action and negotiation, the weakness of the smallest and poorest countries is only too apparent. Such countries have a limited income—often equivalent to no more than that of a small town in a major country. They usually have at most a handful of underpaid experts with time and professional skills to analyze the implications of global proposals for their countries. In contrast, the rich developed countries often have hundreds of well-paid professionals—ready to be called on to analyze the finer specifics of a particular clause in some trade dispute or some case at issue in global regulation of patent protection.

These vast imbalances in wealth, power, and professional capacity define one of the most important roles of the UN in matters of Third World development. However weak and inadequate it may be, the UN stands as a bulwark against these strong forces of power, finance, and specialized manpower of the rich countries, often standing alone in the international system. Even when it is powerless to act, the UN's analysis of the inequalities of the global system and how the poorest countries are being affected serves to raise awareness. How effectively the UN fulfils this role will depend on its ability to identify its own areas of comparative advantage and create and maintain an environment in which creative relevant thinking and policymaking can flourish. On both these issues, the UN's record of the past half-century offers important lessons.

First, to make an impact, the UN needs to work in and build on key areas of comparative advantage. These include exploring and building on perspectives from all parts of the world, especially on the needs and concerns of the poorest and weakest countries and people. This inevitably will involve the willingness to take on controversial and pioneering issues—controversial because many will not be popular with the major powers of the time and pioneering because the necessary look to the future must involve the exploration of new possibilities and new approaches. The UN's work will need to remain multidisciplinary and human-centered, in line with human rights and the UN Charter. One way to achieve this would be for the UN to strengthen a diversity of relationships with universities, NGOs, and other parts of civil society in all regions of the world. These relationships should be two-way interactions, both drawing on and interacting with these institutions and groups, and through them, helping to disseminate international thinking and concerns and stimulate work on these issues within their own countries.

Second, in order to exploit to the full these areas of comparative advantage, the UN must reach out with a major and special role in promotion and dissemination of the UN's knowledge, research, and reports, both nationally and internationally. For all its weaknesses, the UN has a voice with global legitimacy. The best of UN reports still attract media attention on a global scale. At times, such reports have demonstrated their ability to mobilize opinion and give legitimacy to minority concerns. This is an important dimension of the UN's contributions to thinking and ideas that needs to be promoted even better in future.

Third, the UN needs to develop stronger and better-balanced relationships with other international institutions. The contrast between the UN's perspectives and those of the Bretton Woods institutions highlights one advantage of the UN—its long-standing ability to perceive the correct strategy to pursue. At times in the past, these contrasts have been sharp: for instance, in the battles over SUNFED in the 1950s, over structural adjustment in the 1980s, over issues of trade and debt in almost every decade. Though the UN's point of view was often dismissed at the time and criticized for analytical weaknesses, hindsight shows that more often it was the UN who first got it right, and the UN's position was later adopted by the Bank or the IMF. Equally important have been the differences in perspectives that were less publicized but more fundamental: the UN's formal commitment to human rights, its multidisciplinary approaches, and its long-standing concern for the poor and marginalized. Over the years, these differences have enriched international debate and have brought important changes of policy and action, even though there has often been a time lag.

These differences exist for good reason. In contrast to the Bretton Woods institutions, the UN is formally concerned with human rights and has multidisciplinary sectoral agencies. Above all, the UN has a different voting structure based on one country, one vote as opposed to one vote per million dollars of contributions. This makes for a fundamental difference in focus and approach.

Over the years, the World Bank and the IMF have gotten certain crucial issues wrong; most recently, structural adjustment, the need to accelerate debt relief, and the excessive emphasis they placed on freeing capital markets. In the early days, as the record has shown, there were equally egregious mistakes—the opposition to providing loans at below-market rates for the poorest countries, the long delays in providing support for primary education, the failure to recognize least-developed countries as a priority category for support. These mistakes have not happened because of a lack of professional expertise or technical brilliance. Rather, they reflect the way the interests and positions of the richer countries, mediated through the different voting structures, have served to bias and put blinders on much of the work of the Bretton Woods institutions. The WTO, though it has a more democratic voting system, will suffer something of the same weakness because of the overwhelming bargaining power of the industrial countries.

These factors underline why the UN has a continuing and ever-more-important responsibility to fill the gaps and offset these weaknesses. Indeed, one can argue that the end result is better for the debate engendered. The UN has also made many mistakes. Its biases and blinders have led to the omissions and distortions noted in Chapter 11.

The value of these debates to all parties needs to be remembered and recognized in the years ahead, especially when, in other respects, closer working relationships between the UN and the Bretton Woods institutions, the WTO, and OECD are being strongly encouraged by governments and are being actively pursued by staff of both sets of institutions.

Maintaining a UN Environment in Which Creative Thinking and Policy Analysis Can Flourish

In addition to focusing on the right issues, there is the need to ensure a lively environment within which to pursue them. Once again, some important lessons for the future emerge from the past. The UN must:

- Employ professionals of outstanding quality and give them opportunities to think independently
- Support research and research workers with adequate finance
- Strengthen multidisciplinary approaches and dialogue
- Enrich analysis by drawing on and learning from country and regional experiences
- Avoid dogma and orthodoxies, whether of the Washington Consensus or of other political groups or viewpoints
- Provide working environments which encourage original thinking and policy analysis as opposed to routine report production

Past experience shows that these six priorities have been less frequently achieved than one would like or one might expect. Our history has focused on the high points, the successes and the failures, rather than on the routine. Following these six principles can lead to dramatic and important results.

Employing persons of quality is one of the most important lessons. Not all staff can be of Nobel Prize–winning quality, though the award of the laureates demonstrates that the UN has on a number of occasions employed persons of this intellectual quality and distinction in the past. Systems of UN recruitment, promotion, and personnel management all need to be continually watched to ensure that they recognize and encourage the employment of persons of distinction.

It is sometimes said that the UN fails to attract such people because of limitations of salary and employment conditions. We would disagree. Our interviews and our analysis of leading UN contributors show that motivations of other sorts are almost always more important than salaries and formal conditions of work. Many of the UN's most distinguished staff members—and, no doubt, many others—have been attracted by the opportunities of working for an institution committed to global peace and justice, whose development work is focused on ensuring that human rights are fulfilled on a global scale. These motivations are fundamental.

Another requirement for maintaining a stimulating working environment is creative independence and freedom from political or petty administrative censorship and restraints. The UN's work on trade and aid in the 1950s, on the ILO World Employment Programme in the 1970s, and on the UNDP Human Development Reports in the 1990s are all examples of pioneering activities which gave full scope to the intellectual capacities of professionals of creativity and distinction. In each case, strong UN leadership and protection from the deadening hand of bureaucratic control encouraged and made possible new thinking. The ILO country missions in the 1970s were not subject to the normal internal ILO review. The Human Development Reports of the UNDP were issued with the important disclaimer that they did not necessarily represent the views of the UNDP. By such mechanisms, the UN has been enabled to speak out, avoiding the restraints and hesitations which more bureaucratic approaches might have created.

Drawing firsthand on a wide diversity of country and regional experience has also been important. Because of its field staff and its regional commissions, the UN at its best has been much more in touch with country experience than other more centralized international institutions. This is a quality that needs to be protected.

Financial support without strings is another important lesson. As the basic UN budgets have become squeezed, innovative projects often survived or were brought to birth only through special funding. Though in principle this is always a second best, in practice it has often made possible some of the UN's most effective contributions. The willingness of key donors to provide such resources without strings has added to the effectiveness of innovative projects and research.

Priorities for Development in the Twenty-First Century

In the year 2000, the Secretary-General presented *Vision for the New Millennium: We the Peoples: The Role of the United Nations in the 21st Century.*[4] This document set out the challenges of improving international governance in the emerging global world economy. The report identified some basic priorities: sustainable growth, poverty reduction, employment generation, combating HIV/AIDs, upgrading of slums, bridging the digital divide—in short, building structures for global equity and greater solidarity.

The report also set out basic priorities to ensure security on a global basis: prevention of conflicts, protecting individuals from gross violations of human rights, strengthening peace operations, targeting sanctions more accurately, reducing arms stockpiles, and addressing the dilemma of intervention and national sovereignty when the rights and lives of people are threatened on a mass scale.

With echoes of President Roosevelt's "four freedoms"[5] from the years when the first ideas of the UN were being fashioned, the Secretary-General referred to these actions as necessary to achieve freedom from want and freedom from fear. But he added new priorities for sustaining the future that were not identified when the UN was created: coping with climate change, confronting the water crisis, defending the soil, and preserving forests, fisheries, and biodiversity.

The Secretary-General argued that pursuing these goals would require building a new ethic of stewardship—through public education, "green accounting," more accurate scientific data, new regulations, and better incentives.

Finally, the Secretary-General set out new priorities for renewing and strengthening the United Nations: identifying its core strengths and building on them, networking for change, using the new international technologies, and advancing the quiet revolution toward a new awareness and ethic of global solidarity.

These priorities provide a framework for the UN's work on development policy and analysis in the years ahead. Within this frame, there are other specifics for the short to medium term as well as some for the medium to longer term. And the challenge of developing a better system of management of globalization will require an evolving agenda of creative ideas and analysis.

Priorities for Development Ideas and Analysis in the UN

The Millennium Summit endorsed an immediate and special focus on poverty reduction. This led to an unprecedented international consensus on the need to make rapid progress toward the Millennium Development Goals.[6] These include the goals of halving the proportion of the world's population suffering from extreme poverty and hunger by the year 2015 and making accelerated progress toward six related goals: to ensure that all children everywhere—boys and girls alike—are able to complete a full course of primary education by 2015; to eliminate gender disparity in primary and secondary education (preferably) by 2005 and in all levels of education by 2015; to reduce infant and child (those under five) mortality rates by two-thirds between 1990 and 2015; to reduce maternal mortality rates by three-quarters between 1990 and 2015; to halve the incidence of HIV/AIDS; and to halve the proportion of the world's population without access to safe water and adequate sanitation by 2015.[7]

There is also an eighth goal—developing a global partnership "to create an environment—at the national and global levels alike—which is conducive to development and the elimination of poverty."[8] This final goal underpins all the others. It embraces not only additional aid but speedy and adequate action on debt, trade, and foreign investment, brought together in what is seen as a new approach to partnership between donor and recipient countries. This history has made clear that the notion of partnership for development over the last half-century is not new. It remains to be seen whether this time the richer and developed countries can mobilize sufficient commitment and political support to ensure that these brave words are carried forward into action.

The Millennium Declaration also contained some other less-quantitative goals: to halt and begin to reverse the spread of HIV/AIDS; to halt and begin to reverse the incidence of malaria and other major diseases; to integrate the principles of sustainable development into country policies and programs and reverse the loss of environmental resources; and to achieve a significant improvement in the lives of at least 100 million slum dwellers by 2020.

These goals represent a remarkable and unprecedented coalition of international commitment and a big step forward. The goals are specific and time bound, they are focused on the poorest people of the earth, they are directly related to the reduction of poverty and human deprivation on a global scale, and they define an immediate program of action and monitoring by each country. The international system—the UN, including the World Bank and the IMF, together with the donor countries—is organized to provide support for individual countries to move toward the goals as never before. Compared with the early UN commitments to human rights on a global scale, the economic goals of the (First) Development Decade of the 1960s, or even the goal-oriented programs of the WHO in the 1960s and UNICEF in the 1980s and 1990s, these goals are more serious and broader in range than anything seen before.

The Millennium Development Goals and the process of working to fulfill them define a priority agenda for UN policy and analysis. There is a need to investigate success-story countries where rapid progress toward these goals has already been achieved or is under way, to explore cost-effective approaches, and to develop low-cost systems to monitor progress and ensure sustainable results. There is also a need to analyze the links between broader economic strategy and the conditions for making progress toward the goals, especially in a manner which can be sustained. If the goals are to be approached in ways that strengthen democratic empowerment at the local level, the political economy of the process also needs to be tracked and analyzed.

But these goals raise other issues that are less obvious, more subtle, and more fundamental. These issues also will need attention—not to take away from the immediate priority focus on the goals, which are indeed an unprecedented point of global consensus, but to explore the wider implications of working toward them. What can be done to achieve the goals in the poorest and least-developed countries, especially in those where economic growth has been failing for two or three decades? How can the goals be achieved in countries that are beset by conflict? Can pursuit of the goals be used as a step toward resolving the conflict? Health as a bridge to peace was a WHO program in Central America in the midst of the civil conflict of the 1980s. A program for "Days of Tranquility" was initiated by UNICEF in 1984 in El Salvador in order to stop all fighting one Sunday a month for successive months so that children could be immunized. This program continued for several years and was later extended to Uganda, Sudan, Lebanon, Iraq, and other countries in 1991.[9]

Moreover, goals for poverty reduction, though of great importance, are only part of the agenda for development. The UN will need to explore other issues, some of which are closely related and some of which return to the wider agenda of development, including issues that have long been a matter of UN and international debate. Examples are macrolevel strategies for long-run sustainable development; sectoral policy across the whole economy, including agriculture, industry and services; strategies to increase self-reliance and bring about fairer trade policies; and strategies to ensure democratic control and transparency in the whole economy. Poverty reduction, though a priority, does not remove these and many other issues from the agenda of developing countries, nor from the agendas of industrial countries.

Toward a New and More Flexible Concept of Development

The UN will need to ask many questions when it comes to broader issues of development theory and practice. One of the first is whether the development approach adopted up until now has been comprehensive enough or is still too economistic. Another relates to the problem of homogeneity—that is, how far development policies must be adapted and changed to fit the culture of a given region or country. In other words, the UN must face the question of whether there is one development theory and one practice for the entire world, with a little tinkering at the margins to take account of regional differences, or whether there can and should be many theories and many practices to tailor development policies to the culture and habits of countries and regions.

There is a growing awareness of the neglect of culture in the development process and of the cultural assumptions inherent in development theory and practice. Some critics ask Are development models determined culturally by each region or by the culture of one region, namely the West?[10] Culture is here defined in the broad sense, as a way of life and living together, including the values people hold, their tolerance with respect to others (race, gender, foreigners), their outward versus inward orientations and inclinations, and so forth.

The thesis of those who are in favor of more variety in development policies so they can be linked to local cultures, institutions, and habits goes something like this: (1) Western culture has held an iron grip on development thinking and practice; (2) this influence has tended to increase further during the past twenty years; but (3) alternative development models based on a different cultural and institutional historical background do exist; and (4) these alternatives are likely to multiply in the era of globalization that may, therefore, paradoxically witness more diversity than uniformity.

Indeed, globalization already seems to be stimulating localization. Cultural pluralism is becoming an all-pervasive characteristic of societies, and ethnic identification is emerging as a common response to pressures of globalization. People turn to culture as a means of self-definition and mobilization. Participation and empowerment are also closely related to both cultural and economic rights and equality. Participation in the decision-making process—a human right—is one of the key objects of cultural and economic policy, because it opens up both the economy and culture to as many people as possible. Moreover, one of the greatest drivers of globalization—the technological revolution that includes the computer, the Internet, and e-mail—makes it possible to establish connections at local and global level simultaneously.

Is it not desirable, therefore, to search for a range of development models based on local cultural differences? Here we use the word "local" rather than the word "national" because most societies are multicultural in composition. Is it wrong to equate cultural identity with national identity? Should not the UN take more account of these efforts to examine the cultural underpinnings of development?

There are already some starting points. East Asia can be seen as a case of economic and cultural differentiation from the mainstream that is based more on actual practice than on theory. Others want to raise more fundamental questions. This school is best illustrated by the "deconstructionist" approach of Arturo Escobar.[11] Development as practiced today, he argues, is not only a method of the powerful to exercise "economic control" but is also a discursive strategy. Development has proceeded by finding "problems" and then trying to solve them, and in the "solving" it has actually created more problems.

In straightforward language, what this school of thought is pleading for is differentiated development policies based on the cultural, institutional, and historical characteristics of a given region as determined by the participation and empowerment of the people. It is a bottom-up approach pushed to its extreme. However, even if the extremes are discarded, what remains is a vision of important policy alternatives; namely, the desirability of including local variations on national, regional, and global development themes. The "realistic" approach here takes as a starting point the alleged fact that development policies are to a very large extent top down, ethnocentric, and technocratic and treat people and cultures as abstract concepts. They are composed of a series of technical interventions that are supposed to be universally applicable. The alternative is to be much more sensitive to local social and cultural practices; this approach is producing local models of economic activity. In other words, "the remaking of development must thus start by examining local constructions, to the extent that they are the life and history of a people, that is, the conditions of and for change."[12]

According to this school of thought, development theory and practice has paid too little attention, if any at all, to the cultural dynamics of incorporating local thinking and practice into the global orthodoxy of economic thought. Nor has it attempted to make visible the local constructions that exist side by side with the might of global forces. There is, therefore, no question of proposing grand alternatives here—that is, alternatives that can be applied to all places and all situations. In a sense, the proponents of this version of "deconstruction" go farther than that by introducing many local variations on the general theme (any general theme) that in turn will affect the global orthodoxy.

Sensitivity to the diversity of cultures and traditions may require us to re-think much conventional analysis, including the Washington Consensus, but not necessarily the fundamentals of human development. Amartya Sen has argued that a universal approach to development is both possible and desirable, as long as development thinking and policy cover a wide surface by bringing on board issues of human rights—political, civil, and cultural as well as economic and social. Sen attaches fundamental importance to democratic tolerance and pluralism: "To see political tolerance merely as a 'Western liberal' inclination seemed to me a serious mistake."[13] In *Development as Freedom,* Sen allows for diversity of development, providing that this diversity is built on a bedrock of democracy and human rights, principles that lie at the heart of the UN.

Priorities for UN Ideas and Thinking about the Global Economy

One of the most important areas for the UN's future work and analysis will concern better and fairer management of the global economy. In the 1940s, as we saw, the need to avoid repetition of the Great Depression was a major motivation in fashioning the new global institutions—the World Bank, the IMF, and the UN. National and international action in support of policies to pursue full employment was built into the structure and mandates of these bodies. The first three major economic reports of the UN each contained bold analysis about the international conditions and structures needed to implement their recommendations.

The boldness of global vision and commitment to purposeful action to achieve it has been largely lost, replaced by calls for marginal adaptations and sometimes, from the more conservative, for withdrawal from even the attempt to manage globalization in any way. But the need to do so is vital, especially for the poorest and weakest countries. As emphasized in Chapter 7, over the last two decades, some sixty to eighty developing and transition countries have suffered declines in their levels of output and living standards that have been longer lasting and often relatively deeper than anything suffered by the industrial countries during the Great Depression. In the 1980s, the international community offered structural adjustment as the answer. Sharp contractions in demand often compounded the problems—and economic growth failed in most cases to recover. In spite of continuing expansion in the developed countries and, in the 1990s, the most sustained boom that the United States had ever experienced, the situation in many developing countries continued to be extremely difficult. By the year 2000, some forty-five developing countries had per capita income below that of ten to twenty-five years earlier, as did more than twenty transition countries.[14] Not one developed country was in this position.

The international community urgently needs to address these issues, with the UN working in cooperation with the World Bank and the IMF. Goals for the reduction of poverty are important, but they are not enough. Without a substantial and sustained resumption of growth, they will not succeed, especially in the poorest and least-developed countries. Nor are aid and debt relief on the present scale enough to ensure resumed growth over the full range of the countries concerned.[15] It is nothing short of scandalous that the international dimensions of the prolonged failures of growth in so many developing and transition countries have received so little attention. Instead, the failures of much of the developing world have been hidden behind the promises of globalization.

Globalization in the last two decades has, of course, advanced by leaps and bounds. Almost every country has faced the challenges. For some, particularly the larger and stronger countries, the new opportunities seem to have far outweighed the problems. The opportunities to use the new communications technologies, import capital and technology, and increase production and expand exports have been transforming their economies and their societies.

But many other developing countries have been getting the raw end of the stick, particularly the smaller and weaker ones. For them, few of the promised possibilities have opened up, even when they have liberalized their economies. Little if any new investment has flowed in, capital has flowed out, and new and often enormous instabilities have arisen. Some of their citizens, especially those who are better educated, may have personally escaped the worst by emigration. But the long-persisting problems of low export earnings, high debt, and scarcity of resources of all sorts seem only to have gotten worse, severely holding back the resumption of growth, even in the countries which are acknowledged to have been running their economies in accordance with the dictates of the IMF and the international community. To people caught in these countries, including many of the poorest countries, globalization seems a nightmare of false promises and deceit.

For the UN, all of this raises new challenges to improve international economic management, the global economy, and the process of globalization. In recent years, UNCTAD, the UNDP, the ILO, UNRISD, WIDER and other UN organizations and institutions have analyzed the new challenges and issued reports[16] and proposals for action. Consistent with their mandates, they have explored ways to ensure that more of the benefits of globalization go to poorer countries and poorer people, including national and international measures to control the risks and negative repercussions, such as those which followed the dramatic reversals of capital inflows during the Asian crisis.

Nonetheless, changes in global policy and global management have been weak and limited and, as experience has demonstrated, insufficient to restore rapid economic growth in the poorest sections of the global economy. Since 1980, some sixty to eighty countries have traveled the equivalent distance in time from 1919 to 1939, yet the world has learned none of the lessons about how to help them avoid the equivalent of a Great Depression worse than any experienced by the developed countries themselves or how to enable deteriorating countries to recover from it.

The UN and its Bretton Woods partners urgently need to explore and develop ways in which international institutions can be better adapted to the new problems of the global economy and the special problems of the poorest and least developed. The UN remains the main international body that starts with human needs, gives special attention to the poorest and weakest countries, and provides a forum in which the views of all countries have the right to be heard with equal voice.

In addition to the restoration of economic growth on a more balanced global basis, the UN in the years ahead needs to explore a number of other issues central to the better management of the global economy. Among the priority concerns are the following:

- Ensuring environmental sustainability on a global scale
- Providing global public goods, including new sources of finance for their support
- Ensuring a stronger voice and fairer participation of poorer and weaker countries in global governance, including measures to offset their weakness in global negotiations
- Narrowing global economic gaps over the longer run
- Exploring new issues of global injustice

This is not the place, at the end of this volume, to start a long exposition of these issues. Some, such as the conditions for ensuring environmental sustainability, have been the subject of major global conferences and detailed recommendations. Some of these are already being implemented; others are still under debate. The point here is to emphasize that these issues will not fade away—rather, they are likely to grow in intensity in the years ahead. The UN will be challenged to keep abreast of them and help provide focus and guidelines on the actions required to deal with them.

All five issues relate directly to the better management of the global economy. Though this issue has been sidelined on the official agenda of global economic policy and debate for the last twenty-five years, we believe it will return. Indeed, as global communication becomes more instantaneous and all encompassing, the outrage of those marginalized under the operations of the global system will become more strident. Just as accommodation to the demands of the poor and marginalized had to be reached in the early stages of industrialization in the developed countries, so accommodation to the demands of the marginalized must become a political necessity in the global economy of the future. The UN will need to preside over this process to ensure that it proceeds smoothly and effectively. The UN should even now be undertaking analysis of the economic and political adjustments which will be required.

As part of this process, other issues will be raised. Global public goods have already been the topic of pioneering work within the UN.[17] The effective management of the global economy will require support for a number of public goods at the global level—many of which share the need for global financing but by their very nature as public goods have benefits which cannot be restricted only to those who help pay. In fact, this can be an advantage. The need to ensure finance for global public goods in ways which are not possible to achieve through market mechanisms alone will open the door to debate and eventually, one can only hope, to agreement on global financing instruments which take account of the capacity to pay as well as the distribution of benefits.

Some generation of global revenue will certainly be required. There are many ways in which such revenue can be raised and there can also be potential benefits from by-products of new mechanisms. Better management of the global economy, including incentives for meeting the challenges of sustainability, presents opportunities for raising revenue as mechanisms for achieving greater global efficiency. One can also envisage charging market rents for frequency bands for broadcasting; allocating mining rights to undersea bed resources, which offers opportunities for royalties and rents that could accrue to the UN; and levying some Tobin tax on short-run capital movements, applied as a measure to discourage speculation but which as a by-product could generate many billions of international revenue.[18] Each of these strategies can be envisaged on the international agenda of the future. Even now, the UN and others need to be exploring the implications and the possibilities of such ideas.

So far, we have looked ahead to issues already on the agenda of academic debate, though such issues are far from being items on the present UN agenda or acceptable to some of the more powerful governments as matters for acceptable debate. Nonetheless, in our view, the UN ought to have the mandate and the encouragement to explore such issues, without requiring any commitment from the organization as to whether and when the issues should be put forward for more formal consideration or action.

The Statistical Needs for Improving Management of the Global Economy

As part of improving management of the global economy, the UN has both a need and obligation to develop a supporting global statistical system that can provide the up-to-date information required for better tracking of the international system. The priority goals would be to have statistics that help improve efficiency and effectiveness at a global level, to avoid serious preventable risks, to move toward long-term sustainability, and to provide support and fair opportunities for the poorest and least-developed countries, including the long-term aim of narrowing global gaps in income and living standards. In addition to economic dimensions, the system should cover human, social, cultural, and political dimensions.

Some forty-eight indicators to monitor progress toward the goals for poverty eradication have already been identified as a necessary part of such a system. These include seven goals for monitoring global environmental sustainability, including some related to greenhouse gases and global warming.[19] But other indicators are needed, including the development of broader and improved statistics on the operations of transnational corporations, whose operations straddle many countries and are often incompletely reported when statistics gathering relies only on national sources of data. Economically much less important but internationally significant are the operations of the larger international NGOs.

In its early years, several institutions of the UN played a major role in setting up several global statistical systems, assembling sets of national data into a global compilation which provided information on the world economy, global food production, world health, and other key areas of national and international policy. It is extraordinary that nothing equivalent has been created for the global economy.

What is now needed is the construction of a coherent global statistical system that brings the various specialized and partial statistical components together in a consistent, focused, and up-to-date manner which can serve various actors as a guide to international and national policymaking.

Improving Implementation

Translating thinking into practice—implementation—is critical. It is one thing to launch ideas; it is quite another to translate those into doable policies and projects.[20] Within the same organization, thinking and practice often do not meet. This is certainly true of the UN in its headquarters. How much more probable is this between UN ideas and practice on the ground, in the countries where they count. For instance, the world conferences of the 1970s and the summit conferences of the 1990s have been instrumental in bringing important issues—such as the environment, gender, and human rights—to the attention of political leaders around the globe. The UN organizations have been much less successful in following up the global goals with well-focused programs of action and support country by country. This is not to confuse the role of the UN with the ultimate responsibilities of governments. Good examples already show the valuable role of the UN in providing advocacy and catalytic support to countries to encourage and enable them to implement better the commitments they have made in international meetings. The expansion of primary education in the 1960s, the eradication of smallpox, and the mobilization of over 100 countries in the 1980s toward the goal of universal child immunization by 1990 are examples.

The collaboration of UNICEF and the WHO in support of immunization over the 1980s is perhaps the clearest recent example. Building collaboration around the shared pursuit of goals is certainly needed for implementation of the Millennium Development Goals. It is also required in many other areas to ensure closer links between actions approved in UN bodies and the role of the various UN funds and organizations in providing practical support to countries in carrying them into action.

The approach that is needed can be broken down into seven guidelines for translating global goals into country action:[21]

1. Leadership—both in the UN and nationally—is essential. Without leaders who have both vision and a sense of detail, nothing of importance is likely to happen.

2. The goals need to be articulated in terms of a vision of inspiring goals that are specific enough to be readily understood and conveyed through the media. The goals also need to be broken down into time-bound doable propositions which inspire and make clear the action required at local as well as national and international levels.

3. Commitment must be mobilized both within and outside the UN. This will to move ahead needs to be mobilized and sustained nationally and internationally.

4. Enlightened UN leadership must create the conditions which build up strong collaboration and play down unproductive rivalries and competition between UN agencies, shifting the focus to the achievement of shared goals. Concerted action is essential.

5. Rapid changes of policy are unproductive. Priorities need to be chosen and maintained. Extreme ideologies are neither required nor desirable. They are spectacular but not very effective. This is another reason why broad goals must be translated into concrete and doable steps to be achieved in the political lifespan of national decision makers.

6. Participatory decision making is also essential. Strong leadership does not mean imposing goals on national, regional, and local communities. Countries and communities must adopt and adapt the goals in their own way and decide how best to move toward them.

7. Strong leadership within the UN must also imply that steps will be taken to make national and international governance consistent. If a resource-poor country adopts international goals and seriously puts in motion national actions to achieve them, it must be able to count upon extra international support if the international economic environment turns against it—whether through a decline in commodity prices, a rise in international interest rates, or other changes beyond its capacity to influence. Good *national* governance must be backed up and supported by good *international* governance.

Conclusions

As Max Weber remarked, "Interaction creates ideas, imposing kills them."[22] In the social sciences, ideas rarely come to the isolated individual shivering in the cold of his or her room in the attic. They rather come through the interaction of many individuals and groups in the warm rice fields of Asia, for instance. The Green Revolution is an illustration of this thesis. Listening to grassroots movements, to neighborhood groups, may well result in getting or sharpening ideas. It is here that the UN has a comparative advantage because of its role as the universal global forum and its many field workers all over the globe. It requires humility on the part of the professional to listen to those local workers from another culture and with another mindset. It is at this point that we join what was said above about identity and global ideas or, as we called it, the need for local variations on a global theme.

But let us not make a secret about it; in the end, wealth and power count a great deal when it comes to which ideas come to the fore and which are implemented. A telling illustration is the experience of the policy ideas that were to guide the transition countries in East Europe and the former Soviet Union in their transformation into capitalist societies. The idea that finally won was not necessarily the best but the one with money to back it up. In the end, ideas without the backing of wealth and power will struggle to see the light of day. Here is one of the most important roles of the UN—to ensure that such ideas see the light of day and prevent them from being sidelined.

What lessons can the UN learn from this analysis? Inspired leadership is essential, as is humility to learn from the richness and diversity of experience around the world and from people on the ground. These are the fruitful fields that in the long run can result in improving the lives and living conditions of people around the world and in improving national and international development policies and actions. Identifying them takes an open mind, much curiosity, and the will and leadership to bring them to the attention of the world. Long may the UN remain at the center of this challenge, a challenge that is at once human and global.

Appendix: Country Categories and Distribution of Population and GDP by Regions

Developing Countries

Algeria
Argentina
Bahrain
Bolivia
Botswana
Brazil
Cameroon
Chile
China
Colombia
Congo
Costa Rica
Cote d'Ivoire
Cuba
Dominican
Ecuador
Egypt
El Salvador
Gabon
Ghana
Guatemala
Honduras
India
Indonesia
Iran
Jamaica
Jordan
Kenya
Lebanon
Mauritius
Mexico
Mongolia

Morocco
Namibia
Nicaragua
Nigeria
Oman
Pakistan
Panama
Paraguay
Peru
Philippines
Puerto Rico
Qatar
Saudi Arabia
South Africa
Sri Lanka
Swaziland
Syria
Trinidad
Tunisia
Turkey
Uruguay
Venezuela
Viet Nam
Zimbabwe
(56 countries or areas)

Least-Developed Countries

Angola
Bangladesh
Benin
Cambodia
Cape Verde

Central African Republic
Chad
Comoros
Djibouti
Gambia
Haiti
Lao
Madagascar
Mali
Mauritania
Mozambique
Nepal
Niger
Rwanda
Senegal
Sierra Leone
Sudan
Tanzania
Togo
Uganda
Zambia
Yemen
(27 countries or areas)

Tigers

South Korea
Malaysia
Singapore
Thailand
Taiwan
(5 countries)

OECD	Portugal	Estonia
	Spain	Georgia
Australia	Sweden	Hungary
Austria	Switzerland	Kazakhstan
Belgium	United Kingdom	Kyrgyzstan
Canada	United States	Latvia
Denmark	*(23 countries or areas)*	Lithuania
Finland		Poland
France		Republic of Moldova
Germany	*Eastern Europe and*	Romania
Greece	*Former USSR*	Russian Federation
Iceland		Slovakia
Ireland	Albania	Slovenia
Italy	Armenia	Tajikistan
Japan	Azerbaijan	TFYR Macedonia
Luxembourg	Belarus	Turkmenistan
Netherlands	Bulgaria	Ukraine
New Zealand	Croatia	Uzbekistan
Norway	Czech Republic	*(25 countries or areas)*

Distribution of Population and GDP by Regions (1998)

	OECD	Tigers	Eastern Europe and Former USSR	Developing Countries	Least-Developed Countries
Population	15%	3%	7%	68%	7%
GDP	54%	4%	5%	35%	1%

Source: Angus Maddison, *The World Economy: A Millennial Perspective* (Paris: OECD Development Centre Studies, 2001).

Notes

Foreword

1. Devesh Kapur, John P. Lewis, and Richard Webb, eds., *The World Bank: Its First Half Century,* vol. 1, *History* (Washington, D.C.: Brookings Institution, 1997).

2. Louis Emmerij, Richard Jolly, and Thomas G. Weiss, *Ahead of the Curve? UN Ideas and Global Challenges* (Bloomington: Indiana University Press, 2001), xi.

3. Midge Decter, *The Liberated Woman and Other Americans: On Being a Woman, on Being a Liberal, on Being an American* (New York: Coward, McGann & Geoghegan, 1971), 135.

1. Has There Been Progress?

1. "Human rights" is used here for all rights—economic, social, and cultural as well as political and civil.

2. See Louis Emmerij, Richard Jolly, and Thomas G. Weiss, *Ahead of the Curve? UN Ideas and Global Challenges* (Bloomington: Indiana University Press, 2001), 212–213.

3. "Declaration on the Right to Development," General Assembly resolution A/RES/41/128, 4 December 1986.

4. "United Nations Millennium Declaration," General Assembly resolution A/RES/55/2, 18 September 2000.

5. Charter of the United Nations, Preamble.

6. Ibid., Chapter I, Article 1 (4), 5.

7. Ibid., Chapter IX, Article 55, 37.

8. Emmerij, Jolly, and Weiss, *Ahead of the Curve,* Chapter 1.

9. Cynics would no doubt replace such brave adjectives with "gross contradictions with policy and action by the major powers of the time." But emphasizing the contradictions misses the point and underplays the increasing influence of these declarations over the years that followed. Not at once but gradually and unevenly, in country after country, the various rights of the Universal Declaration have had a significant and spreading effect. This is being elaborated in the forthcoming volume in this series, Roger Normand and Sarah Zaidi, *The Unfinished Revolution: Human Rights in the United Nations* (Bloomington: Indiana University Press, forthcoming).

10. Universal Declaration of Human Rights, Article 2. Available online at http://www.un.org/Overview/rights.html.

11. Ibid., Articles 28 and 29 (1).

12. Outside the UN, it was the 1970s before a few pioneers started emphasizing the ethical dimensions and dilemmas of development. See Denis J. Goulet, *The Cruel Choice: A New Concept in the Theory of Development* (New York: Athenaeum, 1971); Godfrey Gunatilleke, Neelen Tiruchelvam, and Radhika Coomaraswamy, eds., *Ethical Dilemmas of Development in Asia* (Lexington and Toronto: Lexington Books, 1988); N. Dower, *What Is Development? A Philosopher's Answer,* Centre for Development Studies Occasional Paper Series 3 (Glasgow: University of Glasgow, 1988); David Crocker, "Toward Development Ethics," *World Development* 19, no. 5 (May 1991): 479–483. More recently, there is N. Dower, *World Ethics: The New Agenda* (Edinburgh: Edinburgh University Press, 1998).

13. On this point, see Arthur Lewis's claim in his *The Theory of Economic Growth* (London: Allen and Unwin, 1955): "The authoritarian governments are in this respect at an advantage in comparison with the democratic governments. They can push the government's share up to twenty or thirty percent of the national income, and use half the proceeds for capital formation, without bothering about what will happen in the ballot box, if there is a ballot box. The democratic governments are in greater difficulty. Here and there a great democratic leader is able to carry his people through a phase of relative privation for the sake of building up the nation. But such leaders are rare. In many other countries democracy is an obstacle to speeding up the rate of economic growth. Perhaps this is as it should be; we are not concerned in this chapter with the desirability or otherwise of economic growth" (401).

14. See "Convention on the Elimination of All Forms of Discrimination against Women," General Assembly resolution A/RES/34/180, 19 December 1979; and the Convention on the Rights of the Child, General Assembly resolution A/RES/44/25, 20 November 1989.

15. Following the establishment in 1950 of the Office of UN High Commission for Refugees on a temporary basis, the UN General Assembly adopted several treaties concerning refugees and stateless persons. See the Convention Relating to the Status of Refugees (28 July 1951), the Convention Relating to the Status of Stateless Persons (28 September 1954), and the Convention on the Reduction of Statelessness (30 August 1961).

16. See the work done by the ILO and "International Convention on the Protection of the Rights of All Migrant Workers and Members of Their Families," General Assembly resolution A/RES/45/158, 18 December 1990.

17. "International Covenant on Civil and Political Rights," UN General Assembly resolution A/RES/2200A (XXI), 16 December 1966.

18. "International Covenant on Economic, Social and Cultural Rights," UN General Assembly resolution A/RES/2200A (XXI), 16 December 1966.

19. Theo van Boven, "Human Rights and Development: The UN Experience," in *Human Rights and Development: International Views,* ed. David P. Forsythe (Basingstoke: Macmillan, 1989), 121.

20. Declaration on the Right to Development, Article 1 (1).

21. For the main declarations made by the UN regarding human rights and development, see van Boven, "Human Rights and Development."

22. Lewis, *The Theory of Economic Growth*.

23. See Paul Streeten, "Basic Needs: Some Unsettled Questions," *World Development* 12, no. 9 (1984): 973–978. Basic needs was an attempt to move away from the utilitarian tradition in the theory of economic development, but it lacked strong theoretical foundations, which made it unfit to provide a sound alternative to the utilitarian foundations of economic theory. See Chapter 3 of *Ahead of the Curve*.

24. The pioneering contribution in development was Esther Boserup, *Women's Role in Economic Development* (New York: St Martin's Press, 1970).

25. There is a vast range of more recent writings, but see especially Caroline Moser, *Gender Planning and Development: Theory, Practice, and Training* (London: Routledge, 1993); and Cecile Jackson and Ruth Pearson, eds., *Feminist Visions of Development: Gender Analysis and Policy* (London: Routledge, 1998), from which the quotation is taken.

26. Mahbub ul Haq, the founder and architect of the first seven Human Development Reports, set out his own perspectives in his book *Reflections on Human Development* (New York and Oxford: Oxford University Press, 1995). See also Meghnad Desai, "Human Development: Concepts and Measurement," *European Economic Review* 35 (1991): 350–357.

27. The links between human development and human rights are set out most clearly in the UNDP's *Human Development Report 2000* (New York: Oxford University Press, 2000) on the theme "Human Development and Human Rights." See also Amartya Sen, *Development as Freedom* (New York: Knopf, 1999). Sen has been associated with the Human Development Reports since the first report in 1990.

28. "United Nations Millennium Declaration," UN General Assembly resolution A/RES/55/2, 18 September 2000.

29. Ibid., Part I, Para. 3.

30. Ibid., Part I, Para. 6.

31. United Nations, *Agenda for Development* (New York: United Nations, 1997).

32. As Martha Nussbaum has analyzed, women frequently exhibit "adaptive preferences," preferences that have adjusted to second-class status. Reference to human rights provides an objective standard against which to consider whether a person's choices are being systematically constrained by social pressures and tradition. See Martha Nussbaum, *Women and Human Development: The Capabilities Approach* (Cambridge: Cambridge University Press, 2000).

2. The History of Development Thinking from Adam Smith to John Maynard Keynes

1. For instance, Walt Whitman Rostow, *Theorists of Economic Growth from David Hume to the Present: With a Perspective on the Next Century* (New York: Oxford University Press, 1990). See also Robert Dorfman's interesting "Review Article: Economic Development from the Beginning to Rostow," *Journal of Economic Literature* XXIX, no. 2 (June 1991): 573–591. For a more sociological and philosophical angle, see

Michael P. Cowen and Robert W. Shenton, *Doctrines of Development* (London and New York: Routledge, 1996). For a somewhat older review, see Walter Eltis, *The Classical Theory of Economic Growth* (New York: St. Martin's Press, 1984).

2. Adam Smith, *An Inquiry into the Nature and Causes of the Wealth of Nations*, ed. Edwin Cannan (Chicago: University of Chicago Press, 1976). The first edition was published in 1776.

3. Ibid., 11.

4. Ibid., 17.

5. Ibid., 405.

6. Ibid., 432–433.

7. Ibid., 23.

8. The complete quotation is: "It is not from the benevolence of the butcher, the brewer, or the baker that we expect our dinner, but from their regard to their own interest. We address ourselves not to their humanity but to their self-love." Ibid., 18.

9. Ibid., 75.

10. Ibid., 148.

11. Ibid., 232.

12. Ibid., 325.

13. Mark Blaug, *Economic History and the History of Economics* (Washington Square: New York University Press, 1986), xvi.

14. The first edition of Adam Smith's *The Theory of Moral Sentiments* was published in 1759 by A. Millar, London.

15. Adam Smith, *The Theory of Moral Sentiments* (1759), from a collection of quotes compiled by the University of Bristol at http://www.ecn.bris.ac.uk/het/smith/moral.6.

16. Ibid.

17. Thomas Robert Malthus, *An Essay on the Principle of Population* (London: J. Johnson, 1798). The second edition, from 1803, contains a much longer and revised text; the sixth and last edition in Malthus's lifetime (1826) has further changes but does not alter fundamentally the thesis set out from the beginning.

18. Thomas Malthus, *An Essay on the Principle of Population* (New York: Penguin, 1985), 77.

19. Ibid., 79.

20. Ibid., 86.

21. Mark Blaug, *Economic Theory in Retrospect*, rev. ed. (Homewood, Ill.: Richard D. Irwin, 1968), 140.

22. David Ricardo, *The Principles of Political Economy and Taxation* (London: Everyman's Library, 1965). This work was first published in 1821.

23. Ibid., 81.

24. Blaug, *Economic Theory in Retrospect*, 100–104.

25. Ibid., 52–53.

26. Friedrich List, *Das nationale System der politischen Ökonomie*, vol. I, *Der internationale Handel, die Handelspolitik und der deutsche Zollverein* (Stuttgart/ Tübingen: F. G. Cotta, 1841).

27. Friedrich List, *The National System of Political Economy,* trans. Sampson S. Lloyd (New York: Longmans Green and Co., 1928), 108.

28. Ibid., 117.

29. Ibid.

30. On this, see Dorfman, "Review Article: Economic Development from the Beginning to Rostow," 578–579.

31. For a strong recent statement on the way today's developed countries have forgotten their own earlier positions, see Ha-Joon Chang, *Kicking Away the Ladder: Development Strategy in Historical Perspective* (London: Anthem Press, 2002).

32. Ibid., 127.

33. Ibid., 175.

34. Ibid., 93.

35. Ibid., 119.

36. Ibid., 8.

37. Charles Dickens, *Hard Times: For These Times* (London: Bradbury & Evans, 1854).

38. There is little point in reading any edition of John Stuart Mill's *Principles of Political Economy: With Some of Their Applications to Social Philosophy* earlier than the third edition published in London by Parker & Son in 1852. Important alterations were introduced in the second and third editions. The seventh People's Edition published in London in 1871 was the last to be revised by Mill in person.

39. John Stuart Mill, *Principles of Political Economy* (New York: A. M. Kelley, 1965).

40. Ibid., 21–25.

41. John Stuart Mill, *Autobiography,* available online at http://www.wesleyan.edu/css/readings/Barber/chapter4.htm.

42. Mill, *Principles of Political Economy,* 120–122.

43. Ibid., 698.

44. Ibid., 696–697.

45. Ibid., 578.

46. Ibid., 581.

47. Ibid., 678.

48. Ibid., 199–217.

49. Ibid., 400–401.

50. Ibid., 403–404.

51. Ibid., 406.

52. Ibid., 916–940.

53. Free compulsory education was not adopted in England until 1870.

54. Mill, *Principles of Political Economy,* 953–956.

55. Karl Marx, *Das Kapital: Kritik der politischen Ökonomie,* vol. I, *Der Produktionsprozess des Kapitals* (Hamburg: Otto Meissner Verlag, 1867); vol. II, *Der Zirkulationsprozess des Kapitals* (Hamburg: Otto Meissner Verlag, 1885); and vol. III, *Der Gesamtprozess der kapitalistischen Produktion* (Hamburg: Otto Meissner Verlag, 1893).

56. On all this, see the fascinating chapter on "Marxian Economics," in Blaug, *Economic Theory in Retrospect,* 227–297.

57. Karl Marx, *Capital: A Critique of Political Economy,* vol. I, *The Process of Capitalist Production,* translated from the 3rd German edition by S. Moore and E. Aveling (New York: International Publishers, 1967), 595.

58. The socially necessary quantity of labor is the amount of labor actually necessary for the production of commodities.

59. Marx, *Capital,* I: 371.

60. "Capitals" is the term used by Marx.

61. Marx, *Capital,* I: 762–763.

62. For the up-to-date text, including the prefaces written by Marx and Engels subsequent to the 1848 edition, see Karl Marx and Friedrich Engels, *The Communist Manifesto,* ed. David McLellan (Oxford; New York: Oxford University Press, 1998).

63. Vladimir Illyich Lenin, *Imperialism: The Highest Stage of Capitalism* (New York: International Publishers, 1939), 63.

64. See Dorfman, "Review Article: Economic Development from the Beginning to Rostow," 573–591. Alfred Marshall, *Principles of Economics,* vol. 1 (London: Macmillan, 1890). His *Principles* went into eight editions during his lifetime—the eighth edition was published in 1920 as *Principles of Economics: An Introductory Volume* (London: Macmillan, 1920).

65. See Joseph A. Schumpeter, *The Theory of Economic Development* (New York: Oxford University Press, 1961). This text was first published under the title *Theorie der wirtschaftlichen Entwicklung* (Leipzig: Duncker & Humblot, 1911).

66. Schumpeter, *The Theory of Economic Development,* 62–65.

67. Ibid., 66.

68. See Joseph Alois Schumpeter, *Capitalism, Socialism, and Democracy* (New York; London: Harper & Brothers, 1942).

69. Joseph Alois Schumpeter, *Capitalism, Socialism, and Democracy* (New York: Harper and Row, 1962), 61.

70. Ibid., 143.

71. Ibid., 123.

72. Ibid., 125.

73. Ibid., 125–126.

74. Ibid., 127.

75. Ibid., 157.

76. Ibid., 161–162.

77. John Maynard Keynes, *The General Theory of Employment, Interest and Money* (New York: Harcourt Brace Jovanovich, 1964), viii.

78. The various versions of Keynes's proposals for an international clearing union are in Donald Moggridge, ed., *The Collected Writings of John Maynard Keynes,* vol. XXV (London: Macmillan, 1980).

79. John Maynard Keynes, *The General Theory of Employment, Interest and Money* (New York: Cambridge University Press, 1973), 24.

80. Ibid., 317.

81. See John Maynard Keynes, *The Economic Consequences of the Peace* (London: Macmillan, 1919).

82. Paul Streeten, "Global Governance for Human Development," a paper made available by the UN at http://meltingpot.fortunecity.com/lebanon/254/streeten.htm.

83. See, for instance, Devesh Kapur, John P. Lewis, and Richard Webb, eds., *The World Bank: Its First Half Century*, 2 vols. (Washington, D.C.: Brookings, 1997).

84. The "third way," typical of "New Labour" under Tony Blair, is a modern version of social democracy.

85. Smith, *The Wealth of Nations* (1776), available online at http://socserv2.socsci.mcmaster.ca/~econ/ugcm/3ll3/smith/wealth.

86. See Louis Emmerij, Richard Jolly, and Thomas G. Weiss, *Ahead of the Curve? UN Ideas and Global Challenges* (Bloomington: Indiana University Press, 2001), Chapter 6.

87. Adam Smith, *The Theory of Moral Sentiments* (1759), from a collection of quotes compiled by the University of Bristol at http://www.ecn.bris.ac.uk/het/smith/moral.6.

3. The 1940s and 1950s

1. Harry S. Truman, "Inaugural Address," 20 January 1949, reproduced in *Documents on American Foreign Relations* (Princeton, N.J.: Princeton University Press, 1967). Available online at http://www.trumanlibrary.org/calendar/viewpapers.php?pid=1030.

2. Gustavo Esteva, "Development," in *The Development Dictionary: A Guide to Knowledge as Power*, ed. Wolfgang Sachs (London: Zed Books, 1992), 7.

3. See, for example, Daniel Lerner, *The Passing of the Traditional Society* (Glencoe, Ill.: Free Press, 1962); and Berthold Frank Hoselitz, ed., *The Sociological Aspects of Economic Growth* (Glencoe, Ill.: Free Press, 1960).

4. William Arthur Lewis, "Economic Development with Unlimited Supplies of Labour," *The Manchester School of Economic and Social Studies* XXII, no. 2 (May 1954): 155.

5. Eugene Staley, *World Economic Development* (Montreal: ILO, 1944); Kurt Mandelbaum, *The Industrialisation of Backward Areas* (Oxford: Basil Blackwell, 1945).

6. Paul N. Rosenstein-Rodan, "Industrialization of Eastern and South-Eastern Europe," *Economic Journal* LXVI (March 1943): 23–48.

7. ECLA, *The Economic Development of Latin America and Its Principal Problems* (New York: UN, 1950).

8. ECLA, *Economic Survey of Latin America, 1949* (New York: UN, 1951).

9. UN, *Measures for the Economic Development of Underdeveloped Countries: Report by a Group of Experts Appointed by the Secretary-General of the United Nations* (New York: UN, 1951).

10. Amartya Sen, "What's the Point of a Development Strategy?" DERP Discussion Paper no. 3, Development Economics Research Programme, London School of Economics, 1997, 1.

11. Albert O. Hirschman, "The Rise and Decline of Development Economics," in *Essays in Trespassing: Economics to Politics and Beyond*, ed. Albert O. Hirschman (New York: Cambridge University Press, 1981), 375.

12. Ibid., 14.

13. There were of course exceptions, notably Peter Bauer. See his contribution in Gerald M. Meier and Dudley Seers, eds., *Pioneers in Development* (New York: Oxford University Press, 1984), 25–44.

14. Tibor Scitovsky, *Papers on Welfare and Growth* (Stanford, Calif.: Stanford University Press, 1964).

15. "Economic Development of Under-developed Countries," General Assembly resolution 198 (III), 4 December 1948.

16. See "Subcommissions of the Economic and Employment Commission," ECOSOC resolution 1 (III), 1 October 1946.

17. ECOSOC Economic and Employment Commission, Sub-Commission on Economic Development, *Report—First Session 17 November to 16 December 1947* (New York: UN, 1947).

18. Ibid., 11.

19. Roy F. Harrod (1900–1978) and Evsey D. Domar (1914–) independently developed a major model of economic growth in 1948, which later came to be known as the Harrod-Domar model. The model, which relates savings, investments, and economic growth, built upon Keynes's theory and demonstrates the conditions under which growth is possible at a steady and sustained rate.

20. William Arthur Lewis, "Industrialisation of the British West Indies," *Caribbean Economic Review* 2, no. 1 (1950): 36.

21. Paul N. Rosenstein-Rodan, *The Objectives of United States Economic Assistance Programs* (Cambridge, Mass.: MIT Press, 1957), 70.

22. Hans W. Singer, "Aid Not Trade? The Evolution of Soft Financing in the Early Years in the United Nations," in *Effective Negotiation: Case Studies in Conference Diplomacy*, ed. Johan Kaufmann (Dordrecht: Martinus Nijhoff, 1989), 268.

23. UN, *Relative Prices of Exports and Imports of Under-Developed Countries* (New York: UN, 1949); UN, *Relative Prices of Primary Products and Manufactures in International Trade: Report by the Secretary-General*, ECOSOC document E/2455, 8 June 1953.

24. UN, *Relative Prices of Exports and Imports*.

25. Hans Singer, "The Distribution of Gains between Investing and Borrowing Countries," *American Economic Review* 11, no. 2 (May 1950), reprinted in Hans Singer, *International Development Growth and Change* (New York: McGraw-Hill, 1964), 165.

26. "Financing of Economic Development through the Establishment of Fair and Equitable International Prices for Primary Commodities and through the Execution of National Programme of Integrated Economic Development," General Assembly resolution 623 (VII), 21 December 1952.

27. UN, *Relative Prices of Exports and Imports*.

28. John Toye and Richard Toye, *The UN and Global Political Economy: Trade, Finance, and Development* (Bloomington: Indiana University Press, 2004).

29. ECLA, *The Economic Development of Latin America*.

30. For a detailed and fascinating account of the roles played by Singer and Prebisch in the development of the Prebisch-Singer thesis, see Toye and Toye, *The UN and Global Political Economy*.

31. Singer, "The Distribution of Gains between Investing and Borrowing Countries," 167.

32. See ECLA, *The Economic Development of Latin America*, 1 and 10.

33. Ibid., 2.

34. Ibid., 6.

35. Toye and Toye, *The UN and Global Political Economy*.

36. Al Fishlow, *The State of Latin American Economics* (Berkeley, Calif.: Stanford-Berkeley Joint Center for Latin American Studies, 1985), 123.

37. See Nehru's speech in Lok Sabha on 15 December 1952, reproduced in Jawaharlal Nehru, *Planning for Development* (New Delhi: The Publication Division, 1962), 4–5.

38. "Full Employment: Report of the Group of Experts Appointed by the Secretary-General under Council Resolution 221E (IX) on National and International Measures Required to Achieve Full Employment," ECOSOC resolution 290 (XI), 15 August 1950.

39. UN, *Measures for the Economic Development of Underdeveloped Countries*.

40. Ibid., 93.

41. Ibid., 21.

42. UN, *Technical Assistance for Economic Development* (New York: UN, 1949), 8.

43. Peter Bauer, "The United Nations Report on the Economic Development of Under-Developed Countries," *Economic Journal* 63 (March 1953): 213.

44. UN, *Measures for the Economic Development of Underdeveloped Countries*, 84.

45. UN, *Economic Development of Underdeveloped Countries: Analytical Summary of Various Suggested Means of Accelerating Economic Growth in Less Developed Countries through International Action: Report of the Secretary-General* (New York: UN, 1959), 26.

46. UN, *National and International Measures for Full Employment* (New York: UN, 1949).

47. UN, *Measures for International Economic Stability* (New York: UN, 1951). The work of the 1949–1951 expert groups that produced these pioneering reports is presented in more detail in Toye and Toye, *The UN and Global Political Economy*.

48. UN, *Commodity Trade and Economic Development* (New York: UN, 1954).

49. The total fertility rate is defined in the UNDP, *Human Development Report 2002* (New York: Oxford University Press, 2002) as the "average number of children a woman would bear if age-specific fertility rates remained unchanged during her lifetime" (264).

50. UN, *Commodity Trade and Economic Development*, 11.

51. See "Economic Development of Under-Developed Countries," ECOSOC resolution 416 (XIV), 23 June 1952.

52. Mandelbaum, *The Industrialisation of Backward Areas*.

53. Mandelbaum later went by the name of Kurt Martin.

54. Kurt Martin, "Comments," *Development and Change* 10, no. 4 (1979): 511.

55. "Integrated Economic Development," ECOSOC resolution 461 (XV), 23 April 1953.

56. UN, *Processes and Problems of Industrialisation in Underdeveloped Countries* (New York: UN, 1955).

57. Ibid., 3.

58. Ragnar Nurkse, "Some International Aspects of the Problem of Economic Development," *American Economic Review* XLII, no. 2 (May 1952): 571–583.

59. Arthur Lewis, "Economic Development with Unlimited Supplies of Labour," *The Manchester School of Economic and Social Studies* XXII, no. 2 (May 1954): 155.

60. For instance, see UN, *Measures for International Economic Stability* (New York: UN, 1951).

61. UN, *Methods of Financing Economic Development in Underdeveloped Countries* (Lake Success, New York: UN, 1949); UN, *Domestic Financing of Economic Development* (New York: UN, 1950); UN, *Report on a Special United Nations Fund for Economic Development* (New York: UN, 1953); ECAFE, *Mobilization of Domestic Capital* (Bangkok: ECAFE, 1953).

62. UN, *National and International Measures for Full Employment.*

63. ECOSOC Economic and Employment Commission, Sub-Commission on Economic Development, *Report of the First Session 17 November to 16 December 1947,* 9.

64. Celso Furtado, *The Economic Development of Latin America: Historical Background and Contemporary Problems* (New York: Cambridge University Press, 1976), 37.

65. Harry S. Truman, "Inaugural Address," available online at http://www.trumanlibrary.org/calendar/viewpapers.php?pid=1030.

66. A detailed account of the early years will be found in Üner Kirdar, *The Structure of United Nations Economic Aid to Underdeveloped Countries* (The Hague: Martinus Nijhoff, 1966).

67. See "Technical Assistance for Economic Development," General Assembly resolution 200 (III), 4 December 1948.

68. Following, respectively, "Economic Development of Under-developed Countries," ECOSOC resolution 179 (VIII) and "Technical Assistance for Economic Development," ECOSOC resolution 180 (VIII), both adopted on 4 March 1949.

69. "Economic Development of Under-Developed Countries," General Assembly resolution 222 (IX), 4 December 1948.

70. Margaret Joan Anstee, "The Field Office and How It Grew," in UNDP, *Generation: Portrait of the United Nations Development Programme* (New York: UNDP Division of Information, 1985), 20.

71. Oral History Interview of Janez Stanovnik, 7–8 January 2001, 19, in the Oral History Collection of the United Nations Intellectual History Project, The Graduate Center, The City University of New York.

72. UN, *The EPTA: A Forward Look—Report of the Technical Assistance Board* (New York: UN, 1956).

73. "Consolidation of the Special Fund and the Extended Programme of Technical Assistance in a United Nations Development Programme," ECOSOC resolution 1020 (XXXVII), 11 August 1964.

74. "Consolidation of the Special Fund and the Extended Programme of Technical Assistance in a United Nations Development Programme," General Assembly resolution 2029 (XX), 22 November 1965.

75. Stephen Klingebiel, *Effectiveness and Reform of the United Nations Development Programme* (London: Frank Cass, 1999), 394.

76. UNDP, Robert Jackson, *A Study of the Capacity of the United Nations Development System*, 2 vols. (Geneva: UN, 1969). A full and fascinating account of the report, and the process of preparing it, is given by Margaret Joan Anstee, who was chief of staff and the main drafter of the report, in *Never Learn to Type: A Woman of the United Nations* (Chichester: John Wiley, 2003).

77. Ibid., 1: 12–13.

78. See also UNDP, *Generation: Portrait of the United Nations Development Programme.*

79. Dudley Seers offered an influential early critique in "Why Visiting Economists Fail," *Journal of Political Economy* 70, no. 4 (August 1962): 325–338. A more recent review presenting new approaches is Sakiko Fukuda-Parr, Carlos Lopez, and Khalid Malik, eds., *Capacity for Development: New Solutions to Old Problems* (London: UNDP/Earthscan, 2002).

80. The experts appointed by the Secretary-General to study the international flow of private capital had published a report, *The International Flow of Private Capital, 1946–1952* (New York: United Nations Department of Economic Affairs, 1954), and concluded that private capital was not being invested in the underdeveloped countries on any substantial scale and that there was little likelihood of improvement. This view was confirmed by "Economic Development of Under-developed Countries," ECOSOC resolution 512 B (XVII), 30 April 1954, and by studies prepared by the Secretary-General on SUNFED and the international flow of private capital.

81. V. K. R. V. Rao, "Financing of Basic Economic Development," reprinted in Annex IV of *Economic Development of Underdeveloped Countries: Methods of Financing the Economic Development of Underdeveloped Countries* (New York: UN, 1949), 17.

82. Ibid., 20.

83. UN, *National and International Measures for Full Employment.*

84. "Financing of Economic Development of Under-Developed Countries," General Assembly resolution 400 (V), 20 November 1950.

85. UN, *Measures for the Economic Development of Underdeveloped Countries.*

86. Ibid., 95.

87. *Economic Development of the Under-Developed Countries: ECOSOC Report*, ECOSOC document A/C.2/SR.147, 20 November 1951, 15–16.

88. *Economic Development of the Under-Developed Countries: ECOSOC Report*, ECOSOC document A/C.2/SR.152, 26 November 1951, 53.

89. UN, *Special United Nations Fund for Economic Development* (New York: UN, 1953).

90. UN, *United Nations General Assembly Ninth Session Official Records* (New York: UN, 1954).

91. "Economic Development of Under-Developed Countries," General Assembly resolution 724B (VIII), 7 December 1953.

92. UN, *Special United Nations Fund for Economic Development*, Final Report by Raymond Scheyven (New York: UN, 1954).

93. "Questions of the Establishment of a Special United Nations Fund for Economic Development," General Assembly resolution 822 (IX), 11 December 1954.

94. UN, *United Nations Fund for Economic Development: Report of the Committee of Experts* (New York: UN, 1955).

95. "Questions of the Establishment of a Special United Nations Fund for Economic Development," General Assembly resolution 923 (X), 9 December 1955.

96. UN, *Final Report of the Ad Hoc Committee on the Question of the Establishment of the SUNFED* (New York: UN, 1957).

97. Paul G. Hoffman, "Blueprint for Foreign Aid," *New York Times Magazine,* 17 February 1957, 11.

98. Press release of 30 July 1957 of the United States delegation to the 24th session of ECOSOC.

99. UNDP, *Generation: Portrait of the United Nations Development Programme,* 23.

100. Paul Hoffman, "The Challenge of Economic Development," *International Development Review 1959,* reprinted in *Development* 40, no. 1 (March 1997): 22.

101. Paul Hoffmann presented the *Reports of the Governing Council of the Special Fund,* ECOSOC document E/SR.1324, 21 July 1964, 59.

102. George Davidson, "The Year of the Breakthrough," *United Nations Review* 5 (September 1958): 21.

103. "Establishment of the United Nations Capital Fund," General Assembly resolution 2186 (XXI), 13 December 1966.

104. See Johan Kaufmann, *United Nations Decision Making* (Rockville, Md.: Sijthoff & Noordhoff, 1980).

105. Edward Mason and Robert Asher, *The World Bank Since Bretton Woods* (Washington, D.C.: Brookings Institution, 1973), 569.

106. Oral History Interview of Hans Singer, 11 and 13 October 1995, 47, in the Oral History Collection of the United Nations Intellectual History Project, The Graduate Center, The City University of New York.

4. The 1960s

1. "Address by Mr. John F. Kennedy, President of the United States of America," in *GAOR,* 16th session, 1013th plenary meeting, 25 September 1961, 55–59.

2. President John F. Kennedy, speech of 25 September 1961, reproduced in U.S., *Public Papers of the President of the United States, J. F. Kennedy, 20 January to 31 December 1961* (Washington, D.C.: U.S. Government Printing Office, 1962), 623.

3. Oral History Interview of Hans Singer, 20, 21, and 26 August 1997, 15, in the Oral History Collection of the United Nations Intellectual History Project, The Graduate Center, The City University of New York.

4. "United Nations Development Decade: A Programme for International Economic Cooperation (I)," General Assembly resolution 1710 (XVI), 19 December 1961.

5. Ibid.

6. See oral history interview of Hans Singer, 20, 21, and 26 August 1997, 18.

7. "Reaffirmation of General Assembly resolution 1522 (XV) on the Accelerated Flow of Capital and Technical Assistance to the Developing Countries," General Assembly resolution 1711 (XVI), 19 December 1961, preamble.

8. UN, *The United Nations Development Decade: Proposals for Action* (New York: UN, 1962), 8. In fact, with hindsight, average population growth was closer to 2.5 percent per annum in both low- and middle-income developing countries, though if China and India were excluded, the rate would be slightly higher. Some fifteen to twenty countries recorded a rate of 3 to 3.5 percent over the 1960s. See World Bank, *World Development Report, 1980* (Oxford; New York: Oxford University Press, 1980), 142–143.

9. UN, *The United Nations Development Decade*, 12–13.

10. "Economic and Social Consequences of Disarmament," ECOSOC document E/3593, 28 February 1962.

11. Ibid., 10 and 59.

12. General Assembly resolution 1710 (XVI), 19 December 1961.

13. UN, *The United Nations Development Decade*.

14. Ibid., 5.

15. Ibid., 13.

16. See Chakravarty Sukhamoy, *Development Planning: The Indian Experience* (Oxford: Clarendon Press, 1987).

17. Ragnar Nurkse, *Problems of Capital Formation in Underdeveloped Countries* (Oxford: Basil Blackwell, 1953).

18. Albert O. Hirschman, *The Strategy of Economic Development* (Cambridge, Mass.: Harvard University Press, 1958).

19. François Perroux, "Note on the Concept of Growth Poles," in *Economic Policy for Development: Selected Readings*, ed. Ian Livingstone (Harmondsworth: Penguin, 1955).

20. Albert O. Hirschman, "A Dissenter's Confession," in Albert O. Hirschman, *Rival Views of Market Society* (Cambridge, Mass.: Harvard University Press, 1992), 12.

21. ECAFE, "Economic Development and Planning in Asia and the Far East," *Economic Bulletin for Asia and the Far East* (November 1955): 63.

22. Oral History Interview of Hans Singer, 20, 21, and 26 August 1997, 29.

23. Though Bauer is correctly considered to be a brilliant exponent of the benefits of the market, even he was able to support some aspects of planning. See Peter Bauer, *Dissent and Development* (London: Weidenfield & Nicolson, 1971).

24. UN, *Planning for Economic Development* (New York: UN, 1963), iv.

25. UN Committee on Programme Appraisal, *Five-Year Perspective, 1960–1964* (New York: UN, 1960), 95.

26. See our companion volume by Michael Ward, *Quantifying the World: UN Ideas and Statistics* (Bloomington: Indiana University Press, 2004).

27. UN Center for Development Planning, Projections, and Policies, *Some Problems of Implementation in the Private Sector of the Economy*, ECOSOC document E/AC.54/L.10, 1967.

28. Center for Development Planning, Projections, and Policies, *Some General Conditions for the Effective Implementation of Plans*, ECOSOC document E/AC.54/L.8, 1967.

29. UN, *World Economic Survey,* Part 1, *Trade and Development: Trends, Needs and Policies* (New York: UN, 1963).

30. Ibid.

31. UN, *World Economic Survey,* Part 2, *Current Economic Development* (New York: UN, 1963).

32. UN, *Studies in Long-Term Economic Projections for the World Economy: Aggregate Models* (New York: UN, 1964).

33. For the ideas coming out of the UN regional commissions, see our companion volume by Yves Berthelot, ed., *Unity and Diversity in Development Ideas: Perspectives from the UN Regional Commissions* (Bloomington: Indiana University Press, 2004).

34. Michal Kalecki, *Essays on Developing Countries* (New York: Harvester Press, 1976), 32.

35. Jan Tinbergen, *The Design of Development* (Baltimore: Johns Hopkins University Press, 1958).

36. Richard Symonds and Michael Carder, *The United Nations and the Population Question, 1945–1970* (New York: McGraw-Hill Book Company, 1973), xiv.

37. See ECOSOC, *ESCOR,* 31st session, 1140th meeting, 24 April 1961, para. 40, 14–15.

38. See, for example, the *Population Bulletin of the United Nations,* nos. 6 and 7 (1962 and 1963); and UN, *Demographic Aspects of Manpower* (New York: UN, 1963).

39. UN, *Development and Utilisation of Human Resources in Developing Countries* (New York: UN, 1967), 11.

40. Hans W. Singer, "Education and Economic Development," paper prepared for the Conference of African States on the Development of Education in Africa, Addis Ababa, 15–25 May 1961, reproduced in Hans W. Singer, *International Development* (London: McGraw-Hill Book Company, 1964), 66.

41. Established in 1964 as an ECOSOC committee.

42. See Advisory Committee on the Application of Science and Technology to Development (ACAST), *Third Report,* May 1966, ESCOR, 41st session, supplement no. 12, (E/4178), para. 7.

43. *World Plan of Action for the Application of Science and Technology to Development: Note by the Secretary-General,* ECOSOC document E/AC.52/L.68, 14 October 1969; see also Lester Pearson and the Commission on International Development, *Partners in Development* (New York: Praeger, 1969). The Sussex Group was a group of academics at the Institute of Development Studies at the University of Sussex (UK).

44. For a more recent collection of papers, see Hans W. Singer, Neelamber Hatti, and Rameshwar Tandon, eds., *Globalization, Technology and Trade in the 21st Century,* Part 1 (Delhi: B. R. Publishing Corporation, 2001).

45. See the comprehensive story of the WFP made by D. John Shaw in *The UN World Food Programme and the Development of Food Aid* (New York: Palgrave, 2001).

46. See Theodore W. Schultz, "The Economics of U.S. Foreign Aid," *Bulletin of the Atomic Scientist* 39, no. 8 (1983): 24–27.

47. Antonio Malintoppi and Philippe Cahier, dirs., *L'Organisation des Nations Unies pour l'Alimentation et l'Agriculture (FAO)* (Genève: Institut Universitaire de Hautes Etudes Internationales, 1986), 72.

48. "Provision of Food Surpluses to Food-Deficient Peoples through the United Nations System," General Assembly resolution 1496 (XV), 27 October 1960.

49. See "World Food Programme," General Assembly resolution 1714 (XVI), 19 December 1961.

50. FAO, *Development through Food: A Strategy for Surplus Utilisation* (Rome: FAO, 1961).

51. Ibid., 8.

52. Ibid., Appendix 2, 110.

53. Frances Stewart, "Food Aid: Pitfalls and Potentials," *Food Policy* 11, no. 4 (November 1986): 316; and Theodore W. Schultz, "Value of US Farm Surpluses to Underdeveloped Countries," *Journal of Farm Economics* 42, no. 5 (1960), cited in Hans W. Singer, "Food Aid: Development Tool or Obstacle to Development?" *Development Policy Review* 5, no. 4 (1987): 332.

54. Hans W. Singer, "A Pioneer's Response to Food Aid Critics," *Ceres: The FAO Review* 123, 21, no. 3 (1988): 47.

55. World Food Programme, "How WFP Fights the Global War on Hunger," www.wfp.org/index.asp?section=1.

56. Celso Furtado, "US Hegemony and the Future of Latin America," *The World Today* 22 (1966): 375.

57. Raúl Prebisch, *Towards a Dynamic Development Policy for Latin America* (Santiago: UN, 1963), 71.

58. Albert O. Hirschman, "The Political Economy of Import-Substituting Industrialisation in Latin America," *The Quarterly Journal of Economics* LXXXII, no. 2 (1968): 1–32.

59. Werner Baer, *The Brazilian Economy: Growth and Development* (New York: Praeger, 1989). See also Lloyd Reynolds, *Economic Growth in the Third World, 1850–1980* (New Haven, Conn.: Yale University Press, 1988).

60. Heinz Wolfgang Arndt, *Economic Development: The History of an Idea* (Chicago: University of Chicago Press, 1989).

61. Fernando Henrique Cardoso and Enzo Faletto, *Dependency and Development in Latin America* (Berkeley: University of California Press, 1979); Osvaldo Sunkel, "National Development Policy and External Dependence," *Journal of Development Studies* 6, no. 1 (1969): 132–176; Celso Furtado, "The Concept of External Dependence in the Study of Underdevelopment," in *The Political Economy of Development and Underdevelopment,* ed. C. K. Wilber (New York: Random House, 1973), 118–123.

62. André G. Frank, "The Development of Underdevelopment," *Monthly Review* 18, no. 4 (1966): 23–28; Ruy Mauro Marini, *Dialéctica de la Dependencia* (Mexico City: Ediciones Era, 1973); Theotonio Dos Santos, "The Crisis of Development Theory and the Problem of Dependence in Latin America," in *Underdevelopment and Development,* ed. Henry Bernstein (Harmondsworth: Penguin Books, 1973).

63. Oral History Interview of Samir Amin, 30 April 2002, 19, in the Oral History Collection of the United Nations Intellectual History Project, The Graduate Center, The City University of New York. (Translation by the author.)

64. GNP per capita grew at 4.0 percent per annum from 1965 to 1980 in East and Southeast Asia and at 3.8 percent over the same period in Latin America and the Caribbean. Data from UNDP, *Human Development Report 1991* (Oxford and New York: Oxford University Press, 1991), 168–169.

65. Cardoso, *Dependency and Development in Latin America.*

66. The "infant mortality rate" is defined in the UNDP, *Human Development Report 2002* (New York: Oxford University Press, 2002) as the "probability of dying between birth and exactly one year of age expressed per 1,000 live births" (265).

67. The joint declaration is annexed to the "United Nations Conference on Trade and Development," General Assembly resolution 1897 (XVIII), 11 November 1963.

68. "Report of the UN Conference on Trade and Development," ECOSOC document E/CONF.46/L.28/Add.1, 26 June 1964.

69. Ibid., 3.

70. Sidney Dell, "The Origins of UNCTAD," in *UNCTAD and the South-North Dialogue,* ed. Michal Zammit Cutajar (New York: Pergamon Press, 1985), 19. See also UNCTAD, *The History of UNCTAD: 1964–1984* (New York: UN, 1985).

71. Oral History Interview of Gamani Corea, 1 February 2000, 55, in the Oral History Collection of the United Nations Intellectual History Project, The Graduate Center, The City University of New York.

72. John Toye and Richard Toye, *The UN and Global Political Economy: Trade, Finance, and Development* (Bloomington: Indiana University Press, 2004).

73. See UN, *World Economic Survey,* Part 1, *The Developing Countries in the 1960s: The Problem of Appraising Progress* (New York: UN, 1970).

74. Ibid., 7.

75. Oral History Interview of Francis Blanchard, 6 and 8 October 1999, 43, in the Oral History Collection of the United Nations Intellectual History Project, The Graduate Center, The City University of New York.

76. Oral History Interview of Hans W. Singer, 20, 21, and 26 August 1997, 42, in the Oral History Collection of the United Nations Intellectual History Project, The Graduate Center, The City University of New York.

77. Dudley Seers, "The Meaning of Development," *International Development Review* 11, no. 4 (1969): 3.

78. Ibid.

79. Committee for Development Planning, "International Development Strategy for the Nineteen Seventies: A Preliminary Sketch," ECOSOC document E/AC.54/L.30, 2 October 1968.

80. For a wider range of perspectives on the first three decades of development, see the important collection of retrospectives in Gerald Meier and Dudley Seers, *Pioneers in Development* (New York: Oxford University Press, 1984).

5. The 1970s

1. The term "employment" is used here to refer to the whole array of associated problems such as open unemployment, disguised unemployment, underemployment, inadequate remuneration, and so forth.

2. Dudley Seers, "The Meaning of Development," *International Development Review* 11, no. 4 (December 1969): 3.

3. Gunnar Myrdal, *The Challenge of World Poverty* (London: The Penguin Press, 1970).

4. Hans W. Singer, "Dualism Revisited: A New Approach to the Problem of the Dual Society in Developing Countries," *Journal of Development Studies* 7, no. 1 (October 1970): 70–71.

5. David Turnham and Ingelies Jaeger, *The Employment Problem in Less Developed Countries: A Review of Evidence,* Development Centre Studies, Employment Series no. 1 (Paris: OECD Development Centre, 1971).

6. Bagich S. Minhas, *Planning and the Poor* (New Delhi: S. Chand, 1974).

7. ILO, *World Employment Programme: Report of the Director-General* (Geneva: ILO, 1969).

8. ILO, *Poverty and Minimum Living Standards: The Role of the ILO,* Report of the Director-General, Part 1 (Geneva: ILO, 1970), 1.

9. "The Elimination of Mass Poverty and Unemployment through the Adoption of National Development Strategies and the International Development Strategy," ECOSOC resolution 1727 (LIII), 28 July 1972.

10. For the goals and objectives concerning employment and education, see "International Development Strategy for the Second Development Decade," General Assembly resolution 2626 (XXV), 24 October 1970, para. B.

11. The Experimental World Literacy Programme "was introduced from 1967 to 1973 with the financial contribution of UNDP; this programme was intended to demonstrate the advantages of literacy from the economic and social standpoints. Twenty-two countries took part in this programme; eleven had selected projects." See www.unesco.org/education/educprog/50y/brochure/tle/124.htm.

12. The WHO published a comprehensive and most thorough account of smallpox in history and of the setting of the goal of eradicating the disease, the implementation of the eradication strategy, and the remarkable achievement of eradication in 1977. Frank Fenner et al., *Smallpox and Its Eradication,* History of International Public Health no. 6 (Geneva: WHO, 1988).

13. The "Freedom from Hunger Campaign," ECOSOC resolution 743c (XXVIII), was formally adopted on 31 July 1959.

14. IFAD became a specialized agency of the UN on 15 December 1977 by an agreement between the governing council of IFAD and the UN General Assembly, "with the objective of mobilizing additional resources to be made available on concessional terms for agricultural development in developing member States." UN/DPI, *Yearbook of the United Nations 1977* (New York: UN, 1980), 1161.

15. The World Employment Programme was launched in 1969 during the fifty-third session of the International Labour Conference in Geneva.

16. A full list of the reports is in ILO, *Employment Growth and Basic Needs: A One-World Problem: Report of the Director-General of the ILO* (Geneva: ILO, 1976). This report was prepared for the Tripartite World Conference on Employment, Income Distribution and Social Progress, and the International Division of Labour. See also

ILO, *Meeting Basic Needs: Strategies for Eradicating Mass Poverty and Unemployment* (Geneva: ILO, 1976).

17. Hollis Chenery et al., *Redistribution with Growth: Policies to Improve Income Distribution in Developing Countries in the Context of Economic Growth* (London: Oxford University Press, 1974).

18. ILO, *Employment, Incomes and Equality: A Strategy for Increasing Productive Employment in Kenya* (Geneva: ILO, 1972). See also David G. Davies, "A Critical Discussion of the ILO Report on Employment in Kenya," *Pakistan Development Review* XII, no. 3 (Autumn 1973): 283–292.

19. A pioneering and influential study outside the UN was Irma Adelman and Cynthia T. Morris, *Economic Growth and Social Equity in Developing Countries* (Stanford, Calif.: Stanford University Press, 1973).

20. Amilcar O. Herrera et al., *¿Catástrofe o Nueva Sociedad? Modelo Mundial Latinoamericano* (San Carlos de Bariloche: Fundación Bariloche, 1977).

21. Dag Hammarskjöld Foundation, *What Now? Another Development* (Uppsala: Dag Hammarskjöld Foundation, 1975).

22. ILO, *Employment, Growth and Basic Needs: A One-World Problem* (Geneva: ILO, 1976). See also Glen Sheehan and Mike Hopkins, *Basic Needs Performance: An Analysis of Some International Data* (Geneva: ILO, 1979); Dharam Ghai, A. R. Khan, and Eddy Lee, *The Basic-Needs Approach to Development: Some Issues Regarding Concepts and Methodology* (Geneva: ILO, 1977).

23. World Employment Conference, *Declaration of Principles and Programme of Action* (Geneva: ILO, 1976).

24. See especially reports of employment missions: ILO, *Employment and Income Policies for Iran* (Geneva: ILO, 1973); ILO, *Sharing in Development: A Programme of Employment, Equity and Growth for the Philippines* (Geneva: ILO, 1974); ILO, *Generación de Empleo Productivo y Crecimiento Económico* (Geneva: ILO, 1975); ILO, *Growth, Employment and Equity: A Strategy for Sudan* (Geneva: ILO, 1976); ILO, *Towards Full Employment: A Programme for Colombia,* prepared by an interagency team organized by the International Labour Office (Geneva: ILO, 1970); ILO, *Matching Employment Opportunities and Expectations: A Programme of Action for Ceylon* (Geneva: ILO, 1971); ILO, *Employment, Incomes and Equality*; Erik Thorbecke, "The Employment Problem: A Critical Evaluation of Four ILO Comprehensive Country Reports," *International Labour Review* 107, no. 5 (May 1973): 393–423.

25. ILO, *Employment, Growth and Basic Needs,* 32.

26. World Employment Conference, Declaration of Principles.

27. See "International Development Strategy for the Third United Nations Development Decade," General Assembly resolution 35/56, 5 December 1980, Annex, I, Preamble, para. 8.

28. Paul Streeten et al., *First Things First: Meeting Basic Human Needs in Developing Countries* (New York: Oxford University Press, 1981). But critiques were also strong; see T. N. Srinivasan, "Development, Poverty, and Basic Human Needs," *Food Research Institute Studies* 16, no. 2 (1977): 16–28; and R. M. Sundrum, "Development, Equality and Employment," *The Economic Record* 50, no. 131 (September 1974): 430–443.

29. Andrew Coulson, *Tanzania: A Political Economy* (Oxford: Clarendon Press, 1982).

30. TANU, *The Arusha Declaration* (Dar es Salaam: Government Printer, February 1967); Julius Nyerere, *Freedom and Socialism: A Selection from Writings and Speeches, 1965–1967* (Dar es Salaam: Oxford University Press, 1968).

31. Julius Nyerere, *Socialism and Rural Development* (Dar es Salaam: Government Printer, 1967).

32. World Bank, *Tanzania Economic Report: Towards Sustainable Development in the 1990s,* vol. 1 (Washington, D.C.: World Bank, 1991).

33. ILO, *Employment, Incomes and Equality,* Chapter 13.

34. Paul E. Bangasser, "The ILO and the Informal Sector: An Institutional History," Employment Paper 2000/9, International Labour Organization, Geneva, 2000. See also ILO, *Women and Men in the Informal Economy: A Statistical Picture* (Geneva: ILO, 2002).

35. These themes can be found in Devesh Kapur, John P. Lewis, and Richard Webb, eds., *The World Bank: Its First Half Century,* vol. 1, *History* (Washington, D.C.: Brookings, 1997). McNamara, World Bank president from 1968 to 1981, was the first to make poverty reduction an explicit "direct" objective of the Bank (215). When Clausen succeeded McNamara in 1981, "the poverty theme, which had been faltering, was abruptly muted in Bank decision-making" (331), though in public statements poverty reduction was presented as an important objective. Conable, who took the presidency in 1987, was an "enthusiastic activist for causes such as poverty alleviation but [in practice] . . . much of what was being demanded could be accommodated by rhetoric" (369). In the late 1990s with Wolfensohn, poverty reduction was again made an explicit and direct objective, linked initially to the Poverty Reduction Strategy Papers and, after the UN Millennium Summit in September 2000, to the Millennium Development Goals and much closer cooperation with the UN system.

36. "Declaration on the Establishment of the New International Economic Order," General Assembly resolution 3201 (S-VI), 1 May 1974.

37. For the Programme of Action, see General Assembly resolution 3202 (S-VI), 1 May 1974.

38. Jeffrey A. Hart, *The New International Economic Order* (London: Macmillan, 1983). See also William Cline, ed., *Policy Alternatives for a New International Economic Order* (New York: Praeger, 1979).

39. For the summary records of these meetings, see *GAOR,* 6th special session, 10 April–1 May 1974, 20–103.

40. A good overview of how the debt crisis developed is in Devesh Kapur, John P. Lewis, and Richard Webb, eds., *The World Bank: Its First Half Century,* 1: 595–682.

41. Oral History Interview of Gamani Corea, 1 February 2000, 31, in the Oral History Collection of the United Nations Intellectual History Project, The Graduate Center, The City University of New York.

42. Oral History Interview of Gert Rosenthal, 3 January 2001, 27, in the Oral History Collection of the United Nations Intellectual History Project, The Graduate Center, The City University of New York. In 1984, ECLA (the Economic Commission for

Latin America) was expanded to include the Caribbean region and was renamed ECLAC (the Economic Commission for Latin America and the Caribbean).

43. Brandt Commission, *North-South: A Programme for Survival* (London: Pan Books, 1980), 8.

44. UNDP, *Human Development Report 2002* (New York: Oxford University Press, 2002), 202.

45. For the "Summary by the Co-Chairmen of the International Meeting on Cooperation and Development," see annex in the General Assembly document A/36/631, 28 October 1981.

46. Rachel Carson, *Silent Spring* (Boston: Houghton Mifflin, 1962).

47. Donella H. Meadows et al., *The Limits to Growth: A Report for the Club of Rome's Project on the Predicament on Mankind* (New York: Universe Books, 1972).

48. UN, *Problems of the Human Environment: Report of the Secretary-General* (New York: UN, 1969), 4.

49. Ibid. Note, however, that the UN never made the mistake of suggesting that population growth was the only or even the major cause of environmental problems. See also Paul R. Ehrlich and Anne H. Ehrlich, *The Population Explosion: From Global Warming to Rain Forest Destruction, Famine, and Air and Water Pollution—Why Overpopulation Is Our #1 Environmental Problem* (New York: Simon and Schuster, 1990).

50. On May 28, 1968, ECOSOC accepted a proposal from Sveker Astrom, the Swedish ambassador to the UN, to explore the possibility of holding an international conference on humans in the environment. See *Stockholm Thirty Years On, Progress Achieved and Challenges Ahead in International Environmental Co-operation: Proceedings from and International Conference 17-18 June 2002* (Stockholm: Ministry of the Environment, 2002).

51. Ibid., 55.

52. Maurice Strong, *Where on Earth Are We Going* (New York: Texere, 2001), gives a full personal account of the process toward Stockholm and the run-up to Rio.

53. UN, *Development and Environment: Report of a Panel of Experts* (UN: Founex, 1971), reprinted in UN, *Proceedings of the United Nations Conference on the Human Environment: Development and Environment* (New York: UN, 1972).

54. UN, *Report of the United Nations Conference on the Human Environment* (New York: UN, 1973).

55. See "Institutional and Financial Arrangements for International Environmental Cooperation," General Assembly resolution 2997 (XXVII), 15 December 1972, part III, Environment Fund.

56. William H. Matthews, ed., *Outer Limits and Human Needs* (Uppsala: Dag Hammarskjöld Foundation, 1976).

57. UN, *Report of Habitat: United Nations Conference on Human Settlements* (New York: UN, 1976), 4. See also Barbara Ward, *The Home of Man* (London: A. Deutsch, 1976).

58. See Nico Schrijver, *The United Nations and Global Resource Management* (Bloomington: Indiana University Press, forthcoming).

59. Agenda 21, Programme of Action for Sustainable Development (1992) was adopted by the conference on 14 June 1992.

60. UNEP, *Environmental Perspectives to the Year 2000 and Beyond* (Nairobi: UNEP, 1988). See more recently Swedish Ministry of the Environment, *Stockholm Thirty Years On: Proceedings from an International Conference, 17–18 June 2002* (Stockholm: Elanders, 2002). Available online at http://www.sweden.se/templates/Publication____5530.asp.

61. IUCN/WWF/UNEP, *World Conservation Strategy: Living Resource Conservation for Sustainable Development* (Gland: IUCN, 1980).

62. UNDP, *Human Development Report 1998* (New York: Oxford University Press, 1998).

63. World Commission on Environment and Development, *Our Common Future* (London: Oxford University Press, 1987), 8–9.

64. In particular in the framework of the World Conservation Strategy by the IUCN, UNEP, and the WWF in 1980.

65. David Brooks, "Beyond Catch Phrases: What Does Sustainable Development Really Mean?" *IDRC Reports* (October 1990): 24–25.

66. A UNIHP companion volume will provide a fuller treatment; Devaki Jain, *Women Enrich the United Nations and Development* (Bloomington: Indiana University Press, forthcoming).

67. John Stuart Mill, *The Subjection of Women* (London: Longmans, 1924) is the exception.

68. Esther Boserup, *Women's Role in Economic Development* (New York: St. Martin's Press, 1970).

69. See UN, *The United Nations and the Advancement of Women, 1945–1996,* Blue Book Series VI, rev. edition (New York: UN, 1996). A well-organized survey of the UN's contributions since the UN Decade for Women (1976–1985) is in Hilkka Pietilä and Jeanne Vickers, *Making Women Matter: The Role of the United Nations* (London and Atlantic Highlands, N.J.: Zed Books, 1996).

70. Quoted in UN, *The United Nations and the Advancement of Women,* 13.

71. The texts of these milestones can be found in UN, *The United Nations and the Advancement of Women,* 103ff.

72. See General Assembly resolution 34/180, 18 December 1979.

73. See UN Economic Commission for Africa, Social Development Section, *Status and Role of Women in East Africa* (New York: United Nations, 1967).

74. More details will be found in the chapter by Adebayo Adedeji on the ECA in the UNIHP companion edited by Yves Berthelot, *Unity and Diversity in Development Ideas: Perspectives from the UN Regional Commissions* (Bloomington: Indiana University Press, 2004). A full and detailed account of these pioneering initiatives can be found in Margaret C. Snyder and Mary Tadesse, *African Women and Development: A History* (London and Atlantic Highlands, N.J.: Zed Books, 1995).

75. For a history of UNIFEM, see the account by its founder and director, Margaret Snyder, *Transforming Development: Women, Poverty and Politics* (London: Intermediate Technology Publications, 1995).

76. INSTRAW was established by ECOSOC resolution 1998 (LX), 12 May 1976.

77. See the surge of publications from UNIFEM, INSTRAW, and UNRISD. See also UNSO, *The World's Women: Trends and Statistics* (New York: United Nations

Statistical Division, 2000); UN Division for the Advancement of Women, *Women Go Global: The United Nations and the International Women's Movement 1945–2000,* an interactive, multimedia CD-ROM (New York: United Nations, 2002), Sales No. E.01.IV.1.

78. Convention (no. 100) Concerning Equal Remuneration for Men and Women Workers for Work of Equal Value, adopted on 29 June 1951 by the General Conference of the ILO.

79. See *Report of the Secretary-General to the CSW on Discrimination against Women in the Field of Political Rights,* ECOSOC document E/CN.6/131, 15 March 1950.

80. UNDP, *Human Development Report 1992* (New York: Oxford University Press, 1992); UNDP, *Human Development Report 1995* (New York: Oxford University Press, 1995).

81. UNDP, *Human Development Report 1995* (New York: Oxford University Press, 1995).

82. UNIFEM, *Progress of the World's Women 2000* (UNIFEM: New York, 2000).

83. Luisella Goldschmidt-Clermont, *Unpaid Work in the Household* (ILO: Geneva, 1982); UN, *The World's Women, 1970–1990: Trends and Statistics* (New York: UN, 1991); Martha Fetherolf Loutfi, ed., *Women, Gender and Work* (Geneva: ILO, 2001).

84. UNDP, *Human Development Report 1995,* 97.

85. As examples of the broader agenda, see Janice Jiggins, *Changing the Boundaries: Women-Centered Perspectives on Population and the Environment* (Washington, D.C.: Island Press, 1994); Cynthia Meillon, ed., *Holding on to the Promise: Women's Human Rights and the Beijing +5 Review* (New Brunswick, N.J.: Center for Women's Global Leadership, 2001).

86. Many other conferences outside the UN helped mobilize opinion and awareness. See, for instance, Khadija Haq, *Dialogue for a New Order* (New York: Pergamon Press, 1980).

87. UN, *Report of the World Conference of the International Women's Year, Mexico City, 19 June–2 July 1975* (New York: UN, 1975).

88. See UN, *The UN and the Advancement of Women,* 187.

89. UN, *Report of the World Conference of the UN Decade for Women: Equality, Peace and Development, Copenhagen, 14–30 July 1980* (New York: UN, 1980). Though these data strike home with force and represent broad orders of magnitude which seem correct, their statistical foundations have never been demonstrated.

90. UN, *Report of the World Conference to Review and Appraise the Achievements of the UN Decade for Women: Equality, Development and Peace, Nairobi, 15–16 July 1985* (New York: UN, 1985).

91. UN, *Report of the World Conference on Women, Beijing, 4–15 1995* (New York: UN, 1995).

6. The 1980s

1. See UNCTAD, *Trade and Development Report: Report by the Secretariat of the United Nations Conference on Trade and Development* (Geneva: UNCTAD, 1981–).

2. The G-7, or Group of Seven, consists of the United States, Japan, Germany, France, Britain, Italy, and Canada. The leaders of these nations, which represent the world's largest market economies, have met each year to discuss political and economic policy since the mid-1970s. In 1998, the Russian Federation was added and the group is now called G-8.

3. The Pearson Commission on International Development report devoted an entire chapter to the debt problem. See Lester Pearson et al., *Partners in Development: Report* (New York: Praeger, 1969).

4. UNCTAD, *Handbook of International Trade and Development Statistics* (Geneva: UN, 1995).

5. UNCTAD, *Trade and Development Report, 1985* (Geneva: UNCTAD, 1985).

6. Ibid.

7. UNCTAD, *Handbook of International Trade and Development Statistics.*

8. Dharam Ghai, "Structural Adjustment, Global Integration and Social Democracy," in *Market Forces and World Development,* ed. Renee Prendergast and Frances Stewart (London: Macmillan Press, 1994), 17.

9. UNCTAD, *Handbook of International Trade and Development Statistics, 1990* (Geneva: UNCTAD, 1990).

10. OECD, *Historical Statistics, 1960–1989* (Paris: OECD, 1991).

11. UNCTAD, *Trade and Development Report, 1987* (Geneva: UNCTAD, 1987). See also Khadija Haq, ed., *Crisis of the '80s: World Monetary, Financial and Human Resource Development Issues* (Washington, D.C.: North-South Roundtable, 1984); and Susan George, *A Fate Worse Than Death: The World Financial Crisis and the Poor* (New York: Grove Weidenfeld, 1990).

12. UNCTAD, *Trade and Development Report, 1997* (Geneva: UNCTAD, 1997), 54.

13. The Paris Club is the forum in which creditor governments meet to negotiate the rescheduling of the debts owed to them—mainly aid loans and guaranteed export credits. The London Club is a general term for rescheduling negotiations on commercial bank debts. Unlike the Paris Club, the London Club has no fixed membership and no permanent secretariat. The London Club is a concept rather than an institution.

14. See Giovanni Andrea Cornia, Richard Jolly, and Frances Stewart, eds., *Adjustment with a Human Face* (Oxford and New York: Oxford University Press, 1987); UNCTAD, *Trade and Development Report, 1997* (Geneva: UNCTAD, 1997), 54.

15. Dharam Ghai and Cynthia Hewitt de Alcantara, "The Crisis of the 1980s in Africa, Latin America and the Caribbean: An Overview," in *The IMF and the South: The Social Impact of Crisis and Adjustment,* ed. Dharam Ghai (London: Zed Books, 1991), 11–42.

16. The Baker Plan was proposed in 1985 by U.S. Treasury Secretary James Baker as a tool to reduce the debt-service obligations of developing countries.

17. See, for example, Patrick Conway, "Baker Plan and International Indebtedness," *World Economy* 10, no. 2 (June 1987): 193–204; Paul-Gunther Schmidt, "Baker, Brady and the Banks: Questionable Recipes to Ease the Debt Burden," *Development and Cooperation,* no. 6 (1990): 12–15.

18. See UNCTAD, *The Least Developed Countries 2000 Report* (Geneva: UNCTAD, 2000).

19. Jubilee 2000 was a successful international campaign which mobilized 24 million people over a five-year period to cancel the unpayable debts of the poorest countries by the year 2000.

20. At the time of writing, the highly indebted poor countries were: Angola, Benin, Bolivia, Burkina Faso, Burundi, Cameroon, Central African Republic, Chad, Comoros, Congo, Cote d'Ivoire, Democratic Republic of Congo, Ethiopia, Gambia, Guinea-Bissau, Guyana, Honduras, Kenya, Lao PDR, Liberia, Madagascar, Malawi, Mali, Mauritania, Mozambique, Myanmar, Nicaragua, Niger, Rwanda, Sao Tome and Principe, Senegal, Sierra Leone, Somalia, Sudan, Tanzania, Togo, Uganda, Vietnam, and Zambia.

21. UNCTAD, *The Least Developed Countries 2000 Report.* Gold sales and the creation of SDRs were not of course new. See John Williamson, *A New SDR Allocation?* (Washington, D.C.: Institute for International Economics, 1984).

22. See the in-depth discussion of debt in the *Trade and Development Reports* of 1985 and 1987, and the resolution 165 (S-IX) on the debt problems of developing countries adopted at the ninth special session of UNCTAD in Manila. The text is contained in UN, *Proceedings of the United Nations Conference on Trade and Development,* Fifth Session, vol. III (New York: UN, 1978).

23. UNCTAD, *Trade and Development Report 1987.*

24. Ibid., 59.

25. Such guidelines had been put forward in "Debt and Development Problems of Developing Countries," UNCTAD Trade and Development Board resolution 222 (XXI), 27 September 1980; and "Strengthened International Economic Cooperation Aimed at Resolving External Debt Problems of Developing Countries," General Assembly resolution 41/202, 8 December 1986.

26. See ECLAC, *Finding Solutions to the Debt Problems of Developing Countries,* ECLAC document LC/L.1230, 20 May 1999, 28.

27. Ibid., 15–27.

28. Ibid., 25–26.

29. UNCTAD, *The Least Developed Countries 2000 Report,* 141–148. For a recent evaluation with recommendations, see Nancy Birdsall, John Williamson, and Brian Deese, *Delivering on Debt Relief: From IMF Gold to a New Aid Architecture* (Washington, D.C.: Center for Global Development Institute for Economic Affairs, 2002).

30. World Bank, *World Development Report 1991: The Challenge of Development* (New York: Oxford University Press, 1991).

31. See Milton Friedman, *Essays in Positive Economics* (Chicago: University of Chicago Press, 1953); Milton Friedman, *Capitalism and Freedom* (Chicago: University of Chicago, 1962); Gary Becker, *The Economic Approach to Human Behaviour* (Chicago: University of Chicago Press, 1976).

32. Friedrich A. von Hayek, *The Road to Serfdom* (London: Routledge & Sons, 1944).

33. Hla Myint, *Theories of Welfare Economics* (Cambridge, Mass.: Harvard University Press, 1948); Hla Myint, *The Economics of the Developing Countries* (London: Hutchinson & Co., 1964); Peter Bauer, *Economic Analysis and Policy in Underdeveloped Countries* (Durham, N.C.: Duke University Press, 1957); Harry G. Johnson, *Economic Policies towards Less Developed Countries* (London: George Allen and Unwin, 1967).

34. Bela Balassa, *Economic Growth, Trade and Balance of Payments in Developing Countries, 1960–1965* (Washington, D.C.: World Bank, 1968); Ian Little, Tibor Scitovsky, and Maurice Scott, *Industry and Trade in Some Developing Countries* (London: Oxford University Press, 1970); Jagdish Bhagwati and Anne Krueger, *Foreign Trade Regimes and Economic Development: Liberalization Attempts and Consequences* (Cambridge: Ballinger, 1978); Deepak Lal, *Against Dirigism* (San Francisco: ICS Press, 1994).

35. See the series of World Development Reports issued by the World Bank in the 1980s and early 1990s, especially the *World Development Report 1991: The Challenge of Development* (New York: Oxford University Press, 1991); and World Bank, *The East Asian Miracle* (New York: Oxford University Press, 1993).

36. Javier Martinez and Alvaro Diaz, *Chile: The Great Transformation* (Washington, D.C.: Brookings Institute, and Geneva: UNRISD, 1996).

37. Alejandro Foxley and Claudio Sapelli, "Chile's Political Economy in the 1990s: Some Governance Issues," in *Chile: Recent Policy Lessons and Emerging Challenges,* ed. Guillermo Perry and Danny Leipziger (Washington, D.C.: World Bank, 1999), 393–424.

38. Klaus Schmidt-Hebbel, "Chile's Take Off: Facts, Challenges, Lessons," in Perry and Leipziger, eds., *Chile: Recent Policy Lessons and Emerging Challenges,* 63–108.

39. UN, "Dilemmas of Macro-Economic Management: Stabilization and Adjustment in Developing Countries," in *Supplement to World Economic Survey, 1990–1991* (New York: UN, 1992).

40. John Williamson, "The Washington Consensus Revisited," in *Economic and Social Development into the Twenty-first Century,* ed. Louis Emmerij (Baltimore: John Hopkins University Press, 1997), 48–61.

41. "International Development Strategy for the 3rd United Nations Development Decade," General Assembly resolution A/35/56, 5 December 1980.

42. See, for example, ECLAC, *The Economic Crisis: Policies for Adjustment, Stabilization, and Growth* (Santiago: ECLAC, 1986); Alexander H. Sarris, *Agricultural Stabilization and Structural Adjustment Policies in Developing Countries* (Rome: FAO, 1987).

43. See Commission on Global Governance, *Our Global Neighborhood: The Basic Vision* (Geneva: The Commission, 1995), 279–283.

44. UNICEF, *State of the World's Children* (New York: Oxford University Press, 1984), 169–172.

45. UNICEF, *The Impact of World Recession on Children* (New York: UNICEF, 1983).

46. See Cornia, Jolly, and Stewart, *Adjustment with a Human Face* (New York: Oxford University Press, 1987), Part 1, especially Chapters 1 and 2.

47. The phrase "adjustment with a human face" was first used by Richard Jolly in 1985 as the title of the second Barbara Ward Memorial Lecture at the Society of International Development in Rome.

48. See Lance Taylor, *Varieties of Stabilization Experiences: Towards Sensible Macroeconomics in the Third World* (London: Oxford University Press, 1988), v.

49. See Ghai, ed., *The IMF and the South*; Martinez and Diaz, *Chile: The Great Transformation.* A devastating evaluation of the Social Dimensions of Adjustment Project is in UNDP, *The Social Dimensions of Adjustment (SDA) Project: An Interim*

Evaluation, vol. I, *Main Report* and vol. II, *Report to the Governing Council of the UNDP* (New York: UNDP, 1991).

50. For more information on the Washington Consensus, see Louis Emmerij, Richard Jolly, and Thomas G. Weiss, *Ahead of the Curve? UN Ideas and Global Challenges* (Bloomington: Indiana University Press, 2001), Chapter 5.

51. For more information on this issue, see ibid., Chapter 6; and Yves Berthelot, ed., *Unity and Diversity in Development Ideas: Perspectives from the UN Regional Commissions* (Bloomington: Indiana University Press, 2004), Chapter 2.

52. Prewar Czechoslovakia was perhaps the sole exception.

53. Keith Griffin, *Alternative Strategies for Economic Development* (London: Macmillan Press, 1989), Chapter 8.

54. Carmelo Mesa-Lago, *The Economy of Socialist Cuba* (Albuquerque: University of New Mexico Press, 1981); Manuel Pastor Jr. and Andrew Zimbalist, "Waiting for Change: Adjustment and Reform in Cuba," *World Development* 23, no. 5 (May 1995): 705–720.

55. Dharam Ghai, Cristobal Kay, and Peter Peek, *Labour and Development in Rural Cuba* (London: Macmillan Press, 1988), 119.

56. Carmelo Mesa-Lago, *Are Economic Reforms Propelling Cuba to the Market?* (Miami: University of Miami, 1994); Pastor and Zimbalist, "Waiting for Change: Adjustment and Reform in Cuba"; Solon Barraclough, "Protecting Social Achievements During Economic Crisis in Cuba," in *Social Development and Public Policy: A Study of Some Successful Experiences,* ed. Dharam Ghai (London: Macmillan and Geneva: UNRISD, 2000), 229–276.

57. Dharam Ghai, Christobel Kay, and Peter Peek, *Labor and Development in Rural Cuba* (London: Macmillan Press, 1988); and Solon Barraclough, "Protecting Social Achievements During Economic Crisis in Cuba, " 245.

58. Emmerij, Jolly, and Weiss, *Ahead of the Curve,* Table 6.1, 164.

59. Ibid., 155.

60. Olivier Blanchard et al., *Post-Communist Reform: Pain and Progress* (Cambridge, Mass.: MIT Press, 1993).

61. Vaclav Klaus, *Renaissance: The Rebirth of Liberty in the Heart of Europe* (Washington, D.C.: Cato Institute, 1997); Leszek Balcerowicz, *Socialism, Capitalism, Transformation* (Budapest: Central European University Press, 1995).

62. See Berthelot, *Unity and Diversity in Development Ideas,* Chapter 2.

63. ECE, *Economic Survey of Europe 1989–1990* (Geneva: UN, 1990).

64. Ibid.

65. See Berthelot, *Unity and Diversity in Development Ideas,* Chapter 2.

66. See Carl Riskin, *China's Political Economy: The Quest for Development Since 1949* (New York: Oxford University Press, 1987).

67. Dharam Ghai, Cristobal Kay, and Peter Peek, *Labour and Development in Rural Cuba* (London: Macmillan Press, 1988), 119.

68. Emmerij, Jolly, and Weiss, *Ahead of the Curve,* 128.

69. See UN, *Yearbook of the United Nations, 1964* (New York: UN, 1966), 205–206.

70. UN, *Enlargement of the Exchange Economy in Tropical Africa* (New York: UN, 1954); UN, *Scope and Structure of Money Economies in Tropical Africa* (New York: UN, 1958); UN, *Economic Survey of Africa Since 1950* (New York: UN, 1959).

71. See UNCTAD resolution 24 (II), 26 March 1968.

72. For their reports on the LDCs, see "Report of Group of Experts on Special Measures in Favour of Least Developed Among Developing Countries," UNCTAD document TD/B/288, 24 November–5 December 1969; and the second report, UNCTAD document TD/B/349/Rev.1, 26 April–5 May 1971.

73. See General Assembly resolution 2724 (XXV), 15 December 1970. The CDP's work on a definition of LDCs can be found in CDP, *Report on the Seventh Session, 22 March–1 April 1971*, ECOSOC document E/4990, May 1971, Part II.

74. Afghanistan, Benin, Bhutan, Botswana, Burundi, Chad, Ethiopia, Guinea, Haiti, the Lao Democratic People's Republic, Lesotho, Malawi, Maldives, Mali, Nepal, Niger, Rwanda, Somalia, Sudan, Uganda, Tanzania, Upper Volta (now Burkina Faso), Samoa, and the Yemen Arab Republic.

75. While the Bretton Woods institutions have their own typology of developing countries, they also give priority to the poorest and least-developed countries, but without formally recognizing the category of least-developed countries.

76. UNCTAD, *The Least Developed Countries 2000 Report* (New York and Geneva: UN, 2000), 234.

77. Ibid., 243.

78. UNCTAD, *The Least Developed Countries 2000 Report*, Chapters 4 and 6.

79. See UNCTAD resolution 122 (V), 3 June 1979; and UN, *Yearbook of the United Nations, 1979*, (New York: UN, 1982), 568–569.

80. United Nations Conference on the Least Developed Countries, *Report of the Second United Nations Conference on the Least Developed Countries: Paris, 3–14 September 1990* (New York: United Nations, 1991).

81. Ibid., 3.

82. See *Report of the Second United Nations Conference on the Least Developed Countries.*

83. Ibid.

84. Ibid.

85. UNCTAD, *The Least Developed Countries Report 2002: Escaping the Poverty Trap* (New York and Geneva: UN, 2002), 268.

86. Ibid.

87. UNCTAD, *The Least Developed Countries 2000 Report*, v.

88. "Report of the Third United Nations Conference on the Least Developed Countries, held in Brussels, Belgium, from 14 to 20 May 2001," General Assembly document A/CONF.191/13, 20 September 2001, 7–86.

89. Ibid., 8, para. 9 of the "Brussels Declaration."

90. Ibid., 81.

91. Ibid., 82–83.

92. UNCTAD, *The Least Developed Countries 2000 Report*, viii.

93. Ibid., viii–ix.

94. Ibid., ix.

95. Ibid., xii–xv.

96. Oral History Interview of Gerald Karl Helleiner, 4–5 December 2000, 74, in the Oral History Collection of the United Nations Intellectual History Project, The Graduate Center, The City University of New York.

7. The 1990s

1. Boutros Boutros-Ghali, *An Agenda for Peace, 1995* (New York: UN, 1995); the first edition was published in 1992 under the title *An Agenda for Peace: Preventive Diplomacy, Peacemaking, and Peace-keeping.*

2. Boutros Boutros-Ghali, *An Agenda for Development* (New York: UN, 1995).

3. John Williamson, "The Washington Consensus Revisited," in *Economic and Social Development into the Twenty-First Century,* ed. Louis Emmerij (Baltimore: John Hopkins University Press, 1997), 48–61.

4. For a summary see UNDP, *Human Development Report 1999* (New York: Oxford University Press, 1999), 38–39. The World Bank, *World Development Report 2003* (New York: Oxford University Press, 2002) states that "income inequality is rising. Average income in the wealthiest 20 countries is 37 times that in the poorest 20 countries—twice the ratio in 1970" (183).

5. Guy Standing, "Social Protection in Central and Eastern Europe: A Tale of Slipping Anchors and Torn Safety Nets," in *Welfare States in Transition,* ed. G. Esping-Andersen (London: Sage, 1996).

6. Alan Roe and Harmut Schneider, *Adjustment and Equity in Ghana* (Paris: OECD Development Centre, 1992).

7. In 1987 the government of Ghana, in cooperation with the World Bank and other agencies, launched the Programme of Action to Mitigate the Social Costs of Adjustment (PAMSCAD), aimed at supporting the government's social programs to alleviate social tension resulting from the adoption of structural adjustment programs. Funding for the program came mainly from donors. This program emphasized community initiatives, employment generation through public works and food-for-work projects, training and placement services for public-sector workers, and basic-needs provision such as wells, low-cost sanitation, and essential drugs. Various reviews of PAMSCAD revealed that it suffered from too wide a spectrum of program activities and from overly time-consuming and complex reporting requirements stipulated by the various participating donor agencies; thus, the program proved to be much slower to implement than originally expected.

8. Sérgio Pereira Leite et al., *Ghana: Economic Development in a Democratic Environment* (Washington, D.C.: IMF, 2000); World Bank, *World Development Report,* various years.

9. Pereira Leite, *Ghana: Economic Development in a Democratic Environment,* 9.

10. OECD-DAC, *Shaping the 21st Century: The Contribution of Development Co-operation* (Paris: OECD, 1996).

11. Unpublished paper by Sakiko Fukuda Parr and Selim Jahan (1996). In 1995, the Japanese delegation to OECD requested it to prepare a paper on development goals. The resulting paper was judged by the delegation to be uninspiring and lacking in specifics. The Japanese delegation then turned to the Human Development Report Office of the UNDP to informally prepare a report. The subsequent document contained many of the goals for 2015 later adopted as the Millennium Development Goals. The 1996 paper also drew on some of the goals agreed at the World Summit for Children though extended to 2015, as had earlier been done by the UNFPA for the Conference on International Population and Development in Cairo, 1994.

12. See "United Nations Millennium Declaration," General Assembly resolution A/RES/55/2, 8 September 2000.

13. See UN, *The United Nations and Human Rights: 1945–1995,* The United Nations Blue Books Series, vol. VII (New York: UN, 1995).

14. General Assembly resolution 217 (III) A, 10 December 1948.

15. See General Assembly resolution 260 (III) A, 9 December 1948.

16. See General Assembly resolution 317 (IV), 2 December 1949.

17. This convention was adopted on 28 July 1951 by the UN Conference of Plenipotentiaries on the Status of Refugees and Stateless Persons convened pursuant to General Assembly resolution 429 (V), 14 December 1950. For the full text of the Convention relating to the Status of Refugees, see *United Nations Treaty Series* 189, no. 2545 (1954): 137.

18. See General Assembly resolution 640 (VII), 20 December 1952.

19. See General Assembly resolution 1763 (XVII) A, 7 November 1962.

20. This convention was adopted by General Assembly resolution 34/180, 18 December 1979 and entered into force on 3 September 1981.

21. See General Assembly resolution 1386 (XIV), 20 November 1959; and the "Convention on the Rights of the Child," General Assembly resolution 44/25, 20 November 1989. The convention entered into force in 1990.

22. See General Assembly resolution 2200 (XXI) A, 16 December 1966.

23. UN, *The United Nations and Human Rights: 1945–1995,* 38.

24. See General Assembly resolution 2106 (XX) A, 21 December 1965.

25. See General Assembly resolution 39/46, 10 December 1984.

26. This convention was adopted by General Assembly resolution 3068 (XXVIII), 30 November 1973, which entered into force on 18 July 1976.

27. See "Declaration on the Rights of the Persons Belonging to National or Ethnic, Religious and Linguistic Minorities," General Assembly resolution 47/135, 18 December 1992; and "International Human Rights Instruments" in the UN High Commissioner for Human Rights website at http://www.unhchr.ch/html/menu3/b/d_minori.htm.

28. See "Draft United Nations Declaration on the Rights of Indigenous Peoples," Sub-Commission on Prevention of Discrimination and Protection of Minorities resolution 1994/45, 26 August 1994; and other documents included in the "Indigenous Peoples" section of the UNHCHR website: www.unhchr.ch.

29. See "International Convention on the Protection of the Rights of All Migrant Workers and Members of Their Families," General Assembly resolution 45/158, 18 December 1990.

30. See General Assembly resolution 41/128, 4 December 1986.

31. It was established by the Commission on Human Rights resolution 1993/22, 4 March 1993.

32. At the 4th session of the Working Group on the Right to Development in February 2003, some developed-country delegates argued that the right to development was a completely national matter and did not involve any obligation on the part of the international community. They even argued that the working group should be terminated! See South Centre, "Human Rights: Questioning the Right to Development," *South Bulletin* 55 (15 April 2003): 10–11.

33. See the Vienna Declaration and Programme of Action, Section I, para. 14, in *Report of the World Conference on Human Rights: Report of the Secretary-General,* General Assembly document A/CONF.157/24, Part I, 13 October 1993, 24.

34. UNDP, *Human Development Report 2000* (New York: Oxford University Press, 2000).

35. ILO, *Report of the Director-General: Decent Work* (Geneva: ILO, 1999).

36. Ibid., 3.

37. World Bank, *Sri Lanka: Recapturing Missed Opportunities* (Washington, D.C.: World Bank, 2000); Godfrey Gunatilleke, "Sri Lanka's Social Achievements and Challenges," in *Social Development and Public Policy,* ed. Dharam Ghai (London: Macmillan, and Geneva: UNRISD, 2000), 141–145.

38. Lal Jayawardena, "Sri Lanka," in Hollis Chenery, the World Bank, and the University of Sussex, *Redistribution with Growth: Policies to Improve Income Distribution in Developing Countries in the Context of Economic Growth* (London: Oxford University Press, 1974), 274.

39. Gunatilleke, "Sri Lanka's Social Achievements and Challenges," 164.

40. World Bank, *World Development Report 2000/2001: Attacking Poverty* (Washington, D.C.: World Bank, 2000).

41. UNDP, *Human Development Report 2000,* 20.

42. Ibid., 22.

43. Ibid., 24.

44. Information about the UN work on governance can be found at www.un.org/partners/civil_society/m-gov.htm.

45. Commission on Global Governance, *Our Global Neighborhood: The Basic Vision* (Oxford; New York: Oxford University Press, 1995).

46. For a review of work relevant to poverty and development, see Caroline Thomas, *Global Governance, Development and Human Security* (London: Pluto Press, 2000).

47. See *Gemeinsame Verantwortung in den 90er Jahren: die Stockholmer Initiative zu globaler Sicherheit und Weltordnung—Die Charta der Vereinten Nationen [Common Responsibility in the 1990s: The Stockholm Initiative on Global Security and Governance—The Charter of the United Nations]* (Bonn: Stiftung Entwicklung und Frieden, 1991).

48. "Security in the Global Neighbourhood," The Second Global Security Lecture by Sir Shridath Ramphal, co-chairman, The Commission on Global Governance, University of Cambridge, June 1995.

49. Commission on Global Governance, *Our Global Neighborhood,* 2.

50. Authors' translation from the oral history interview of Boutros Boutros-Ghali, 5 May 2001, 58, in the Oral History Collection of the United Nations Intellectual History Project, The Graduate Center, The City University of New York.

51. Mahbub ul Haq, the founder-originator of the Human Development Report, set out his thinking in *Reflections on Human Development* (New York: Oxford University Press, 1995). For further elaboration of these ideas, see Amartya Sen, *Development as Freedom* (Oxford: Oxford University Press, 1999); Amartya Sen, *Commodities and Capabilities* (Amsterdam: North Holland, 1985); Amartya Sen, *On Ethics and Economics* (Oxford; New York: B. Blackwell, 1987).

52. Much of the UNRISD work in the 1960s and 1970s was devoted to developing, refining, and classifying social indicators for intercountry comparisons. While the authors developed several profiles of social development performance, for methodological reasons they had hesitations about constructing a composite index. See D. McGrahanan et al., *Contents and Measurement of Socio-Economic Development: An Empirical Enquiry* (New York: Praeger, 1970); and D. McGrahanan, Eduardo Pizarro, and C. Richard, *Measurement and Analysis of Socio-Economic Development* (Geneva: UNRISD, 1985).

53. UNDP, *Human Development Report 2000,* 2.

54. Oral History Interview of Jacques Polak, 15 March 2000, 41, in the Oral History Collection of the United Nations Intellectual History Project, The Graduate Center, The City University of New York.

55. For further details and analysis of world conferences over the past thirty years, see Louis Emmerij, Richard Jolly, and Thomas G. Weiss, *Ahead of the Curve? UN Ideas and Global Challenges* (Bloomington: Indiana University Press, 2001), Chapter 4.

56. Rachel Carson, *Silent Spring* (Boston: Houghton Mifflin, 1962); Donella H. Meadows et al., *The Limits to Growth: A Report for the Club of Rome's Project on the Predicament of Mankind* (London: Pan Books, 1972).

57. Esther Boserup, *Women's Role in Economic Development* (London: Allen & Unwin, 1970).

58. See "Institutional and Financial Arrangements for International Environmental Cooperation," General Assembly resolution 2997 (XXVII), 15 December 1972.

59. The International Research and Training Institute for the Advancement of Women (INSTRAW) was established by General Assembly resolution 3520 (XXX), 15 December 1975.

60. The United Nations Development Fund for Women (UNIFEM) was established by General Assembly resolution 39/125, 14 December 1984.

61. See *Report of the World Food Conference, Rome, 5–16 November 1974* (New York: United Nations, 1975); and "World Food Conference," General Assembly resolution 3348 (XXIX), 17 December 1974.

62. For the final report, see the *Report of the World Conference on Human Rights: Report of the Secretary-General.*

63. Emmerij, Jolly, and Weiss, *Ahead of the Curve,* Chapter 4.

64. See Gus Edgren and Dharam Ghai, *Capacity Building for Eradicating Poverty in Vietnam: An Impact Evaluation of UN System Activities in 1985–97* (2001), available online at www.un.org/esa/coordination/coordocs/Vietnam_rep.pdf.

65. See Kofi Annan, *We the Peoples: The Role of the United Nations in the 21st Century: Report of the Secretary-General* (New York: United Nations, 2000).

66. "United Nations Millennium Declaration."

67. Oral History Interview of Gert Rosenthal, 3 January 2001, 44, in the Oral History Collection of the United Nations Intellectual History Project, The Graduate Center, The City University of New York.

68. Ignacy Sachs summarized the need in relation to the United Nations University (UNU), which he believed had let the world down in terms of international research of quality: "The UNU in theory has the intellectual independence necessary for it to criticize one Agency or another from a substance point of view. Au lieu de ronronner comme on ronronne dans toutes les évaluations intérieures." Author's translation from the oral history interview of Ignacy Sachs, 9 May 2000, 22, in the Oral History Collection of the United Nations Intellectual History Project, The Graduate Center, The City University of New York.

8. Building the Human Foundations

1. WHO, *The World Health Report 1998: Life in the 21st Century—A Vision for All* (Geneva: WHO, 1998), 19.

2. UNESCO, *World Education Report 2000: The Right to Education—Towards Education for All Throughout Life* (Paris: UNESCO, 2000), 16 and Annex 1, 91–109.

3. The "Declaration Concerning the Aims and Purposes of the International Labour Organization" was adopted in Philadelphia on 10 May 1944 by the General Conference of the International Labour Organization; for the text, see UN, *Yearbook of the United Nations, 1946–1947* (New York: UN, 1947).

4. The Convention on the Elimination of All Forms of Discrimination against Women was adopted by the General Assembly on 18 December 1979; see *United Nations Treaty Series* 1249, no. 20378 (1983): 13.

5. "Convention on the Rights of the Child," General Assembly resolution 44/25, 20 November 1989. This text can also be found in UNICEF, *First Call for Children* (New York: UNICEF, 2000).

6. Convention on the Rights of the Child, Articles 24 and 28.

7. Data from the UN Population Division data files, 2000, as quoted in Louis Emmerij, Richard Jolly, and Thomas G. Weiss, *Ahead of the Curve? UN Ideas and Global Challenges* (Bloomington: Indiana University Press, 2001), 18, Table 1.1.

8. Ibid., 17.

9. See UNESCO, *Report of the Director-General on the Activities of the Organization in 1948* (Paris: UNESCO, 1948), quoted in Richard Symonds and Michael Carder, *The United Nations and the Population Question, 1945–1970: A Population Council Book* (New York: McGraw-Hill, 1973), 31.

10. Population figures and projections taken from WHO, *The World Health Report 1998* (Geneva: WHO, 1998), 2 and 119.

11. World Bank, *World Development Indicators 2000* (Washington, D.C.: World Bank, 2000), 33.

12. See "Population Commission," ECOSOC resolution 3 (III), 3 October 1946.

13. UN, Population Division, Department of Social Affairs, *The Determinants and Consequences of Population Trends: A Summary of the Findings of Studies on the Relationships between Population Changes and Economic and Social Conditions,* Population Studies, no. 17 (New York: UN, 1953), 160–162.

14. The actual projection was by Colin Clark, who predicted that the world population would grow at 1 percent per annum to reach 3.480 billion in 1990. This would imply 3.844 billion in 2000. See Colin Clark, "The World's Capacity to Feed and Clothe Itself," *The Way Ahead* II, no. 2 (1949), 75.

15. UN, "The Past and Future Growth of World Population: A Long-Range View," *Population Bulletin,* no 1 (December 1951): 1–12.

16. See Symonds and Carder, *The United Nations and the Population Question, 1945–1970.* Chapter 1 gives a good summary of the widespread concerns in many European countries with falling birth rates and the prospect of declining population. At the same time, they note that in the immediate postwar period, some distinguished conservationists were drawing attention to the exploding population growth and warning "often in tones of deep gloom, of the dangers to the human environment of continued rapid population growth." They cite Sir Frank Fraser Darling in Britain and Fairfield Osborn and William Vogt in the United States (ibid., Chapter 4, 36).

17. In 1931, the Indian census commissioner had pointed out that the rate of population increase was from most points of view a cause for alarm rather than for satisfaction. The report of the 1931 census noted that Madras already had a Neo-Malthusian League with two maharajahs, three High Court judges, and four men very prominent in public life as its sponsors. Symonds and Carder, *The United Nations and the Population Question,* ix.

18. Ibid., xiv.

19. Ibid., 11–19.

20. Ibid., 21.

21. This of course was not the first time the links between women's status and fertility had been stressed. The 1974 World Population Plan of Action had called on governments to formulate population and development policies that would respond to women's needs, and similar concerns were expressed at the International Women's Year Conference in Mexico a year later.

22. UN, Department of International Economic and Social Affairs, *Review and Appraisal of the World Population Plan of Action: 1984 Report* (New York: UN, 1986).

23. U.S. Bureau of the Census, quoted in Bjorn Lomborg, *The Sceptical Environmentalist: Measuring the Real State of the World* (Cambridge: Cambridge University Press, 2001), 47.

24. Chapter titled "Asia and the Pacific," in Nafis Sadik and the UN Fund for Population Activities, *Population: The UNFPA Experience* (New York: UN, 1984), 34.

25. In East Asia and the Pacific. The average for all of Asia is about the same as for Latin America and the Caribbean. See UNDP, *Human Development Report 2001* (New York: Oxford University Press, 2001), 157.

26. Sadik, *Population*, 1–2.

27. See the "Proclamation of Teheran," Final Act of the International Conference on Human Rights, Teheran, 22 April–13 May 1968, General Assembly A/CONF. 32/41 at 3 (1968), para 16. Available online at http://heiwww.unige.ch/humanrts/instree/l2ptichr.htm.

28. Quoted in Symonds and Carder, *The United Nations and the Population Question*, 175.

29. UN, *Report of the United Nations World Population Conference 1974* (New York: UN, 1975), 11.

30. Devesh Kapur, John P. Lewis, and Richard Webb, eds., *The World Bank: Its First Half Century* (Washington, D.C.: Brookings, 1997), 1: 348. The earlier conversion is well described in Symonds and Carder, *The United Nations and the Population Question*, Chapters 15–17.

31. UN, *Review and Appraisal of the World Population Plan of Action: 1984 Report*, 148.

32. ECOSOC called for the International Health Conference, which met in New York from 19 June to 22 July 1946; see International Health Conference, *Economic and Social Council Report of the International Health Conference: Held in New York from 19 June to 22 July 1946* (Lake Success, New York: United Nations, 1948).

33. UN, *Review and Appraisal of the World Population Plan of Action: 1984 Report*, 67.

34. See "Population Growth and Social and Economic Development," ECOSOC resolution 1048 (XXXVII), 15 August 1964, item 21; "Work Programs and Priorities in Populations Fields," ECOSOC resolution 1084 (XXXIX), 30 July 1965, item 19; "Population Growth and Economic Development," General Assembly resolution 2211 (XXI), 17 December 1966.

35. The World Population Plan of Action was adopted by the conference on 30 August 1974; text of the plan in UN, *Report of the United Nations World Population Conference 1974*, Part I, Chapter 1.

36. UN, *Review and Appraisal of the World Population Plan of Action: 1984 Report*, 27.

37. The UN undertook a careful comparison of the Cairo Program of Action with the Bucharest World Population Plan of Action and the Mexico City Recommendations. This concluded that "the contribution of the [Cairo] Program of Action stands out not as an isolated landmark but rather as a highly important and timely incremental step on the road that began at Bucharest in 1974." Department for Economic and Social Information and Policy Analysis, Population Division, *Population Consensus at Cairo, Mexico City and Bucharest: An Analytical Comparison* (New York: UN, 1995), 7.

38. E. Burnet and W. A. Aykroyd, "Nutrition and Public Health," *Quarterly Bulletin of the Health Organisation of the League of Nations* 4, no. 2 (June 1935): 1–52.

39. Cited in John Boyd Orr, *As I Recall: Memoirs of a Nobel Prize Peace Winner* (New York: Doubleday, 1967), 119–120.

40. League of Nations, *Final Report of the Mixed Committee of the League of Nations on the Relation of Nutrition to Health, Agriculture and Economic Policy*, League of Nations document A.13, 1937, Part II. Economic and Financial.

41. See United Nations Conference on Food and Agriculture, *United Nations Conference on Food and Agriculture: Hot Springs, Virginia, United States of America, 18th May–3rd June, 1943. Section Reports of the Conference* (London: H. M. Stationery Office, 1943).

42. This account relies heavily on Boyd Orr, *As I Recall,* especially 160–195.

43. Second session of the FAO Conference held in Copenhagen, 2–13 September 1946; see FAO, *Report of the Second Session of the Conference held at Copenhagen, Denmark, 2–13 September 1946* (Washington, D. C.: FAO, 1946).

44. The full story of the World Food Programme will be found in breadth and detail in D. John Shaw, *The UN World Food Program and the Development of Food Aid* (New York: Palgrave, 2001).

45. J. M. Cohen and M. J. Cohen, *The Penguin Dictionary of Twentieth-Century Quotations* (London: Penguin Books, 1993), 214.

46. See UN, *Human Rights: A Compilation of International Instruments,* vol. 1, 2nd part: *Universal Instruments* (New York; Geneva: UN, 1994), 531–536. The declaration was adopted on 16 November 1974 by the World Food Conference and endorsed by General Assembly resolution 3348 (XXIX) of 17 December 1974.

47. See "World Food Conference," General Assembly resolution 3848 (XXIX), 17 December 1974.

48. See FAO, *Report of the World Food Summit 1996* (Rome: FAO, 1997).

49. Ibid.

50. FAO, *The State of Food Insecurity in the World, 1999* (Rome: FAO, 2000).

51. George H. Beaton, "UNA-CC Sub Committee on Nutrition," *SCN: The First 21 Years,* unpublished manuscript, March 1998.

52. The conceptual framework was the creation of Urban Jonsson, who was with the nutritional program of the UN University for about ten years, following which he became director of nutrition and regional director for UNICEF.

53. Alfred Sommer and Keith P. West Jr., *Vitamin A Deficiency: Health, Survival and Vision* (New York: Oxford University Press, 1996).

54. WHO, *The World Health Report 2002: Reducing Risks, Promoting Healthy Life* (Geneva: WHO, 2002), 55.

55. UNICEF, *Progress Since the World Summit for Children: A Statistical Review* (New York: UNICEF, 2001), 17; and UNICEF, *State of the World's Children 2002* (New York: UNICEF, 2002), 87.

56. V. R. Fuchs, "Health Economics," in *The New Palgrave: A Dictionary of Economics,* ed. John Eatwell, Murray Milgate, and Peter Newman (London: Macmillan, 1987), 615.

57. Kapur, Lewis, and Webb, *The World Bank: Its First Half Century,* 1: 265.

58. Ibid., 326–327.

59. WHO, *The World Health Report, 1998,* 23.

60. Ibid., 144.

61. Universal Declaration of Human Rights (1948), Article 25.

62. See WHO, *Basic Documents,* 45th edition (Geneva: WHO, 2001), 1.

63. Norman Howard-Jones, "The Scientific Background of the International Sanitary Conferences, 1851–1938," in WHO, *History of International Public Health,* vol. 1 (Geneva: WHO, 1975).

64. See *Venice Sanitary Conference, 1891–1893,* FO 83/1280-4, 1573 (London: Her Majesty's Stationery Office, 1893).

65. See ECOSOC, *Report of the International Health Conference* (1946); and WHO, *Basic Documents,* 5–10.

66. WHO, *The World Health Report, 1998,* 45 and 95.

67. UNICEF, *Progress Since the World Summit for Children,* 9.

68. See WHO and UNICEF, *International Conference on Primary Health Care, 6–12 September 1978, Alma-Ata, USSR* (Geneva: WHO/UNICEF, 1979).

69. See WHO, *The World Health Report 1998,* Chapter 5.

70. UNICEF, *Progress Since the World Summit for Children,* 141.

71. See, for instance, the data given in UNDP, *Human Development Report 2000* (New York: Oxford University Press, 2000), Statistical Tables 16 and 14.

72. Universal Declaration of Human Rights, Article 26.

73. UNESCO, *Basic Facts and Figures: International Statistics Relating to Education, Culture, and Mass Communications 1958* (Paris: UNESCO, 1959), 11.

74. International Covenant on Economic, Social and Cultural Rights, Article 13, cited in UNESCO, *World Education Report 2000,* 18.

75. UNESCO, *EFA Global Monitoring Report 2002: Education for All: Is the World on Track?* (Paris: UNESCO, 2002), 16.

76. Ibid., 245.

77. This plan was adopted by thirty-one African states and territories and four European nations during a conference on the development of education in Africa held at Addis Ababa in May 1961; see UN, *Yearbook of the United Nations 1961* (New York: UN, 1963), 610.

78. See UNESCO, *World Education Report 2000,* 46–47.

79. Kapur, Lewis, and Webb, *The World Bank: Its First Half Century,* 1: 259–260.

80. Ibid., 260.

81. Jan Tinbergen et al., *Econometric Models of Education: Some Applications* (Paris: OECD, 1965).

82. "Eradication of Illiteracy in Non-Self-Governing Territories," General Assembly resolution 330 (IV), 2 December 1949, cited in UNESCO, *World Education Report 2000,* 29.

83. Ibid., 33.

84. Ibid., 34.

85. Ibid., 32.

86. Ibid., 68.

87. UNESCO, *Learning to Be: The World of Education Today and Tomorrow* (Paris: UNESCO, 1972), 57.

88. "Recommendation concerning Education for International Understanding, Co-operation and Peace and Education relating to Human Rights and Fundamental Freedoms," UNESCO General Conference, 18th Session, Paris, 19 November 1974. Available online at http://www.unesco.org/education/nfsunesco/pdf/Peace_e.pdf.

89. See the final report of the conference, which was held in Geneva on 3–8 October 1994: *International Conference on Education, 44th Session* (Paris: UNESCO, 1994), 23, point 3.4.

90. Economic theory was used to suggest that a backward-sloping supply curve might exist for peasant labor. This, it was argued, would explain why peasants who were "target workers"—aiming to earn only a fixed amount of income—would show interest in working only a few hours and, indeed, even fewer hours if the rate of pay was increased. The idea of a backward-sloping supply curve for labor in developing countries was soon discredited after empirical studies found it difficult to identify many target workers who acted in the manner described. Perhaps this failed attempt to bring cultural factors into the economics of development disillusioned economists about the value of even trying to take account of culture. Instead, the idea of the rational peasant took hold—and still remains strong, not without a good deal of empirical evidence to support it. But the main conclusion which should be drawn from this whole episode is what is shown about the ignorance of the lives of poor men and women in colonial countries.

91. UN Charter, Chapter IX, Article 55 (b).

92. Universal Declaration of Human Rights, Articles 22 and 27.

93. UNESCO, *World Culture Report 2000* (Paris: UNESCO, 2000), 19.

94. Ibid., 18.

95. Lourdes Arizpe, "The Intellectual History of Culture and Development Institutions," Conference Papers, 25 February 2002, available at www.cultureandpublicaction.org/conference/papers.htm.

96. Jomo Kenyatta, *Facing Mount Kenya: The Tribal Life of the Gikuyu* (New York: Random House, 1962).

97. See Bhikhu Parekh, *Colonialism, Tradition, and Reform: An Analysis of Gandhi's Political Discourse,* rev. ed. (Newbury Park, Calif.: Sage, 1999).

98. Oscar Lewis, *Five Families: A Mexican Case Study in the Culture of Poverty* (New York: Basic Books, 1975).

99. Katy Gardner and David Lewis, *Anthropology, Development, and the Post-Modern Challenge* (Chicago, Ill.: Pluto Press, 1996).

100. Arizpe, "The Intellectual History of Culture and Development Institutions."

101. But note that ordinary people have just as much art and intellect as the elite, though their art and intellect may not be recognized as such because they are excluded by current notions of "culture." These notions imply that if it is high culture, only the elite have it, and if it is exotic culture, only primitive peoples studied by Western anthropologists have it.

102. Of course, traditional cultures as much as contemporary ones have been influenced by power and wealth, although these were more the power and wealth of local hierarchies than of global structures. However, cultures were rarely bounded and immutable, even when there was much less global interaction.

103. Preamble of the Constitution of the United Nations Educational, Scientific and Cultural Organization, which came into force on 4 November 1946; see UN, *Yearbook of the United Nations, 1946–47,* 712.

104. UNESCO, *Les Conférences de l'UNESCO* (Paris: UNESCO, 1947), 2, quoted by Arizpe, "The Intellectual History of Culture and Development Institutions."

105. Arizpe, "The Intellectual History of Culture and Development Institutions."

106. Yudhishthir Raj Isar, "Unpacking the Cultural Policy Discourse: An International Perspective," unpublished manuscript, April 2002.

107. UNESCO, *World Culture Report 2000,* 154.

108. UNESCO, *Recommendation Concerning the Protection, at National Level, of World Cultural and Natural Heritage: Adopted by the General Conference at Its Seventeenth Session, Paris, 16 November 1972* (Paris: UNESCO, 1972).

109. The convention was adopted during UNESCO's 1972 General Conference and was drawn up by UNESCO in cooperation with the International Union for Conservation of Nature and Natural Resources; see UN, *Yearbook of the United Nations 1972* (New York: UN, 1975), 759.

110. UNESCO, *World Culture Report 2000,* 153.

111. Ibid., 156.

112. Jean Meynaud, *Social Change and Economic Development* (Paris: UNESCO, 1963).

113. Ibid., 5–6.

114. UNESCO, *Cultural Policy: A Preliminary Study* (Paris: UNESCO, 1969).

115. UNESCO, *A Study of Cultural Policy in the United States* (Paris: UNESCO, 1969).

116. See UNESCO, *World Conference on Cultural Policies, Mexico City, 26 July–6 August 1982* (Paris: UNESCO, 1982).

117. See ibid., Preamble of the "Mexico City Declaration on Cultural Policies."

118. Ibid., para. 16.

119. The commission was established at the request of the General Conference of UNESCO during its 26th session in 1991.

120. World Commission on Culture and Development, *Our Creative Diversity: Report of the World Commission on Culture and Development* (Paris: UNESCO, 1995).

121. Ibid., 15.

122. Ibid.

123. Mahbub ul Haq was the founder of the UNDP's Human Development Report and Keith Griffin and Lourdes Arizpe had been closely associated as consultants, especially in the first few years. All three were members of the commission.

124. Amartya Sen, "Culture Economics and Development," a paper contributed to the World Commission on Culture and Development, May 1995, cited in World Commission on Culture and Development, *Our Creative Diversity,* 22.

125. World Commission on Culture and Development, *Our Creative Diversity,* 46.

126. The words of Federico Mayor, the director-general of UNESCO, cited in World Commission on Culture and Development, *Our Creative Diversity,* 45.

127. UNESCO, *World Cultural Report 1998* (Paris: UNESCO, 1998), quoted in UNDP, *Human Development Report 1998* (New York: Oxford University Press, 1998), 33.

128. Ibid., 33.

129. Dag Hammarskjöld, Address at the Inauguration of the 25th Anniversary of the Museum of Modern Art, October 19, 1954, in *Public Papers of the Secretaries-General of the United Nations,* ed. Andrew W. Cordier and Wilder Foote (New York: Columbia University Press, 1972), 2: 375.

130. We are grateful to Lourdes Arizpe for the draft of this box on interpreters.

131. See "Rules of Procedure Concerning Languages: Report of the First Committee: Resolution," *Official Records of the First Part of the First Session of the General Assembly,* 10 January–14 February 1946, Item 40.

132. International Association of Conference Interpreters, *The Interpreters: A Historical Perspective* (New York: IACI, 1996), video.

133. UN Population Division, Department of Economic and Social Affairs, *World Population Prospects: 2002 Revision Highlights,* available online at http://www.un.org/esa/population/publications/wpp2002/WPP2002-HIGHLIGHTSrev1.PDF. This is based on the median projection of world population reaching 8.9 billion in 2050. The high projection is for world population to reach 10.6 billion in 2050, the low variant 7.4 billion.

134. See, for example, the final report of the Intergovernmental Conference on Cultural Policies for Development held in Stockholm, 30 March–2 April 1998, available online at http://www.unesco.org/culture/laws/stockholm/html_eng/113935eo.pdf.

9. Structural and Sectoral Change

1. FAO, *FAO: The First 40 Years, 1945–85* (Rome: FAO, 1985), 3.

2. Asher Hobson, *The International Institute of Agriculture: An Historical and Critical Analysis of its Organization, Activities and Policies of Administration* (Berkeley: University of California Press, 1931).

3. International Institute of Agriculture, *International Yearbook of Agricultural Statistics* (Rome: C. Colombo, 1922).

4. International Institute of Agriculture, *The First World Agricultural Census (1930)* (Rome: C. Colombo, 1939).

5. Several individuals played leading roles in arguing that the FAO should have a broad mandate. These include John Boyd Orr, who had led the work on nutrition in the League of Nations; Stanley Bruce, a former Australian prime minister, then high commissioner to London; and his economic advisor, Frank McDougall. Lester Pearson, later to be Canadian prime minister, who was then Canadian ambassador to the U.S., chaired the first FAO conference in Quebec.

6. Edouard Saouma, *FAO in the Front Line of Development* (Rome: FAO, 1993), 1.

7. Ibid., 5.

8. For the text of the constitution, see Appendix III in FAO, *Report of the First Session of the Conference,* held at the City of Quebec, Canada, 16 October–1 November 1945 (FAO document FAO 630 F687).

9. See FAO, *Report of the 5th Session of the Conference* (Washington, D.C.: FAO, 1950), 10–14.

10. See FAO, *Report of the 8th Session of the Conference, 4–25 November 1955* (Rome: FAO, 1956), paras. 47–58.

11. D. John Shaw, *The UN World Food Programme and the Development of Food Aid* (Basingstoke: Palgrave, 2001). Chapter 2 describes the antecedents of the World Food Programme.

12. John Boyd Orr, *As I Recall: Memoirs of a Nobel Peace Prize Winner* (New York: Doubleday, 1967), 193–194.

13. Ibid.

14. Saouma, *FAO in the Front Line,* 1.

15. Ibid., 2.

16. Ralph W. Phillips, *FAO: Its Origins, Formation and Evolution, 1945–1981* (Rome: FAO, 1981), 78.

17. Ibid., 79.

18. See Saouma, *FAO in the Front Line,* 24.

19. See ibid., 5–6.

20. Phillips, *FAO: Its Origins,* 153–154.

21. See "World Food Day," FAO resolution 1/79, 28 November 1979.

22. FAO, *World Food Survey* (Washington, D.C.: FAO, 1946).

23. Ibid.

24. FAO, *FAO: The First 40 Years,* 73.

25. *Joint FAO/WHO Expert Committee on Nutrition, Report on the First Session,* Technical Report Series, no. 16 (Geneva: WHO, 1950), 24.

26. For a critique suggesting that the standards have been heavily influenced by politics as well as science, see Nathalie Avery, Martine Drake, and Tim Lang, *Cracking the Codex: An Analysis of Who Sets World Food Standards* (London: National Food Alliance, 1993).

27. FAO, *FAO: The First 40 Years,* 75.

28. See "International Undertaking on Plant Genetic Resources," FAO Resolution 8/83, adopted 23 November 1983, at the 22nd session of the FAO Conference, Rome, 5–23 November 1983. The full text of the document is available online at ftp://ext-ftp.fao.org/ag/cgrfa/Res/C8-83E.pdf.

29. Saouma, *FAO in the Front Line,* 92.

30. Ibid., 93.

31. "Establishment of a Commission on Plant Genetic Resources," FAO resolution 9/83, 23 November 1983.

32. The convention was signed on 5 June 1992 and entered into force on 29 December 1993. For the text, see "Convention on Biological Diversity," *United Nations Treaty Series* 1760, no. 30619 (1992): 79.

33. FAO, *Report of the 7th Session of the Conference, 23 November–11 December 1953* (Rome: FAO, 1954), para. 87.

34. A detailed account can be found in D. John Shaw, *The UN World Food Programme and the Development of Food Aid* (New York: Palgrave, 2001), Chapter 2.

35. See UN, *Report of the World Food Conference, Rome, 5–16 November 1974* (New York: United Nations, 1975).

36. See "Food Sovereignty: A Right For All, Political Statement of the NGO/CSO Forum for Food Sovereignty," approved 13 June 2002 at the FAO World Food Summit, Rome, Italy, 8–13 June 2002, available online at http://www.viacampesina.org/IMG/_article_PDF/article_36.pdf; and Marcel Mazoyer and FAO, *Protecting Small Farmers and the Rural Poor in the Context of Globalization,* June 2002, available on the FAO Web site, www.fao.org. See also FAO, *The Right to Food in Theory and Practice* (Rome: FAO, 1998).

37. See Article 25, "Everyone has the right to a standard of living adequate for health and well-being of himself and of his family, including food."

38. See "International Covenant on Economic, Social and Cultural Rights," General Assembly resolution 2200 (XXI) A, 16 December 1966, Article 11.

39. Paragraph 61, objective 7.4: (e) of the "World Food Summit Plan of Action," available online with the "Rome Declaration on World Food Security" at http://www.fao.org/docrep/003/w3613e/w3613e00.htm.

40. "The Right to Adequate Food (Art. 11): Committee on Economic Social and Cultural Rights General Comment 12," CESCR document E/C.12/1999/5, 12 May 1999. Available online at http://www.unhchr.ch/tbs/doc.nsf/099b725fe87555ec8025670c004fc803/3d02758c707031d58025677f003b73b9?OpenDocument#Notes.

41. *Declaration of the World Food Summit: Five Years Later,* para. 10, adopted at the World Food Summit held at Rome, 10–13 June 2002, available online at www.fao.org/worldfoodsummit/english/index.html.

42. "World Food Summit Plan of Action," para. 1.

43. See UN, *Report of the World Food Conference, Rome, 5–16 November 1974.*

44. Shaw, *The UN World Food Programme.*

45. See "World Food Programme," General Assembly resolution 1714 (XVI), 19 December 1961.

46. See Sir Hans Singer, "Foreword" in Shaw, *The UN World Food Programme,* xx.

47. See "International Fund for Agricultural Development," World Food Conference resolution XIII, 16 November 1974, in UN, *Report of the World Food Conference,* 12–13.

48. See the final report of the external review team on *The Results and Impact of IFAD Operation,* available online at http://www.ifad.org/pub/external/english.pdf.

49. IFAD became the fifteenth UN specialized agency by an agreement concluded on 15 December 1977; see UN, *Yearbook of the United Nations 1977* (New York: UN, 1980).

50. IFAD, *Annual Report 2000: Working with the Rural Poor* (Rome: IFAD, 2001), 26–27 and 31. Since 1978, IFAD has made $6.9 billion in loans in support of nearly 600 projects. Many of the loans were co-financed with other donors and with support of over $7 billion from domestic resources in the countries concerned—adding up to a total of over $27 billion.

51. Ibid., 21.

52. See, for example, IFAD, *The Rural Poor: Survival or a Better Life? The Choice between Destruction of Resources and Sustainable Development* (2002), available online at http://www.ifad.org/events/wssd/e/index.htm.

53. IFAD, *Rural Poverty Report, 2001: The Challenge of Ending Rural Poverty* (Oxford: Oxford University Press, 2001).

54. See Press Release at http://www.transparency.org/pressreleases_archive/2003/2003.03.06.nigeria_anti_corr_act.html.

55. O. Aboyade, "The Economy of Nigeria," in *The Economies of Africa,* ed. Peter Robson and Denis A. Lury (London: George Allen and Unwin, 1969).

56. David Bevan, Paul Collier, and Jan Willem Gunning, *Nigeria and Indonesia* (New York: Oxford University Press and Washington, D.C.: World Bank, 1999).

57. UNDP, *Human Development Report 2002* (New York: Oxford University Press, 2002), 155.

58. Angus Madison, *Monitoring the World Economy, 1820–1992* (Paris: OECD Publications and Information Center, 1995), 237.

59. Stephen C. Smith, *Industrial Policy in Developing Countries* (Washington, D.C.: Economic Policy Institute, 1991); and Ajit Singh, "How Did East Asia Grow So Fast? Slow Progress towards an Analytical Consensus," *UNCTAD Discussion Paper,* no. 97 (Geneva: UNCTAD, 1995), 1–56.

60. For example, UN industrial development activities were discussed at the eighteenth session of the General Assembly. See the summary of the debates in UN, *Yearbook of the United Nations 1963* (New York: UN, 1965), 230–232.

61. Sandrine Tesner argues that UNIDO was created "despite American opposition." This opposition, she explains, "stemmed from the reluctance of placing another UN economic agency under the control of the developing countries." She adds that "the United States did not agree with the rationale of separating industrial development from the overall formulation of development policy, a view that has been reiterated in recent efforts to reform UNIDO and place it under the mandate of a larger UN body." See *The United Nations and Business: A Partnership Recovered* (New York: St. Martin's Press, 2000), 18 and 166.

62. Personal communication from François Legay.

63. UN, *The United Nations Development Decade: Proposals for Action* (New York: UN, 1962), 54. This rate of growth was the equivalent of an average of 8.7 percent per year.

64. See "Activities of the United Nations in the Field of Industrial Development," General Assembly resolution 1712 (XVI), 19 December 1961.

65. See UNIDO's Web site, www.unido.org/en/doc/3323.

66. See UNIDO, *Report of the International Symposium on Industrial Development* (New York: UN, 1969).

67. See the draft resolution presented by more than sixty countries at the Special International Conference of UNIDO, Vienna, Austria, 1–8 June 1971, UNIDO document ID/SCU/L.1, 4 June 1971.

68. The constitution was adopted on 8 April 1979 at the 2nd session of the UN Conference on Establishment of UNIDO as Specialized Agency and opened for signature on same date. See General Assembly document A/CONF.90/19, 8 April 1979.

69. See the text of the Lima Declaration and Plan of Action on Industrial Development and Co-operation, in UNIDO, *Report of the Second General Conference of the United Nations Industrial Development Organization,* UNIDO document ID/CONF.3/31, 9 May 1975.

70. See "Programme of Action on the Establishment of a New International Economic Order," General Assembly resolution 3202 (S-VI), 1 May 1974, Section III: Industrialization.

71. See UNIDO, *Report of the Second General Conference.*

72. These proposals for action were elaborated in UNIDO, *Industry 2000—New Perspectives* (New York: United Nations, 1979).

73. Ibid., 94.

74. Calculated from data on the GDP and the share of value added in industry, in World Bank, *World Development Indicators 2002* (Washington, D.C.: World Bank, 2002), Table 4.2, 208–210.

75. These are all countries which have averaged 4 percent or more per capita real GDP growth from 1975 to 1999. See UNDP, *Human Development Report 2001* (New York: Oxford University Press, 2001), 178–180.

76. UNDP, *Human Development Report 2002* (New York: Oxford University Press, 2002), 165.

77. Commission on Global Governance, *Our Global Neighborhood: The Basic Vision* (New York: Oxford University Press, 1995), 281–282.

78. The commission contained fourteen members from developing countries, two from transition countries, and ten from industrial countries.

79. See "Relationship between Disarmament and Development," General Assembly resolution 39/160, 17 December 1984, preamble.

80. World Bank, *World Development Indicators 2002,* Table 5.7, 304–306.

81. *Report of the International Conference on the Relationship between Disarmament and Development, New York, 24 August–11 September 1987,* General Assembly document A/CONF.130/39, 22 September 1987.

82. UN, *The Relationship between Disarmament and Development: Report of the Secretary-General* (New York: UN, 1982). Hereafter referred to as the Thorsson Report.

83. Devesh Kapur, John P. Lewis, and Richard Webb, eds., *The World Bank: Its First Half Century* (Washington, D.C.: Brookings, 1997), 533.

84. Dag Hammarskjöld, *The Economic and Social Consequences of Disarmament: Report of the Secretary-General* (New York: UN, 1962).

85. UN, *The United Nations Development Decade: Proposals for Action* (New York: UN, 1962).

86. Ibid., 12–13; see also 24–25.

87. See UN, *The Relationship between Disarmament and Development.*

88. Ibid.

89. The Thorsson Report, as quoted in Mac Graham et al., *Disarmament and World Development* (Oxford: Pergamon Press, 1986), 235.

90. Ibid.

91. Ibid.

92. Ibid.

93. Speech of President Ronald Reagan, 8 March 1983, quoted in Robert Andrews, *Cassell Dictionary of Contemporary Quotations* (London: Cassell, 1998), 26.

94. Klein has made these arguments in several places. A good summary can be found in the Oral History Interview of Lawrence R. Klein, 4 January 2002, in the Oral History Collection of the United Nations Intellectual History Project, The Graduate Center, The City University of New York. Klein has used the LINK model, which he originated to make estimates of the orders of magnitude of the impact of the beneficial peace dividend in developing countries.

95. UNDP, *Human Development Report 1994* (New York: Oxford University Press, 1994). Though note that the 1989 *Report on the World Social Situation* (New York:

United Nations, 1989) presented many of their issues in terms of the need for improving security in many social situations.

96. UNDP, *Human Development Report 1999* (New York: Oxford University
Press, 1999).

10. The Record of Performance

1. See our companion volume, Michael Ward, *Quantifying the World: UN Ideas
and Statistics* (Bloomington: Indiana University Press, 2004).

2. Angus Maddison, *The World Economy: A Millennial Perspective* (Paris: OECD
Development Centre Studies, 2001). This source has been used for the data in the
following six paragraphs.

3. Calculations made from data in Table A-a and Table A3-b in Maddison, *The
World Economy*, pages 173 and 214, respectively.

4. World Bank, *World Development Report 2003* (Washington, D.C.: World Bank,
2002), 2 and 183. The size of the global gaps depends considerably on which measures
for income are used, $PPP or $US GNP per capita. GNP per capita measures, which
involve international conversion at foreign exchange rates, generally lead to larger
estimates of the gaps between richer and poorer countries. Purchasing power parity
($PPP) measures convert income per capita in one country to that of another—for
example, the U.S.—using an estimate based on purchasing power equivalence.
Generally, this leads to smaller measures of global gaps. Because of index-number
problems, there is no certain or simple answer to which of these comparisons is
"correct."

5. David S. Landes, *The Wealth and Poverty of Nations* (New York: W.W. Norton
& Co., 1998), xx.

6. Data on human advance is taken from UNDP, *Human Development Report
1990* and *2002* (New York: Oxford University Press, 1990 and 2002) and for 1955 from the
UN Population Division data files, as cited in Table 1.1 in Louis Emmerij, Richard Jolly,
and Thomas G. Weiss, *Ahead of the Curve? UN Ideas and Global Challenges*
(Bloomington: Indiana University Press, 2001), 18.

7. See Mahesh S. Patel, "Reducing Social Distance between Nations," in Surendra
J. Patel, Krishna Ahooja-Patel, and Mahesh S. Patel, *Development Distance between
Nations*, International Development Studies Series no. 1 (New Delhi: Ashish Publishing
House, 1995), 139.

8. See, for instance, Carlo A. Corsini and Pier Paolo Viazzo, eds., *The Decline of
Infant Mortality in Europe, 1800–1950: Four National Case Studies* (Florence: UNICEF
International Child Development Centre, 1993).

9. UNICEF, *State of the World's Children Report* (New York: Oxford University
Press, 1989), 84. On average, infant mortality in the industrialized countries in 1950 was
estimated to be 64. See UNICEF, *Statistical Review of the Situation of Children in the
World* (New York: UNICEF, 1986), Table 2.

10. UNDP, *Human Development Report 2000* (New York: Oxford University Press,
2000), 5.

11. Ibid., 51. The Convention against Torture and Other Cruel, Inhuman or Degrading Treatment or Punishment is the sixth and least ratified of the major human rights instruments—ratified in 2000 by only 119 out of 194 countries.

12. Eric Hobsbawm, *The Age of Extremes: A History of the World, 1914–1991* (New York: Pantheon Books, 1994), 13.

13. Economic growth figures for the least-developed countries are from UNDP, *Human Development Report 2002* (New York: Oxford University Press, 2002), Table 5, 162–165 and Table 12, 190–193.

14. World Bank, *World Development Report 2003*, 183. See also Raffer Kunibert and Hans W. Singer, *The Economic North-South Divide: Six Decades of Unequal Development* (Cheltenham: Edward Elgar, 2001).

15. The World Summit for Children, held in New York on 29–30 September 1990, adopted the World Declaration on the Survival, Protection, and Development of Children and the Plan of Action for Implementing the World Declaration in the 1990s; see UN document A/45/625, Annex. Both declarations can be found on the UNICEF Web site at http://www.unicef.org/wsc.

16. UNICEF, *Progress Since the World Summit for Children: A Statistical Review* (New York: UNICEF, 2001).

17. Ibid., 27.

18. See "Proclamation of the International Drinking Water Supply and Sanitation Decade," General Assembly resolution A/35/48, 10 November 1990. The statistical results are summarized in WHO, *Drinking Water and Sanitation, 1981–1990: A Way to Health* (Geneva: WHO, 1981) and for 1990–2000 in WHO, UNICEF, and Water Supply and Sanitation Collaborative Council, *Global Water Supply and Sanitation Assessment, 2000 Report* (Geneva: WHO, 2000).

19. UNICEF, *Progress Since the World Summit for Children*, 9.

20. See, for example, "The Needs of Asia in Primary Education," UNESCO *Educational Studies and Documents*, no. 41 (1961): 8–29. For statistics, see UNESCO, "A Summary Statistical Review of Education in the World 1960–82," UNESCO document ED/BIE/CONFINTED 39/Ref. 1, 12 July 1984, summarized in UN Department of International Economic and Social Affairs, *1985 Report on the World Social Situation* (New York: United Nations, 1985), 40.

21. UNESCO, *EFA Global Monitoring Report 2002, Education for All: Is the World on Track?* (Paris: UNESCO, 2002).

22. See *World Declaration on Education for All and Framework for Action to Meet Basic Learning Needs* (New York: Inter-Agency Commission, 1990) adopted by the World Conference on Education for All—Meeting Basic Learning Needs, 5–9 March 1990, Jomtien, Thailand. The Inter-Agency Commission consists of representatives from the UNDP, UNESCO, UNICEF, and the World Bank.

23. UNESCO, *EFA Global Monitoring Report 2002*, 15.

24. See OECD-Development Assistance Committee, *Development Co-operation Committee, 2002 Report* (Paris: OECD, 2002) for full statistics. UNDP, *Human Development Report 2002* (New York: Oxford University Press, 2002), 202, provides a summary of ODA data for 1990 and 2000 in Table 15.

25. Moises Syrquin and Hollis B. Chenery, *Patterns of Development, 1950–1983,* World Bank Discussion Paper no. 41 (Washington, D.C.: World Bank, 1989).

11. UN Contributions and Missed Opportunities

1. Country records of UN support have recently been prepared in China and Cuba and are under way in Kenya under UNDP auspices.

2. UN Charter, Preamble.

3. See, for example, ILO, *Agrarian Reform and Employment* (Geneva: ILO, 1971).

4. The World Conference on Agrarian Reform and Rural Development, held in Rome from 12 to 20 July 1979, adopted a declaration of principles, a programme of action, and a resolution for follow-up. See *Report of the World Conference on Agrarian Reform and Rural Development, Rome, 12–20 July 1979* (Conference report WCARRD/REP), transmitted to the members of the General Assembly by a note by the Secretary-General (General Assembly document A/34/485); and FAO, *Fighting Rural Poverty: FAO's Action Programme for Agrarian Reform and Rural Development* (Rome: FAO, 1983).

5. "Reaffirmation of General Assembly Resolution 1522 (XV) on the Accelerated Flow of Capital and Technical Assistance to the Developing Countries," General Assembly resolution 1711 (XVI), 19 December 1961.

6. See *International Development Strategy. Action Programme of the General Assembly for the Second United Nations Development Decade* (New York: UN, 1970) and "International Development Strategy for the Third United Nations Development Decade," General Assembly resolution 35/56, 5 December 1980, Annex.

7. UN, *Measures for the Economic Development of Underdeveloped Countries: Report by a Group of Experts Appointed by the Secretary-General of the United Nations* (New York: UN, 1951).

8. Economic and Employment Commission, Sub-Commission on Economic Development, *Report, First Session—17 November to 16 December 1947,* ECOSOC document E/CN.1/47, 18 December 1947.

9. See UNCTAD resolution 24 (II), 26 March 1968.

10. See *International Development Strategy. Action Programme of the General Assembly for the Second United Nations Development Decade.*

11. The Lomé Treaty is the development arm of the European Union and covers the so-called ACP countries (Africa, the Caribbean, and the Pacific). Stabex is a European Union fund that compensates the ACP countries when their agricultural sectors encounter serious declines in export earnings.

12. For a spirited but carefully analyzed account, see OXFAM, *Rigged Rules and Double Standards: Trade, Globalization, and the Fight against Poverty* (Oxford: OXFAM, 2002), 112. This estimated agricultural subsidies to rich-country farmers at $245 billion in 2000.

13. The one success obtained through negotiations conducted under UNCTAD was the system of trade preferences, under which developed countries imposed lower or no tariffs on most manufactured goods. However, the category of sensitive products mentioned in the text remained outside the purview of the system of trade preferences.

14. UN, *The Relationship between Disarmament and Development: Report of the Secretary-General* (New York: UN, 1982), 7.

15. UNDP, *Human Development Report 2002* (New York: Oxford University Press, 2002), Table 17, 207–210.

16. *Problems of the Human Environment: Report of the Secretary-General* (New York: UN, 1969).

17. UNEP, *In Defense of the Earth, the Basic Texts on Environment: Founex, Stockholm, Cocoyoc* (Nairobi: UNEP, 1981).

18. ECE, *Economic Survey 1990* (Geneva: UN, 1990).

19. See, for instance, the series of reports on the world nutrition situation, issued in 1987, 1992, 1997, and 2000 by the Sub-Committee on Nutrition of the UN Administrative Committee on Coordination—the UN system's Forum for Nutrition. The latest of these professional documents is ACC/SCN, *The Fourth Report of the World Nutrition Situation* (Geneva: UN, 2000).

20. Most of the basic university textbooks on development now have a section dealing with human development that refers to the Human Development Indices and to the UNDP's Human Development Reports.

21. Most notably, Amartya K. Sen, *Choice, Welfare, and Measurement* (Oxford: Blackwell, 1982); Amartya K. Sen, *Resources, Values, and Development* (Oxford: Blackwell, 1984). A more recent overview is given in Amartya K. Sen, *Development as Freedom* (New York: Knopf, 1999).

22. These issues are explored further in Sakiko Fukuda-Parr and A. K. Shiva Kumar, eds., *Readings in Human Development* (New York: Oxford University Press, 2003).

23. The national human development reports are listed in UNDP, *Human Development Report 2002* (New York: Oxford University Press, 2002), 276–277.

24. See Chapter 7 of Louis Emmerij, Richard Jolly, and Thomas G. Weiss, *Ahead of the Curve? UN Ideas and Global Challenges* (Bloomington: Indiana University Press, 2001).

25. It could take a leaf out of the European Union book (agriculture, multi-fiber accords) and more recently out of the United States book; on 5 March 2002, President Bush imposed temporary tariffs on steel imports under Section 201 of U.S. trade law to help the U.S. steel industry adjust to foreign competition.

26. For instance, Joseph E. Stiglitz, *The Ninth Raúl Prebisch Lecture* (Geneva: UNCTAD, 1998).

27. UN, *Measures for the Economic Development of Underdeveloped Countries.*

28. The founder of Transparency International was a staff member of the World Bank who resigned because of the standoffish attitude of the Bank with respect to large-scale corruption. The idea for Transparency International was first promoted in the UNDP, *Human Development Report 1991* (Oxford; New York: Oxford University Press, 1991), 50, in a box entitled "Corruption." The box was drafted by Paul Streeten, who often referred to his proposal as creating an agency called "Honesty International."

29. See Lamond Tullis, *Handbook of Research on the Illicit Drug Traffic* (New York: Greenwood Press, 1991); Francisco E. Thoumi, *Political Economy and Illegal Drugs in Colombia* (Boulder: Lynne Rienner Publishers, 1995); James Painter, *Bolivia and Coca* (Boulder: Lynn Rienner Publishers, 1994); Maria Celia Toro, *Mexico's "War" on Drugs:*

Causes and Consequences (Boulder: Lynne Rienner, 1995); LaMond Tullis, *Unintended Consequences: Illegal Drugs and Drug Policies in Nine Countries* (Boulder: Lynn Rienner, 1995).

30. See "Joint and Co-Sponsored United Nations Programme on the Human Immunodeficiency Virus/Acquired Immunodeficiency Syndrome (HIV/AIDS)," ECOSOC resolution 1994/24, 26 July 1994.

31. See "Fact Sheet. The United Nations and the Global Fund to Fight AIDS, TB and Malaria," available online at http://www.unaids.org/en/media/fact+sheets.asp.

32. See Emmerij, Jolly, and Weiss, *Ahead of the Curve,* Chapter 9.

33. Fernand Braudel, *Civilization and Capitalism, 15th–18th Century: The Perspective of the World* (London: Fontana Paperbacks, 1985), 536–556.

34. Ibid., 632.

12. Lessons for the Future

1. Louis Emmerij, Richard Jolly, and Thomas G. Weiss, *Ahead of the Curve? UN Ideas and Global Challenges* (Bloomington: Indiana University Press, 2001), 179, Table 7.5.

2. Expenditure data calculated from World Bank, *World Development Indicators 2002* (Washington, D.C.: World Bank, 2002), 322, Table 5.11. Patent data from UNDP, *Human Development Report 2001* (New York: Oxford University Press, 2001), 3.

3. South Centre, *For a Strong and Democratic United Nations: A South Perspective on UN Reform* (Geneva: The South Centre, 1996).

4. Kofi Annan, *We the Peoples: The Role of the United Nations in the 21st Century* (New York: United Nations, 2000).

5. From President Roosevelt's address to Congress on 6 January 1941. The four freedoms were freedom of speech, freedom of worship, freedom from want, and freedom from fear.

6. "United Nations Millennium Declaration," General Assembly resolution A/RES/55/2, 8 September 2000.

7. The numbering of the various goals differs a bit in different documents and resolutions. This is taken from *Road Map towards the Implementation of the United Nations Millennium Declaration: Report of the Secretary-General,* General Assembly document A/56/326, 6 September 2001. Note that the sanitation goal was not part of the original set of Millennium Development Goals but was formally approved at the World Summit on Sustainable Development in Johannesburg in September 2002, www.un.org/events/wssd/pressreleases/sanitation.pdf.

8. "United Nations Millennium Declaration," para. 12.

9. Varindra Tarzie Vittachi, *Between the Guns: Children as a Zone of Peace* (London: Hodder & Stoughton, 1993), 15–31. See also the chapter by Richard Reid, "Stopping Wars for Children," in *Jim Grant: UNICEF Visionary,* ed. Richard Jolly (Florence: UNICEF, 2001), 89–109.

10. See, for instance, Arturo Escobar, *Encountering Development: The Making and Unmaking of the Third World* (Princeton, N.J.: Princeton University Press, 1995). See also Rajeev Bargava, Amiya Kumar Bagchi, and R. Sudarshan, eds., *Multiculturalism, Liberalism, and Democracy* (New Delhi: Oxford University Press, 1999).

11. Escobar, *Encountering Development*. See also Majid Rahnema and Victoria Bawtree, eds., *The Post-Development Reader* (London: Zed Books, 1997).

12. Escobar, *Encountering Development*, 98.

13. "Autobiography of Amartya Kumar Sen," available online at www.nobel.se/economics/laureates/1998/sen-autobio.html.

14. Calculations from UNDP, *Human Development Report 2002* (Oxford and New York: Oxford University Press, 2002), Table 12, 190–193.

15. Robert Lensink and Howard White, "Assessing Aid: A Manifesto for Aid in the 21st Century?" *Oxford Development Studies* 28, no. 1 (February 2000): 5–18.

16. Gerald K. Helleiner, "Markets, Politics and Globalization: Can the Global Economy Be Civilized?" UNCTAD 10th Raúl Prebisch Lecture delivered at the Palais des Nations, Geneva, 11 December 2000, text online at http://www.unctad.org/en/docs/prebisch10th.en.pdf; Peter Stalker, *Workers without Frontiers: The Impact of Globalization on International Migration* (Geneva: ILO, 2000); UNRISD and UNDP, *Adjustment, Globalization and Social Development: Report of the UNRISD/UNDP International Seminar on Economic Restructuring and Social Policy* (Geneva: UNRISD, 1995); UNRISD, *States of Disarray: The Social Effects of Globalization* (Geneva: UNRISD, 1995).

17. Notably in the volume by Inge Kaul, Richard Stern, and Isabelle Grunberg, eds., *Global Public Goods* (Oxford; New York: Oxford University Press, 1999).

18. Tobin was a Nobel Prize winner in economics. He proposed that a small tax be levied on capital movements that would come into and leave a country within a matter of months. The tax would be a disincentive for speculative movements.

19. See *Road Map towards the Implementation of the United Nations Millennium Declaration*, Annex, 55–58.

20. In this connection, many have criticized the problem of the two World Banks: the World Bank of presidential speeches, the World Development Reports, and the many analyses produced by its research department with many lofty ideas about poverty, income distribution, and the role of the state, and the World Bank of the bankers, the people who make the loans and do the actual negotiating with their counterparts in the developing countries. This is quite a different world and often is far from the world of ideas and speeches. This problem is explored in Devesh Kapur, John P. Lewis, and Richard Webb, eds., *The World Bank: Its First Half Century* (Washington, D.C.: Brookings Institution Press, 1997). Volume 1, Chapter 5, "Poverty Moves Up," refers to "a notable contrast between McNamara's forceful calls for more equitable development and the organization's slow, relatively unheralded reshaping of lending and advisory work" (233), and to McNamara's speeches that "were efforts to present 'state of the art reports,' or navigational fixes, on what became a meandering, decade-long quest for ways to do more than lament the fact of mass poverty" (235).

21. These guidelines paraphrase the "Ten Commandments of Jim Grant's Leadership for Development" by Kul Gautam in Jolly, ed., *Jim Grant: UNICEF Visionary*, 137–144.

22. Max Weber, *Essays in Economic Sociology* (Princeton, N.J.: Princeton University Press, 1999).

Index

Page numbers in *italics* indicate tables and charts.

About the Authors

Richard Jolly is Senior Research Fellow at The CUNY Graduate Center, where he is co-director of the United Nations Intellectual History Project and Research Associate and Honorary Professor at the Institute of Development Studies, University of Sussex. Until mid-2000, he was special advisor to the UNDP administrator and architect of the widely acclaimed Human Development Report. Before this, he served for fourteen years as UNICEF's deputy executive director for programs, and prior to that he served for a decade as the director of the Institute of Development Studies at the University of Sussex. Publications to which he has contributed include *Development with a Human Face* (1998); *The UN and the Bretton Woods Institutions: New Challenges for the Twenty-First Century* (1995); *Adjustment with a Human Face* (1987); and *Disarmament and World Development* (1978). With Louis Emmerij and Thomas G. Weiss, he co-authored *Ahead of the Curve? UN Ideas and Global Challenges,* the first volume in the UNIHP series, and more recently he edited *Jim Grant: UNICEF Visionary* (2001). He was knighted in 2001 in recognition of his services to international development.

Louis Emmerij is Senior Research Fellow at The CUNY Graduate Center, where he is co-director of the United Nations Intellectual History Project. Until 1999 he was special advisor to the president of the Inter-American Development Bank. Before that he had a distinguished career as president of the OECD Development Centre, rector of the Institute for Social Studies in The Hague, and director of the ILO World Employment Program. Among his recent books are *Ahead of the Curve? UN Ideas and Global Challenges* (with Richard Jolly and Thomas G. Weiss); *Economic and Social Development into the 21st Century* (1997, editor); *Limits to Competition* (1995, co-author); *Nord-Sud: La Grenade Degoupilée* (1992); *Financial Flows to Latin America* (1991, co-editor); *Science, Technology and Science Education in the Development of the South* (1989); *One World or Several?* (1989, editor); and *Development Policies and the Crisis of the 1980s* (1987).

Dharam Ghai is advisor to the International Labour Organization. His previous positions include Director of the United Nations Research Institute for Social Development, the World Employment Programme Research at the ILO, and the Institute for Development Studies at the University of Nairobi. He served as coordinator of the Transition Team of ILO Director-General Juan Somavia in 1998–1999. He was also a member of the Pearson Commission on International Development; a Visiting Fellow at the Economic Growth Centre, Yale University; and Chief of the Secretariat for the World Employment Conference in 1976. He has written extensively on employment, poverty, rural and social development, social indicators, structural adjustment, and social dimensions of globalization and the environment. His recent books include *Monitoring Social Progress in the 1990s: Data Constraints, Concerns and Priorities* (1993, co-editor with David Westendorff); *Development and Environment: Sustaining People and Nature* (1994, editor); and *Renewing Social and Economic Progress in Africa* (2000, editor).

Frédéric Lapeyre is Professor at the Institute of Development Studies, Catholic University of Louvain, and a member of the United Nations Intellectual History Project. He is a former Associate Professor at the Graduate Institute of Development Studies in Geneva and a Fulbright Fellow at Brown University. He has contributed to the work of the World Commission on the Social Dimension of Globalization established by the International Labour Organization in February 2002. Prior to that, he participated in the Council of Europe and ILO research programs on poverty and social exclusion. Publications to which he has contributed include: *Poverty and Exclusion in a Global World* (1999, with A. S. Bhalla), *Les défis de la globalisation: Babel ou Pentecôte?* (2001, with J. Delcourt and P. de Woot), *Palestinians' Public Perception of Their Living Conditions: The Role of International and Local Aid during the Second Intifada* (2003, with R. Bocco), and numerous articles on development issues.

About the Project

The United Nations Intellectual History Project was launched in mid-1999 to fill a gaping hole in the literature about the world organization. The project is analyzing the origins and evolution of the history of ideas cultivated within the United Nations family of organizations and of their impact on wider thinking and international action. Certain aspects of the UN's economic and social activities have of course been the subject of books and articles; but there is no comprehensive intellectual history of the world organization's contributions to setting the past, present, or future international agenda.

This project is examining the evolution of key ideas and concepts about international economic and social development born or nurtured under United Nations auspices. Their origins are being traced and the motivations behind them as well as their relevance, influence, and impact are being assessed against the backdrop of the socioeconomic situations of individual countries, the global economy, and major international developments. Indiana University Press will publish fourteen books about human rights and key economic and social ideas central to UN activity.

The project also has conducted in-depth oral history interviews with leading contributors to crucial ideas and concepts within the UN system. Excerpts are being published in a volume entitled *UN Ideas: Voices from the Trenches and Turrets*.

For further information, the interested reader should contact:

UN Intellectual History Project
Ralph Bunche Institute for International Studies
The CUNY Graduate Center
365 Fifth Avenue, Suite 5203
New York, New York 10016-4309
212-817-1920 Tel
212-817-1565 Fax
UNHistory@gc.cuny.edu
www.unhistory.org